Community Identity

Community Identity

Dynamics of Religion in Context

Edited by

Sebastian C. H. Kim and Pauline Kollontai

Published by T&T Clark

A Continuum imprint

The Tower Building, 11 York Road, London SE1 7NX
80 Maiden Lane, Suite 704, New York, NY 10038

www.continuumbooks.com

British Library Cataloguing-in-Publication Data
A catalogue record for this book is available from the British Library

ISBN-10: HB: 0-567-03156-X
PB: 0-567-03157-8
ISBN-13: HB: 978-0-567-03156-3
PB: 978-0-567-03157-0

Typeset by Kenneth Burnley, Wirral, Cheshire
Printed on acid-free paper in Great Britain by
Cromwell Press Ltd, Trowbridge, Wiltshire

Contents

Contributors

Richard Andrew is a Methodist Minister and Director of York Institute for Community Theology, a Methodist Training Institution based at York St John University. After a period working in industry and training at Cambridge he served as a Circuit Minister in Sheffield before joining the Institute in 2002. His academic interests relate to the mission and theology of the Church, spirituality and political theology.

Philippa Baird gained a BSc (Hons) in Psychology from Leeds University in 2005, while working part-time for Professor Ian Rivers on his Bullying in Schools project. During 2005/6 she worked as Research Assistant on the Islamophobia Research Project. She presented posters on the Project at the Annual British Psychological Society Conference 2006. She is currently studying for an MSc in Cognitive Neuroscience at the University of York.

Johan Bergström-Allen lives and works in the northern English city of York where he is a member of the Carmelite Third Order (Secular). He teaches as an Executive Board Member of the Carmelite Institute of Britain & Ireland and is on the editorial team of the international journal of Carmelite Studies, *Carmelus*. He has published articles about Carmelite history and spirituality and regularly gives talks in Europe and North America. He has been a major contributor to the Order's lay formation programme in Britain.

Adrian Brockett is Principal Lecturer in the Faculty of Education and Theology, York St John University. He is the author of various articles on Middle Eastern and Islamic issues. His current research focuses on Islamophobia and interfaith values.

Stephen Friend is currently a Senior Lecturer in Theology and Religious Studies, York St John University, York. His current research includes exploring 'lived religion' and the creative aspects of life in fishing communities, and he has published on fishing communities and religion. A recent development of this research has included the video-recording of women's stories in fishing communities.

Sari Harenwall has been employed in the Faculty of Education and Theology, York St John University, since 2006, working as Research Assistant on the Islamophobia Research Project. She gained a BSc (Hons) in Psychology from Leeds University in 2004, and a Certificate in Counselling from York St John University in 2005. Her special interests are in Social, Clinical and Counselling Psychology. For four years she has also worked in SNAPPY (Special Needs Activities and Play Provision in York), for which she is currently Scheme Co-ordinator.

Greg Hoyland is Senior Lecturer in Theology and Religious Studies in York St John University's Faculty of Edcation and Theology. An ordained Anglican, he has spent several years teaching Christian and Biblical studies in Higher Education after parish work in Bradford and the Yorkshire Dales. His research interests focus on contemporary Christianity with a particular interest in the Anglican tradition and the role of institutional religion in a 'non-institutional' age.

Sebastian Kim is Professor of Theology and Public Life in the Faculty of Education and Theology of York St John University. He is a Fellow of the Royal Asiatic Society and the author of *In Search of Identity: Debates on Religious Conversion in India* (Oxford University Press, 2003). His research interests include public theology; world Christianity; theology of mission; community and identity; contextual theologies; and religion in contemporary society.

Pauline Kollontai is Deputy Dean in the Faculty of Education and Theology at York St John University. She teaches in the area of world religions and religious studies. Her research covers various aspects of religion in the contemporary world. Her most recent publications include 'Messianic Jews and Jewish Identity', *Journal of Modern Jewish Studies* 3.2 (July 2004) and 'Between Judaism and Christianity: The Case of Messianic Jews', *Journal of Religion and Society* 8 (January 2006).

Antony Lester has been Provincial Superior of the British Province of Carmelite Friars since 2002, prior to which he served for seven years as Roman Catholic Chaplain to the University of York. As a Carmelite Friar he has been engaged in retreat ministry and spiritual direction as well as inner-city parish ministry in London. He is a trustee of the Archbishop Oscar Romero Trust.

Esther McIntosh is currently Lecturer in Religion, Gender and Ethics at the University of Leeds, Assistant Editor of the *International Journal of Public Theology* and Research Associate at York St John University. Her most recent publications include *John Macmurray: Selected Philosophical Writings* (Exeter: Imprint Academic, 2004), 'Religious Voices in Public Places: John Macmurray on Church and State', *Journal of Scottish Thought* 1.1 (forthcoming 2007) and 'The Possibility of a Gender-Transcendent God: Taking Macmurray Forward', *Feminist Theology* 15.2 (January 2007).

Chris Maunder is the Head of Programme for the BA in Theology and Religious Studies at York St John University. He has for many years undertaken research in Mariology and the cult of Mary. He has been the chair of trustees of the Centre for Marian Studies (now based at the University of Wales, Lampeter) since its foundation in 1996. He has published several articles and reviews in Marian Studies, and has appeared in television programmes on Mary. His most notable publication, however, is the third edition of Henry Bettenson's *Documents of the Christian Church* (Oxford: Oxford University Press, 1999).

Richard Noake is currently Head of Theology and Religious Studies and Director of the Centre for Church School Education at York St John University. His teaching and research are in the areas of Religious Studies and Religious Education.

Nathalie Noret is a lecturer in Developmental Psychology at York St John University. Her main research interests include relationships in adolescents, in particular the prevalence and nature of bullying in schools. Her most recent publications focus on the nature and prevalence of cyberbullying and Nathalie is currently a member of a Department for Education and Skills (DfES) taskforce set up to develop strategies to tackle cyberbullying.

Ian Rivers is Professor and Head of Psychology at Queen Margaret University, Edinburgh. He is the author of various books and resources focusing upon discrimination at school, and is the recipient of the British Psychological Society's 2001 Award for Promoting Equality of Opportunity in the UK for his research on bullying behaviour. Ian currently serves on a number of advisory groups for the Scottish Executive and the voluntary sector, and recently co-authored a guide book for teachers and parents on tackling bullying effectively.

Rob Warner is currently Lecturer in Sociology of Religion and Practical Theology at the University of Wales, Lampeter. His primary specialism is contemporary Christianity in the UK. Recent publications include 'Pluralism and Voluntarism in the English Religious Economy', *Journal of Contemporary Religion* 21.3 (October 2006), pp. 389–404 and 'Autonomous Conformism: The Paradox of Entrepreneurial Protestantism?' in L. Woodhead and A. Day (eds), *Religion and the Individual* (Aldershot: Ashgate, 2007).

Gary Wilton is Head of the Postgraduate Programme in Theology and Religious Studies at York St John University. He was previously Associate Principal at Church Army's Wilson Carlile College in Sheffield. He is currently a member of the enabling groups for the North North East and Yorkshire Regional Training Partnerships. Gary's research interest is in theological education and he has recently authored two articles looking at the Hind Report and other key documents shaping Church of England theological education.

Sue Yore is a Senior Lecturer in Theology and Religious Studies at York St John University. She teaches Religions in the Contemporary World, Religion and the Visual Arts, Religion and Gender, Christianity and Culture, and Islam. Her current research interest is focused on the development of creativity in the Theology and Religious Studies curriculum in Higher Education.

Acknowledgements

The editors would like to acknowledge those who have contributed to the project. We thank Thomas Kraft of T & T Clark, for his sustaining support in the project, Dominic Mattos and Slav Todorov for their cooperation, and Sarah Norman for her efficient correction of the manuscripts. At York St John University, we appreciate the support and encouragement of Dianne Willcocks, David Maughan-Brown and John Spindler, and other members of staff in Theology and Religious Studies. In particular, we are indebted to Louise Redshaw for her excellent work in proofreading and her editorial suggestions, which have made this volume better shaped and focused.

Introduction

Sebastian C. H. Kim and Pauline Kollontai

In recent years, the in-depth study of the concept of identity has come to prominence in the academic disciplines of anthropology, sociology, cultural and political studies. It is the thesis of this book that many contemporary conflicts between communities have to be examined in two dimensions: the focus needs to be on *community* identity as well as *individual* identity, and the issues need to be looked at from *theological and religious* perspectives in addition to socio-anthropological analysis.

The importance of understanding the concept of identity in relation to community in assessing the dynamics of modern and post-modern contemporary society has been recognized in several academic studies in recent years. For example, in her stimulating book *Europe – The Exceptional Case: Parameters of Faith in the Modern World* (2002) Grace Davie deals with the changing identity of contemporary European Christians. The basis of her argument that Europe is 'exceptional' lies in the unique development of religious patterns in (Western) Europe. Taking the example of Britain, she points out that, though church attendance has drastically declined, the British have not abandoned 'their deep-seated religious aspirations or a latent sense of belonging', but instead 'religious belief is inversely rather than directly related to belonging' and as the institutional disciplines decline 'belief not only persists, but becomes increasingly personal, detached and heterogeneous' (2002: 2–8). Her study helps us to understand the dynamics of Christian communities in Europe, particularly in Britain, and shows that the sense of religious identity of Europeans is distinctive and peculiar to Europe.

On the other hand, an exclusive self-understanding of identity of one's own community, coupled with a hostile attitude towards other communities, often leads to communal conflicts, and in some cases results in devastating consequences – as we have witnessed in the history of communal and ethnic conflicts. Furthermore, it is important to notice the significance of religion in the re-shaping of community identities in this process. When it comes to religious conflicts, though in most cases the issues are not exclusively 'religious' and are often entwined with other complicated political and social matters, the situation becomes more acute when religious beliefs endorse or reinforce the legitimization of violent action against others. For example, in conflict between communities, fundamentalist attitudes to other beliefs often lead to aggressive approaches to others. This is because fundamentalists tend to produce a self-identity that has been 'threatened, made anxious and uncertain and reacts aggressively' or has 'such total and unassailable aims and faith that they can no longer accept other convictions and attitudes alongside their own' (Küng and Moltmann 1992: 20, 103). It is not an exaggeration to say that most contemporary conflicts are somehow related to religious, as well as ethnic and political, identities of different communities, and we witness conflicts driven by fundamentalist religious attitudes towards identity.

Though there is considerable literature from sociological and anthropological perspectives on the topic of identity, the religious dimensions of identity are often neglected. Therefore these studies do not give a satisfactory explanation for conflicts in which community identity is influenced, or even formed, by religious affiliation. Despite the predictions of secularists that religion would become far less significant in late modern and post-modern societies, the present context shows otherwise, and the reality of the phenomena of growing religious fervour and the rise of fundamentalisms is apparent. Aspects of community identity formulated out of religious commitment tend to be far deeper and more consolidating than that from any other source. It is therefore vital for contemporary scholarship to examine the origins and mechanisms of identity in a religious community, and the interaction of these communities with others, in order to understand how religious allegiance plays in relation to the wide spectrum of individual and community life.

This issue is also related to the current debate on 'multi-culturalism', which encourages the cultural and religious identity of communities. In recent years this policy has come under scrutiny, especially in the aftermath of the 7 July bombings in London. It appears that although the motivation of each individual was complex, the religious identity of the suicide bombers overrode their national identity. Its opponents insist that this policy of 'multi-culturalism' results in the segregation of particular religious groups and the encouragement of the separate self-identity of communities, which often leads to conflicts with the common interest of the wider community. This contemporary situation, both in British society and more widely, demands that the issue of identity, including religious identity, is addressed in looking at the causes of conflicts.

With this understanding, the present volume focuses first on *communal* or *corporate* understandings of identity as, for example, the source of identity; the basic components of a sense of belonging; and the way the community operates and interacts with other communities. These involve the community's understanding of their scriptures and tradition, and the ethnic and socio-cultural traditions for forming community identity. Second, this volume assesses the topic of identity from the perspectives of *theology* and *religious studies*. This involves not only using traditional methodologies of the above academic disciplines, but also engaging with other disciplines. Third, the volume investigates the *dynamics of interaction* between religious communities and wider society, and the causes of tension and resolutions. For this purpose, various religious communities, especially in and near Yorkshire, are chosen for our studies to demonstrate the formation of self-understanding of community identities and the interaction with wider society of actual living communities.

The volume has been divided into two sections: perspectives on community identity and community identity in local contexts. The former deals with establishing theories or discussing issues on the topic, and the latter engages with a particular community for the task of investigation.

Perspectives on Community Identity

On the basis of the notion that, in post-modern contexts traditional discourses of theological language, text and mode have to be re-shaped, Sue Yore (Chapter 1) explores the possibilities of creative writing for the development of an integrated theology. She looks at the distinctive ways in which creative writing has a spiritual or theological focus and argues that this provides insights for the renewal of theological methodologies and of theological communities. The integrated theology towards which she is working draws on the whole of human experience. In order to demonstrate this point, she discusses how the writings of Iris Murdoch, Denise Levertov and Annie Dillard can function as vehicles of integration between existential and conceptual polarities, and how an engagement with literary resources can provide workable proposals for theological method. She argues that literary texts have the means to create words that move beyond mere human experience and official doctrines, and that human identity must be imagined as something that is in a perpetual process of becoming rather than a permanent fixed state of being. In particular, this is important for our discussion on identity because it deals with the plural nature of identities in post-modern contexts, and encourages us to move beyond traditional modes of theologizing – confined to the official doctrines and traditions. Instead of a something static and exclusive, there is a need for a more creative and liquid form of interacting and to be open to the possibility of widening the concept of identity.

Seeking for theological identity in the public sphere, Richard Andrew (Chapter 2) examines the dynamics of interaction between Christianity and public space within the theology of Karl Barth, which he sees as the interaction between identity and recognition. He argues that the 'binary reciprocity' (von Balthasar) of God and humanity is a central feature of Barth's theological project and has consequences for the conception of 'public space'. For Barth, questions of identity and recognition are meaningful within the context of God's identity and act in Jesus Christ. This seemingly counter-intuitive proposal contains significant resources for exploring the question of identity, both rupturing it at its core and re-establishing it as a question concerning freedom for fellowship. Here he offers a significant insight for our quest for community identity: according to Barth, deep commitment to the concentration of God in Christ provides 'recognition and reciprocity', which leads humanity into the appreciation of the dignity of the other, along with recognition that one's own community is 'broken and fragmented'. A deep sense of community identity does not necessarily lead to an exclusive or even hostile attitude towards others: when it is rooted in a realization of humility, it fosters far-reaching positive outcomes.

The question of what is the process of shaping and changing community identity in an alien context is the subject Pauline Kollontai (Chapter 3) discusses. She argues that the transplantation process plays a crucial role in defining religious belief and practice, and the expression of identity of a minority religious group. In this process, people take with them a host of social, cultural, political, philosophical and religious phenomena, both consciously and subconsciously, and as a result, this shapes the features of the new community they become and the identity being constructed and expressed. In addition to Kim Knott's theory of the factors in forming (or maintaining) group identity (home traditions; host traditions; nature of migrant process; nature of migrant groups; and nature of host response), she suggests the 'host world view' plays an important role in forming the identity of religious communities which have not originated in the host context. This area is open for further exploration since Europe is undergoing a complex process of demographic change due to migration. In order for a healthy relationship to develop between different religious groups and also wider society, identifying their aspirations and difficulties by critical examination of the process of adaptation and formation of community identity in a new environment is vital.

Examining the concept of community in contemporary political and social contexts, Esther McIntosh (Chapter 4) takes us through the differing concepts of community used by contemporary politicians, and argues that John Macmurray's understanding of community is important to consider. She characterizes the philosophical meaning of community articulated by Macmurray as 'inclusive community' and relates the Macmurrian concept of community to an example of a non-political, religiously and culturally plural community in Leeds, West Yorkshire, leading to the conclusion that Macmurray's understanding of community is a relevant and effective response to a religiously plural society. The significant contribution of Macmurray's thought is that religion based on sets of rules or morals or on fear does not produce authentic and open community but rather exclusive, static and institutionalized religious society. This is particularly relevant in the context of the rising phenomenon of fundamentalist groups within religious traditions on the one hand, and the ill-prepared and ill-informed response of some contemporary politicians on the other. As McIntosh argues, communities are not artificially created, but based on intimate relationships with one another, welcoming diversities and expressing justice and care.

Within the academic community of theology, there is often a certain tension between the confessional and academic dimensions of teaching and learning, and the shift of emphasis on either side can affect the identity of an academic community. Gary Wilton (Chapter 5) explores Thomas Kuhn's influential theory of paradigm shifts in science, and adapts this in his discussion of David Kelsey's 'Athens' and 'Berlin' models of theological education. Building on Kelsey's approach, he develops generic versions of the 'Athens' (i.e. faith-based theological education) and 'Berlin' (i.e. academic study of theology in universities) paradigms to analyse some contemporary theological communities. Through his personal experience of involvement in church training institutions and church institutions of higher education, he perceives the latter can bridge the gap between the 'Athens' and 'Berlin' models. His point is important to consider for the formation of academic community in church institutions (and other religious traditions), as holding the balance between the two models is always not easy. Nevertheless, he suggests it is possible to develop a creative tension, in which an academic community, while holding the faith values of a particular religion, is still open to intellectual encounter with academic vigour without losing its identity.

Often in multi-religious contexts, the concept of identity varies from community to community and Sebastian Kim (Chapter 6) looks into this area of dynamics of changing concepts of community identity. He examines the recent controversial Racial and Religious Hatred Bill presented to the House of the Commons in UK in June 2005 and, after going through various stages of amendments, was passed by the House on 31 January 2006. He examines the arguments for and against the Bill and draws out the understandings of community behind the arguments. As a result of this investigation, he argues that Britain is both a secular and a multi-religious society, and that religion is integral to many religious communities and individuals should be respected. However, he continues, this identity should not be asserted in the form of legislation which could result in the reverse effect of preventing healthy interaction between communities. He suggests instead the active engagement in critical dialogue between those who hold differing views of community identity.

Community Identity in Local Contexts

The interaction between global and local identities is a fascinating area to examine for our purpose. Chris Maunder (Chapter 7) explores the ways in which Marian shrines help to maintain Roman Catholic identity in contemporary Yorkshire and North Lincolnshire. With extensive field research and interaction with historical literature on the trends of Catholic identity since Vatican II, in contrast to pre-Vatican II Britain, he discusses how Catholic identity has changed and formed various strands within the English context. He argues that in the history of English Catholics shrines play an important role in expressing Catholic culture and identity. He convincingly argues that, within the process of globalization, the shrines are important expressions of localization or inculturation of Catholic theology and identity. He further suggests that people who are associated with them place more cultural and historic value on the shrines themselves than their counterparts in continental Europe, where shrines feature various forms of miracles. His research well illustrates in our study of community identity that, while the process of globalization of theology, literature, doctrines and rituals is forming an official and institutionalized community, at the same time particular communities have a strong tendency to hold on to local aspirations and values – and these are vital to the quest for community identity.

Johan Bergström-Allen and Antony Lester (Chapter 8) discuss the development of the concept of community of the Carmelite Order in York. In tracing Carmelite identity, they identify the spirituality and heritage of 'Carmel', the religious family which emerged in the Holy Land before 1215. They discuss the main events and texts in the Carmelite Family's global quest to construct an identity of 'self' through surveying their history and the contemporary ministries of the Carmelite community in York today. They argue that Vatican II is an important landmark in the movement of Carmelite understanding of identity from exclusive community to active engagement with contemporary hopes and concerns in the modern context. Belief in universal brotherhood and standing in solidarity with their fellow men and women have been vital for the spirituality of Carmelites, and furthermore, the sense of belonging to a wider community of praying people of God is a key part of their identity, along with commitment to prayer and service. The upholding of a distinctive spirituality as the key to community identity is a very positive contribution in relation to other communities considered here, and especially to the wider secular society.

Greg Hoyland (Chapter 9) focuses his attention on contemporary Anglicans in York, arguing that it is vital to examine the changing nature of what they believe in addition to sociological and historical analysis of the demographic trends in their congregation. He notes three points in relation to Anglican York. First, numerical decline is not a new phenomenon: in fact, there is little evidence of a strong and confident community identity at any time; it has tended to be fragile and fluctuating. Second, there is a remarkable degree of resilience and adaptability in Anglican attitudes to theological and social changes taking place inside and outside the community. And third, there has been constant interaction with new denominations and groups, which in turn has shaped the Anglican identity in York. He discusses what makes Anglicans stay in spite of the trends of modernity and post-modernity as he sees that identity is something to do with allegiance extended through time, and this needs to be observed over a longer period of generations. He further argues that many of the newly emerging churches are not necessarily new ways of being church but rather of doing church, and observes that Christian identity has less and less to do with denominational identity. He argues the strength of the Anglican form of community is a looser form of affiliation, which he believes could be a model for contemporary British society. His insights on Anglican identity are helpful in understanding how a religious community adapts and evolves in a new context and, as he persuasively argues in the case of Anglican community, the loose form of affiliation and permeation into the wider society is a distinctive built-in characteristic; and this should be seen as the positive aspect of their identity and not as the area of concern on the basis of decline in numbers as some sociologists have expressed it.

This Anglican diversity of identity is further explored by Rob Warner (Chapter 10), who examines evangelical and charismatic groups in York. He describes the leading role played by St. Michael-le-Belfrey Church in the renewal movement of the 1970s and subsequent developments. He examines the empirical data on church attendance among evangelicals and charismatics in York during the last quarter century, and explores the extent to which this sector reflects the general trend to church decline or indicates, at least to some degree, the emergence of an entrepreneurial free market in expressive and voluntarist religion. He further discusses the rise of coalitions among evangelicals and charismatics, which are centred around Anglican charismatics and neo-Pentecostals. This research gives us a perspective on how the charismatic movements in the 1970s have not only shaped the identity of their members but also, by their engagement with other groups, have created unique networks of those who hold a similar theology and mode of worship. As Warner observes, the form of community developed by evangelicals and charismatics is resilient to the changing situation of pluralism, competition and secularization. The effect of this is not only limited to the members of that particular theological orientation, but to the whole Christian community in York.

How do members of a community maintain and develop their sense of religious identity in the midst of dominant traditional religiosity? Stephen Friend (Chapter 11) explores the relationship between religion and identity in Yorkshire fishing communities by examining the way in which members have made sense and meaning of their lives of uncertainty. Using extensive interviews, field research and interaction with theoretical literature on the field, he explores church and community links, rites of passage, folk customs and superstitions. His research enables us to see how a community relates to its religious and spiritual heritage without the preconceptions of a dualistic perspective. It gives insights into how a community formed by geography and occupation, and not by religious affiliation, utilizes its shared religiosity in the formation of a distinctive identity.

Richard Noake (Chapter 12) focuses on the Sikhs living in York. He examines the ways in which they create and maintain their identity, and raises the question of whether they constitute a community. He begins by setting their story within the story of Sikhs in Britain – a story that is a diasporic one – and traces something of the history of Sikh diaspora and the arrival and establishment of the Sikh community in Britain. Using extensive interviews with some of the Sikhs in York, and illustrating his points using examples of recent cultural and religious activities in and around York St John University, he shows how the Sikh community in York are instrumental in bringing various religious communities together. His study is very useful for our investigation, in that the Sikh community in York has to interact with several other communities in defining their identity: the larger Sikh communities in neighbouring cities, Hindu communities, other religious communities and wider society. The Sikh community in York seems to play a major role in inter-faith dialogue, not by asserting their own identity but by being an inclusive community.

Perhaps the most controversial issue relating to religious community in recent years is the relationship between Muslim communities and the wider society in the West. Adrian Brockett and others (Chapter 13) examine adolescent attitudes in York towards Muslims, Islam and the Middle East through empirical research conducted among 1,500 school pupils and college students in York. The purpose of this research is to assess some of the causes of tension in the interactions between religious communities and wider society, and so to contribute to a deeper understanding of communal conflicts. The subject of questions includes the level of respondents' knowledge and their sources of information; their attitude towards Muslims after 9/11; their attitude towards Muslims after the invasion of Iraq; their measure of agreement with views of the British National Party; their attitudes regarding the wearing of headscarves in their schools and colleges. There are some important findings: for example, older groups demonstrate a less tolerant attitude towards Muslims and Islam than younger ones, and males are less tolerant then females. Their study demonstrates an important indication of the direction of this future research: the focus should not only be on how the wider community perceives a minority religious community, but also on the causes of these perceptions, how they are formed and what can be done to promote healthy interaction between communities.

The project that produced this book started in April 2005 and involves most of the academic members of Theology and Religious Studies in York St John University and others who are specialists in the topic in other institutions. This project has encouraged members to focus on an aspect of religion in contemporary society which is urgent for not only those who engage in the academic study of community relations, but also for the general public, for whom untangling the ways and means in which community identity is formed and transformed is of crucial importance at the present time. Through our collective engagement in research on the topic of community identity, we have been able to identify some common points for discussion and suggestions for further research. First, due to the dynamic and complex nature of identity, it is vital to develop comprehensive tools from socio-cultural, historical and religious perspectives. These need to include the use of creative, unofficial and interactive discourse, as Yore suggests by showing that literary writings are an important way of exploring the formation of theological identity in the post-modern context. Kollontai underlines the importance of understanding the reasons for changes of community identity in the process of moving into different contexts. In his exploration of the religiosity of fishing communities, Friend helps us to appreciate their religious and spiritual aspirations.

Second, there is always tension between affirming self-identity and being open to engaging with other communities or wider society. Our research suggests that the former does not necessarily lead to the breakdown of community relations or to communal conflict. This is demonstrated by Andrew, who shows how the Barthian notion of commitment to faith leads to respecting the dignity of others. Warner reveals how the evangelical and charismatic communities have been instrumental in helping the wider Christian community to respond to the secular environment in recent years. Wilton presents the tensions but also suggests ways to bridge the gaps between theological and academic institutions without sacrificing theological integrity. And Bergström-Allen and Lester see that the unique ministry and spirituality of Carmelites make a positive contribution to wider society. These studies show that having a strong faith commitment does not lead to exclusivity but rather becomes a launch pad for constructive engagement with other communities.

Third, while affirming self-identity, all the communities desire to be part of wider society by actively engaging in both religious and secular activities. For example, Hoyland sees the inclusive nature of Anglican identity as a strength of that tradition and a positive feature of religious community; while McIntosh's discussion on Macmurrian community and illustration of cooperation between communities establishes not only models to follow but ways and means to interact with other communities. In addition, Kim suggests that, when it comes to conflicting views and differing concepts, the engagement between religious communities and wider society requires constant efforts to pursue dialogue.

Fourth, there are constant interplays between globalization and localization in forming the identity of religious communities. Maunder's study on the role of Marian shrines illustrates this point very well as they are an example of inculturation of the Catholic tradition involving local culture and history; while Noake's study of the Sikh community in York exhibits this interaction between the global and the local identities. The empirical research done by Brockett and others is set in the context of both global conflicts (i.e. 9/11 and war in Iraq) and local tensions (i.e. BNP and wearing headscarves), and shows how these are closely interconnected. The above findings are not comprehensive, and we can draw many more lessons from individual chapters. We expect this will lead to ongoing debates and further research.

We trust that this book is a small step towards making our expertise and research on religion in contemporary society available to other academic communities, religious communities and wider society so that these findings may be an instrument in achieving a healthy and positive relationship between diverse communities. We are confident that this cooperative work will be a seedbed for many active and exciting ventures in the coming years.

References

Davie, Grace (2002), *Europe – The Exceptional Case: Parameters of Faith in the Modern World* (London: Darton, Longman & Todd).

Küng, Hans, and Jürgen Moltmann (eds) (1992), *Fundamentalism as an Ecumenical Challenge* (London: SCM).

Part I

Perspectives on Community Identity

1

Theological Identity in Post-modernity through a Literary Lens

Sue Yore

Introduction

The notion of identity asserted within the modernist agenda imagined the perfect human self as rational and autonomous. It equally sought to seek out master theories that encapsulated the Truth through absolute meta-narratives. The contextual and diverse realities that constitute human existence in post-modernity are progressively subverting this. Today we are increasingly aware that there is not one story, but many. In spiritual and theological circles it is once again being recognized that some of the most spiritual and insightful moments of human endeavour stem from the irrational or creative part of human nature and that there are aspects of lived reality over which we have no control. Life and the events it throws at us are still, despite our best efforts, largely random and chaotic, often with no discernible meaning or purpose. Further to this, as theologian Philip Sheldrake has remarked, it is because post-modernity

> resists attempts to reduce events or people to mere instances of some overarching theory, postmodernism defends the otherness, particularity and difference of all people . . . [so that] the post-modern image of the self exists in a complex and mobile network of relationships, there cannot be said to be such a thing as a complete or completed self. (2001: 12–13)

Human identity, and especially spiritual or theological identity, is therefore something that is in perpetual process of becoming rather than a permanent fixed state of being. Theological reflection on identity must consequently reflect the plural nature of diverse realities, and an acceptance that only partial or temporary 'truths' concerning the self are attainable. Contemporary theologians (Tracy 1994; McFague 1997; Sheldrake 1998, 2001; Soelle 2001) are increasingly recognizing that theological identity has to be worked out through encounters with strangers and all the mysteriousness that the face of the Other – whether it be peoples of other religions, or the Sacred – represents.

Further to this, Sheldrake argues that both theological language espoused by the Church and contemporary consumerist-led spiritualities fail to address contemporary needs, calling for a 'language or practices that facilitate true communion between persons in and through communion with the sacred or the divine' (Sheldrake 1998: 199). The focus of this discussion will be on the development of an integrated theological approach to identity that draws on the whole of human experience, the central objective of which is to contribute towards a joyful, just and peaceable future for all. As such I shall argue that the 'practice' of literary writing is a suitable means to create words that move beyond on one hand personal experience and on the other official doctrine that ignores individual lives to 'create space for transcendence and communion' (Sheldrake 1998: 201).

Such a theology might be called a theology of integration and is offered as a more holistic and realistic alternative model for theological reflection on identity in post-modernity. The aim of this chapter is to demonstrate how the writing of one medieval writer and theologian, Julian of Norwich, and three contemporary literary writers, Iris Murdoch, Denise Levertov and Annie Dillard, can function as a vehicle of integration between individual, existential lives and theological, conceptual polarities. As such, the notion of integration is intended to differentiate between the goal of spiritual escapism either in this life or the next and the more feasible integration of body, mind and soul as being essential for theological identity in postmodernity. A consequence of this reorientation is a notion of theological identity that is positioned outside of abstract philosophical thought and more integrated into socio-political realities. Such a position is more readily aligned with that of the mystic.

In the classical mystical tradition, spiritual progression through the stages of the *via negativa* and the *via positiva*[1] ultimately leads to the *via unitiva*, or to the experience of unity with God. This signifies the point 'where the self ceases actively to surrender itself and instead suffers the blindingly superabundant presence of God' (McIntosh 1998: 191). Similarly, in Platonic mysticism the ultimate goal is to emerge from the cave into the full light of the sun or 'truth'. Interpretations of both scenarios imply that there is a hierarchical movement away from the body, from matter generally, toward the spiritual realm. Underlying this largely pre-modern worldview is the assumption that God or the Good exists above and beyond reality.

From the Protestant Reformation onwards, and more than ever following the establishment of Enlightenment ideals, the individual, as an autonomous, thinking being, was central to any Western theology. Personal faith developed into a key focus of religious belief and practice. In such a world, especially following the rapid rise of scientific discovery and the changes wrought by the Industrial Revolution, the model of 'mechanistic progress' dominated the discussion. This model created an imaginary 'picture of an upward line, graphing the abundant life in terms of consumer goods for more and more of the world's people' (McFague 2001: 43–45). However, both views, theological and worldly, represent a single vision that eclipses the realities of non-Westerners and of non-traditional religious conceptions as well as the material or embodied nature of existence.

Whilst earlier mysticisms, especially those articulated by male religious leaders, tended to deny the corporal element of reality, post-modern consumer culture celebrates it, and therefore, spiritual experience becomes a commodity like everything else. Jeremy Carrette and Richard King explain the difficulties inherent in this transformation:

> Our understanding of the self and its desires is lost . . . when [Eastern practices such as yoga and Buddhist meditation are] transformed in modern western societies into an individualised spirituality of the self, or as we are increasingly seeing, repackaged as a cultural commodity to be sold to the 'spiritual consumer'. (Carrette and King 2004: 16)

Moreover, in this scenario, the realities of marginalized peoples are ignored at the expense of attaining pleasure in the accumulation of consumer goods. Despite the focus on the self, pleasure in post-modernity largely represents a *dis*-integration, or fragmentation, of self-identity. Dualistic constructs that debase the natural world and our bodies have proved to be detrimental to the psychic health of individuals and to the sustainability of the earth's ecosystems. An integrative approach to theological identity represents an alternative and more holistic theological model to the Plotinian image of the 'flight of the Alone to the Alone'.[2] It also resists forms of contemporary 'holistic' spirituality that would aspire to repudiate 'oppressive material worlds' but can 'paradoxically reinscribe the forces of isolation by focusing upon the individual' (Carrette and King 2004: 82).

To develop an integrated theology that draws on the insights of writers such as Murdoch, Levertov and Dillard, I will firstly posit Julian's reflections as an espousal of a theology of integration. In fact, her sense of the undivided 'double' nature of human beings in relation to God provides a useful spiritual blueprint for theological identity in post-modernity. Secondly, I will explore the philosophical categories of being, knowing and acting — or ontology, epistemology and ethics — through the lens of integration. To finish, I will posit a model of relationship as encapsulated in the doctrine of the Trinity for its 'unusual capacity to hold unity and difference together' (Sheldrake 1998: 67).

The Example of Julian

Grace Jantzen aptly describes Julian as 'an outstanding example of an integrated theologian, for whom daily life and religious experience and theological reflection are all aspects of the same whole' (2000: 91). An overriding vocational aim that Julian expresses in her theological reflections on her mystical visions, *Showings*, is her desire to help people become whole by healing the fragmented nature of the human self. Her response to what she saw as a universal human longing is an image of humanity's relationship with the Creator:

> I saw that we have, naturally from our fullness, to desire wisely and truly to know our own soul, through which we are taught to seek it where it is, and that is in God. And so by leading through grace of the Holy Spirit we shall know them both in one; whether we are moved to know God or our soul, either motion is good and true. (Julian 1978: 288)

The increased attention to the humanity of Christ and awareness that human beings are made 'in the image and likeness' of God were seen in the late medieval period as proof that humans are 'inextricably joined with divinity' (Bynum 1982: 129–30). So Julian assures us that 'our substance is in God . . . and God is in our sensuality' that it is as sensual bodily creatures that we perceive God (Julian 1978: 288). Our 'substance' or essential selves remain united with God, but it is our 'sensuality', or 'consciousness and behaviour', which loses touch with God (Julian 1978: 148–49). Jantzen notes that the way that 'bodily reality is integrated into . . . [her] spirituality' differentiates Julian and other female mystics from male expressions of mysticism (Jantzen 1995: 147). That is, rather than a flight from the material realm to the spiritual, the spiritual is realized within the material.

Because of the conjoining of the human and divine soul and the belief that God is the ground of our being, to Julian's mind, it follows that to know ourselves at a deep level is to know God:

> And so I saw most surely that it is quicker for us and easier to come to the knowledge of God than it is to know our own soul. For our soul is so deeply grounded in God and so endlessly treasured that we cannot come to knowledge of it until we first have knowledge of God, who is the Creator to whom it is united. (Julian 1978: 288)

Julian appears to suggest that it is only by embracing the human condition and a persistent striving for a unified consciousness that humans can overcome the false separation between the body and soul, which is not to say that we are totally pure. As Julian recognized, the human potential for sin blocks the possibility of receiving God's grace. She thought that a life's spiritual task should be to 'know and see, truly and clearly, what our self is, then we shall truly and clearly see and know our Lord God in the fullness of joy' (Julian 1978: 258).

Behind Julian's revelations, and her years of pondering them, are the reality of God and the unfathomable mystery of love. The only way to transcend sin is through the power of love. Love is what binds the creature to the Creator. Indeed, Julian concludes that the meaning of her revelations was precisely 'love':

> So I was taught that love is our Lord's meaning. And I saw very certainly in this and in everything that before God made us he loved us, which love was never abated and never will be . . . In our creation we had beginning, but the love in which he created us was in him from without beginning. In this love we have our beginning, and all this shall we see in God without end. (1978: 342–43)

Murdoch shared Julian's sense of the power of love as reflected in her interest in 'the ways that love makes for wholeness of perception, wholeness of being', but she was equally interested in love's failings (Conradi 2001: 324). It is chiefly though her belief that poetry is an incarnation that links Levertov to Julian's integrated vision of reality. She insists that '[t]he substance, the means, of an art, is an incarnation – not a reference but phenomenon. A poem is an indivisibility of "spirit and matter"' (Levertov 1973: 50). The human imagination or soul is where this fusion takes place. Annie Dillard's engagement with Julian is perhaps the most challenging. She uses the experience of watching a moth burn to death in a candle flame as a metaphor for a nun in post-modernity (Dillard 1998: 16–17). Like Julian, she yearns for an experience of the sacred but knows this does not come without being willing to look suffering and death in the face. The fact that the body of the dead moth continues to burn and give light after its death is a symbol of sacrifice. For Dillard, surrendering oneself to the blinding presence of God is not about escape from this world, but a deeper encounter with reality.

Spiritual Being and Wholeness

There is an etymological link between the word 'wholeness' and 'holiness' in the Old English words *hal* for health and *halig* for holy. For a human being to be whole, or in full health, the body, mind and spirit need to be in an integrated state. Like Julian, Soelle appreciates that the overriding religious concern for human beings is the desire 'to be whole and not fragmented' (1984: 137). This need extends to all creation wherein 'the wish of growing love is to bind and join together even larger entities' (ibid.). In post-modernity, this has urgent ethical repercussions, as individuals, in the first world in particular, have become 'enemies of the earth, enemies of the sky above us, and enemies of ourselves' (Soelle 2001: 192). In other words, we have lost a sense of relationship to creation, to the transcendent, and between our spiritual and material selves.

Theologian Sallie McFague, in the same way, states that 'the category "human being" is a construction with fuzzy edges; it is a category that makes no sense apart from the history of life on our planet and the interlocking networks of support that keep all of us in existence' (McFague 2001: 46). She is adamant that the Enlightenment ideal of the rational autonomous individual who has the potential to force matter to give up its secrets through scientific discovery rests on an ontological mistake. Yet, despite the damaging effect of mechanistic thinking in the past, a scientific paradigm in post-modernity, in McFague's view, is still able to provide crucial insights for theology. Specifically, she refers to the scientific discovery that there is a 'continuum between matter and energy (or more precisely, the unified matter/energy field), which overturns traditional hierarchical dualism' (McFague 1993: 16). Not least is the fact that we are minds as well as bodies and that the former emerges from the latter (ibid.). The categorical quality of the language is different, but the mystical essence is the same as Julian's sense of love that exists 'in him from without beginning', through the conjoining of human and divine matter.

In post-modernity, humans tend to experience themselves progressively in terms of isolation from those around them. Murdoch was acutely aware of this disunity between self and the external world, contending that, '[t]o do philosophy is to explore one's own temperament, and at the same time to attempt to discover the truth' (Murdoch 1970: 46). Philosophy's aim is to discover what is inside us as well as that which resides beyond the tangible world. At a basic level, philosophy (and much of theology, we should add) is the human attempt to resolve these feelings of separation and disunity. Conradi points out that one of Murdoch's perennial problems was 'how to marry the inner and the outer worlds, how to create fictions that honour both a strict causality and a strict sense of privacy and "freedom" that the moral agent may experience himself as endowed with' (Conradi 2001: 325). At a subjective level, an existential tension exists between the self as an autonomous unique being and the larger world that appears to operate through randomness and chance, which creates an unresolved tension within the human mind. In one sense, humans have a unique awareness of their freedom, but in another they cannot escape the knowledge that we are all subject to events over which the individual has little influence.

As a novelist and philosopher, Murdoch sought to mediate a path between absolute principles (whether philosophical or religious) and human consciousness. Murdoch does not resolve existential anxieties, but she offers, through her novels, a way to acknowledge that, while death and randomness is real, so is goodness. Like Julian, Murdoch intuited that a part of human consciousness was always orientated toward the Good but our lower desires could lead us into immoral behaviour. In other words, although we need to foster our higher eros, we still need to keep our feet on the ground. The temptation to escape into pseudo-spirituality is a constant temptation within a consumerist construction of spirituality, one that would be robustly criticized by Murdoch as pertaining to fantasy and escapism if she were still with us today.

Murdoch believed that a fundamental orientation towards the Good was present in human nature. In *Metaphysics as a Guide to Morals*, she imagines the Platonic notion of the Good as something 'distant and apart' that operates as 'a source of energy'. Further, she describes it as 'an active principle of truthful cognition and moral understanding in the soul, the inspiration of the love-object of Eros' (Murdoch 1992: 474). It is not an object as such, or a person as in traditional beliefs about God, but rather, Murdoch depicts the Good as a 'reality principle whereby we find our way about the world' (ibid.). Fundamental to her task as a novelist was her desire to re-orientate people towards the Good, which is how she understands conversion or, in relation to the discussion here, a reintegrated self, so that, by definition, Murdoch's way is one of integration.

In her poem 'Sojourns in the Parallel World', Levertov gives us her interpretation of how the two worlds of the material and the supernatural intermingle and she dissuades us from a mysticism of escapism. In the same poem, she tells the reader of the transcendental realm where 'we lose track of our own obsessions,/our self-concerns' and our earthly existence, where 'our lives of human passions,/cruelties, dreams, concepts' occur. She concludes that, however joyous the experience of the mystical realm is, 'we must/return, indeed to evolve our destinies' (Levertov 1998: 49). As Linda Kinnahan reminds us, Levertov never 'occupies a place of separation from the world nor embodies a self innocent of its systems of power' (Kinnahan 1992: 156). Furthermore, Levertov was acutely aware at all times of her own complicity in systems of oppression. Her close friend, the Jesuit priest and peace activist Daniel Berrigan, argues that, through her writing, she helped to restore the balance in the seventies between American writing that was 'disproportionately passionate about the self, and correspondingly numb . . . toward the public weal and woe' (Berringan 1993: 175).[3] Levertov's poetry represented a synthesis of subjective insight and ethical concern for others.

One seemingly mundane incident in *Pilgrim at Tinker Creek* depicts Annie Dillard's sense of herself as wholly integrated as a human and with her surroundings. It happens whilst she stops at a gas station during a long drive on a hot day. She takes a coffee outside, finds herself alone, and dazzled by the mountainous landscape before her eyes, she notices that

> the bare forest folds and pleats itself like a living protoplasm before my eyes . . . I am more alive than all the world. This is it, I think, this is it, right now, the present, this empty gas station, here, this western wind, this tang of coffee on the tongue, and I am patting a puppy, I am watching the mountain. And the second I verbalize this awareness in my brain, I cease to see the mountain or feel the puppy. I am opaque, so much black asphalt. (Dillard 1998: 79–80)

Sharon Chirban, who positions herself on the border between culture and clinical practice in psychology, finds in Dillard's *Pilgrim at Tinker Creek* a sound example of the experience of what she calls 'oneness'. This state of wholeness is achieved through attention to an individual dog in parallel with the broader landscape. In particular, she points to Dillard's experience of patting a puppy as an example of 'oneness experience', noting that 'it is this area of experiencing in the space between that Dillard's sense of self and the many stimuli emitted from the mountain contribute to form the substance of an oneness experience' (Chirban 2000: 253). Ross-Bryant similarly states that 'Dillard experiences herself as part of a supportive matrix which is more than herself and yet includes herself' (1990: 88). As such, 'human meaning, as Dillard presents it, depends on being open to and true to the experience of the other' (1990: 91). Murdoch, Levertov and Dillard clearly maintain that it is only by engaging with others that we get a fuller sense of self.

Seeing Others through a Literary Lens

McFague believes that good art can help us to pay attention to others:

> Art frames fragments of our world: paintings, poetry, novels, sculpture, dance, music help us to look at colors, sounds, bodies, events, characters – whatever – with full attention. Something is lifted out of the world and put into a frame so that we can, perhaps for the first time, *see* it. Most of the time we do not see: we pass a tree, an early spring crocus, the face of another human being, and we do not marvel at these wonders, because we do not see their specialness, their individuality, their difference. (1997: 29)

It is only with the help of the artist, who captures the duality of existence, that we can begin to discern truth. In McFague's ecological model, the categories of knowing, being and acting must include the 'otherness of the other . . . [as a] total way of being in the world' (1997: 149). She further points out that the difficult task of attending to another fundamentally means paying attention to difference (1997: 28). This section explores how Murdoch, Levertov and Dillard attempt to bridge the gap between self and others.

A central feature of Murdoch's moral philosophy is her notion of 'loving attention'. Her view on pornography demonstrates her reasoning behind this assertion. She opposed the sex industry generally because it 'displays . . . [a] lack of honour and restraint', arguing that sexual promiscuity is to be discouraged because people do not really care for each other (Fletcher and Bove 1994: 209). In *The Sovereignty of Good*, Murdoch expresses her opinion that art provides more appropriate clues for the apprehension of reality:

> The great artist sees his objects . . . in a light of justice and mercy. The direction of attention is, contrary to nature, outward, away from self which reduces all to a false unity, towards the great surprising variety of the world, and the ability so to direct attention is love. (Murdoch 1970: 66)

Murdoch states that 'looking at other people is different from looking at trees or works of art'; looking at people has an extra layer of meaning or power dynamics whereby 'a loving just gaze cherishes and adds substance, a contemptuous gaze withers' (1992: 463). Pornography falls into the latter category. In her view, the way we look at others actually takes effect in the world and has the potential to empower or disempower others.

As a case in point, Gabriele Griffen suggests that the portrayal of women in Murdoch's novels appears to represent them as 'externalisations of male needs, men who need women as mother figures, virgins, whores or goddesses' (1993: 8). Similarly, women's issues are raised marginally and female characters are cast in conventional roles of femininity (1993: 7). Most notably, women function as mirrors of men's needs where their individual being is not fully recognized.[4] Murdoch indicates in several novels that men are unable to 'see' women as separate individual beings. *The Sandcastle* illustrates a universal characterization of the male ego, where Bledyard explains to Mor, who is married but has a fixation on another woman, that

> there is no such thing as respect for reality. You are living on dreams now, dreams of happiness, dreams of freedom. But in all this you consider only yourself. You do not truly apprehend the distinct being of either your wife or Miss Carter. (Murdoch 1957: 213)

The ability to 'see' another person is primarily bound to the ability to love others, and, undoubtedly, her assertion that the 'inner' life of others needs attending to was influenced by the writings of Simone Weil. When someone tries to assess another's situation, there may be no comprehension of the introspective life.[5] Much space is given over to such inner musings in her novels. The inclusion of insight into moral reasoning, in Murdoch's language, means that the capacity for empathy has more to do with 'vision' than 'choice'. In other words, the ability to 'see' or empathetically enter into another's world enables more advanced moral insight than does reason alone. The mystical or imaginative approach to morality is equally present in Levertov's writing.

Levertov expresses an affiliation with Albert Schweitzer's doctrine of Reverence for Life, with the recognition of 'oneself *as life that wants to live* among other *forms of life that want to live*' (Levertov 1973: 53, original emphasis).[6] Levertov further maintains that there can be 'no self-respect without respect for others, no love and reverence for others without love and reverence for oneself; and no recognition of others is possible without the imagination' (ibid.). It is uniquely through attention that this reverence or compassion for other life is achieved. In 'Watching, Dark Circle', Levertov highlights this through portraying our inability to feel the pain of others (1986: 37). Here she refers to an actual event through the graphic description of the use of pigs for testing the effects of a nuclear blast. She quite rightly points out that 'the Pentagon wants to know something a child could tell it: it hurts to burn', and she criticizes the notion that the deliberate harm done to these animals can be called a 'simulation' because the agony is real for the pigs. Instead, she suggests that the so-called simulation is in fact 'the simulation of hell' (1986: 37).

In order to imagine a more mutual understanding between sentient beings, McFague develops the metaphor of vision through the idea of 'locking eyes'. 'When we lock eyes something happens: we become two subjects, not subject and object . . . so that we relate to others more like a Thou than an It' (1997: 35).[7] In this subject–subject relationship, the 'other' may be human or non-human. An example of a 'locking of eyes' was experienced by Dillard while sitting by a pond, through a sudden encounter with a weasel:

> He had two black eyes I did not see, any more than you see a window. The weasel was stunned into stillness as he was emerging from beneath an enormous shaggy wildrose bush four feet away. I was stunned into stillness, twisted backward on the tree trunk. Our eyes locked, and someone threw away the key.
>
> Our look was as if two lovers, or deadly enemies, met unexpectedly on an overgrown path when each had been thinking of something else: a clearing blow to the gut. It was also a bright blow to the brain, or a sudden beating of brains, with all the charge and intimate grate of rubbed balloons. It emptied our lungs. It felled the forest, moved the fields, and drained the pond; the world dismantled and tumbled into that black hole of eyes. If you and I looked at each other that way, our skulls would split and drop to our shoulders. But we don't. We keep our skulls. (1988b: 67)

This is illustrative of Buber's concept of an 'I–Thou' relationship as opposed to an 'I–It'; one that relates to the meeting of two equals rather than an objective gaze that seeks to dominate.

On an epistemological level, Murdoch, Levertov and Dillard portray encounters with other beings in a manner that challenges dualistic constructions. If others are seen as objects rather than subjects in their own right, it affords them no moral significance and allows the justification and continuation of abuse and exploitation. A theology of integration prioritizes radical engagement with other beings. While there is no denying the fact that human existence consists of duality, shifting to one extreme is disastrous for the individual, society and the natural environment as the balance is tipped in favour of those with the most power.

Blurring the Boundaries of Knowledge

By definition, a theology of integration subverts dualistic thinking or ways of explaining human existence. The separation between love and knowledge, between reason and imagination, is not evident in Julian's theology, and that separation is also absent in Murdoch, Levertov and Dillard's work. In fact, in post-modernity, it is perhaps more important to acknowledge that we must interrogate and assimilate knowledge within a context that values both individual existential knowledge as well as considering global implications.

Matthews suggests that a mystical person in post-modernity becomes a 'liminal witness' (2000: 139). As *limen* is Latin for 'threshold' this implies that this 'witness' is someone who operates as a mediator between various social, religious and disciplinary groups, particularly those on the margins. It is important to note, therefore, that Murdoch, Levertov and Dillard draw upon many academic disciplines and literary genres to incorporate an eclectic range of knowledge and thought into their work. Murdoch was a respected philosopher, but she was also well versed in theological and religious studies. Levertov, whilst heavily steeped in her literary heritage and Judeo-Christian context, had a good knowledge of a range of spiritual traditions.[8] Dillard brings insights from natural history, philosophy, literature, biblical exegesis, theology and science into her mysticism. In fact, more of a generalist than a specialist, Dillard is the hardest to contain within any particular genre or discipline.

Knowledge about God, due to the invisible nature of the subject matter, can never be purely a matter of rational discourse but must draw equally on imaginative and emotive elements of an embodied life. Beginning with the late medieval period and extending through to the Enlightenment there was an increased separation of the creature from the Creator in metaphysical thought, and predominantly in the Protestant tradition, God became a transcendent object, distant and outside of Creation in order to preserve God's sovereignty. McIntosh sums up this theological stance:

> God is a particularly powerful and invisible subject who acts over against human subjects, and must withdraw in order to permit their freedom to act autonomously . . . Likewise the human person comes to be understood as human subject over against whom exists the range of objects for potential mastery and subordination. (1998: 211)

Hence, God and the human subject are mutually exclusive, each with power over others. The human mind, by virtue of its radical capacity for self-consciousness, becomes the source and centre of meaning, whilst God ceases to be perceptible in creation. This results in the dualistic separation of the object and subject as characterized in the modernist agenda, and brings with it an elevated notion of the free and autonomous individual. In short, the over-emphasis on God as Other has resulted in both denying God and an exaggerated view of human power.

If God as a moral absolute moves further and further out of the picture, correspondingly, moral thinking becomes more and more relative. The claims that the autonomous individual has superseded absolutes and universal laws in post-modernity present the real possibility that ethics as a set of virtues and moral values common to all could disappear before a horizon of free choice in a consumer society. Murdoch, through her model of the spiritual journey toward the Good, intends to pre-empt such a decline; Levertov refuses to separate faith from political agency; while Dillard aspires to bring an unpredictable God devoid of human construction back into the picture.

Systematic theologians provide a thematic, or systemized, summary of the main doctrinal positions in Christian theology, and by so doing, they seek to provide a unified vision of biblical teachings relevant for contemporary contexts. Often, in order to achieve such a systematic description, there is inevitably some selective pruning in order to achieve a sense of coherence.[9] In this manner, theology tends to adopt a somewhat blinkered and unhelpful response to the human condition by bracketing off anything that sits outside its field of vision. In the main, this systematic approach requires the use of reason and logic to characterize and identify key terms and concepts. A mystic, or as we have seen, a creative writer, is more likely to use the senses, emotion, intuition or imagination to apprehend and describe the sacred. Within the former category, there are clear boundaries such as the difference between right and wrong and between the divine and human. In the latter category, the boundaries blur so that knowledge is dialectical and flexible and does not therefore provide rigid structures of thought. Likewise, mystical perception relies on paradoxical and ambiguous language, terms that suggest 'an encompassing, elemental, or ultimate unity through a juxtaposition of opposites that frustrate the analytic intellect's conventional attempt to join them' (Keller 1983: 5). While Murdoch, Levertov and Dillard build bridges between bipolar opposites using their imaginations, they do not offer easy answers or find permanent resolutions to life's conundrums.

The Role of the Creative Imagination in Theological Identities

According to Lorna Sage (1992: 72), Murdoch's writing occupies what she terms the 'middle-ground'. As such, Murdoch creates and inhabits a mediating space between the symbolic narratives of orthodox philosophy and the popular genre of the novel. Her philosophy relates to a conceptual space, while her novels occupy a cultural space. Murdoch's focus is on the concept of the Good, which, although similar to God and Kant's Universal Law, is unrepresentable and transcendent and is based on an aspiration towards perfection in lived experience. She asserts that the 'intellect naturally seeks unity', and it is only through the intellect and emotions together that progress towards the Good can be made (Murdoch 1970: 57). She does not seek to replace reason with emotion but, rather, to enter into a creative space of dialogue between the two.

There is, as Dipple demonstrates, an important point of separation in Murdoch's philosophy, which departs from Plato's ideal of the absolute in favour of a realization of our 'entrapment in a perpetual, flawed selfhood almost entirely incapable of moral advancement' (1982: 78). In 'The Fire and the Sun' Murdoch comments that:

> Plato spent some extremely valuable time (*Parmenides*, *Theaetetus*, *Sophist*) dismantling his earlier imagery, but then invented some more, marvellous, entirely new, mythological but still explanatory images in the *Timaeus* . . . However, his failures do not lead him (as they might lead a later, Christian or liberal, thinker) to conclude humbly or tolerantly that the human mind is essentially limited and fallible. They lead rather to a firmer sense of Hierarchy. Wisdom is *there*, but belongs to gods and very few mortals (*Timaeus*, *Laws*). (Conradi 2001: 445–46)

This highlights the major flaw in Plato's thought that is corrected by the humility of mystics such as Julian. A single-minded focus on wisdom outside of the world leads to the false belief in the potential of humans to escape their imperfect nature. Instead, as Murdoch demonstrates through her novels, overcoming our fallibility is a continual struggle.

Undoubtedly, philosophical reflection spills over into Murdoch's novels, so that the difference between truth and fiction become blurred.[10] Yet her attention to detail and local particularities question the logic of dualistic or oppositional thinking, which radically separates the mind from experience. In other words, thought and emotion move together to create a scepticism towards the bipolar separation of good and evil, right and wrong, or truth and fiction.

Likewise, Levertov continually breaches the boundary between imagination and intellect. When properly utilized, she argues, imagination is the key to moving beyond what might be termed 'the feel-good factor' or an artificial consolation.

> The action of imagination, if unsmothered, is to lift the crushed mind out from under the weight of affliction. The intellect by itself may point out the source of suffering; but the imagination illuminates it; by that light it becomes more comprehensible . . . Though imagination's wings can lift the individual out of private pits of gloom, it is a *creative* function, producing new forms and transforming existing ones; and these come into being *in the world*, autonomous objects available to others, and capable of transforming *them*. (1992: 145–46, original emphasis)

In Levertov's (1992: 147) reasoning, intellect, although invaluable to comprehend things, remains a passive and static force if not 'illuminated' by imagination. Poetry that accurately depicts the horrors of our time can only make readers really know by appealing to imagination and emotion, by 'giving flesh to the abstract'. More succinctly she puts it thus, '[j]ust to tell the tale and walk away isn't enough' (1992: 146). She sums up her own stance by denying that she is 'specifically an intellectual'. An artist, she suggests, has to '[draw] upon a wider range of intelligence – sensory, intuitive, emotional – than the term intellect connotes' (1992: 239). In the final instance, Levertov's intellectual creed was an aesthetic that was 'bound up with artistic integrity' (1992: 240).

Indeed, Levertov feels that it is her responsibility as a poet to inhabit the space between different realities, causing her to write in 'The Life of Art': 'the borderland – that's where, if one knew how,/one would establish residence. That watershed . . .' (1989: 85). She acknowledges that as a creative poet she needs to be constantly aware of what is happening in the world and to offer interpretations, thereby becoming, from a position on this borderland, a 'locus of change' (Harris 2000: 22). This balance is a rare and difficult thing to obtain though: '. . . there's an interface,/immeasurable, elusive – an equilibrium/just attainable, sometimes, when the attention's rightly poised' (Levertov 1989: 85). So this 'equilibrium' that remains 'elusive' is something to be strived for in the creative working life. It is from this position on the borderland that the writer can transcend both themselves and the contingent in order to see 'what lies beyond the window, past the frame, beyond . . .' in order to offer new insights (ibid.). The poet then operates in the tension between what is factual and what is ideal – moves to 'some place part fantasy, part truer-than-fact, where the life of the imagination supersedes commonplace activity' (Wagner-Martin 1991: 1). Yet it is only by holding firmly onto reality that the ideal can be aspired towards – to let go of reality opens the way for escapism into the world of fantasy.

Dillard describes the end of the *via negativa* as 'the lightless edge where the slopes of knowledge dwindle, and love for its own sake, lacking an object, begins' (1988b: 46). This is the recognition that the mystical search must ultimately move past the intellect and reason and move towards love, that knowledge is only a means to an end – not the end in itself. Earlier in the same text she raises her fears that language may not be able to convey any real meaning beyond individual understanding when she asks:

> Is the search for meaning among the high heaps of the meaningless a fool's game? Is it art's game? What is (gasp) the relationship between the world and the mind? Is *knowledge* possible? Do we ever discover meaning, or do we make it up? (Dillard 1988b: 14)

The claim that 'true' knowledge is never possible is self-evident to mystics.

The same notion is present in *Holy the Firm*, where she states: 'Knowledge is impossible. We are precisely nowhere, sinking on an imaginary ice floe, into entirely imaginary seas themselves adrift' (Dillard 1988a: 46). Language, although always imprecise, is the only means available to us. It follows that fluctuations of an imperfect world will necessitate a continual requirement to revision the notion of the sacred, for to treat anything in the finite world as beyond criticism is to render language idolatrous. This is what has tended to happen in religious discourse, where the dynamic functions of metaphors and symbols have become concretized and operate as idols rather than means to go beyond familiar interpretations of things they represent. Conversely, the potential for a symbol to 'act at the level where the scarcely understood fades into the unknown', in Dillard's view allows it to act as 'an instrument of new knowledge' (1988b: 168–69). She elaborates:

> Symbol does not only refer; it acts. There is no such thing as a *mere* symbol. When you climb to the higher level of abstraction, symbols, those enormous, translucent planets, are all there is. They are at once your only tools of knowledge and that knowledge's only object. It is no leap to say that space-time is itself a symbol. If the material world is a symbol, it is the symbol of mind, or of God. Which is more or less meaningless – as you choose. But it is not *mere*. In the last analysis, symbols and art objects do not stand for things; they manifest them, in their fullness. You begin by using symbols, and end by contemplating them. (1988b: 170)

Symbols and metaphors are the only means available to us by which we can articulate our sense of the sacred. Even philosophy, in the end, has to rely on metaphor to speak about its concepts. For Dillard, symbols and metaphors step in 'at the rim of knowledge where language falters' (1988b: 170).

Although Dillard recognizes that each progressive generation has the task of dedicating themselves 'to more comprehensive forms of beauty and understanding' (1988b: 170) she tends to be sceptical about what she calls the 'human emotional stew' because it might provide a false egocentric view of the world (Dillard 1998: 181). Additionally, Dillard is unusual in that she fuses a scientific approach with a mystical one in the contemplation of nature. Susan Felch observes that *Holy the Firm* contains a 'reflection thoroughly informed by modern physics' (1989: 2). If science tells Dillard one thing, it is that life is chaotic and random; '[n]othing temporal, spatial, perceptual, social or moral is fixed' (Dillard 1988b: 24). In other words, she has confidence in the ability of science to broaden our mystical understanding of the world, and, for example, suggests that Newton's discovery of gravity under the apple tree provides an interesting parallel to Buddha's enlightenment under the Bo tree and aligns herself with both (Dillard 1998: 186).

Time and space is a further continual fascination to Dillard. Stephen Webb notices that, in Dillard's thought, 'the irregularities of time and place are hyperbolically condensed to produce a sudden illumination, sublime, mystical and yet troubling' (1994: 435–36). An epiphany is produced through 'a disruptive suspension of ordinary time, a moment of eternity in the here and now' (ibid.). These moments appear to be unstable, yet as Sandra Humble-Johnson notes, 'the illuminated moment has the potential to steady a wobbling universe' (1992: 20). It is in fact her knowledge of Einstein's work that encourages her to seek this timeless moment that is an in between place. It was Dillard's belief that spiritual intuition and creative writing, as with Einstein's hypothesizing, could lead to '*true* knowing' (1992: 21). However, developing knowledge and understanding only functions as a transformative power if it transposes onto practical or political matters.

Towards a Theology of Integration

Because the notion of dualism is so firmly ingrained in Western culture, one of the overriding problems that theologians faces in post-modernity is that of merging conceptual opposites such as theory and practice, secularism and spirituality, intellect and emotion, and what approach to take to insights from other world religions. Here the model of relationship is evoked to imagine a theological integration of these polarities. This effectively enables personal spiritual experience to feed into the wider communal theological enterprise, thus avoiding the exclusive, ego-ridden journey of individual faith.

Since the 1960s, liberation theologians have endorsed the belief that theology cannot be divorced from political reality by adopting a hermeneutics of praxis. The word *praxis* stems from the Greek verb *prassien*, which means 'to do'. By definition, praxis involves the integration of ideas and actions, of theory and practice. I suggest that mystical praxis is about paying attention to the world around us, continuing the quest for spiritual insights, taking ethical responsibility for our actions, and having the courage to speak out – ultimately reaching out to others. The Greek term *phronesis*, which means to act truly and rightly, perhaps captures this best. This is a term developed by Aristotle as an alternative way of knowing, standing in contradistinction to *sophia*, which means to be more concerned with universal truths. *Phronesis* is usually translated as 'practical wisdom' and refers to the development of a habitual or virtuous way of living that will inevitably include a concern to further the well-being of all.

A crucial dimension of theological identity in post-modernity is the ability to build a bridge between the outer or active life and the inner or contemplative life. Historically, Mary who sits at Christ's feet in quiet contemplation has been valued over Martha, who attends to his bodily needs. In theological terms, this relates symbolically to the elevation of theory over praxis. Eckhart, however, did not separate 'Martha's acting from Mary's contemplative devotion but rather, conceiving of Mary in Martha' as the more spiritually developed. The point that Soelle makes is that the aim of the mystic (or religious) life should not be

> to practice an introverted mysticism nor to engage in an extroverted critique of the age alone, but to find one's *vita mixta* in this sense between contemplation and activity . . . This combination of contemplating and acting is rooted in the mystical understanding of the relationship to God as a mutuality of receiving and giving. (2001: 200–1)

The fact that Julian wrote in the vernacular so that 'even Christians' could share her revelations as well as acting as a spiritual advisor exemplifies this dual achievement of the mystic.

Murdoch's approach, while not explicitly political or radical, inspires moral action at a public and private level. Her attempts to recover Plato's concept of the

Good contribute to ideological restructuring at a communal level, while her concerns about illusion and self-deception encourage a reorientation of individual consciousness. Of our three literary writers, Levertov is the most overtly political. She felt obliged to work for peace and justice, and for her, prayer and politics play an equal role in Christian discipleship. Burton Carley (2000) depicts Dillard as 'an axe for the frozen sea within us . . . breaking through the frozen separating the modern self from the world'. The goal is not just to bring comfort to their readers, but rather, like Julian, these writers want their audiences to learn from and act upon their experiences.

For Murdoch, contrary to beliefs concerning the centrality of personal salvation, a theological identity in post-modernity must direct humans away from the self and towards others. She believed that people are not one-dimensional, but varied and complex, and it is only by incorporating a spiritual element into their lives, which she defines as 'attention' towards others, that people can make sense of the world. Abstract theory does not account for real people's lives. In the real world, people have a tendency to use other people for their own ends. A focus on the self, whether it is selfish love or lust, guilt, anger or intellectual pursuits, distracts us from reality. In few words, Murdoch's moral philosophy can be summed up in the phrase 'loving attention'.

Levertov demonstrates a more proactive understanding of love that leads to action through her political activities during the seventies. For her, to transform the world through love means being vocal, being active and being prepared to break the law in the name of peace and justice. Cary Nelson observes that, within Levertov's poetic vision, there emerges a 'moral commitment to practical action *outside* poetry [which] enters the poetry itself' (1993: 162, original emphasis). Levertov was involved in 'Ban the Bomb' demonstrations in the fifties, but her leftist political views did not appear in her poetry until the late sixties. Patricia Hampl describes Levertov as 'a reporter or witness at the political front . . . a *soul* at the front' (1993: 167, original emphasis). As Hampl realizes, Levertov feels acute guilt for being alive at all; as long as someone on earth was suffering and dying, she felt guilt for having herself survived. Moreover, she feels complicitous in human-caused suffering. For example, she feels implicated in the American involvement in the war in Vietnam. At times, her anger spills over into her poetry, which she argued should not be the purpose of poetry, but it was as if she could not contain her rage at injustice. This is something she had to overcome to live and work at her full potential.

During the Vietnam War, Levertov adopted an anti-war stance that was, largely, contrary to popular opinion in America at the time. Although there were growing voices of dissent, especially from the younger generation, the average American was firmly committed to their country's involvement in the conflict. It was only through the concerted efforts of committed pacifists, in whose number Levertov can be counted, that the American public gradually became aware of atrocities inflicted on the Vietnamese people in the name of democracy. The fact that a poet engaged in what is essentially a political issue through poetry led to disagreement among artists and politicians alike, but Levertov believed passionately that she was morally obligated to respond to issues of inhumanity and injustice that she perceived to be all around her.

Unlike Levertov, Dillard does not attempt political polemic or moral teaching. She said, 'I don't write at all about ethics. I try to do right and rarely do so. The kind of art I write is shockingly uncommitted – appallingly isolated from political, social, and economic affairs' (Yancy 1978: 960). To many, her policy of non-intervention is problematic. Pamela Smith (1995) speculates that this could partly be due to a feeling of 'estrangement . . . of an overwhelming sense of separateness'. In addition, she offers no alternative visions of Western thought and practice. But she does urge her readers through her reflections on her own experience to become fully alive and awake through an evocation of consciousness (Carley 2000). Above all, she wants to make her readers conscious of the supernatural, and surely to grow in consciousness means to become more aware. Although Dillard concentrates on her own personal growth (leaving her open to the criticism of egocentrism), the contemplative requirements of a mystic discussed previously pre-empt too much navel gazing.

Julian's teachings are undoubtedly entrenched in the Augustinian tradition and the doctrines of the Church. More importantly, however, her theology is fundamentally Trinitarian, for the Trinity is the expression of integration *par excellence*. Philip Sheldrake, in his exposition of the divorce between spirituality and theology, suggests that the Trinity represents 'a creative tension within God that is inherently dynamic rather than static . . . [As such] it holds together unity and diversity, oneness and distinction, communion and individuality, fixed ground and fluid relations' (1998: 49).

Although the Christian Trinity as a metaphysical reality is not of great significance for Murdoch, Levertov and Dillard, its metaphorical implications are evident. Indeed, it is interesting to note that ways of knowing and being tend to be represented by triadic structures in more holistic viewpoints rather than binary oppositions as found in mechanistic modes of understanding the world. Trinities are common metaphors in world religions to represent the idea of the one and the many, or the sense of unity at the heart of creation.[11] This represents a perceived unity present within the universe. It is also a model of relationship. It is a metaphor for the mysterious and inexhaustible mystery of God. It is also a metaphor for the human being made in the image of God. An integrated view of the human person would include body, mind and soul, and, in short, triadic structures resist dualistic modes of thinking by suggesting a more holistic or integrated vision of reality and the self in relation to it.

Any perception of a Transcendent Absolute, whether we call it the Good or God, or anything else, cannot materialize in the 'dress' of language without the combined efforts of both mind and heart. Moreover, without a corporeal body, humans would be unable to think or write. We can conclude, therefore, that our cognitive faculties (mind), our emotions (heart) and physical attributes (body) are three interlinked and necessary components to make the conveyance of a mystical consciousness possible. Language, particularly mystical language, has the potential to provide the bridge between these ontological realities. The poem, according to Levertov, is a 'communion . . . between the maker and the needer within the poet; the makers and needers outside him . . . and between the human and divine in both poet and reader' (1973: 47).

Sallie McFague has made her most prominent mark on the theological enterprise through her reconfigured Trinitarian model of God as Lover, Mother and Friend as outlined in *Models of God* (1987) and *Body of God* (1993). This conceptualization of the trinity reflects her view that relationship is an ontological reality. Humans are literally made from stardust and are part of the same 'primal explosion' as is the rest of the cosmos, and thus emblematic of inter-relationship in the extreme (McFague 1993: 104). Salvation in McFague's theology is within this world, and sin is categorized as 'turning away not from a transcendent power but from interdependence with other beings, including the matrix of being from whom all life comes' (McFague 1987: 139). By the time McFague writes *Life Abundant*, she has changed her metaphors for the Trinity to 'Creator, Sustainer and Liberator'. The metaphors will no doubt continue to change, but the Trinity as a metaphor for relationship in the context of unity and diversity has much potential. The relationship that individual humans have with multiple others is but one dimension of this.

Identity in Post-modernity from a Theological Perspective

The totality of human existence consists of both the universal and the particular; every living thing has its own peculiarities whilst at *the same time* participating in the whole of all that is – and theology must relate to and express both. Murdoch persuades us that

> [o]ur pilgrimage (in the direction of reality, good) is not experienced only in high, broad or general ways (such as in increased understanding of mathematics or justice), it is experienced in all our most minute relations with our surrounding world, wherein apprehensions (perceptions) of the minutest things (stones, spoons, leaves, scraps of rubbish, tiny gestures etc., etc.) are also capable of being deeper, more benevolent, more just (etc., etc.). (1992: 474)[12]

So, like Julian, Murdoch recognizes that both our 'substance and sensuality' are part of a larger unity. In an attempt to provide moral inspiration, however, Murdoch includes, through the personal fable, a means by which individual vision enters into a dialogue with public moral debate at a time when religious belief appeared to be in decline. Murdoch questions the logic of universal rules by suggesting that certain stories 'incarnate a moral truth that is paradoxical, infinitely suggestive and open to continual reinterpretation' (Conradi 2001: 91). In particular, the space given to ambiguity and paradox in her novels effectively highlights the complexities of many moral choices. Moral reasoning is not a fixed absolute but, rather, is in continual flux.

Perhaps more accurately stated, she creates contexts that enable an objective reflection on moral and ethical concerns. Her oft-quoted metaphor of a 'great hall of reflection where we can all meet and where everything under the sun can be examined and considered' offers an interesting divergence from Plato's myth of the cave (Conradi 2001: 461). In Plato's thought, the conception of ideas only takes place outside the cave away from illusion, whilst Murdoch, conversely, 'sees thinking as rooted in body-language' (Sage 1992: 83). Murdoch here calls into question the idea of the disembodied intellect. Through attention to the 'stuff' of an ordinary life, she similarly denounces the notion of an abstract individual that dominates Western philosophy. It is only through our interaction with others as part of different communities that moral or mystical insight occurs.

It took Levertov many years and much wrestling with her conscience to harmonize the relationship between her personal life and the public world of politics. Lorrie Smith puts it succinctly when she concludes that

> Not until she learns to live with paradox, relinquishing the desire to reconcile good and evil, can Levertov move beyond defeat toward new, though diminished, forms of affirmation. Her deep yearning for synthesis gradually moderates into a sort of détente which eases the polarized tension between the personal life and public contingency, lyric revelation and didactic statement . . . Though 'inner' and 'outer' are often painfully separate in Levertov's fallen world, they are also paradoxically united because one person suffers and another records the dissonance. Her most successful political poems neither collapse the distinctions between these terms nor flatly oppose them, but sustain an equilibrium in which the integrity of each is preserved and enlarged by the other. (1993: 181)

In Levertov's affirmative vision, 'her knowledge of evil is mitigated by a deep reverence for earthly life' (Smith 1993: 192). She does not attempt to offer specific solutions to problems but, as a socially engaged poet, she feels equally compelled to point out that which is worthy of praise and that which should be protested against. Hampl also makes the point that, unlike feminist poets such as Adrienne Rich and Marge Piercy, who hoist a large part of the blame on the Vietnam War onto men and patriarchy, Levertov recognizes herself 'as a citizen of an oppressive nation, rather than as a victim of it . . . [so] she could not separate herself physically from that paralyzing guilt that war brought with it' (Hampl 1993: 170–71). In other words, for Levertov, true liberation happens at both the personal and political levels and as a member of the community, not in separation.

The fact that Dillard moves from her solitary experience in *Pilgrim at Tinker Creek* to include the experiences of others in *Holy the Firm* and *Teaching a Stone to Talk* prompts Ronda to assert that 'a kind of tension is created between personal vision and collective insight' (Ronda 1984: 1064). It is particularly in her essays 'Expedition to the Pole' and 'Total Eclipse' in the latter of these that this is evident. In *Teaching a Stone to Talk*, Dillard, through dialogue with the Other, treads the *via media* between self-absorption and communal loyalties so that an engagement with others 'completes the incomplete self' (Ronda 1984: 1066). An essential element of Dillard's writing that is often overlooked due to the solitary nature of her work is her sense of community. One of the most memorable of Dillard's accounts of her forays into nature is 'Total Eclipse', which appears in *Teaching a Stone to Talk*. She gathers with a crowd 'of rugged individualists' on a mountain in Washington State to watch the event and describes how 'wrong' the world looked once the sun was covered up.

> The sky snapped over the sun like a lens cover. The hatch in the brain slammed. Abruptly it was dark night, on the land and in the sky . . . There was no sound. The eyes dried, the arteries drained, the lungs hushed. There was no world. We were the world's dead people rotating and orbiting around and around, embedded in the planet's crust, while the earth rolled down. Our minds were light years distant, forgetful of almost everything. (Dillard 1992: 13–18)

Time stood still on that mountainside, and Dillard, in the face of 'the power and indifference of nature', here 'claim[s] a place with others'. Ronda (1984) suggests that she imagines this as an apocalyptic scenario similar to a nuclear disaster, but what is clear is that Dillard wants to be with others, and in fact, in other writings, she has identified herself, 'however ambivalently, [with] the Christian community'. For Dillard in this piece, her revelation is somewhat sinister and provides a prophetic insight into the outcome of thinking ourselves too powerful. However, I would argue that, by situating herself with others, Dillard emphasizes the communal aspect of mysticism. After the eclipse she and her companion go back to a restaurant and eat among some of the other watchers, reinforcing the fact that she perceived herself as part of the human community. In fact, a young man suggests that the eclipse 'looked like a Life Saver up in the sky'. Dillard agrees with him and describes him as a 'walking alarm clock' who brings her back to the world of reality, ready for 'the mind to begin its task' (Dillard 1992: 23–24). This helps her to realize that the 'vision' is useless unless she continues in her task of waking people up, through her creative ability to manipulate language, to the sacred.

An Integrated Theological Identity in Post-modernity

This discussion has suggested that theological expression must include both emotion and rational argument as a way of living in a dialectical tension between our private and public selves in post-modernity. Moreover, this chapter has argued that contemporary writers such as Murdoch, Levertov and Dillard are examples of creative writers that can provide clues that help us to achieve this because they incorporate the *whole* of human experience into their spiritual/theological reflections in their writing just as Julian of Norwich did before them. At the microcosmic level, the writings of Murdoch, Levertov and Dillard contain a subjective view of the world through their individual spiritual quests. At the macrocosmic level, however, their voices are prophetic by protesting against injustice and reading the signs of the time. In other words, they recognize both the personal and communal aspects of theological identity.

The reader should now be also aware of how literature, such as the examples cited here, is capable of creating what Sheldrake defines as space for communion with others and transcendence (1998: 201). Following on from this, human self-understanding is by necessity diminished in order to fully apprehend the Other, and the category of Truth becomes both plural and unstable. Both human identity and the process of theology that reflects on its relationship to the Transcendent are therefore never fixed or finalized. Instead it is recognized to be, as the French Jesuit priest Michel De Certeau puts it, 'in a perpetual state of departure' (1992: 99). We are always on the way to what we are to become. I suggest that a dynamic engagement with this is better facilitated through creative texts rather than official doctrine at one end of the spectrum or, at the other end, consumerist-led spiritualities that ultimately diminish the self into a passive consumer.

Notes

1 These two terms have become associated with the Christian mystical tradition. The *via positiva* or Affirmative Way is the belief that God can be known through His creation and results in affirming all we can say about God. The *via negativa* or Purgative Way is characterized as the way of not knowing and darkness, and the fact that all language fails to capture what God is. See McGinn 1991: x–xx.
2 This metaphor of ascent written by Plotinus, in *Enneads* VI.9 is typically found in Christian and Platonic mysticism and tends to imply the flight of the soul from the corporeal body.
3 Daniel Berrigan and Denise Levertov travelled to Hanoi together during the Vietnam War.
4 See also Daly 1990.
5 See Murdoch's (1970: 17–23) example of a mother-in-law who feels hostility towards her daughter-in-law but learns to see her in a good light.
6 Levertov does not reference Schweitzer here but she most probably refers to the sentence 'The most immediate and comprehensive fact of consciousness is that I am life which wills to live, in the midst of life that wills to live' (1987: 310).
7 McFague refers to the Jewish theologian Martin Buber's phrase from his publication of the same name here.
8 Levertov published a book with Edward C. Dimock, Jr. of translated Vaishnava poetry from the Indian religious traditions, *In Praise of Krishna: Songs from the Bengali* (1965).
9 Rosemary Radford Ruether would be a typical example of this theological method. She has pruned away everything that she sees as being unhelpful or inherently sexist or able to support systems of domination from the Judaeo-Christian tradition to provide a form of Christianity liberated from colonial or patriarchal biases.
10 Although Murdoch herself disputed this – see Murdoch 2001: 4–5.
11 Trinities exist in most world mythologies as a natural metaphor of the concept of the tension or space between opposites. Trinities typically represent the idea of the one and the many, or the sense of unity at the heart of creation. In Mahayana Buddhism, for example, the *dharmakaya* represents the cosmic body of Buddha, *nirmanakaya* the cosmic body incarnate in Gautama Buddha, and *sambogakaya* is the cosmic body present in the intersessionary bodhisattvas. In ancient Egyptian mythology, there was the Osirus–Isis–-Horus trinity. Another example would be the Hindu *trimurti* of Brahma, Vishnu and Shiva as aspects of the universal Brahmin.
12 It is poignant that at the end of her life Murdoch took to collecting bits of rubbish like old envelopes and cigarette ends. See Bayley 2000: 2.

References

Bayley, J. (2000), *Elegy for Iris* (New York: Picador).
Berrigan, D. (1993), 'Denise Levertov's Prose', in A. Gelpi (ed.), *Denise Levertov: Selected Criticism* (Ann Arbor: University of Michigan Press).
Bynum, C.W. (1982), *Jesus as Mother: Studies in the Spirituality of the High Middle Ages* (Berkeley; Los Angeles; London: University of California Press).
Carley, B. (2000), 'Anne Dillard: Getting a Feel for the Place', *The Journal of Liberal Religion* 2:1. http://www.meadville.edu/gibbons_2_1.html
Carrette, J., and R. King (2004), *Selling Spirituality: The Silent Takeover of Religion* (London: Routledge).
Chirban, S.A. (2000), 'Oneness Experience: Looking Through Multiple Lenses', *The Journal of Applied Psychoanalytic Studies* 2.3: 247–64.
Conradi, P.J. (2001), *Iris Murdoch: The Saint and the Artist* (London: HarperCollins, rev. edn).
Daly, M. (1990), 'The Looking Glass Society', in A. Loades (ed.), *Feminist Theology: A Reader* (London: SPCK).
De Certeau, M. (1992), *The Mystic Fable* (trans. Michael B. Smith; Chicago and London: University of Chicago Press).
Dillard, A. (1988a), *Holy the Firm* (New York: HarperPerennial).
—— (1988b), *Living by Fiction* (New York: HarperPerennial).
—— (1992), *Teaching a Stone to Talk* (New York: HarperPerennial).
—— (1998), *Pilgrim at Tinker Creek* (New York: HarperPerennial, rev. edn).
Dipple, E. (1982), *Iris Murdoch: Work for the Spirit* (London: Methuen).
Felch, S.M. (1989), 'Annie Dillard: Modern Physics in a Contemporary Mystic', *Mosaic* 22.2: 1–14.
Fletcher, J., and C. Bove (1994), *Iris Murdoch: A Descriptive Primary and Annotated Secondary Bibliography* (New York and London: Garland).
Griffen, G. (1993), *The Influence of the Writings of Simone Weil on the Fiction of Iris Murdoch* (San Francisco: Mellen Research University Press).
Hampl, P. (1993) 'A Witness of our Time', in A. Gelpi (ed.), *Denise Levertov: Selected Criticism* (Ann Arbor: University of Michigan Press).
Harris, V. (2000), 'Denise Levertov and the Lyric of the Contingent Self', in A.C. Little and S. Paul (eds), *Denise Levertov: New Perspectives* (West Cornwall, CT: Locust Hill Press).
Humble-Johnson, S. (1992), *The Space Between: Literary Epiphany in the Work of Annie Dillard* (Kent, OH, and London: Kent State University Press).
Jantzen, G. (1995), *Power, Gender and Christian Mysticism* (Cambridge: Cambridge University Press).
—— (2000), *Julian of Norwich* (London: SPCK, rev. edn).
Julian of Norwich (1978), *Showings* (trans. Edmund College, OSA and James Walsh, SJ; Mahwah, NJ: Paulist Press).
Keller, J. (1983) 'The Function of Paradox in Mystical Discourse', *Studia Mystica* 6.3: 3–19.
Kinnahan, L. (1992), *A Poetics of the Feminine: Authority and Literary Tradition* (Cambridge: Cambridge University Press).
Levertov, D. (1973), *The Poet in the World* (New York: New Directions).
—— (1986), *Oblique Prayers* (Newcastle upon Tyne: Bloodaxe Books).
—— (1989), *A Door in the Hive* (New York: New Directions).
—— (1992), *New and Selected Essays* (New York: New Directions).
—— (1998), *Sands of the Well* (Newcastle upon Tyne: Bloodaxe Books).
Levertov, D., and E.C. Dimock, Jr. (trans.) (1965), *In Praise of Krishna: Songs from the Bengali* (Chicago: University of Chicago Press).

Matthews, M. (2000), *Both Alike to Thee: The Retrieval of the Mystic Way* (London: SPCK).
McFague, S. (1987), *Models of God* (Philadelphia: Fortress Press).
—— (1993), *The Body of God* (London: SCM Press).
—— (1997), *Super, Natural Christians* (Minneapolis: Fortress Press).
—— (2001), *Life Abundant* (Minneapolis: Fortress Press).
McGinn, B. (1991), *The Foundations of Mysticism* (London: SCM Press).
McIntosh, M.A. (1998), *Mystical Theology* (Oxford: Blackwell).
Murdoch, I. (1957), *The Sandcastle* (London: Penguin).
—— (1970), *The Sovereignty of Good* (New York and London: Routledge).
—— (1992), *Metaphysics as a Guide to Morals* (London: Penguin).
—— (2001), 'Literature and Philosophy: A Conversation with Bryan Magee', in Conradi 2001: 4–5.
Nelson, C. (1993), 'Levertov's Political Poetry', in A. Gelpi (ed.), *Denise Levertov: Selected Criticism* (Ann Arbor: University of Michigan Press).
Ronda, B.A. (1984), 'Annie Dillard's Fictions to Live By', *Christian Century* 101.35: 1062–1066.
Ross-Bryant, L. (1990), 'The Silence of Nature', *Religion and Literature* 22.1: 79–94.
Sage, L. (1992), *Women in the House of Fiction* (London: Macmillan).
Schweitzer, A. (1987) *The Philosophy of Civilisation* (trans. C.T. Campion; New York: Macmillan, 1950; repr., New York: Prometheus Books).
Sheldrake, P. (1998), *Spirituality and Theology* (London: Darton, Longman and Todd).
—— (2001), *Spaces for the Sacred* (London: SCM Press).
Smith, L. (1993), 'Songs of Experience: Denise Levertov's Political Poetry', in A. Gelpi (ed.), *Denise Levertov: Selected Criticism* (Ann Arbor: University of Michigan Press).
Smith, P.A. (1995), 'The Ecotheology of Annie Dillard: A Study in Ambivalence', *Cross Currents* 45.3: 341–59. http://www.crosscurrents.org/dillard.htm (accessed 29 June 2002).
Soelle, D. (1984), *Suffering* (trans. E.R. Kalin; Philadelphia: Fortress Press).
—— (2001), *The Silent Cry: Mysticism and Resistance* (Minneapolis: Fortress Press).
Tracy, D. (1994), 'Theology and the Many Faces of Postmodernity', *Theology Today* 51.1: 104–14.
Wagner-Martin, L. (1991), *Critical Essays on Denise Levertov* (Boston, MA: G K Hall & Co).
Webb, S.H. (1994) 'Nature's Spendthrift Economy: The Extravagance of God in Pilgrim at Tinker Creek', *Soundings* 77: 429–51.
Yancy, P. (1978), 'A Face Aflame', *Christianity Today* 22: 960–61.

2

Binary Reciprocity: Karl Barth, Christological Identity and the Politics of Religion

Richard Andrew

Introduction

> Jesus Christ as attested to us in Holy Scripture is the one Word of God whom we must hear and whom we must trust and obey in life and in death. (CD IV/3.1: 3)[1]

This chapter explores some of the resources and dynamics within the theology of Karl Barth for examining one aspect of the interaction between Christianity and public space; namely the question of identity and its correlate, the question of recognition. On first inspection Karl Barth seems an unlikely candidate with whom to investigate this theme. His legacy is regarded by many as deeply flawed and at best ambiguous. Indeed Barth himself conceded that his life's work seemed 'to lack a certain power of attraction; indeed one characteristic of it seems to be a certain explosive or any rate centrifugal effect'. Yet, in the same breath, he was able to admit to finding 'new friends and sometimes very good ones along the way' (Busch 1976: 249).

This response to Barth is instructive for it has parallels in the history of his reception into the theological canon. The quotation at the head of this chapter illustrates the tension. For one group of readers, Barth's christological concentration, which reaches its climax in volume IV of the *Church Dogmatics*, seems so highly particular that it is unable to sustain a theological vision that is comprehensive (or catholic) enough to engage meaningfully in the public sphere. A variation on this theme might view Barth's statement with suspicion; merely the continuation of Christianity's long history of asserting power over other traditions and narratives which give unity, purpose and meaning to life.

On closer inspection, however, the theo-political force of Barth's statement becomes apparent. The sentence repeats words from the first article of the Barmen Declaration, itself largely written by Barth, adopted by the confessing church in Nazi Germany on 31 May 1934. In this instance the exclusiveness of loyalty suggested by the statement forms the basis for the theological and political resistance of a minority against totalitarianism. Indeed Barmen provides the inspiration for subsequent confessional documents associated with opposition to tyranny (for example, the *Kairos* document in South

Africa). The particularity of christological identity in this instance provides the basis for a praxis of resistance.

This reading suggests that there is more at stake in the identification of our loyalties in the public sphere. If it is granted that one feature of our context is that it is characterized by a variety of views which conceive public space in plural (and sometimes contradictory) ways then a counterpoint must be made; such standpoints are not neutral. Translated into the public sphere they are associated with concrete decisions which include or exclude, emancipate or alienate others. At some point any quest which seeks to give unity and purpose to life needs to give an account of how it analyses power, the kinds of reciprocity and solidarity it envisages between people of different outlook and how it contributes to human flourishing: it must, in other words, make judgements of worth.

> A common tradition, a common way of life, is not sustained by discussion alone. It requires the structuring of common experience, and the pursuit of agreed goals and purposes in common action. Any movement or way of life which is to sustain its identity and vitality, *as* a movement, has to be able to decide and declare what it stands for. And if a movement or way of life is concerned with meanings and values that are central to human need and human flourishing, then, in the measure that it calls in question the operations and the legitimacy of the 'powers that be', it can expect to meet not merely with 'disagreement' but with more practically enacted forms of resistance. (Lash 1986: 22)

This chapter is concerned with how one 'particular' theology conceives the dynamics of the interaction between the Christian community and the public square, defying its limits to 'echo the hope and anguish of *all* humanity' (Buckley 1992: 160, original emphasis). The first section locates Barth in relation to a debate concerning the nature of recognition in public life. Following that, the chapter offers an interpretation of Barth in two stages, indicating how his approach illuminates some of the issues at stake in a politics of identity. For Barth the dynamics of the interaction between the Christian community is one centred in Jesus Christ, the identity of whom provides the ontological basis for a vision of a unified yet differentiated public square in which particular kinds of reciprocity and recognition find their ground.

Reciprocity and the Public Square: The Problem of Recognition

What type of universality is at stake in Barth's claim that Jesus Christ is the one Word which the Church must hear, trust and obey? It is noticeable that this statement links together different stages of Barth's mature theological work (see, for example, his commentary on *Barmen* in CD II/1: 172–78). Although the Barmen Declaration was written in a period of acute political crisis, the repetition of its theme at several junctures indicates that its central concern was not a passing whim but represented a deeply held conviction.

Yet even if Barmen can be read as the 'basic text of Barth's theology' (Jüngel 1986: 43), given the recurrence of the first thesis, it must be viewed in the wider context of his thought. For some commentators the christological concentration of Barmen is its chief strength, a 'permanent thorn as well as . . . comfort' (Blaser 1984: 303); for others its voice is completely alien. Barth's particularist bent leads, so the argument goes, to a kind of revelatory captivity. However, it is questionable whether such a reading, at least in a strong form, can be sustained. The monumental scope of the *Church Dogmatics* is itself testimony to the fact that for Barth the particular identity of Jesus Christ can be unfolded in a number of related but differentiated ways. The concern with the particular identity of Jesus Christ is not an attempt to elaborate a principle, method or system which fills the interpretative horizon. Rather, Barth's theology represents an attempt to unfold the nature of revelation as a 'gift' in such a way that its universal character is specified in Jesus Christ, 'free of any unfortunate dichotomy between the deity of God and the humanity of humankind' (Jüngel 1986: 127). In other words, Barth is concerned to think God and humanity together not as abstract polarities but in related but differentiated ways in Jesus Christ. In arguing this viewpoint, Barth runs counter to a number of intellectual traditions which have dominated discussions of identity since the Enlightenment. Whilst Barth can only be understood in the context of a response to those traditions, it is, nevertheless, possible to understand why some commentators have chosen to describe Barth as the first post-modern theologian. The target of his indignation, in this respect, is the development of an Enlightenment ideal of the unlimited, 'absolutist' human person who 'discovers his own power, his own ability, the potential that slumbers in his . . . humanity simply as such, and who understands this as something . . . in itself justified and mighty, and who therefore sets this potential in . . . motion in every direction' (Barth quoted in Jenson 1989: 26). Barth rejects the identification of humanity which lies behind this construction and hence of any notion of identity divorced from its christological ground, the concrete person in whom God binds himself to human history. This claim is clearly profoundly counter intuitive for, as Wolf Krötke notes,

> This principle of theological anthropology is particularly provocative today because it does not at first appear to show how it can be connected with what we already know generally about the human being. And without such a connection, all statements of theological anthropology are in danger of hanging isolated in space, simply incomprehensible outside of theological discourse. (Krötke 2000: 159)

The qualification 'at first' is crucial, as Krötke goes on to demonstrate. Nevertheless, the fact that Barth has been read in this way suggests that his use in elaborating a public theology presents some challenges. A particular set of concerns helps to clarify one dimension of the issues at stake. One reading of modern society suggests that it lacks the conditions for securing consensus; it is irreducibly pluralist. Whether or not this thesis can be maintained (or indeed whether the conditions for reaching consensus on the nature of a common life are entirely absent), such a context poses a dilemma for any tradition which makes a claim to universality or 'publicness'. Alistair McFadyen points out the acuteness of the problem:

> [W]e are bound to dialogue in plurality; to go round in circles, explaining, exploring and elaborating perceived theological truth in dialogue with other basic commitments with their own truths, believing as we do so that we somehow serve the truth, yet knowing that truth can never become clear in plurality, can never get spelt out or made clear in terms that can be agreed on by all. (McFadyen 1993: 437)

Yet the dilemma can be sharpened further: what is at stake is not just a question of how conditions for reciprocal communication can be established. It is also about how concrete decisions can be taken in the political sphere, even in the absence of consensus, especially when confronted with the type of absolutism the Barmen Declaration confronted in the 1930s.

The relationship of 'publicness' to various kinds of universalism forms part of the logic of the explorations of the Canadian philosopher Charles Taylor into what he calls the 'politics of recognition'. In a wide-ranging essay on this theme, Taylor traces the evolution of modern notions of identity and their connection to ideas of recognition. He points out that recognition is essential to a person's self-understanding:

> The thesis is that our identity is partly shaped by recognition or its absence, often by the *mis*recognition of others, and so a person or group of people can suffer real damage, real distortion, if the people or society around them mirror back to them a confining or demeaning or contemptible picture of themselves. (Taylor 1994: 25)

Taylor charts the development of two strands within the modern conception of identity that generate the concern for recognition. The displacement of traditional forms of society based on hierarchies of honour by societies based on the principle of dignity represents a shift towards a universal and egalitarian sense of recognition. The principle of dignity manifests itself in the public sphere in a politics of universalism characterized by what is held to be universally and equally the same in all people. At the same time, the theme of identity is modified by a parallel development, from the end of the eighteenth century onwards, of an ideal of authenticity. The subjective turn of Enlightenment culture issues in a principle of originality, the assertion that each one of us has our own 'original' way of being human. At first the ideal of authenticity has a moral accent: it sits easily with a notion of relationship with God or the good. Gradually this attachment was displaced so that moral importance attached itself increasingly to the self. As Taylor notes, in a discussion of Herder, in this view, 'Not only should I not mold my life to the demands of external conformity; I can't even find the model by which to live outside myself. I can only find it within' (1994: 30).

This ideal of originality has both an individual and a public face. In the personal sphere it is expressed as a desire for (or right to) self-fulfilment or self-realization; its parallel in the public sphere is the self-fulfilment or self-realization of the culture that 'bears' a particular people. This latter idea underpins the development of various forms of nationalism including the idea of a *Volk* true to itself and its own culture which emerges in a malignant form in Nazi Germany.

Taylor indicates the monological direction of this development and highlights its dialogical modification in the modern era: 'We define our identity always in dialogue with, sometimes in struggle against, the things our significant others want to see in us' (1994: 33).

Nevertheless, even in its modified form, the principle of authenticity is premised on a universalist basis: each person is entitled to be recognized for their own identity and to be protected from 'other-induced distortions' (1994: 37). Taylor indicates the tensions within the 'universalisms' that constitute the modern politics of recognition. The discourse of recognition means two things: a politics of universalism which focuses upon what is universally the same in all people which, to that extent, is 'difference blind' (1994: 43); and a politics of difference which recognizes distinct identities but on a universal basis, i.e. it is premised on the universal application of the principle of originality. One draws upon the notion of a universal capacity (each person is equally worthy of respect); the other upon a universal potential (the potential to form one's own identity must be respected):

> These two modes of politics, then, both based on the notion of equal respect, come into conflict. For one, the principle of equal respect requires that we treat people in a difference-blind fashion. The fundamental intuition that humans command this respect focuses on what is the same in all. For the other, we have to recognize and even foster particularity. The reproach the first makes to the second is just that it violates the principle of nondiscrimination. The reproach the second makes to the first is that it negates identity by forcing people into a homogenous mold that is untrue to them. (1994: 43)

But the latter form of politics frequently issues in a further claim: the politics of equal dignity is itself the expression of the hegemony of a particular culture. Underlying this critique is the idea that various forms of liberal culture are themselves nothing more than 'particularism masquerading as the universal' (1994: 44). The key claim of radical forms of the politics of difference is that in practice a politics of equal dignity can be discriminatory: it is minority cultures that are forced to take on characteristics which are alien to their 'authentic' nature; 'difference-blind' liberalism is itself the political expression of a particular kind of culture.

This tension between different forms of universality is instructive for it highlights some of the fault lines within contemporary discussions of identity and the politics that accompany it. Indeed many of the anxieties within the current spate of 'culture wars' result from a nervousness about how to handle these distinct elements of public discourse. What heightens the problem is that the first pole ('difference-blind' liberalism) assumes that the absence of differentiation is crucial to the development of a common life. A balanced other-dependence (or reciprocity), in this view, necessitates a unified purpose, common projects, a common self (1994: 49). On the other side of the equation, such forms of reciprocity (or other-dependence) are incompatible with the idea of differentiation: a politics of universal capacity proves to be a politics of homogeneity (1994: 51).

The remainder of Taylor's essay begins to address the question of how this tension can be resolved. The specific issue concerns what a balanced reciprocity might look like: what grounds public space in a way that enables both unity of purpose (a common life) and differentiation? In an aside towards the end of his essay, Taylor holds out the tantalizing possibility that the answer might be a religious one. He even makes use of Herder's view that the idea of providence provides a basis for differentiation leading to harmony (1994: 72). There is a hint here that a secularized discourse of recognition (dignity and authenticity) has its equivalent, and possibly its roots, in theological discourse.

One possible theological response to these issues claims that 'in God's singularity and universality the world's plurality does achieve a unity (though not necessarily a uniformity)' (McFadyen 1993: 442). Though unity, in this sense, has an eschatological flavour, it does suggest that it is possible to embrace difference within a theological framework and that approximations, or anticipations, of an ultimate unity of purpose might be glimpsed in the present. If a universal claim is intrinsic to the identity of Christianity, as I believe it is, a basic commitment necessitated by faith in Jesus Christ, then some argument of this form seems to be essential. Yet even if this commitment cannot, or should not, easily be placed on one side, there remains a nagging question: what sort of universality or publicness is appropriate to Christian faith? The richness of Taylor's account of the politics of recognition highlights some issues that need to be addressed within a Christian description of universality and 'publicness'. Clearly, such an account is not a neutral one: but what kind of reciprocity emerges from such an account? How does it negotiate the boundaries between unity of purpose and distortion of the other?

The remainder of this chapter traces the potential of Barth's theology for a politics of recognition. Of course, Taylor's precise questions and context are not those of Barth. Nevertheless, a concern with identity, more specifically with the identity of Jesus Christ, the 'ontologically constitutive' (Webster 1995: 1) centre of God's dealings with humanity (*God's* humanity; God's *humanity*), suggests that there are at least implicit resources within his theology which can illuminate aspects of the discussion. The claim to universality in this context implies that the horizon within which the problem of recognition functions has a theological character. The tensions within a politics of recognition are not simply to do with bridging a rhetorical or communicative gap: they represent a distance, a 'theological space between us and Trinity' (Willimon 2005: 4). In that sense, Barth's contribution to the discussion can be understood as an attempt to offer an ontology of human identity (and recognition) within the context of God's identity and act in Jesus Christ, electing, creating, reconciling and redeeming. The corollary of this is an account of human action corresponding to divine action which provides the theological conditions for reciprocity, recognition and unity of purpose (a common life) within public space.

The sheer scope of Barth's work demands some kind of limiting method in order to draw out its major features. John Webster (1995: 2–5) draws attention to two inter-related aspects of Barth's thought in the period of the *Church*

Dogmatics. First, Barth's theology is an intense reflection upon the meaning and universal implications of the statement, 'God is'. For Barth, God is not conditioned, determined or derived from anything outside of Godself (CD II/1: 307). Second, because 'God is', theology is 'the-anthropology': God is God only in the particular form of the history of Jesus Christ. As Webster puts it, 'God moves towards humanity by establishing covenant fellowship between himself and his creatures; God is true God "only in this movement"' (Webster 1995: 3, quoting CD II/2: 7). Webster's concern is for the possibilities of Barth's thinking for a 'moral ontology' (ibid.). In parallel with this, one might argue, Barth offers an ontology within which it is possible to make sense of a politics of recognition in terms of what von Balthasar (1992: 177) describes as the 'binary reciprocity' of God and humanity, a reciprocity within which it is possible to conceive of the relationship between God and humanity and between human beings and other human beings in both differentiated and related ways. In tracing through the implications of this insight, it is essential that the inter-related themes that Webster draws attention to remain in view.

In what follows, Barth's concern for the 'binary reciprocity' of God and humanity implied in Webster's analysis is examined first under the heading binary reciprocity as the rupture of recognition and secondly, binary reciprocity as God's 'freedom for fellowship' (Webster 1995: 3). Integral to each stage of interpretation, each linked to the first Barmen thesis, is the assumption that the conditions for reciprocity, and hence for a politics of recognition, are pure gift: in other words they are dependent upon the prior, gracious initiative and activity of God.

Binary Reciprocity as the Rupture of Recognition

> Jesus Christ as attested to us in Holy Scripture is the one Word of God whom we must hear and whom we must trust and obey in life and in death. (CD IV/3.1: 3)

Essential to the construction of a politics of recognition in Taylor's account is an assumption of some form of anthropological normativity. Though, as Taylor (1994) demonstrates, the precise way in which humanity is 'normed' is disputed within the politics of recognition, on different sides of the debate there is at least tacit agreement: it is what humanity is thought to be, how it is 'normed', that grounds particular kinds of universality and shapes the view of what constitutes identity and recognition in both its private and public dimensions. Identity and recognition, in other words, have an anthropological character.

How, then, is this framework articulated theologically? One possible response, dominant since the Enlightenment, suggests that a theological account of identity and recognition advances by locating a common, shared discourse about humanity before asking the question of God, a procedure validated (or not) by the 'perceived measure of overlap between natural experience of the world and that which is articulated in Christian doctrine' (Webster 1995: 59). A variation of this response argues that theological accounts of identity and recognition must correlate closely with (at least some) anthropological claims that are made by others. In this view, Christian claims gain purchase in the public sphere by attempting to demonstrate how particular claims concerning identity and recognition make sense when rooted in God as their ground.

Yet for a theologian like Barth such approaches are highly problematic. Barth perceives a difficulty in any 'normative' anthropology which begins with the human subject: 'We are totally and not just partially incapable of occupying any independent vantage point from the height of which we might penetrate and judge ourselves' (CD III/2: 30). The inference is that Barth rejects certain ways of grounding identity and the kinds of recognition and universality associated with it. The statement 'God is' represents an interruption of the discourse of identity:

> [W]ith the advent of the truth of God, the structure of language has been ruptured at the very core. In relation to this divine interruption, the interruption of all interruptions, deliberate paradox or conjunction of opposites is the fitting vehicle of expression. (Hunsinger 1991: ix)

Hunsinger's statement highlights the importance of reading Barth with a dialectical imagination. He indicates how Barth prioritizes the language of mystery over the language of experience and reason, implying a deep respect for the limits of human language in conveying the reality of God. On one side of the dialectic, this 'rupture' illuminates the pathos of certain ways of construing the private and public face of human authenticity, originality and dignity. These ideas represent a fiction, an abstraction, to the extent that they are divorced from 'real' humanity as it is made known on the other side of the dialectic, in the gracious encounter between God and humanity in Jesus Christ.

For Barth, Christology has an ontological and epistemological priority from which anthropological considerations are derived. As a consequence, a discourse of recognition is one which has its prior determination in the knowledge of humanity made possible because humanity 'stands in the light of the Word of God. The Word of God is thus its foundation' (CD III/2: 20). This position needs only to be stated for us to recognize how radical and counter-intuitive it seems. Yet for Barth this christological claim not only reflects reality as it really is but relativizes the attempt to 'norm' humanity on any other basis, '. . . disrupting all efforts at metaphysical closure' (Hunsinger 2000: 9).

Further, Barth's seemingly counter-intuitive conclusions are due not, as one might be tempted to think, to cultural barbarism; an abandonment of any engagement with wider intellectual culture. Indeed Barth's writing is full of such engagement, especially in the closely argued notes which accompany the main body of the argument in the *Church Dogmatics*. Rather, it is more accurate to say that a key feature of his theology is its rejection of certain features of modernity, especially the terms in which it frames the debate about the nature of the relationship between God and humanity. Even whilst his theology arises in dialogue with the intellectual culture of the Enlightenment (i.e. it does not represent a return to pre-modern ways of thinking), Barth's thinking represents a departure from some of its most cherished notions. In particular, he rejects the turn towards the subject which typifies not only the intellectual climate he is responding to but also the notion of identity which is its correlate. It is important to recognize that the reason why Barth distances himself from this approach is theological. As Robert Jenson indicates:

> Barth's objection to the Enlightenment's passion for autonomous humanity is not so much to the ideal of the autonomous human as to the eighteenth century's identification of who this human person is. (1989: 27–28)

For someone like Barth, then, the key problem with a politics of recognition is a problem of (mis)identification:

> Wherever the human being is supposed to be understood theologically in relation to God on a purely human basis, the danger looms of replacing real humanity with a short sighted and constricting image of the human, thereby suppressing and impeding possibilities for the free development of real human being. (Krötke 2000: 162)

The development of this aspect of Barth's thought has deep roots. Initially immersed and nurtured within the nineteenth-century German liberal theological tradition, he came to reject the views of his teachers and to seek a different basis for theology. The grounds for this rejection are complex although Barth later recalled that it was the support of his former teachers, including Adolf von Harnack, for the Kaiser at the outbreak of the First World War that forced him to question radically the basis of his previous theological convictions. 'An entire world of theological exegesis, ethics, dogmatics, and preaching, which up to that point I had accepted as basically credible, was thereby shaken to the foundations' (Barth 1982: 264).

It is important to note what is at stake in this observation. For Barth, a particular mode of theology revealed its ideological hand. Theology had been domesticated, assimilated to a particular type of hegemony (culture Protestantism). It marked the beginning not only of the search for a new basis for theology, but of a thoroughgoing iconoclasm. The response of his teachers represented for Barth not only an attempt to provide religious legitimation for the War effort but the domestication of God within a particular cultural, religious and political framework. This domestication was one which he believed to be symptomatic of any synthesis of Christianity, to the left or right, revolutionary or bourgeois, even whilst politically he remained a socialist to the end of his life. Barth's iconoclasm parallels in certain respects the insights of radical forms of the politics of difference, namely that what claims to be universal can be an expression of hegemony, a particularism masquerading as a universal.

In Barth's reading of the theological tradition since Schleiermacher he observed an attempt to posit a 'given relationality' between humanity and God (Webster 2000: 25). This relationality manifested itself as a given within human experience, history, culture and religion which could be cultivated as an aspect of human and cultural identity without reference to the God who is 'wholly other' than us. Webster notes that construing God's relation to humanity in this way makes God merely a function of the human realm, 'an exalted aspect of creaturely existence' (2000: 25), a point recognized in a different way by the atheistic philosophers of the nineteenth century, such as Feuerbach and Overbeck, who themselves exercised a considerable influence upon Barth. The pinnacle of misidentification is religion, the 'highest possibility of humanity, our quest for that beyond ourselves in which alone we can be fulfilled; but just so it is our attempt to use eternity for our own purposes, and so the denial of it as eternity' (Jenson 1989: 32). It is important to recognize that the primary object of Barth's critique of religion is not the world religions but the human attempt to master God and secure God as a possession or legitimation for human programmes and practice. Bruce McCormack indicates how Barth's early theology represents

> an assault on a central feature of late bourgeois culture: the understanding of the human individual as the creative subject of culture and history . . . Against the divisive individualism which had given rise to class warfare and world war, Barth posited a diviner 'universalism'. (McCormack 1995: 141)

Barth's attack focuses upon the attempt to provide religious (especially Christian) legitimation, in both private and public dimensions, for particular kinds of hegemonic identity. Barth observed in these approaches an idol, a form of human self-righteousness, a titanism which claimed God as its possession. In a letter to his friend and colleague, Eduard Thurneysen, dated 20 April 1920, Barth, in a reference to a form of theology he had himself once espoused, argued that 'the idol totters' (1964: 50). Barth's subsequent theological career can, in part, be characterized as a radical de-ideologization of notions of human identity on the basis of the first commandment and a God who is 'wholly other'. Against a notion of identity rooted in the idea of a common, shared discourse about humanity, Barth opposes God as 'the pure and absolute boundary and beginning of all that we are and have and do . . . distinguished qualitatively . . . from everything human . . . never . . . identified with anything we name, or experience, or worship, as God' (1933: 330–31).

In the polemical and dialectical language of Barth's famous second commentary on Paul's Epistle to the Romans, God is the 'crisis' of human identity: 'The warning is uttered against any position or manner of life or endeavour that WE think to be satisfactory and justifiable, as though WE were able in some way or other to escape the KRISIS of God' (1933: 504).

The nature of God's relationship to humanity is non-given: it cannot be located within any account of human endeavour or within any notion of human nature or identity. God is free, God is Other, God cannot be conformed to any cultural, moral or religious project nor can grace be domesticated within human thought, experience or speech. There is an 'infinite qualitative distinction' (Barth 1933: 10) between God and humanity which is precisely that: a 'distinction' not a repudiation of the relationship. Rather, the relationship between God and humanity is one which is 'constituted solely by the free, disorienting action of God' (Webster 2000: 27). The irreversible character of this relation (God is God and we are human) relativizes human history, culture and religion but does not annihilate it. As Timothy Gorringe points out, the idea of a God who is 'wholly other' does not function as a basis for asserting a metaphysical distance between humanity and God but rather as a 'social-qualifying concept' (1999: 37).

Barth is rejecting a particular way of constructing the relationship between God and humanity and a set of traditions about human history and identity which are its correlate. The consequence of this is to raise a theological question mark about the ways in which a discourse of identity and recognition has come down to us, for this theme has a meta-critical function in Barth's theology: it establishes a priority in the ordering of theological discourse about the nature of the relationship between God and humanity. God is God, different from humanity qualitatively and infinitely, representing a 'crisis' for notions of identity and recognition, for identity is not a quality or capacity which can be possessed or cultivated but is bound up with the identity of a God made known at the 'cross-roads' of human perception in 'the figure of Jesus Christ' (Barth 1933: 10).

In the early stages of Barth's theological development the christological theme is developed through a rhetoric which is provocative, dialectical and paradoxical: he did not at that point possess the dogmatic apparatus which would enable him to develop his theme in a much more positive fashion. Nevertheless, this 'advent of the truth of God' in Jesus Christ has implications for how one conceives a politics of recognition, for the notion of human identity is 'ruptured at the very core', caught up in a dialectic of God and creature, veiling and unveiling, hiddenness and presence. The key to understanding Barth at this point lies in grasping the nature of his thoroughgoing theological realism. Barth's purpose is not to secure particular epistemological privileges for Christianity in the construction of identity. Indeed, the Christian legitimation for certain ways of constructing identity provide the target for much of his polemic. Rather, Barth's theological meditation on the 'Godness' of God supposes particular things which, because of the nature of its object, can be described but not demonstrated: namely, the presence of a reality independent of us which precedes and is not exhausted by what we say about it, and which determines our knowledge of it (not the other way around), and which can be represented in theological language however indirectly (Dalferth 1989: 16–18). As Webster indicates:

> [I]t [the self-revealing God] is real in a way and with a force which entirely eclipse all other claimed realities, realities which it absolutely transcends and encloses within itself, but by which it is in no sense comprehended . . . To be encountered by that reality in its self-positing and radically *new* character is to be faced with a challenge to transgress and reorganise habitual perceptions of the norms for human experience and expression. (Webster 1995: 28, original emphasis)

The main dimensions of this viewpoint are carried forward to the *Church Dogmatics*. It remains axiomatic for Barth that God's 'Godness' ruptures the language of human identity. This approach is expanded descriptively and polemically within the later writings providing a thread which connects his opposition to culture Protestantism at the beginning of the twentieth century, to his opposition to Nazism and natural theology in the 1930s, to his opposition to Rudolf Bultmann's existentialism and various forms of secular anthropology, to the mature outworking of his theological anthropology in the later volumes of the *Church Dogmatics*. At the same time, because God's 'Godness' can never be considered apart from revelation in Jesus Christ, theological language corresponds, however indirectly, to its object, and theology itself is always 'the-anthropology' even when we find Barth at his most polemical. The concern for the 'Godness' of God is equally a concern for the 'real' (as opposed to the distorted) autonomy, dignity and authenticity of humanity.

This insight provides a way of understanding one aspect of the issues at stake for Barth at Barmen and the connections that he makes between particular kinds of theological endeavour (most notably in this instance, natural theologies) and particular distortions of human identity especially insofar as the former provides legitimation for, or grounds for assimilation to, the latter. By his own admission, the purpose of the declaration was, for Barth, 'polemical delimitation' (CD I/2: 460). This 'delimitation' took the form of a radical reaffirmation of central Reformation themes: *solus Christus* (Christ alone), *sola scriptura* (by scripture alone), *sola fide* (by faith alone) (Scholder 1988: 149). Klaus Scholder argues that the primacy of these themes within the Barmen text suggests that the overwhelming concern was theological rather than political (ibid.). Whilst it is true that the text reflects some disagreement and sensitivity towards the Lutheran view of the relationship between Church and state, and that Barth himself admitted (Busch 1976: 235) the narrow remit within which the questions of Barmen were framed, the logic of Scholder's observation that Barmen reaffirms central Reformation concerns points in a different direction. Timothy Gorringe indicates that the text presents an uncompromising affirmation of a central Reformed concern, 'the traditional Calvinist emphasis on Christ's supremacy over every aspect of life without exception. It is the rendering of Christology into politics' (Gorringe 1999: 129).

Gorringe's remark highlights an extremely important element of Barmen: politics and theology are mutually implicated, though it is also important to note that, for Barth, they must not be confused. There is then a connection between the type of theology one propounds and the types of politics that emerge and vice versa. The situation which confronted Barth in the 1930s was one which had political and theological overtones, both of which required diagnosis.

In a discussion of Barmen (CD II/1: 172–78), Barth describes the situation which confronted the Church in 1933. The rise to power of Adolf Hitler led to demands within the Protestant Church to see in these events a specific revelation which required a response of trust and obedience. These demands led to the German Church conflict from which the Declaration emerged. The response of one of Barth's contemporaries and opponents, Emmanuel Hirsch, illustrates the sharpness of the debate that unfolded. Hirsch argued that:

> integration into *Volk* [people] and state is so interwoven with my existence as a human being that I could deny it only by being disobedient to the one who has placed me in it, and could fail to make it the fundamental point of that understanding of *Volk*, state and war which is my task as a theologian only by lapsing into non-existential, i.e. theologically insignificant chatter. (Hirsch, cited in Scholder 1987: 177)

In Hirsch's statement there are echoes of Charles Taylor's depiction of malignant forms of the principle of originality (authenticity), the self-realization or self-fulfilment of a culture bearing a people. Barth observed in remarks such as these and within the wider political movement of the time, 'the proclamation of this new revelation as the only revelation, and therefore the transformation of the Christian Church into the temple of the German nature- and history-myth' (CD II/1: 173).

At the same time Barth draws a parallel with a wider assimilation of theology in preceding centuries. The language of the Barmen text is directed particularly at different forms of natural theology. The danger of natural theology for Barth is precisely because it is close to the truth but nevertheless capable of ideological manipulation. Indeed, Barth notes in *Nein!* the welcome given to Emil Brunner's essay *Nature and Grace* by prominent 'German Christians' (1946: 72). The force of his argument is epistemological. To give priority to any other source of authority is to compromise and domesticate revelation:

> He [Jesus Christ] has ceased to be the measure, but is Himself measured by the other. He no longer speaks the first and last word, but only at best an additional word. As one factor in the assimilated and domesticated theology of revelation, He is caught up into the process of making the Gospel respectable. (CD II/1: 163–64)

Of course, the historical context within which Barmen is framed is one of political extremism. Yet this ambiguity is present for Barth even in seemingly less problematic contexts. As Hunsinger notes:

> The Christ of natural theology is always openly or secretly the relativized Christ of culture. The trajectory of natural theology leads from the Christ who is not supreme to the Christ who is not sufficient and finally to the Christ who is not necessary. Culture-religion, relativization, and domestication or assimilation indicate that the Lordship of Jesus Christ is no longer believed in or understood. (Hunsinger 2000: 80)

The chief target of Barmen's first thesis is an 'assimilated' theology (CD II/1: 163); it is the analysis of theological failure that drives a political response. The religious and ideological character of Nazism could not be countered by a theological approach which, even if closer to the truth, echoed its assumptions. For Barth, theologies which began with an abstract (i.e. abstracted from Christ) account of culture, experience or existence were themselves forms of natural theology and as such shared a similar starting point to theologies of *Volk*, blood and nation which were infiltrating the Church. Barth's objection to natural theologies is not that there is nothing of value outside of the scriptures or the Church: 'God may well speak to us through Russian communism or a flute concerto, a blossoming shrub or a dead dog' (CD I/1: 60). Nor is it Barth's intention to argue that common cultural identities are irrelevant or insignificant. Indeed the logic of the incarnation points towards their significance. Rather, for Barth, 'frontiers, cultures, and languages are all fluid and removable. None of these boundaries are original or final' (Gorringe 1999: 201).

There is, then, continuity between Barth's rejection of culture-religion in the form of liberal individualism and the later denunciation of *völkisch* nationalism: both cases issue in forms of distorted reciprocity or recognition in the public square. In both cases there is a deficient universalism at work, a feature Barth identifies in various forms of theological and secular anthropologies divorced, or abstracted, from a christological ground. In adopting a view of the 'infinite qualitative distinction' (Barth 1933: 10) between God and humanity, Barth acquires a weapon of considerable rhetorical potency which qualifies and relativizes particular conceptions of identity and the politics that accompany them. However, this negative assertion represents a clearing of the ground for what Barth wishes to assert positively. How, then, does the politics of recognition look when relocated within the framework to which faith testifies?

Binary Reciprocity as Freedom for Fellowship

> Jesus Christ as attested to us in Holy Scripture is the one Word of God whom we must hear and whom we must trust and obey in life and in death. (CD IV/3.1: 3)

The repetition of the first *Barmen* thesis at the head of one of the later volumes of the *Church Dogmatics* indicates a substantial continuity between the early and later work. Until relatively recently Barth studies were dominated by a view, influenced by the reading of von Balthasar, which argued that Barth's theological outlook developed in two distinct phases. According to this analysis, the movement in Barth's thought was one from dialectic to analogy, from an account of God and humanity as polar opposites to one of correspondence between God and humanity based on the christological covenant (Webster 2000: 21–23). In recent decades this view has been modified, partly in response to the publication of previously unavailable lecture cycles, but more fundamentally through an increased awareness of the connections between Barth's theological beginnings and his mature dogmatic work. Whilst clearly there is development and change in Barth's thought, the significance of this change in perception is that it locates more clearly the positive intent of the famous second edition of his *Romans* commentary beyond the rhetorical attack upon the cultural, theological and political situation of its time, but also, and this is significant to the present task, demarcates more visibly the sense which remains consistent in the later writings that the distinction between God and humanity is precisely that, a qualitative difference.

In considering the ways in which Barth's later theology transfigures the conditions of recognition it is essential to underline this significant continuity. At the same time, it is clear that as Barth's theology develops the positive thesis comes much more to the fore. The word 'transfigured' hints at the radical way in which Barth re-orientates ordinary language, experience and understanding in the light of what he reads in the biblical narratives (Hunsinger 1986: 359). The language of recognition (or the language of the binary reciprocity of God and humanity in Jesus Christ) follows language about God, not the other way around. In Barth's terms, the politics of recognition makes sense in the context of the covenantal encounter between God and humanity in Jesus Christ, 'the fullness, epitome and standard of all reality' (CD III/4: 27): the identity of the triune God, who binds himself to humanity in Jesus Christ, provides the basis for understanding questions of human identity and recognition. To that extent,

> The *Church Dogmatics* is a single massive description of that specific human person in whom being the human he is and being the Lord and judge of good and evil coincide, who truly is in himself both helped and Helper; and it is a statement of our ontological identity with and in precisely this person. (Jenson 1989: 27–28)

In this sense, von Balthasar's identification of the importance of analogy in Barth's theology, albeit qualified dialectically in the context of God's veiling in unveiling, assumes great importance. The analogy of faith (*analogia fidei*), which Barth appropriates from his reading of Anselm, provides him with a basis for interpreting the whole of reality christologically. This central conviction determines Barth's approach to a number of inter-related themes which mutually interpret one another, including election, creation, providence, anthropology and reconciliation, and profoundly affects Barth's approach to the question of human identity. Yet the tone is not negative. As Gorringe notes, this is an understanding of 'all reality . . . as a product of divine affirmation' (Gorringe 1999: 171).

It is important to recognize, for interpretative purposes, the significance of the inter-relationship of themes in the *Church Dogmatics*. It is characteristic of Barth's theology that he returns to a theme again and again and articulates it from a number of vantage points. Increasingly, as the *Dogmatics* unfolds, Barth turns to narrative as a way of unfolding the distinctiveness of these different motifs in their inter-relatedness. This feature accounts in part for the complexity and length of the *Church Dogmatics* but also indicates the importance of reading Barth at length: the strength of the presentation derives from its cumulative effect and from the complex arrangement and interaction of different themes.

Nevertheless, it is possible to identify a number of key moves which help to clarify the essential characteristics of recognition in Barth's mature theology. The first key to understanding the direction of his thought in this respect lies in a further exposition of the statement 'God is'. Writing on the being and attributes of God in 1937–38, as Nazi power continued to grow, Barth describes God as the one who loves in freedom. Gorringe observes that this provides Barth with the grounds for an engaged politics 'because the God who loves in freedom can and does ground all life-giving action' (Gorringe 1999: 144). Intriguingly, Gorringe connects this insight with the possibility of a liberation theology contrasting the God of life with the lifelessness of an idolatrous regime (1999: 143–44). The actuality of God's freedom is 'a seeking and creation of fellowship without any reference to an existing aptitude or worthiness on the part of the loved' (CD II/1: 278). The statement 'God is', therefore, is not a statement about a God who exists in isolation:

> On the contrary, He is Father, Son and Holy Spirit and therefore alive in His unique being with and for and in another. The unbroken unity of His being, knowledge and will is at the same time an act of deliberation, decision and intercourse. He does not exist in solitude but in fellowship. Therefore what He seeks and creates between Himself and us is in fact nothing else but what He wills and completes and therefore is in Himself. It therefore follows that as He receives us through His Son into his fellowship with Himself, this is the one necessity, salvation, and blessing for us, than which there is no greater blessing . . . That He is God – the Godhead of God – consists in the fact that He loves, and it is the expression of His loving that He seeks and creates fellowship with us. (CD II/1: 275)

This fundamental insight is one which Barth will develop at greater length within his discussions of election, covenant, creation and reconciliation. It is an insight which Webster indicates has significance for an account of humanity: if God's freedom is 'the perfection of his capacity to love, then God is essentially one whose act is directed towards the reciprocal active life of humanity' (Webster 1995: 46). The corollary of this is the divine patience whereby God allows humanity 'space and time for the development of its own existence, thus conceding to this existence a reality side by side with His own, and fulfilling His will towards this other in such a way that He does not suspend and destroy it as this other but accompanies and sustains it and allows it to develop in freedom' (CD II/1: 409–10, cited in Webster 1995: 46–47).

The implications of these remarks acquire greater specificity as Barth unfolds the logic of election in volume II/2. The logic of God for us, God for this other, is expounded in relation to the concrete history of Jesus Christ; in him is disclosed both electing God and elected humanity. Election represents, first and foremost, the irrevocable self-determination of God in eternity to be for humanity in Jesus Christ. As Barth puts it elsewhere, Jesus Christ is the 'humanity of God' so that election has to do with the covenant of grace in which God determines himself for humanity and humanity is determined for God. Jüngel notes how humanity is the 'implicit subject' of Barth's Christology:

> [T]he concrete existence of Jesus Christ . . . constitutes a history in which we cannot speak of God apart from the man Jesus, nor about the man Jesus apart from God. At the same time, we cannot speak of the history of Jesus Christ without speaking of all human beings, for the royal man was there in such a way precisely because he was there for humankind. And insofar as that was the case, God was there for all persons. (Jüngel 1986: 128)

This theological decision has profound implications for the ways in which one might conceive a politics of recognition. Barth's re-orientation of the doctrine of election contains within itself the content and reality of the binary reciprocity of God and humanity in Jesus Christ. The direction of Barth's theology is from this particular towards the general in such a way that the general is included in the concrete history of Jesus Christ in comprehensively particular ways. Gorringe indicates how Barth's discussions of the doctrine of God and election provide him with significant political resources. Barth proposes an 'ontology of freedom' in which human autonomy, dignity and authenticity are constituted not in terms of liberal individualism but by a structural, ontological relationship with God and with others given to us in Jesus Christ:

> Here there are profound resources for those of us whose being is defined by the laws of the market, an election which is not consumption, in which consumer choice is a parody of true choosing in the same way that the *Führerprinzip* was a parody of the election of Jesus Christ. And it is here above all that Barth shows us what it is for theology to be political. (Gorringe 1999: 163; cf. Barth 1961: 72)

There is, in this sense, no human being or realm of human activity that is ontologically godless, for even that which opposes God 'lives only by what it negates', and must only be taken seriously ' . . . within its limits, but only within them' (Barth 1981: 127). The discussion of election also grounds Barth's discussion of dignity: because of God's eternal will to be for us in Jesus Christ we must think of every human being as the brother of Jesus Christ and as one to whom God is Father. This acknowledgment is, for Barth, the basis of human dignity and human rights (Barth 1961: 50; cf. Krötke 2000: 166). In election, God freely elects humanity as covenant partner (CD II/2: 9–10) in such a way that the human creature is taken seriously 'not engulfed and covered as by a divine landslide or swept away as by a divine flood' (CD IV/4: 163). Rather, God's precedence is a summons to freely correspond to God, to enact existence as God's partner (Krötke 2000: 164).

These fundamental principles are carried forward into the remaining volumes of the *Dogmatics*. In volume III, Barth deals specifically with anthropology in the context of the doctrine of creation. His concern in these volumes is to oppose a general view of human nature with the particular form of humanity encountered in Jesus Christ. What cannot be missed here is the radical departure Barth makes from most theological accounts of human being. Rather than proceeding from general pre-theological reflection on anthropological themes which are then correlated with Christian themes, Barth begins from the other direction working from the particular to the general. It is not that such general descriptions are without value but rather that they are like 'knives without edges' (CD III/2: 76). Barth fills out his description of humanity in relation to its particular ontological determination in Jesus Christ. In this sense, notions of identity have a distinctive character for Barth. The history of Jesus Christ is the definitive history between God and humanity in which the words 'God' and 'humanity' acquire their meaning:

> The two subjects – God as Creator, Reconciler, Redeemer, the human partner as creature and as object of, and respondent to, reconciling and redemptive activity – are specific, perceptible, describable realities in Jesus Christ, whose history is not illustrative but definitive of the content of the terms 'God' and 'humanity'. (Webster 1995: 69)

Barth develops the doctrine of creation in a way that enables the covenant to be fulfilled. In his famous formula, the covenant is the internal basis of creation and the creation is the external basis of the covenant (CD III/1: 94ff.). Creation, for Barth, is not a sphere which exists independently of God but a space within which God's covenant with humanity in Jesus Christ can be realized, within which reciprocal encounter between God and humanity can unfold. A key theme within the *Church Dogmatics* is the idea of humanity as genuine partnership with God: God's life calls forth a correspondence, a parallel, an analogy, an answer in human life. Webster notes (drawing upon David Kelsey) that this is an anthropology which focuses upon human agency rather than human beings as subjects of consciousness (1995: 57). As such, this is an anthropology defined in terms of responsibility, a response to the Word of God which is a 'continuous answer' (CD II/2: 641).

This theme acquires further specificity in Barth's discussion of the *imago Dei*. Here this correspondence to God's being is recognized in Jesus Christ who in his humanity is 'the repetition and reflection of God Himself . . . the image of God, the *imago Dei*' (CD III/2: 219). For Barth, the word 'image' expresses a limitation. The humanity of Jesus is indirectly not directly identical with God (ibid.). In this, Barth signals not only the consistent Chalcedonian texture of his Christology but the particular nature of the relationship between God and the reality which is other than him. God is not solitary but exists in relationship with Godself but also in relationship (fellowship) *ad extra* with that which is other than God. In this respect, the humanity of Jesus has a distinctive character which follows this structural pattern; it is fellow humanity. What is true of Christ's humanity (as opposed to his divinity) is true of all humanity elected in him; true humanity is fellow humanity (CD III/2: 324).

This conclusion is an outworking of theological decisions that are evident in several sections of the *Church Dogmatics*, the logical outworking of Barth's discussion of the divine perfections and the doctrine of election. At this point there is a key insight into the essential theological dynamics of a politics of recognition. Jesus Christ, in his humanity, is the 'real' human being before God but he is so in the distinctive way in which in his humanity he is for other human beings: 'humanity in general participates in this correspondence and similarity in such a way that the human person is human only in relation to fellow human beings' (Krötke 2000: 168).

The basic form of the politics of recognition is then the enactment of the life of co-humanity, the life of solidarity. It is this co-relatedness that distinguishes human beings as God's covenant partner. The classic instance of humanity in the image of God as co-humanity is the creation of man and woman (CD III/2: 288ff.). In Barth's exegesis of Genesis 1:26, humanity is as it is depicted in this relationship of partnership; differentiated yet related. Quite rightly, a number of commentators detect a hint of patriarchy in Barth's development of this theme which must be rejected. However, as Krötke notes, it is possible to retain the fundamental insight without following Barth in particular respects. The key focus is an understanding of humanity as a summons to partnership, to see 'the mutual communication of equally human human beings in their otherness as the "basic form of humanity"' (Krötke 2000: 169), the basic form of recognition, a parabolic correspondence to the life of the triune God (CD III/2: 203ff.).

Conclusion

This chapter began with a question about how a particular theology might 'echo the hope and anguish of all humanity' (Buckley 1992: 160). Barth's christological concentration offers a distinctive way of grounding that discussion which addresses humanity in both its weakness and its possibility. The particular narrative of God and humanity in Jesus Christ is understood by Barth as one which has universal significance, providing an ontological basis for recognition and reciprocity in which we are invited to affirm the dignity of the other. At the same time, this identification invites a serious consideration of humanity as it really is before God which, at the same time as mirroring its Creator, is broken and fragmented. It is no surprise that both the anthropological sections and Barth's later development of the doctrine of reconciliation issue in a summons to a 'lived anthropology' (Krötke 2000: 173–74). The Christian community, for all its limitations, as the community of the reconciled, as a community of hope, is called upon to live out and seek better forms of human righteousness, free of ideological distortions of our real humanity, as a provisional representation of the perfected reciprocity which lies in the eschatological future. The final words are Barth's, fragments published after his death:

> They themselves [the Christian community], who as humans are also hidden in all kinds of robes and uniforms and rags, go through life wanting their right, though not demanding it by their own efforts. They do not live by the better, which does not wholly evade them and which they may sometimes achieve in favour of others. They live solely by hope and therefore by the promise that human right, worth, freedom, peace, and joy are not a chimera but have already been actualized by God in Jesus Christ and will finally and ultimately be revealed in their actualization. They have to be witnesses, shining lights of hope, to all men [sic]. (Barth 1981: 270)

Note

1 *Church Dogmatics.*

References

Barth, K. (1956–1977), *The Church Dogmatics* (ed. G.W. Bromiley and T.F. Torrance; Edinburgh: T&T Clark).

—— (1933), *The Epistle to the Romans* (trans. E.C. Hoskyns; Oxford: Oxford University Press).

—— (1946), *Natural Theology Comprising 'Nature and Grace' by Professor Dr. Emil Brunner and the Reply 'No!' by Dr. Karl Barth* (London: Geoffrey Bles).
—— (1961), *The Humanity of God* (London: Collins).
—— (1964), *Revolutionary Theology in the Making: Barth–Thurneysen Correspondence. 1914–1925* (trans. James D. Smart; Richmond: John Knox Press).
—— (1981), *The Christian Life* (trans. G.W.Bromiley; Grand Rapids: Eerdmans).
—— (1982), *The Theology of Schleiermacher* (trans. G.W. Bromiley; Edinburgh: T&T Clark).
Blaser, K. (1984), 'The Barmen Declaration and the Present Theological Context', *Ecumenical Review* 36.3: 299–315.
Buckley, J. (1992), *Seeking the Humanity of God: Practices, Doctrines, and Catholic Theology* (Collegeville: The Liturgical Press).
Busch, E. (1976), *Karl Barth: His Life from Letters and Autobiographical Texts* (London: SCM).
Dalferth, I. (1989), 'Karl Barth's Eschatological Realism', in S. Sykes (ed.), *Karl Barth: Centenary Essays* (Cambridge: Cambridge University Press), pp. 14-45.
Gorringe, T. (1999), *Karl Barth Against Hegemony* (Oxford: Oxford University Press).
Hunsinger, G. (1986), 'A Response to William Werpehowski', *Theology Today* 43: 354–60.
—— (1991), *How to Read Karl Barth: The Shape of his Theology* (Oxford: Oxford University Press).
—— (2000), *Disruptive Grace: Studies in the Theology of Karl Barth* (Grand Rapids: Eerdmans).
Jenson, R. (1989), 'Karl Barth', in D.F. Ford (ed.), *The Modern Theologians: An Introduction to Christian Theology in the Twentieth Century*, I (Oxford: Blackwell), pp. 23–49.
Jüngel, E. (1986), *Karl Barth: A Theological Legacy* (trans. Garrett E. Paul; Philadelphia: Westminster Press).
Krötke, W. (2000), 'The Humanity of the Human Person in Karl Barth's Anthropology', in J. Webster (ed.), *The Cambridge Companion to Karl Barth* (Cambridge: Cambridge University Press), pp. 159–76.
Lash, N. (1986), *Theology on the Way to Emmaus* (London: SCM).
McCormack, B. (1995), *Karl Barth's Critically Realistic Dialectical Theology, its Genesis and Development 1909–1936* (Oxford: Clarendon Press).
McFadyen, A. (1993), 'Truth as Mission: The Christian Claim to Universal Truth in a Pluralist Public World', *Scottish Journal of Theology* 46.4: 437–56.
Scholder, K. (1987), *The Churches and the Third Reich Vol. 1: 1918–1934 (Preliminary History and the Time of Illusions)* (London: SCM).
—— (1988), *The Churches and the Third Reich Vol. 2: The Year of Disillusionment 1934: Barmen and Rome* (London: SCM).
Taylor, C. (1994), 'The Politics of Recognition', in A.Gutmann (ed.), *Multiculturalism* (Princeton: Princeton University Press), pp. 25-73.
Von Balthasar, H. Urs (1992), *The Theology of Karl Barth: Exposition and Interpretation* (trans. E.T. Oakes, SJ; San Francisco: Ignatius Press).
Webster, J. (1995), *Barth's Ethics of Reconciliation* (Cambridge: Cambridge University Press).
—— (2000), *Karl Barth* (London: Continuum).
Willimon, W.H. (2005), *Proclamation and Theology* (Nashville: Abingdon Press).

3

Transplanting Religion: Defining Community and Expressing Identity

Pauline Kollontai

Introduction

This chapter aims to explore the role which the transplantation process plays in constructing, de-constructing and re-constructing religious belief and practice and the expression of community and identity. Over the past two decades there has been a growing body of work both within religious studies and social sciences looking at the transplantation of religions and their communities. Ninian Smart, referring to this transplantation, argues it is important to understand because 'the study of diaspora and their modes of adaptation can give us insights into general patterns of religious transformation' (1999: 421).

The first section of the chapter sets the scene through a brief overview of the nature and scope of migration. This is followed with a discussion of the work of Pye and Knott on the features and dynamics of the transplantation of religion. Then the issue of globalization is looked at to identify what part it plays in the transplantation process and how it contributes to the shaping and expression of community and identity.

Setting the Context: Migration

Since 1975 the number of persons moving across borders has more than doubled. In 2002 over 175 million persons resided in a country other than where they were born and 60 per cent of these live in the more developed regions. The UK has experienced increasing levels of both inward and outward international migration in recent years. Over the past decade, migration into the country increased from 314,000 in 1994 to 582,000 in 2004, with most of the increase occurring after 1997 (UK Office for National Statistics 2001: 1–2).

The movement of people within geographical borders and across them has been a feature of human existence throughout history. Juergensmeyer argues that from the earliest accounts of recorded history there has always been the movement of peoples taking with them their cultures and religions which have changed and adapted (2003: 4–5). Migration has been tribal, national, class and religious driven. Its causes have been climatic, political, economic, religious, or mere love of adventure. It denotes any movement of groups of people from one locality to another, rather than of individual wanderers. Park considers migration as a classic relocation-diffusion mechanism whereby beliefs, values, attitudes and behaviour are spread spatially between people (2005: 443). Tariq Modood states that migration is one of the key factors along with race and ethnicity that shapes the identity of minority groups in British society (2005: 82). Migration is also identified as

> among the most conspicuous agents of change of religious systems because they expose migrants to new ideas, challenge the power and control of religion in places of origin, and raise profound questions of community and personal identity and affiliation. (Chatterjee *et al.* 2002: 23)

Any dispersed group of people take with them a host of social, cultural, political, philosophical and religious phenomena, both consciously and subconsciously, which helps shape the communities they become and the identity they construct and express. The vast array of experiences which face migrating people from the point of their departure from their homeland to the moment they arrive and settle in their new context means that all of these phenomena undergo a process of transplantation and adaptation. Religion is no exception. There are degrees of adaptation which may result in various manifestations of the one and the same religion because the local context will produce local forms and expressions of religion. As Hinnells points out, these are complex processes which can take place over an extended period of time and will not produce new monolithic expressions of community and identity (1998: 688); rather, they will result in community and identity being expressed in a diversity of ways.

Migration can have an effect on both the incoming group of people and the indigenous population in terms of social, cultural, political and religious matters. An example of this is examined in Best's work (2005) on the various ways 'black southerners' transformed African-American religion in Chicago during their Great Migration northward. He shows how the new religious practices and traditions in Chicago were stimulated by migration and urbanization. The migration launched a new sacred order among blacks in the city that reflected aspects of both Southern black religion and modern city life.

Sometimes in relation to pressures of assimilation and having to articulate their practices and beliefs in a different environment, migrant communities 'can tend to become conservative in religious and social matters' (Veer 2001: 9). Some migrant communities find meaning through the construction of a transnational identity. This is shown in the study of the Harari Muslims who are re-located from Ethiopia in Canada and have constructed values that reflect and 'would be relevant in the home and host country' (Gibb 1998: 243–50). The concept and expression of religious community and identity undergo some change and modification in every migrant group. The factors conditioning change and modification involve recognizing pre-migration factors, the nature and experience of migration, the experience of reception and settlement in the new context and the integration of religion and locality. These factors will be looked at in more depth through the work of Pye and Knott to provide an analytical and interpretative theory of how the transplantation of religion is a central factor in the construction and expression of community and identity.

The Transplantation of Religion

The term 'dynamics of religion' was first used by van der Leeuw. He identified five aspects: syncretism, transposition, mission, revival and reformation. All of these could be a product of a combination of either conscious or unconscious activity on the part of the faith adherents (1938: 57). Pye adapted van der Leeuw's model. His starting point is that the transplantation process 'involves a complex relationship between tradition and interpretation' (1969: 236). Tradition refers to the content (teaching, beliefs and rituals) of a religion and interpretation refers to what happens to these things once there is a change in the context in which the religion is operating. Pye identified three principal aspects of the transplantation process: contact, ambiguity and recoupment. It is not always the case that these three aspects occur chronologically. Whilst the aspects may appear chronologically as in the Hellenization of Christianity, they can occur in another order as in the case of Nichiren Buddhism (1969: 238). Pye says that transplantation can be geographical or chronological; the latter he describes 'in the sense that a religion may find itself running on the spot to reassert itself in changing cultural circumstances' (1969: 236). Pye's view of transplantation as being geographical or chronological is also important because although a religion may be deemed as ethnic, migrant or diaspora, the longer a religion remains in a 'new' geographical location the chronological dimension may become more prominent with the growth of subsequent generations. He also makes an important point that transplantation includes 'conscious and unconscious activity' on the part of the adherents of a religion (1969: 238).

The contact aspect, identified by Pye as the first principal aspect of transplantation, is the way in which people present their religion through diverse means of communication and activity in relation to the context or situation (1969: 236–37). One example of the contact principle today would be the popularization of Kabbalah to Jews and non-Jews. Kabbalah, an ancient body of Jewish spiritual wisdom, is said by its followers to contain secrets of the universe as well as the keys to the mysteries of the human heart and soul. The Kabbalistic sages both past and present teach that every human being is born with the potential for greatness and Kabbalah is considered to be the means for activating that potential. Since the latter part of the twentieth century interest in these ancient teachings has grown amongst Jews and non-Jews. Learning Kabbalah is now available through the genre of popular writing, the production of videos/DVDs, the use of the music industry, the opening of Kabbalah Centres and Kabbalists who, at a financial cost, offer their services as life coaches concerning anything from career coaching to diet coaching and crisis coaching through this ancient mystical tradition.

The ambiguity principle, considered to be the second principal aspect, is described by Pye as presenting questions of heresy and orthodoxy because of the prevailing influence and eventual acceptance of certain factors or 'unresolved coexistence of elements belonging to the transplanting tradition and to the situation which is being entered' (1969: 237). One example is seen in the way in which some Buddhist groups in the West such as the Kadampa tradition, which emerged from Tibetan Buddhism, have communal centres where both lay and monastic members live together over extended periods of time. This would not be the case in the Tibetan Buddhist communities of Tibet or Nepal. The Kadampa tradition has adopted a model of community living that reflects both the Christian model of retreat centres and a type of new age worldview that advocates the benefits of community and communal lifestyle for both lay and monastic members. A further example of the ambiguity principle is evident in Muslim communities in the West as regards the practice of arranged marriages. Traditionally within Muslim families parents have been responsible for identifying a marriage partner for their daughter or son. Initially, this involves both sets of parents meeting and agreeing that the marriage is suitable after which the two individuals who are to marry are introduced to one another in the presence of the parents. There may be a small number of further opportunities for the couple to meet but usually this is with members of their respective families present. Amongst second and third generation Muslims living in the West this approach is sometimes modified due to the fact that the concept and practice of arranged marriages in Western society is an alien one. Younger Muslims live and work alongside their non-Muslim counterparts many of whom will have a number of girlfriends or boyfriends before they marry. Thus, the traditional Muslim model that a suitable marriage partner is identified for your child not always on the basis of love but in the hope that love will develop has become increasingly difficult for many young Muslims to accept.

As a result of trying to maintain some adherence to this traditional Muslim family practice and combine to some extent the less controlled approach of the West, a number of agencies (one was set up in Bradford during the early 1990s) have been established within Muslim communities whereby young Muslims in agreement with their parents are allowed to socialize at various events organized by the agency with members of the opposite sex, in the hope that a suitable marriage partner will be eventually identified. This socializing is not supervised by parents but agency staff will be present. These examples also demonstrate that syncretism is present in the sense that there is a blending of religions and cultures into lifestyle practices. Pye does not address the issue of syncretism. However, syncretism would seem to be a part of the transplantation process of religions and a tool by which some religious groups deal with the unresolved coexistence of factors within the transplanting religion and the host context.

Recoupment, the third principal aspect of transplantation, 'involves the reassertion or re-clarification of that which was being transplanted in some adequate way' (Pye 1969: 237). This means that the transplanted religion will be presented in relation to its original form but it will not be absolutely identical with that form because it will be expressed 'in terms of the factors of the situation which it has entered' (1969: 238). The recoupment aspect means that at some stage in the transplantation process there may be an attempt to reassert or re-clarify essential characteristics of a religion in relation to its original incoming expression. This is often due to a recognition that certain factors of the host context may have produced a significant syncretic expression of the transplanting religion and may lead to the dissipation or eventual dying out of a religion. Pye's perspective is that even in the act of reasserting or reclarification of a religion there is a degree of acceptance that there is 'the conscious acceptance of a tolerable amount of ambiguity as the price of successful transplantation' (1969: 239).

An extreme example of the recoupment aspect can be seen in the case of Hasidic Judaism in Britain. In terms of the essential characteristics of their belief there has been no significant incorporation of the doctrines or dogmas of the dominant religion Christianity. Neither has there been adoption of key secular values with regard to the role of women, concept of family, and lifestyle practices. Hasidic communities live a religious and socially contained lifestyle according to their interpretation of Halakah. The Hasidim appear to have minimalized the ambiguity aspect and maximized the recoupment aspect. Whilst elements of Pye's theory benefit understanding of how the process of transplantation impacts on the way in which people express their religion in a different context there are criticisms to be made of his theory. The first is Pye's way of determining what makes a migrant or diaspora religion authentic. He argues that for a migrant or disapora religion to be deemed authentic, irrespective of some cultural adaptation, it must reflect the essential teachings of a religion. In Buddhism the term 'skilful means' relates to the Buddha's use of morally wholesome teachings devised for the purpose of enabling nirvana or enlightenment. On this basis Pye states that the controversial Japanese Buddhist group Aum Shinrikyo was not Buddhism because 'from the viewpoint of skilful means there is no evidence of the important regulatory feature of leading backwards towards central Buddhist conceptions' (Pye 2003: 115). David Kay criticizes Pye's evaluation of Aum Shinrikyo as methodologically unsound:

> First, the appeal to the concept of skilful means to make a scholarly distinction between authentic and inauthentic expressions of Buddhism is problematic. Since skilful means is a religious concept from within the Buddhist tradition, its suitability as a paradigm for academic analysis must be regarded as highly questionable. (Kay 2004: 24)

Pye is criticized here on grounds that his methodology is being informed by and at the same time establishing a normative definition of what constitutes authentic Buddhism. To some extent Pye's methodology appears to contradict a key aspect of his work that the transplantation of a religion involves a complex interplay between 'the content of the religion', and the socio-economic, political, cultural and religious factors of the context into which it has entered (Pye 1969: 236). This would appear to recognize that all religions started in an alien context and have all been shaped to some extent according to the characteristics of that context. Therefore, what does an authentic expression of a religion mean other than human belief in a divine ultimate reality which is shaped and sometimes re-shaped either because of socio-economic, political or cultural changes in the indigenous context or because of the geographical spread or relocation of a religion? Trying to establish the authenticity of a religion through a process whereby the non-presence of a particular belief, ritual or aspect of lifestyle is deemed as not being an authentic expression seems to push back towards the static view of religion. Finally, these aspects of Pye's work serve as an important reminder about the role of the researcher and the way material is gathered and analysed in the context of his or her own subjective views and 'story'. It reminds the researcher to be constantly vigilant in the way that we study and speak about religions that are not our own.

Factors in Religious Transplantation

Building on the work of Pye, Knott has established a theoretical framework to examine how religions change as their followers migrate and to identify what factors contribute to religious change. She writes 'it has been necessary to attempt to construct a framework for understanding what happens to a religious group and its tradition when it moves to a new geographical and social location' and to identify the factors which contribute to 'new patterns and forms of religious behaviour, organisation, experience and self understanding' (Knott 1986b: 10). These factors are grouped together in five categories: (1) home traditions; (2) host traditions; (3) nature of migrant process; (4) nature of migrant group; (5) nature of host response (Knott 1986a: 10–12).

Writing about the first category – home traditions – Knott states that 'People bring with them their own religious and cultural traditions', which will interact 'with the new environment' and produce change in their religion. The character of the change will come partly from '(i) the nature of the religion itself (e.g. its unity or diversity, its universality or its ethnic particularity) and (ii) the nature of the other cultural factors such as language, customs, food and dress etc.' (1986a: 10–11). This category is a reminder of the influence and importance which people's religious and cultural traditions can play when settling in a new location. Undoubtedly, change does take place for many groups because of their new environment, but as previously argued there are examples as with Hasidic Jews living outside their country of origin where there appears to be no change to the central tenants of their religion or culture.

The second category deals with host traditions – 'On arrival and throughout the subsequent period of settlement migrants come into contact in various ways with the established traditions of the "host community", religion, politics, culture, laws, education, welfare and immigration and settlement policies' (1986a: 11).

One point which Knott does not explicitly address here is that the impact of these traditions may vary between the generations because whilst the initial migrants may find aspects of Britain's culture and traditions obscure and strange, they will be considered less so by second, third and subsequent generations as they and their religion and culture may become indigenized.

The third category, the nature of the migrant process, recognizes that all migrants have journeyed to their new location through various routes. 'Some have come from their original homelands; others from other migrant situations' and all have various reasons for making this journey – economic migrants, exiles, refugees, settlers – some plan to stay and other want to return to their country of origin (1986a: 11). The third point identifies the reasons behind why people migrate and recognizes that the actual physical experience can affect the way in which migrants relate to and are seen by the host community. Development of this point would be to assess the impact of the nature of the migration process on subsequent generations. For example, Jews are seen predominantly as a victim diaspora (Cohen 1997: x) with the last episode of being a persecuted minority relatively recent with the events of the Holocaust. But do subsequent generations of Jews identify with the victim diaspora model? According to Cohen, 'However economically or professionally successful, however long settled in peaceful settings, it is difficult for many Jews in the diaspora not to keep their guard up to feel the weight of their history and the cold clammy fear that brings the demons in the night to remind them of their murdered ancestors' (1997: 20). Evidence of this is found amongst many Jews who were not themselves victims of the Holocaust, were born after the event and are part of Jewish communities in West and North Yorkshire. This being the case the framework of analysis needs to address this issue and examine the reasons for the ongoing impact of the original cause of the migration process.

Knott's fourth category looking at the nature of the migrant group recognizes that all migrant groups in terms of religion and culture have their own internal diversity. 'To understand more about the dynamics of the migrant communities it is necessary to give serious consideration to group size, geographical dispersion, division, and cohesion' (Knott 1986a: 11–12). Understanding the nature of the migration process and that of the migrant group provides insights about why people migrate to a new geographical location; how the migration process can impact on how people shape and practise their religion in the new context; and in some situations it can help to gain insights into the relations between ethnic religions. It can also help identify how ambiguity within a religion is managed in terms of group cohesion or division; how any generational expressions of a religion are managed; and what role do the socio-economic backgrounds of individuals play within each migrant community. Helweg's study of south Asian immigrants into Australia during the 1980s is relevant to the latter factor. His study appears to demonstrate that south Asians who have little education coming from a rural, agricultural setting have a different adaptation process to those who are better educated, middle-class professionals who have lived in towns and cities (Helweg 1991: 29).

Knott's fifth and final category explores the nature of the host response – 'The other major set of influences . . . including general social attitudes rather than cultural traditions such as racism, attitudes to assimilation and integration and ecumenism' (Knott 1986a: 12). This final category provides understanding and insight into the expression, practice, character and visibility of religions. The nature of the host response impacts on the very core of a group's identity and sense of community. The work of a number of other scholars also provide interesting insights in this issue. Ballard and Ballard, writing about East African Asians arriving in the UK during the 1970s, argue that 'racism has precipitated a reactive pride in their separate identity' (Ballard and Ballard 1977: 54).

Solomos's study of the experience of first-generation Afro-Caribbean migrants, who arrived during the 1950s and 1960s in the UK, also shows they faced high levels of racial discrimination which are seen as contributing to high rates of crime, unemployment and ghettoization amongst the second generation (Solomos 1989: 83). But as Cohen points out, the evidence presented during the 1990s through government reports indicates that the experience of third-generation Afro-Caribbeans has improved because of better access to education and employment in sport, broadcasting and the performing arts (Cohen 1997: 141).

In 1991 Knott added seven other factors which were seen necessary for an understanding of the future development of South Asian religions in Britain. The seven areas were: (i) language (e.g. English and vernacular; the relationship between ethnic languages and maintaining religion and culture); (ii) transmission of religious belief and culture (e.g. models of family and geographical location); (iii) individual identity (e.g. changes in socio-religious identity due to the impact of Western ideas such as personal choice and autonomy or feminism); (iv) group identity (e.g. issues of caste; the influence of events in the homeland; legal identity of religious-ethnic groups); (v) leadership (e.g. will the religious leaders of diaspora groups continue to be from the countries of origin); (vi) universalisation (e.g. ethnic and sectarian divisions within religion or a striving for unity); (vii) impact of Western religious ideas (Knott 1991: 100–105).

Overall Knott's theoretical framework provides a valuable tool in identifying factors which contribute to understanding how religions are manifest having crossed geographical boundaries and for analysing the complex interactions between these factors. However, there are two factors that I would add to Knott's existing categories and one new category.

First, within the 'home tradition' category, gender and sexuality need to be identified explicitly as one of the factors. A point which also needs to be clarified and elaborated under the 'nature of host response' category is why sometimes a host community, whose dominant religious belief system is that of the migrant, expresses prejudice and discrimination against these people. The examples in the UK of African-Caribbean Christians, Irish Catholics and Sudanese Christians bear witness to this reality. One thing these examples show is that the sharing of a religion in common between host and migrant communities is not always sufficient to overcome the fear of the racial other. In the African-Caribbean case it is possible to use Cohen's argument that the type of diaspora community a group is perceived as will influence the response of the host community to its newcomers. '[T]he peoples of the Caribbean may be thought of as parts of other diasporas – notably the African victim diaspora, the Indian labour diaspora and the European imperial diasporas' (Cohen 1997: 137). These three diaspora views, if held either individually or collectively, provide an image of the African-Caribbean people as those who have suffered at the hands of other nation states either economically, politically, militarily, culturally and religiously. Therefore, a host community's response may be that of wanting to ensure that its African-Caribbean community is not subject to prejudice and discrimination. In the case of the UK as host community it would seem that our historical role in exploiting Afro-Caribbean people was to some extent retained and expressed towards them through racial discrimination in various spheres of British society.

Second, the category 'nature of migrant group' needs to include the generational factor and the impact this has on how religions evolve and groups cohese. For example, whilst the initial migrants can be very religious and culturally traditional, resisting the host culture and traditions, this is often less likely to be the case amongst second, third and subsequent generations as they and their religion and culture become acculturated. Examples of this are found in two studies of East African Gujaratis in Britain. Michaelson (1979) and Tambs-Lyche (1980) show that first-generation East African Gujaratis are intensely religious and culturally very traditional compared with later south Asian migrants.

Finally, I would argue there needs to be a new category: host worldview. This seems extremely relevant to include in a framework looking at the transplantation of religion. To some extent this could be included in the 'host tradition' or 'host response' categories but this does not necessarily give sufficient consideration to the role of foreign policy in the shaping of views and attitudes within a country either on the part of the host community or diaspora communities. A worldview can be described as an individual's psychological framework through which reality is perceived, sense made of life and the world around us. It can be described as the mental thought grid through which a person perceives how things ought to be (prescriptive) and how things are (descriptive). Adding a 'host worldview' category would mean considering the impact of a host country's foreign policy on religious identity, behaviour and practices of ethnic religious groups. For example, one of the current issues would be the extent to which the British government's support to go to war against Iraq has contributed to a new self-consciousness concerning religious identity amongst members of the British Muslim community.

One further development of Knott's work which informs us about issues of community and identity is her claim that all religion is in some sense local. The importance of studying religions in their locality is that it 'enables a researcher to investigate fully the relationship of religion and its context, the impact of aspects of that context on the religion and the active shaping of the locality by the religions within it' (Knott 1998: 284). This work seems to be a logical extension of Knott's initial work on migrant religions because by working with the concept that all religions to a greater or lesser degree become localized there is recognition of the fact that in the majority of cases the religions of minorities will evolve over time, either becoming more indigenized or in some instances more traditional and perhaps fundamentalist. The significance of this work is not just theological but also significant in gaining insight into the role of religion in human relations between diverse groups of people in both the public and private spheres of life.

The other side of the argument that in some sense all religion is local is the argument that all religion is in some sense global. Finally, in looking at the role the transplantation process plays in constructing, de-constructing and re-constructing religious belief and practice, it is important to consider globalization to identify what part it also plays in the transplantation process and how it contributes to the shaping and expression of community and identity.

The Globalization Mechanism

Globalization is visible in a number of spheres which include the economy, politics, culture and religion. In each of these fields there is a tension between forces which, on the one hand, lead to integration in globalization and, on the other, resist it. Cultural, religious and social differences become visible at the same time as one experiences direct or indirect pressure towards increased homogenization and 'free' competition (Spickard 2001: 5). This creates a field of tension where the value of religious belonging as identity forming becomes more important and is rapidly changing. So how does globalization affect religious practice, the expression of identity and community?

This is explored to some extent by McLoughlin who argues that globalization has in some instances reinforced difference and identity amongst and within ethnic groups. He argues that globalization has promoted 'processes of cultural homogenisation and postmodernism has assisted equally with promoting hybridity in all spheres of society' (McLoughlin 2005: 533). The theorization of culture is identified as key to examining the two notions of hybridity and ethnicity because 'Hybridity can be seen in terms of the fusion and intermixture of cultures whereas ethnicity represents the reassertion of cultural distinctiveness' (ibid.). Cultures have become de-territorialized as they 'have become separated from any absolute connection within localities, regions or nations of origin' (ibid.). McLoughlin agrees with Gerhard Baumann's view that culture is something that people practise, that they are in the continual process of making and remaking (Baumann 1996: 87–94). Another important contribution to the discussion of the globalization factor is Cohen's concept of the deterritorialization of social identities as people move across nation-state boundaries. From this there emerges a syncretization of elements of these identities which 'mix and match differently in each setting' (Cohen 1997: 174).

Change can also take place within a religion as a result of active or passive interaction with the country of origin. This is referred to as the tripolar or triadic inter-relatedness of a diasporic situation (Baumann 2000: 327). It can also work the other way: religious traditions back in their place of origin can be impacted upon either through the return of migrants to their home country or through mass global communication. For example, the Sikh diaspora is considered by many Sikhs in the Punjab as a threat to some aspects of traditional practice (Juergensmeyer 2003: 7). Another example is the Muslim diaspora which has contributed to the rise of both Islamic liberalism and Islamic fundamentalism within the Middle East (Arjomand 2003: 32). This two-way process became recognized in the area of Migration Studies during the late 1970s with the work of scholars such as Graves and Graves (1974), Helweg (1983), Bhachu (1985) and Shaw (1988). Helweg, writing in 1991, argued that 'In essence the home, host and migrant communities may mutually influence each other as if they were in the same geographic location' (Helweg 1991: 9). Bhachu took this a step further by arguing that in some cases where people have migrated several times it could be a 'three-way interactional relationship, each place of residence may be exerting an ongoing influence' on the religious and cultural identity of diaspora communities and their religion (Bhachu 1985: 98).

Conclusion

In this chapter I have aimed to show how the transplantation process of religion can impact on community and identity. How people express a sense of community and identity in both the public and private sphere must be seen through a double-focused lens that allows issues of globalization and locality to be considered.

Community and identity can provide the individual with a sense of belonging, stability and meaning. It can also cause a struggle for individuals as they attempt to balance their religious heritage with secular and humanistic concepts and values, or incorporate aspects of other religions into their lives. Examining community and identity in a religious context is important for a number of reasons. It reminds us that there is no one way to be Jewish, Hindu, Muslim, Sikh, Buddhist and it raises the question of what it means to be part of one of these groups in an alien context and about the way in which individuals and their religious communities define themselves.

Finally, exploring community and identity in the context of religion in the post-9/11 world is an essential task because in many parts of the world people remain divided from one another based on nationalist, ethnic, tribal or racial rivalries that are passed from generation to generation. These rivalries are intimately connected to a sense of one's identity and community and whether or not these things are secure or threatened. In the public mind, to discuss religion in the context of the world situation automatically raises the spectre of religious-based conflict. The many other dimensions and impacts of religion tend to be downplayed or even neglected. However, as Appleby writes, 'Religion's ability to inspire violence is intimately related to its equally impressive power as a force for peace' (Appleby 1999: 58). According to this viewpoint religion has the capacity to create cultures in which community and identity are not seen as something to be feared by the other but as expressions of our humanity that at the core seeks to 'Love your neighbour as yourself'.

References

Appleby, R.S. (1999), *The Ambivalence of the Sacred: Religion, Violence and Reconciliation* (Lanham, MD: Rowman & Littlefield).

Arjomand, S.A. (2003), 'Islam', in M. Juergensmeyer (ed.), *Global Religions: An Introduction* (Oxford: Oxford University Press), pp. 29–39.

Ballard, R., and C. Ballard (1977), 'The Sikhs: The Development of South Asian Settlements in Britain', in J.L. Watson (ed.), *Between Two Cultures: Migrants and Minorities in Britain* (Oxford: Basil Blackwell), pp. 46–58.

Baumann, G. (1996), *Contesting Culture: Discourses of Identity in Multi-Ethnic London* (Cambridge: Cambridge University Press).

—— (2000), 'Diaspora: Genealogies of Semantics and Transcultural Comparison', *Numen* 47.3: 313–37.

Best, W.D. (2005), *Passionately Human, No Less Divine: Religion and Culture in Black Chicago 1915–1952* (Princeton: Princeton University Press).

Bhachu, P. (1985), *Twice Migrants: East African Sikh Settlers in Britain* (London and New York: Tavistock Publications).

Chatterjee, N., N. Forner, N. Schiller, and L. Walbridge (2002), *Religion and Migration,*

Report of the Watson Insitutute for International Studies (Providence: Brown University Press).
Cohen, R. (1997), *Global Diasporas: An Introduction* (London: UCL).
Gibb, C. (1998), 'Religious Identification in Transnational Context: Being and Becoming Muslim in Ethiopia and Canada', *Diaspora* 7.2: 243–50.
Graves, N.B., and T.D. Graves (1974), 'Adaptive Strategies in Urban Migration', in B.J. Siegel, A.R. Beals and S.A. Tyler (eds), *Annual Review of Anthropology*, III (Palo Alto, CA: Annual Review Inc.).
Helweg (1983), 'Emigrant Remittances: Their Nature and Impact on a Punjabi Village', *New Community* 10: 435–43.
—— (1991), 'Indians in Australia: Theory and Methodology of the New Immigration', in S. Vertovec (ed.), *Aspects of the South Asian Diaspora*, vol. II, part 2 (Oxford University papers on India; Delhi: Oxford University Press), pp. 19–34.
Hinnells, J. (1998), 'The Study of Diaspora Religion', in J. Hinnells (ed.), *A New Handbook of Living Religions* (London: Penguin Books), pp. 682–89.
Juergensmeyer, M. (2003), 'Thinking Globally about Religion', in M. Juergensmeyer (ed.), *Global Religions: An Introduction* (Oxford: Oxford University Press), pp. 1–9.
Kay, D.N. (2004), *Tibetan and Zen Buddhism in Britain: Transplantation, Development and Adaptation* (London: Routledge Curzon).
Knott, K. (1986a), *Religion and Identity, and the Study of Ethnic Minority Religions in Britain* (Community Religions Project Monograph; Leeds: University of Leeds).
—— (1986b), *Hinduism in Leeds: A Study of Religious practice in the Indian Hindu Community and in Hindu-Related Groups* (Community Religions Project Monograph; Leeds: University of Leeds).
—— (1991), 'Bound to Change? The Religions of South Asian in Britain', in S. Vertovec (ed.), *Aspects of the South Asian Diaspora* (Oxford: Oxford University Press).
—— (1998), 'Issues in the Study of Religion and Locality', *Method and Theory in the Study of Religion* 10.3: 279–90.
Leeuw van der, G. (1938), *Religion in Essence and Manifestation* (London: George Allen & Unwin).
McLoughlin, S. (2005). 'Migration, Diaspora and Transnationalism: Transformation of Religion and Culture in a Globalising Age', in J.R. Hinnells (ed.), *The Routledge Companion to the Study of Religion* (Oxford and New York: Routledge), pp. 530–42.
Michaelson, M. (1979), 'The Relevance of Caste among East African Gujeratis in Britain', *New Community* 7.3: 66–78.
Modood, T. (2005), *Multicultural Politics: Racism, Ethnicity and Muslims in Britain* (Minneapolis: University of Minnesota Press).
Park, C. (2005), 'Religion and Geography', in J.R. Hinnells (ed.), *The Routledge Companion to the Study of Religion* (Oxford: Routledge), pp. 440–52.
Pye, E.M. (1969), 'The Transplantation of Religions', *Numen* 16.1: 234–39.
—— (2003), *Skilful Means: A Concept in Mahayana Buddhism* (London: Routledge).
Shaw, A. (1988), *A Pakistani Community in Britain* (Oxford and New York: Blackwell).
Smart, N. (1999), 'The Importance of Diasporas', in S. Vertovec and R. Cohen (eds), *Migration, Diasporas and Transnationalism* (Aldershot: Edward Elgar), pp. 417–30.
Solomos, J. (1989), *Race and Racism in Contemporary Britain* (London: Macmillan).
Spickard, J. (2001), 'Religion and Globalization', in *Newsletter of the American Sociological Association Section on Religion*, Fall.
Tambs-Lyche, H., (1980), *London Patidors: A Case in Urban Ethnicity* (London: Routledge & Kegan Paul).
UK Office for National Statistics (ONS) (2001), http://neighbourhood.statistics.gov.uk/dissemination/
Veer van der, P. (2001), 'Transnational Religion', paper given to conference on 'Transnational Migration: Comparative Perspectives', Princeton University.

4

Community and Society: John Macmurray (1891–1976) and New Labour

Esther McIntosh

Introduction

The purpose of this chapter is to tease out the meaning of 'community'. Further, since the term is a commonplace in contemporary British politics and the links between Tony Blair and John Macmurray have been claimed repeatedly by the media, this chapter argues that Blair's use of the term is not equivalent to Macmurray's and, moreover, that Macmurray's notion of community is more appropriate and helpful than New Labour's. Next, from the philosophical and conceptual examination of Macmurray's 'community', this chapter expounds and critiques Macmurray's understanding of ethical relations among persons and his related thesis concerning 'real religion'. Finally, the chapter will end with an example of a contemporary 'community' in Leeds, West Yorkshire that satisfies the necessary and sufficient conditions of Macmurray's definition of community, thereby confirming Macmurray's contemporary relevance to religious pluralism. In particular, this chapter will conclude that it is possible to build community across religious boundaries, and that politics can support but not create genuine community.

We use the term community on a daily basis with little thought as to its definition. On the one hand, it is assumed that we intuitively know what we mean by 'community' and that the reference is understood by all those included in it (and perhaps by all those excluded from it as well), hence it needs no further explanation; on the other hand, the term can be used in such a wide variety of ways that attempts to produce a single definition seem futile. In addition, our identity is bound up with those communities of which we would claim to be a part, such that finding oneself outside of a given community is an unsettling process that gives rise to fear, insecurity and crises of identity. Moreover, since George W. Bush announced his 'war on terror' in response to the 11 September 2001 attacks on the twin towers of the World Trade Center, the importance of locating oneself inside or outside of particular communities has become increasingly significant. In contemporary Britain, outward signs of community identity, especially religious ones, have gained political significance. For example, the recent media reports surrounding Jack Straw's views on the wearing of the niqab ('Take off the veil, says Straw – to immediate anger from Muslims', *Guardian*, 6 October 2006, http://www.guardian.co.uk/

frontpage/story/0,,1888966,00.html) used the language of segregation, community division and 'voluntary apartheid' ('Muslim leaders "risking voluntary apartheid" as veil row escalates', *Guardian*, 16 October 2006, http://www.guardian.co.uk/religion/Story/0,,1923309,00.html); similarly, the case of a classroom assistant from Dewsbury, West Yorkshire asked to remove her niqab at work ('Tribunal dismisses case of Muslim woman ordered not to teach in veil', *Guardian*, 20 October 2006, http://education.guardian.co.uk/schools/story/0,,1927251,00.html); and the British Airways check-in worker at Heathrow, who was asked to cover up a small Christian cross ('BA faces legal action over worker's crucifix ban', *Observer*, 15 October 2006, http://www.guardian.co.uk/airlines/story/0,,1922923,00.html) have been making headline news.

Among the media fascination with Muslim integration, and the multiple interpretations of freedom, choice and women's rights in relation to the niqab, we find claims that racial riots may be on the horizon ('Warning over UK race riot danger', BBC News, 22 October 2006, http://news.bbc.co.uk/1/hi/uk_politics/6074286.stm). Furthermore, Polly Toynbee argues that New Labour's moves to add to the current number of faith schools are contributing to increased segregation, despite intentions to the contrary ('Only a fully secular state can protect women's rights', *Guardian*, 17 October 2006, http://www.guardian.co.uk/Columnists/column/0,,1924022,00.html). Thus, while the government recognizes finally the need for 'honest debate about integration and cohesion in the UK' (Nick Cohen, 'Pivotal moments of 2006', *Observer*, 24 December 2006, http://observer.guardian.co.uk/magazine/story/0,,1975982,0.html), the word 'community' is used repeatedly in vague and broad senses. In particular, politicians and the media make frequent reference to the 'Muslim community' in general, without acknowledging the differences among Muslims, and yet female and male Muslims of all ages vary greatly (both in Britain and around the world) in, for example, their interpretation of the religious instruction to dress modestly or their beliefs concerning whether Muslim women have a right to pray inside the mosque with the Muslim men ('Dispatches: women only jihad', Channel 4, 30 October 2006). Likewise, the media refers to Muslims and non-Muslims as 'two communities' ('Straw's veil comments spark anger', BBC News, 5 October 2006, http://news.bbc.co.uk/1/hi/uk_politics/5410472.stm), as if all those who are not Muslim – all humanists, Hindus, Sikhs, Christians, Buddhists, Jews and so on – share an identity. It is against this confused and highly politicized background that the need to define community, and understand the identity-issues associated with existing inside or outside of a given community, is both urgent and of great consequence.

Macmurray on Society

John Macmurray is most widely known for the series of Gifford lectures he delivered in Glasgow University in 1953 and 1954. The lectures were published in two volumes under the title *The Form of the Personal*, with the first volume having the subtitle *The Self as Agent* and the second volume having the subtitle *Persons in Relation*. The first volume, *The Self as Agent*, is an attack on the legacy of Cartesian individualism, which, based on Descartes' famous *cogito ergo sum* (I think therefore I am), defines the human person in terms of the capacity for thought (see Descartes 1968 [1637]: 18–19.54). On the contrary, Macmurray contends that thinking is an activity, and therefore 'we should substitute the "I do" for the "I think" as our starting-point and centre of reference' (1995c [1957]: 84). In essence, Macmurray's starting point reunites mind and body (thought and action) in contrast with the usual mind–body dualism of theoretical philosophy. According to Macmurray, then, the self exists primarily as agent (doer), but this includes necessarily existing as subject (thinker) also (1995c [1957]: 100–103). Furthermore, since action requires that which is acted on, Macmurray argues, counter to the solipsistic individualism of Cartesian philosophy, the self is a person, whose 'existence is *constituted* by the relation of persons' (1995c [1957]: 12, original emphasis).

Macmurray provides empirical support for his thesis in the second volume, *Persons in Relation*, in which he analyses the relationship between the human infant and her or his adult carer(s). According to Macmurray, relationality is a defining characteristic of the person; thus, he insists that, from the initial relationships of dependence into which we are born, we grow into relationships of interdependence with our fellow human beings, rather than becoming entirely independent individuals. He states: '"I" exist only as one element in the complex "You and I"' (1995a [1961]: 24), and in a later work he acknowledges having an affinity with the work of Martin Buber (1995d [1965]: 24; cf. Buber 1959). It is against this backdrop that Macmurray examines the morality of the relations of persons and develops his notion of community.

It is much earlier in his career, however, following the experience of world war, that Macmurray, in the interests of peace, recognizes the importance of defining, expanding and sustaining community (1943: 16–22, 30–31). Nevertheless, it is only now, thirty years after his death, that his ideas are beginning to receive the attention they deserve. In the last decade almost half of Macmurray's books have been reissued; furthermore, two anthologies (Conford 1996; McIntosh 2004), a biography (Costello 2002) and a collection of critical essays (Fergusson and Dower 2002) have been published for the first time. Likewise, Macmurray's name has been cropping up in media circles, since Tony Blair stated: 'If you really want to understand what I'm all about, you have to take a look at a guy called John Macmurray. It's all there' ('The real Mr Blair', *Observer*, 1 May 2005, http://politics.guardian. co.uk/election/story/0,15803,1473993,00.html), although Blair's autobiography refers to only one of Macmurray's articles (1996: 59).

Central to Macmurray's definition of community is its distinction from 'society', a distinction based on the nature of the relationships within the group. Admittedly, Macmurray's earlier work is less consistent in its use of the terms community and society, but it still contains the notion that there are different types of groups of persons distinguishable by examining the operational relationships on which they are founded and through which they are sustained (1941a: 21–24). According to Macmurray, there are 'groups which consist of people co-operating for certain specific purposes' and 'groups which are bound together by something deeper than any purpose' (1941a: 22). By way of illustration, he suggests that trade unions and sports clubs are examples of cooperative groups united around a purpose, whereas families (good ones, of whatever composition) and friendships are examples of groups of people sharing a common life above and beyond cooperation for a purpose. In other words, for Macmurray, both societies and communities are characterized by the intentional relations of human beings, but it is the type of union informing the relationality of the people, in addition to the intentionality, that marks the difference between a community and a society. The term community is applicable only when persons 'are in communion with one another, and their association is a fellowship' (1995a [1961]: 146).

Nevertheless, Macmurray does not employ the terms society and community in a mutually exclusive manner; rather, the terms society and community represent poles on a spectrum along which groups of intentionally related people travel, in either direction. If we consider the (healthy and happy) family (whatever that might mean) as an example of a community – enjoying each other's company, playing together, sharing experiences and having an interest in each others' well-being – it is clear that the family-members also cooperate to achieve specific purposes (such as daily household chores, going on holiday or moving house). Nonetheless, a community can degenerate into a society if the relations that the members have towards one another change from concern with each other's welfare to concern only with each other's functions in the workings of the group. Similarly, if we consider the sports club as an example of a society, while the group comes together through a shared interest in a particular physical activity and works towards the achievement of high scores in sporting fixtures, it is possible and even probable that at least some of the members will share more than a passing interest in the welfare of their team-mates, an interest that stretches beyond their concern with winning trophies and the smooth functioning of the club. Hence, it seems that every community incorporates society within it and, while not every society is a community, every society possesses the potential to become a community, or at least contain smaller communities within it; that is, simply through the act of bringing people into contact with one another, a society, whatever its purpose, provides the opportunity for individuals to develop community-category relationships. Likewise, every community must be conscious of the possibility of losing community-category relations and degenerating into a society. In brief, Macmurray insists that a group of intentionally related people is identifiable as being more like a society or a community on the basis of the 'intensity of the feeling of comradeship' (1941a: 23) found within the group.

Communities come into existence in order to satisfy a fundamental human need for familiarity and intimacy; hence, communities cannot be artificially created. Societies, however, are engineered into existence in order to satisfy contingent needs, applicable only to a selection of people. Consequently, a community is an end-in-itself, whereas a society is a means-to-an-end. In Macmurray's words, communities have 'spontaneous and intrinsic' origins, while societies are founded on 'external and compulsive' constraints (1941a: 23). It is therefore a necessary condition of a community that the people within it are involved in face-to-face or direct relations with one another; community cannot exist at a distance or among people who never meet. While some societies involve direct relations (and direct relations would be required if the opportunity for developing into a community is to be offered), societies can and frequently do exist across distant or indirectly related human beings, so long as there is an intentional as opposed to a merely factual relationship among those counted as members. Within the workplace, societies revolve around the economic management of the world-as-means, including the use of employees as labour and the relations required to make and distribute that which is produced. In essence, an economic society is formed by connecting people who may not have any physical contact with one another and may not even like one another, but who must cooperate for certain material purposes; members of a society are, therefore, related in terms of their function or usefulness. On the contrary, members of a community are concerned with the intrinsic value of each other, engaging in relationships characterized by love and care.

As we have seen, Macmurray argues that humans, by their nature, desire and require community for growth and fulfilment as persons. Consequently, he argues that economic societies, while necessary, are properly justified by reference to community; that is, economic societies are a means to an end and the end is community. Hence, he states: 'The functional life is *for* the personal life; the personal life is *through* the functional life' (1941b: 822, original emphasis). In terms of today's language of work–life balance, then, Macmurray can be taken as arguing that we do not live to work; rather we work to live; our working life provides us with the financial means to pursue our personal life (where 'personal life' refers to meaningful relationships with friends and family, as opposed to the individualistic understanding of personal life that implies activities pursued alone). It is appropriate for economic societies to be concerned with efficiency and productivity, since efficiency and productivity will benefit the personal life, but safeguards are required in order to prevent the economic life from suppressing or overriding the personal life. In this respect, Macmurray states that 'maintaining, improving and adjusting the indirect or economic relations of persons is the sphere of politics' (1995a [1961]: 188) and, moreover, in this role the state achieves justice by subordinating the working life to the personal life.

Blair and New Labour on Community

By examining Macmurray's account of society, we have reached an understanding of its distinction from community and we have hinted at the role of the state in relation to the support of societies and communities. We must now consider the way in which the term community is being used in contemporary British politics. As we have noted, the British Prime Minister, Mr Tony Blair, claims to have been influenced by Macmurray. Moreover, since both Macmurray and New Labour emphasize the importance of community, it might be assumed that it is Blair's notion of community that has come from Macmurray. For example, in the 'Foreword' to Philip Conford's anthology of Macmurray's writings, Blair states:

> [H]e [Macmurray] confronted what will be the critical political question of the twenty-first century: the relationship between the individual and society . . . he [Macmurray] places the individual firmly within a social setting – we are what we are, in part, because of the other, the 'You and I'. We cannot ignore our obligations to others as well as ourselves. This is where the modern political notions of community begin. (1996: 9)

Furthermore, as Sarah Hale highlights, Blair claims, in his speech to the Women's Institute, that 'the renewal of community is the answer to the challenge of a changing world' (2002: 192). Nevertheless, the alleged influence of Macmurray on Blair is called into question by a closer examination of the concept of community employed by Blair; in fact, Macmurray and Blair use the term community in manifestly different senses. According to Hale, Blair's understanding of community is not simply a variant of Macmurray's community; rather, it is 'in stark opposition to it' (2002: 193).

Despite the care Macmurray takes to define and distinguish societies from communities, Blair simultaneously conflates the terms, reducing the notion of community to mere social relations, and he falls foul of the fallacy of equivocation, giving the term community two different meanings. It is also in the 2000 speech to the Women's Institute that Blair demonstrates his muddled and imprecise use of the term community by citing both 'villages, towns and cities' and our 'fulfilment as individuals' as examples of communities. Furthermore, it is not only Blair who is guilty of this confused use of terminology, since in the same year Gordon Brown, in his speech to the National Council for Voluntary Organizations, also refers to 'common needs, mutual interests, shared objectives, related goals' and to the fact that 'we depend upon each other' as examples of community (Hale 2002: 194). Neither Blair nor Brown seem to have grasped Macmurray's distinction between communities and societies; they have failed to realize that villages and/or social networks based on shared objectives are societies rather than communities and, thus, unless they become communities, they will not lead to our fulfilment as persons.

Nevertheless, the sense in which community is used by New Labour, while at odds with Macmurray's concept, is a familiar one. Contemporary philosophical communitarianism is heavily influenced by the founder of the Communitarian Network, Amitai Etzioni, who argues that community would be better served by a closer association between rights and responsibilities (1995 [1993]: 163–208). In Hale's opinion, therefore, Blair fits the communitarian mould because of the prominent place he assigns to duties in relation to rights. That is, the government under Blair has made the honouring of covenants and contracts a central element in accessing rights. (For example, New Labour demands that the unemployed fulfil 'responsibilities' that increase employability, such as acquiring new skills, training in interview techniques, attending application workshops and so on, in order to be granted the 'right' to unemployment benefit.) In addition, as Hale shows, Blair assumes that communities can be fostered by making what is commonly referred to as 'community-work' compulsory for all university students, a measure intended to be attained by the year 2010 (2002: 196).

Macmurray's understanding of responsibility and service are radically different to the versions espoused by Blair. While Macmurray takes responsibility seriously, his understanding of responsibility does not fit the communitarian model. Macmurray understands responsibility as a voluntary act of self-limitation for the benefit of someone else; that is, since persons in a community are concerned with the growth and development of each other, they avoid exercising their freedom in ways that will limit the freedom of others (1995a [1961]: 190–91). Moreover, contrary to Blair's high hopes for compulsory 'community-work', Macmurray is opposed to the ideological promotion of servitude. In fact, in an early work where Macmurray examines the type of morality that 'talks always of service . . . duty . . . to serve others, to serve our country, to serve humanity' (1932: 193), he argues that this is in fact a false morality, since it 'subordinates human beings to organization' (1932: 195). In conjunction with Macmurray's understanding of the correct work–life balance, Macmurray also insists that 'institutions . . . exist for the sake of the personal life' (1995b [1935]: 63); that is, rather than people being made to serve institutions, human-made institutions are there for the benefit of humanity (and should be changed when they cease to be a benefit). True morality, for Macmurray, is 'personal morality' (1995b [1935]: 199); it exists among groups of friends (communities) who relate as equals and therefore have the freedom to grow as persons. Blair's emphasis on service, therefore, is not the sort of morality Macmurray associates with community, but it does fit Macmurray's account of social morality. Consequently, Hale suggests that: 'Far from providing the philosophical basis for New Labour's "communitarianism", Macmurray's writings constitute a very plausible philosophical ground from which to condemn it' (2002: 197).

However, it is not necessarily the case that Macmurray's influence on Blair is as hard to detect as it might seem from the disjunctions in their diverse understandings of community. Whereas Hale uses Macmurray's work to offer a thoroughly negative critique of Blairite rhetoric and policies, Bevir and O'Brien offer a supportive explanation of the alteration that has occurred in the meaning of the term community when being transmitted from Macmurray to Blair (2003: 305–29). They argue that, if we see Macmurray's idea of community as a point within a historical continuum, Blair's notion of community can be understood as the contemporary development of Macmurray's version. As Bevir and O'Brien rightly point out, Blair and his contemporaries have had to grapple with 'the dilemma of multiculturalism' (2003: 327); a problem that Macmurray did not address or envisage. In addition, Bevir and O'Brien argue that multiculturalism is accompanied by an increasing lack of solidarity in a nation, which translates into a loss of votes for political parties that advocate the increased taxation required to fund the sort of welfare state Macmurray advocates (2003: 327). If Bevir and O'Brien are correct, and their claims seem highly plausible, then we can account for the introduction of New Right – the policy that ties benefits to responsibilities – on the basis of multiculturalism and a decrease in solidarity among British citizens. Thus, in agreement with Hale's assessment of New Labour policy, Bevir and O'Brien state that: 'The main role of the welfare state is no longer to provide a uniform and universal set of benefits . . . It is, rather, to enable individuals to improve and to develop themselves' (2003: 327).

Despite reasonable explanations for transforming the traditional perception of a welfare state, it does seem as if Blair has changed Macmurray's community beyond all recognition. In particular, as we have noted, Blair stresses compulsory duties and service as the means by which community will be created and sustained, but this is counter to Macmurray's account in a fundamental respect. First, since communities are made up of friendships, Macmurray insists that they cannot be artificially created (nor maintained by force) and, therefore, politics cannot be the means by which communities are engendered and sustained (1941a: 24–27; 1995d [1965]: 78–79). Second, a Macmurrian community is a meeting of equals, concerned with each other's well-being, whereas 'New Labour offers us a future in which the well-to-do are increasingly free to go their own ways while the poor are subject to increasingly punitive responsibilities' (Bevir and O'Brien 2003: 328). Blair seems to have missed Macmurray's emphasis on the role the state has to play in providing the conditions necessary for communities to flourish. That is, since communities are formed among persons who care for each other as equals, the state can assist this process by seeking justice, including economic justice, through the provision of equality of opportunity and equality of consideration under the law. Blair, however, seems to see political policies as the end rather than a means to an end, ignoring Macmurray's statement that 'the State is *for* the community; the community is *through* the State' (1941c: 856, original emphasis).

Macmurray on Community and Religion

If Macmurray's community is desirable and significant, which it seems that it is if we accept his argument from human nature to the necessity of communal relations, we need to find a way to address the contemporary problems of fragmentation, fear and multiculturalism without losing all resemblance to Macmurray's conception of community. We need, therefore, to look further at Macmurray's account of the development of community.

According to Macmurray, while politics cannot create community, he argues that community is created and sustained by religion (1941a). Against the widespread history of religious wars, schisms and antagonism, however, it seems as if religion is the cause of disrupting rather than creating community and Macmurray is aware of this.[1] Macmurray's argument rests on a serious critique of institutionalized religion and an explanation of that which Macmurray refers to as 'real religion' (1995a [1961]: 170). Macmurray's argument concerning religion is based on the fact of religion; that is, Macmurray assumes that, since every society has a religion(s) of some kind, we can infer that religion has its roots in a common human experience (1956: 916–17). Alternative explanations for the appearance of religion and the increase in secularity (in some places) represent challenges to such a claim; however, the common human experience referred to here is simply the interdependence of persons. Macmurray states:

> The primary religious assertion is that all men [and women] are equal, and that fellowship is the only relation between persons which is fully rational, or fully appropriate to their nature as persons. In this assertion the whole nature of religion is bound up. (1995b [1935]: 124)

Consequently, Macmurray argues that the idea of a private religion practised in solitude – more recently referred to in relation to the secularization thesis as 'believing without belonging' (Davie 1994: 112–14) – is fundamentally mistaken and, further, that individualistic societies are, in fact, irreligious in spite of claims to the contrary (1995b [1935]: 127). Similarly, Macmurray's distinction between real and unreal or 'pseudo-religion' (1935: 45–58) depends on whether or not a so-called religion is affirming and expanding community. That is, since the relation of persons as friends assumes an equality based merely on common humanity, communities are essentially inclusive in intention, such that the admission of new members is welcomed. Hence, Macmurray insists that real religion is 'heterocentric' whereas unreal religion is 'egocentric' (1935: 170). In other words, an unreal religion is inward-looking and concerned with the limitation and preservation of the current membership and is thus prone to stagnation, whereas a real religion is outward-looking or other-centred and recognizes the inconsistency of limiting expansion and the need to expand for the future of the community and, more importantly, to fulfil the human need for fellowship.

Unreality in religion is manifested in idealism and the related dualism of the material and spiritual aspects of life. An unreal religion is either in pursuit of material power at the expense of the spiritual life or it pursues contemplative spirituality in separation from material means and needs, focusing on the notion of an ideal world-to-come instead of effecting changes in this world; its emphasis is otherworldly. On the contrary, a real religion is practical; it is concerned with person-to-person relationships in their material as well as their spiritual aspects. Macmurray makes the bold assertion that:

> Until . . . religion becomes a force for the creation of community, of the conscious community of men and women who know and appreciate and love one another, not merely religion, but the life of mankind is immature and sub-rational. (1995b [1935]: 155)

Community expansion has 'both a quantitative and qualitative side' (Macmurray 1936: 74). That is, while the future of a community requires its enlargement in terms of numbers, this will decrease the quality of the community, which must be attended to in turn otherwise the community will collapse into a society. It is imperative, therefore, that rituals are maintained to facilitate the opportunity for new members to develop friendships and increase the quality of community alongside the increase in quantity (1995a [1961]: 174; 1995d [1965]: 31–33). Ritual is a key part of the reflective aspect of religion serving to emphasize the consciousness of membership of a community. Macmurray argues that the central aim of religion is the 'celebration of communion' (1995a [1961]: 162). Hence, as Macmurray shows, a religious activity is merely an ordinary activity endowed with special significance; for example, eating can be merely functional or it can be part of a sacred meal (1936: 65–66). However, in order for the religious symbolism to be effective, it must represent the extension of the community through time. Nevertheless, rituals only serve to celebrate the present and remember the past, if they have present meaning and are not simply arcane or archaic traditions. Thus Macmurray argues: 'The necessity is . . . for a ritual head, a representative of the unity of the community as a personal reality, so that each member can think his [or her] membership of the community through his [or her] relation to this person' (1995a [1961]: 164). The symbolism of a ritual head is, therefore, an explanation of the idea of god; the idea of god is able to encompass the sense of belonging to a community that encompasses previous and future generations.

According to Macmurray, the true nature of religion comes to the fore when a religion reaches maturity. While inclusivity on the grounds of common humanity is a trademark of a mature religion, exclusivity on the basis of doctrinal disagreement indicates immaturity in a religion (Macmurray 1995b [1935]: 152). At the heart of Macmurray's account of religion, then, is an emphasis on othropraxis rather than orthodoxy, or, as A.R.C. Duncan puts it, Macmurray distinguishes 'between religious belief and religious faith' (1990: 125). Religious belief is denoted by acceptance of the creeds, doctrines and dogmas associated with a particular religion, whereas religious faith, according to Macmurray, is observed through an optimistic attitude that leads to heterocentric behaviour (1995d [1965]: 69–71). On the basis of this definition it seems that a person or community could have religious faith without being members of an institutionalized religion and members of an institutionalized religion could have religious belief without religious faith. In fact, Macmurray argues 'it is a great mistake to identify religion with theology; and it is in principle wrong to make any belief or set of beliefs a test of religious loyalty' (1961: 71).

An over-emphasis on doctrine and creeds stems from the Stoic dualism of reason and emotion; that is, it valorizes the intellect and turns religion into a system of rules and dogmas. This is problematic for three main reasons: first, it fragments the embodied self and ignores the fact of human relationality; second, it assumes that religious doctrines can be understood aside from their practical implications as opposed to relating belief to its outworking in daily practicalities; third, when membership of a religious tradition rests on the ability to assent to a static set of beliefs it becomes unreasonably exclusive, creating division and tension rather than supporting and increasing community. Hence Macmurray states: 'it is a mistake to identify a religious way of life with a set of rules, moral or other . . . In religious behaviour what is important is . . . the right motive' (1961: 71). As we have seen, the right motive, according to Macmurray, is one of love for one's fellows. Moreover, rather than contrasting love with hate, Macmurray contrasts love with fear. Likewise therefore he understands fear to be a hindrance to religious faith, a view he supports with reference to the New Testament account of Jesus' life and teaching.

Macmurray on Fear, Faith and Christianity

For Macmurray, Jesus is a Hebrew prophet and a religious exemplar par excellence (1935: 88), but Macmurray does not comment on whether Jesus has a divine nature. Macmurray's concern is to ascertain Jesus' intention from an examination of his life and teaching without the interpretation being coloured by the Pauline letters or the trends in interpretation thus far. (Since the New Testament report of Jesus' life and teaching is the only report we have to hand, we have to use this report even though we cannot ascertain its historical accuracy.)

Clearly we cannot detach ourselves from our current socio-historical context or from all the scholarship that has informed our understanding to date in order to discover the person referred to as Jesus of Nazareth. Yet, the attempt to read a text again with the aim of rediscovering or even uncovering an interpretation that may have been suppressed or ignored is an admirable one. Furthermore, the endeavour of re-reading sacred text without the reading being contaminated by historical biases has affinities with the approach of feminist biblical scholarship (Fiorenza 1983).

In essence, Macmurray is concerned with eliminating the dualism that separates Jesus' life from his teaching; on the contrary, Macmurray insists that the two must be taken together. According to Macmurray, in the New Testament account of Jesus' life and teaching, Jesus equates the fulfilment of human nature through positive person-to-person relationships with the divine intention for human beings (1938: 101). In religious terms, Macmurray claims that Jesus understands the 'Kingdom of Heaven' as fully positive relationships among persons and, further, that Jesus' life and teaching is the explanation of the way in which that kingdom can be achieved 'on earth' (1935: 62). In particular, Macmurray argues that Jesus identifies fear as the key stumbling block to positive personal relationships, the evidence for which is the repeated question 'why are ye fearful?' (Matt. 8.26 KJV). Furthermore, when Jesus asks this question, it is followed frequently with the saying 'O ye of little faith' (Matt. 8.26). As we have already noted, Macmurray defines faith as an attitude of trust, openness, care of and love for the other, and he defends this view by citing Jesus' respect for the commands in the Hebrew Bible to 'love the Lord thy God with all thine heart, and with all thy soul, and with all thy might' (Deut. 6.5) and to 'love thy neighbour as thyself' (Lev. 19.18). In conjunction with the opinion that love is the foundation of positive personal relationships, Macmurray holds that the fear that prevents positive relations among humans is overcome by love (1979: 6–10). He claims that Jesus advocates the view that love is the means by which fear is subordinated and community is created with the instruction to 'Love your enemies' (Matt. 5.44; Lk. 6.27).

In Macmurray's opinion, therefore, Jesus is more concerned with living life to the full (with fulfilling human nature through positive human relationships) than with moral commands or with an ideal, future world that exists only after death (1973: 11). It follows, for Macmurray, that sin and salvation are to be understood in terms of human relations; that is, sin is the disruption of community and salvation is from the fear that prevents community (1979: 7).

Furthermore, rather than condemnation for wrong-doing, Macmurray draws attention to the motif of forgiveness and Jesus direction to forgive each other 'seventy times seven' (Matt. 18.22), since it is via mutual forgiveness (and repentance) that guilt and shame are overcome and relationships are restored. In addition, Macmurray finds support in Jesus' life and teaching for his insistence that equality is required for genuine community. Equality in person-to-person relationships centres on transcending inevitable functional inequalities and dependencies and eradicating notions of superiority and inferiority. Jesus creates equality by stating: 'whosoever will be chief among you, let him be your servant' (Matt. 20.27), by washing the disciples' feet (Jn 13.5-17) and by referring to his followers as friends (Jn 15.15). As we have seen, the notion of friendship is central to Macmurray's thesis; hence, in drawing corroboration from the life and teaching of Jesus, the language of friendship as opposed to that of master and servant is critical.

Contrary to tradition, then, Macmurray condemns the emphasis on servanthood and self-sacrifice found in institutionalized Christianity. Servants cooperate with their masters from obligation, whereas friends cooperate voluntarily. In Macmurray's interpretation of the New Testament text, therefore, self-sacrifice is that which may be occasionally required, but Jesus does not promote it as the norm, since it is counter to the basic principles of community relations (1979: 4). Friends may make sacrifices, but self-sacrifice or service cannot be the foundation or the modus operandi of free and equal relationships. Moreover, Macmurray interprets Jesus' comment 'Greater love hath no man than this, that a man lay down his life for his friends' (Jn 15.13) to be an affirmation of the value of life rather than a recommendation for martyrdom. Likewise, Macmurray suggests that the saying 'He that findeth his life shall lose it: and he that loseth his life . . . shall find it' (Matt. 10.39) confirms his insistence that friendship is characterized by hetero- rather than egocentric behaviour (1979: 5).

Initially it seems that there are two weaknesses in Macmurray's account: first, it is not obviously the case that Jesus' perception of friendship is unique, and second Macmurray's interpretation of Jesus' life and teaching is at odds with the prevalent Christian tradition. However, Macmurray argues that, while other religions and scholars advocate friendship in relation to human flourishing, such accounts are usually taken to be expressing an ideal which we aim towards but fail to achieve; for Jesus, at least according to Macmurray, friendship is not an unachievable ideal, it is the very essence of human life (1973: 6–7, 10–11). In accordance with Macmurray's distinction between religious belief and religious faith, therefore, Macmurray perceives Jesus' life and teaching as instruction in having a religious attitude of faith rather than consenting to a particular religion's belief system. In keeping with this interpretation, Macmurray contends that, when Jesus is crucified, the disciples' mission is to continue to increase community as opposed to converting others from one religion to another (1995d [1965]: 51–52).

Furthermore, despite the disjunction between Macmurray's interpretation of Jesus' life and teaching and that of the majority of mainstream institutionalized Christianity, there is contemporary support for Macmurray's account. Peter

Harvey, for example, similarly re-interprets the sayings of Jesus to emphasize human fulfilment, and he strongly opposes interpretations that construe Jesus' teaching to be idealism and/or moralism. With striking similarity to Macmurray's approach, Harvey suggests that the phrase 'He that shall lose his life shall find it' invites a rejection of fear, subjection and victimhood in favour of a life lived freely and fully (1991: 80–87). In essence, then, Jesus' life and teaching, for both Macmurray and Harvey, is an example of a life lived with confidence in the face of adversity, such that Jesus affirms his identity and attains his potential as a person.

Macmurray on Ethical Relations

In conjunction with Macmurray's definition of religious faith as an attitude of mind centred on heterocentric action (and therefore the creation and sustenance of community), this is also the standard by which the morality of an act is measured. Thus, Macmurray asserts that: 'The moral rightness of an action . . . has its ground in the relation of persons' (1995a [1961]: 116). Moreover, for action to be properly other-centred (and hence morally right) it needs to be in keeping with the nature of the other.

In other words, if we try to feed a stone or if we keep an eagle in the house, we are not acting in accordance with the nature of the other. Similarly, if we treat people as if they are objects, ignoring the fact that they have physical and emotional needs, then we are not acting in accordance with human nature. As Macmurray states: 'To act rightly, I must know . . . what the properties or characters of the Other are' (1995a [1961]: 113). Consequently, while we may achieve our intentions by treating other persons, in Kantian terms, as mere means to our end (Kant 1948 [1785]: 65–67 [428–29]), or we may satisfy our desire for companionship by treating an object as if it were a person, Macmurray argues that these activities would not be right actions, since the morality of an act is not bound up with its success. He maintains that: 'The most obviously immoral action can be efficiently and skilfully performed' (1995a [1961]: 116).

While inanimate objects cannot resist our actions on them, acting in relation with other persons inevitably leads to tension and conflict, and it is then that the morality of an act is harder to discern. Since our actions affect other persons (and we are aware that this is the case), the morality of our actions depends, Macmurray claims, on our underlying intentions (1995a [1961]: 116–17). We can act with the intention of assisting others in their acts (so long as their acts are heterocentrically motivated), or we can deliberately aim to thwart their action; hence, the morality of our actions is determined, not so much by its actual effects, as by whether we intended to increase or decrease tension and conflict with heterocentric others. Nevertheless, the resolution of conflict is fraught with difficulties. As Macmurray explains, there are two common courses of action in response to conflict; one is aggressive and the other is submissive (1995a [1961]: 118). While aggression aims to prevent the other from acting as intended, submission prevents the self from acting as originally intended. In Macmurray's opinion, neither aggression nor submission results in morally right action since both prevent the friendship relations required for persons to fulfil their nature. In short, 'a morally right action is an action which intends community' (1995a [1961]: 119).

On the one hand, we only fulfil our nature by exercising freedom in our capacity for communal action; yet, on the other hand, since membership of community is conscious, we have to be aware that our actions impinge upon our relations with other members of the community thereby limiting their freedom to act. Hence, while we cannot be held responsible for consequences of our actions of which we could not have had prior knowledge, we are answerable to others for the effects of our actions on them, where advance knowledge of those effects is available. In Macmurray's thesis: 'Freedom and responsibility are . . . aspects of one fact' (1995a [1961]: 119). For Macmurray, then, an individual who unsuccessfully attempts murder is still morally culpable of murder, even though the law makes a distinction between attempted and actual murder (1995a [1961]: 120); this view is consistent with religious and moral systems that focus on thoughts as well as deeds.

Nonetheless, Macmurray does make some allowances concerning moral responsibility in respect of worldviews. That is, since communities operate in a variety of ways and place different expectations on their members, an individual's moral accountability may be mitigated by the shared perceptions of the community. Hence, as persons-in-relation, individuals cannot be held responsible for failing to intend community, if they have intended what their group erroneously views as community, although individuals are not absolved of responsibility if they have not reflected on the shared understanding of their group. Thus, an individual is both shaped by her or his community and potentially able, at least in reflection, to critically assess the workings and assumptions of it. On this basis, Macmurray asserts that 'An agent's morality must be relative to [her or] his own conscience' (1995a [1961]: 120).

There are sociological and philosophical studies that examine the transmission of social norms across generations, both at the level of the family and at a national level, providing support for Macmurray's argument concerning the development and perception of moral action (Bem 1970; MacIntyre 1981). While we cannot always (or even very often) remove ourselves entirely from those influences, we can examine whether that to which we are referring as a community and as communal action is serving to decrease fear and to increase care and love for other persons. As Macmurray states: 'the centre of reference for the agent, when he seeks to act rightly, is always the personal Other' (1995a [1961]: 122).

A Contemporary Community: Hyde Park, Leeds, West Yorkshire, UK

If we are to take Macmurray's account of community seriously, we have to consider whether it is practicable. As we have seen, the contemporary context of cultural and religious pluralism is not foreseen by Macmurray and, at least in Blair's case, can lead to the dilution of the conception of community along with its vague and varied usage. The extent to which Macmurray's theory is of current benefit therefore depends upon whether it is offering a useful and intelligible explanation of the need for and the means of achieving satisfying person-to-person relations.

As with any life work, some of Macmurray's writings are dated and lack adaptability and some concepts are over-worked and lack intelligibility. However, in its essential aspects Macmurray's thesis is both intelligible and utilizable. That is, we cannot deny that human beings crave relations that are more than mere social interaction. Macmurray's argument in favour of friendship for human flourishing is not contentious, neither is the claim that friendship resists superiority and dependence and is made easier by economic equality. However, if we acknowledge that human relations have the power to humanize or to dehumanize, then we are challenged by Macmurray to ensure that our intentions in action are other-centred. It is the rejection of egocentrism that renders Macmurray's theory most at odds with western capitalism and most challenging in terms of moral accountability.

In addition to the moral challenge, since Macmurray's perception of community is of inclusivity, face-to-face relations and celebratory rituals, it might seem that religious and cultural pluralism renders inclusive community impossible or at least implausible. However, inter-religious and non-religious communities are consistent with Macmurray's definition of religion as the 'celebration of communion' rather than the assertion of religious beliefs (whether or not we agree with such a definition), despite his appeal to Christian texts. In my opinion, Unity Day in Hyde Park, Leeds, West Yorkshire, provides a contemporary illustration of an inclusive community that is managing to unite and overcome religious and cultural differences (http://www.myspace.com/hydeparkunityday). The Hyde Park area of Leeds is home to a number of religions and to huge economic disparity. Mosques, Christian Churches and a Hindu Temple are situated in close proximity, as are students, families, the elderly and young offenders. Anyone who wishes to assist with Unity Day can become involved by volunteering; in fact, Unity Day is run entirely by volunteers. Unity Day was envisaged and founded by residents in the Hyde Park area of Leeds with the expressed aim of celebrating 'talent and diversity' in response to the 1995 riots. Over each twelve-month period the Unity Day volunteers hold regular meetings and source local talent, generating an annual celebratory outdoors event of music and activities that attracts people of all ages from all over Leeds.

Perhaps preparatory meetings and an annual event represent less regular rituals than Macmurray envisaged for community, but, aside from this, Unity Day is an especially appropriate illustration of Macmurray's theory, because its central focus is unity and inclusion, as opposed to, for example, an artistic 'community' that excludes those lacking in artistic talent. Moreover, it provides fitting support for Macmurray's understanding of the role that politics has to play in assisting communities. As we have seen, Macmurray argues that politics cannot initiate community, but that it can provide the conditions necessary for communities to be created and to expand. The 1995 riots are testament to the failure, or rather the inability, of politics to create community in the Hyde Park area, whereas the popularity of Unity Day is indicative of the potential for building community out of local heterocentric intentions and action. Unity Day is based on the sharing of a common life and aims to extend fellowship across secular and religious divisions, turning a fragmented and antagonistic society into a community. In keeping with Macmurray's theory, politics provides the means for Unity Day to continue and to grow, since the local government has to grant the necessary entertainment licences for the annual celebration to go ahead.

Conclusion

Nevertheless, the example of Unity Day, which is only one of many possible examples of a contemporary community, does not mean that Macmurray's account of community will be without its critics. On the one hand, any theory that speaks of care, love and community risks being trivial, frivolous or figurative. It is profoundly important to remember therefore that Macmurray is opposed to dualism, idealism and socio-economic injustice. Macmurray avoids trivializing community by emphasizing equality, social action and face-to-face relations, unlike Blair's use of the term to refer to societies that may be too large and/or constituted by members who are too hostile to one another to fit Macmurray's definition of a community.

Nonetheless, Macmurray insists that community is inclusive and therefore has no numerical limit, but talk of universal community sounds vacuous. We need to remember, therefore, Macmurray's assertion that a community of friends is inclusive in intention, as opposed to being actually universal; that is, since genuine friendship is grounded in shared humanity, any human being can, in principle, be included. Significantly, then, Macmurray is not advocating enclosed communities that emphasize the exclusion of those with whom the group does not identify; rather, the identity required for membership in a Macmurrian community is simply that of being a human.[2] In addition, by focusing on the other, Macmurray's community is one which welcomes diversity and the otherness of others, thereby avoiding the sort of conformity and exclusion of social difference in other theories of community that Iris Marion Young, for example, finds problematic (Young 1990: 227).

On the other hand, while the marginalized and exploited would benefit from a greater emphasis on care, an ethic of care runs the risk of being either overburdensome for the carer or smothering of the cared for, as Joan Tronto points out in her critique of the feminist ethics of care (1993: 247–52). Again, Macmurray's stress on justice is vital here; justice prevents the exploitation of the carer and the control of the cared for. Similarly, since a Macmurrian community comprises the relations of equals, it is advocating the kind of care that encourages interdependence and mutuality instead of the kind of care that leads to dependency either through charity or paternalism.[3]

Care and justice are integral to human life in order that the vulnerable are both provided for and protected, but we also have to redress the historical tendency of women in patriarchal cultures to accept and adopt an unequal and repressive care-giving role, as feminists highlight (Friedman 1993: 261–62; Parsons 1996: 209). Consequently, Macmurray's theory could benefit from the addition of concepts of self-care and self-love (see McIntosh 2007); although his version, as we have seen, is opposed to the Christian motif of self-sacrifice and, moreover, his portrayal of community is at odds with the kind of communitarianism in which the individual is subsumed in the group. As Frank Kirkpatrick states:

> Clearly in Macmurray's view of community the individual is not suppressed or subordinated to a greater whole in which [she or] he is only a functional part. The flourishing of the individual with [her or] his own unique gifts and talents is integral to the very meaning of community itself. Individual and community are not polar opposites. (2001: 74)

While Macmurray is not so naïve as to present community as a panacea for all social, emotional and psychological ills, he possesses enough insight to recognize that the yearning for community is fundamental to human nature. He gives politics a role in the support of communities without reducing community to society and, moreover, he combines this with an account of religion that is thoroughly this-worldly, thus offering religion a vital role in human flourishing. Admittedly, Macmurray's account of religion is highly critical of the otherworldly and divisive tendencies of institutionalized religion; yet, by defining religion as the celebration of community, he provides a practical standard by which to measure justice. A real religion, then, will be working towards the eradication of distinctions based on sex, race, class, disability and so on and this, according to Kirkpatrick, is the proper goal of a Christian ethic; it is not a case of religion acquiescing to the demands of secular society (2001: 126).

Furthermore, with recent media reports spotlighting the contemporary problem of fear, including the claim that Britain is afraid of young people ('A nation "fearful of young people"', *Metro*, 22 October 2006, http://www.metro.co.uk/news/article.html?in_article_id=22125&in_page_id=34&in_a_source=; 'British adults "fear youngsters"', BBC News, 22 October 2006, http://news.bbc.co.uk/1/hi/uk/6074252.stm), but more frequently focusing on the perceived threat of Islam by the west ('Islam poses a threat to the west, say 53pc in poll', *Telegraph*, 25 August 2006, http://www.telegraph.co.uk/news/main.jhtml?xml=/news/2006/08/25/nislam25.xml; 'Campus radicals "serious threat"', BBC News, 17 November 2006, http://news.bbc.co.uk/1/hi/education/6155916.stm; 'Threat of Islamic extremism that stretches across Europe', *The Times*, 26 July 2005, http://www.timesonline.co.uk/tol/news/uk/article548063.ece; 'MI5 wants 800 more spies to take on Islamic threat', *The Times*, 13 November 2005, http://www.timesonline.co.uk/tol/news/uk/article589700.ece) and the fear of British Muslims that their religion is under political attack ('Fear, paranoia and being British', *Asian Image*, 28 October 2006, http://www.asianimage.co.uk/search/display.var.980471.0.fear_paranoia_and_being_british.php) or that they will be subject to hate crimes perpetrated by their neighbours ('Calls for calm as fear of severe backlash grows', *Guardian*, 13 July 2005, http://www.guardian.co.uk/attackonlondon/story/0,,1527336,00.html), we need to create and sustain community. As we have seen, politics cannot eliminate fear, but, according to Macmurray, fear can be overcome with love; not a vague love of humanity or the smothering love of sentimentalism, but a love that appreciates the needs and the otherness of the other and, therefore, necessarily consists of persons working together for social justice. Moreover, contrary to the negative image of religion portrayed in the media reports, Macmurray suggests that religion (as he defines it) is the means by which we can rise above fear and develop community.

Macmurray's critique of institutionalized Christianity may be regarded as contentious among mainstream Christian organizations and his portrayal of Jesus as a religious exemplar may be regarded as irrelevant among those who are committed to another religion or have no allegiance to organized religion; however, Macmurray's minimalist definition of religion may appeal to agnostics and it renders his theory adaptable to situations of religious pluralism. Finally, in the contemporary context, where identity is a fraught and contentious issue and where the term community is used in varied and conflicting senses, we need to have a clear understanding of the meaning of community and, as Kirkpatrick contends: 'John Macmurray provides . . . a solid, comprehensive, and metaphysically adequate foundation for a philosophy of community' (2001: 65).

Notes

1 Christianity (and other religions) has a chequered history of engaging in holy wars and doctrinal division; see Chadwick 1993 [1967]; Frost 2004.

2 There is, of course, an ecological argument to be made concerning the ethics of excluding or including other animals and nature, but this is not the subject of this chapter.

3 Obviously dependency is an inescapable issue for those with profound mental and/or physical disabilities, but there is still scope for relationships with the profoundly disabled to engender communal intentions (see Swinton and McIntosh 2000) similar to the parent–child relationship.

References

Bem, D.J. (1970), *Beliefs, Attitudes and Human Affairs* (Belmont: Brooks/Cole).

Bevir, M., and D. O'Brien (2003), 'From Idealism to Communitarianism: The Inheritance and the Legacy of John Macmurray', *History of Political Thought* 24.2: 305–29.

Blair, T. (1996), *New Britain: My Vision of a Young Country* (London: Fourth Estate).

Buber, M. (1959), *I and Thou* (trans. R.G. Smith; Edinburgh: T. & T. Clark).

Chadwick, H. (1993 [1967]), *The Early Church* (London: Penguin, rev. edn).

Conford, P. (1996), *The Personal World: John Macmurray on Self and Society* (Edinburgh: Floris Books).

Costello, J.E. (2002), *John Macmurray: A Biography* (Edinburgh: Floris Books).

Davie, G. (1994), *Religion in Britain Since 1945* (Oxford: Blackwell).

Descartes, R. (1968 [1637]), *Discourse on Method and the Meditations* (trans. F.E. Sutcliffe; London: Penguin).

Duncan, A.R.C. (1990), *On the Nature of Persons* (New York: Peter Lang).

Etzioni, A. (1995 [1993]), *The Spirit of Community: Rights, Responsibilities and the Communitarian Agenda* (London: Fontana Press).

Fergusson, D. and N. Dower (eds) (2002), *John Macmurray: Critical Perspectives* (New York: Peter Lang).
Fiorenza, E.S. (1983), *In Memory of Her: A Feminist Theological Reconstruction of Christian Origins* (London: SCM Press).
Friedman, M. (1993), 'Beyond Caring: The De-moralization of Gender', in M.J. Larrabee (ed.), *An Ethic of Care* (New York: Routledge), pp. 258–73.
Frost, J.W. (2004), *A History of Christian, Jewish, Muslim, Hindu and Buddhist Perspectives on War and Peace* (2 vols; Lewiston: Edwin Mellen Press).
Hale, S. (2002), 'Professor Macmurray and Mr Blair: The Strange Case of the Communitarian Guru that Never Was', *Political Quarterly* 73.2: 191–97.
Harvey, N.P. (1991), *The Morals of Jesus* (London: Darton, Longman and Todd).
Kant, I. (1948 [1785]), *Groundwork of the Metaphysic of Morals* (trans. H.J. Paton; London and New York: Routledge).
Kirkpatrick, F. (2001), *The Ethics of Community* (Oxford: Blackwell).
McIntosh, E. (2007), 'The Concept of Sacrifice: A Reconsideration of the Feminist Critique', *International Journal of Public Theology* 1.2: 210–29.
McIntosh, E. (ed.) (2004), *John Macmurray: Selected Philosophical Writings* (Exeter: Imprint Academic).
MacIntyre, A. (1981), *After Virtue: A Study in Moral Theory* (London: Duckworth).
Macmurray, J. (1932), *Freedom in the Modern World* (London: Faber).
—— (1935), *Creative Society* (London: SCM Press).
—— (1936), *The Structure of Religious Experience* (London: Faber).
—— (1938), *The Clue to History* (London: SCM Press).
—— (1941a), *A Challenge to the Churches* (London: Kegan Paul).
—— (1941b), 'Persons and Functions: 3 – Two Lives in One', *The Listener* 26: 822.
—— (1941c), 'Persons and Functions: 4 – The Community of Mankind', *The Listener* 26: 856.
—— (1943), *Constructive Democracy* (London: Faber).
—— (1956), 'What is Religion About? – 1', *The Listener* 56: 916–17.
—— (1961), *Religion, Art and Science* (Liverpool: Liverpool University Press).
—— (1973), *The Philosophy of Jesus* (London: Friends Home Service Committee).
—— (1979), *Ye Are My Friends and To Save From Fear* (London: Quaker Home Service).
—— (1995a [1961]), *Persons in Relation* (London: Faber).
—— (1995b [1935]), *Reason and Emotion* (London: Faber).
—— (1995c [1957]), *The Self as Agent* (London: Faber).
—— (1995d [1965]), *Search for Reality in Religion* (London: Quaker Home Service).
Parsons, S. (1996), *Feminism and Christian Ethics* (Cambridge: Cambridge University Press).
Swinton, J., and E. McIntosh (2000), 'Persons in Relation: The Care of Persons with Learning Disabilities', *Theology Today* 57.2: 175–84.
Tronto, J.C. (1993), 'Beyond Gender Difference to a Theory of Care', in M.J. Larrabee (ed.), *An Ethic of Care* (New York: Routledge), pp. 240–57.
Young, I.M. (1990), *Justice and the Politics of Difference* (Princeton: Princeton University Press).

5

Paradigm, Community and Theological Education: A Study of Theological Education with Reference to the Work of Thomas S. Kuhn and David H. Kelsey

Gary Wilton

Introduction

The purpose of this chapter is to explore communal formation and identity within theological education. My approach is perhaps more epistemological than sociological. I begin by reviewing Kuhn's concept of 'paradigm' developed in *The Structure of Scientific Revolutions*. Here Kuhn provided a theoretical framework for understanding the shared life of a scientific/academic community: the development of ideas, the induction and formation of community members. I then turn to Kelsey's *Between Athens and Berlin: The Theological Education Debate* to explore his 'Athens' and 'Berlin' paradigms of theological education. Building on Kelsey's approach I develop generic versions of the 'Athens' and 'Berlin' paradigms to analyse some contemporary theological communities. I also reflect further on the Kuhnian concept of paradigm.

Thomas S. Kuhn: Paradigm

The term 'paradigm' entered academic and popular vocabulary as a result of Kuhn's *The Structure of Scientific Revolutions* first published in 1962. Fuller begins his critical work on Thomas Kuhn as follows:

> *The Structure of Scientific Revolutions* by Thomas Kuhn (1922–96) is probably the best-known academic book of the second half of the twentieth century. Thirty-five years after its first publication, *Structure* has sold nearly a million copies and been translated into twenty languages. It remains one of the most highly cited works in the humanities and the social sciences. (Fuller 2000: 1)

Thomas S. Kuhn was a physicist turned historian of science. 'Struck by the number and extent of the overt disagreements between social scientists about the nature of legitimate scientific problems and methods', he argued that science was much more than an 'ever-growing stockpile that constitutes scientific technique and knowledge' (Kuhn 1996: x). He proposed that the history of scientific development needed to be set within its wider social, philosophical and historical context. Most significantly it needed to recognize and engage with the values that practitioners brought to the scientific task. The scientific community placed great store on objectivity and empiricism, yet personal and community values could not help but be brought to bear on the scientific process, and they needed to be accounted for:

> An apparently arbitrary element, compounded of personal and historical accident, is always a formative ingredient of the beliefs espoused by a given scientific community at a given time. (Kuhn 1996: 4)

For Kuhn, a paradigm was an understanding of reality shared by a community of scientists/academics. The opening chapters of *Structure* make repeated references to 'community', 'professional groupings' and 'professional colleagues'. 'Like literature and the arts [science] is the product of a group, a community of scientists' who bring to their experimentation and discovery, the shared values and insights of their peers and predecessors. Such insights and values equipped and yet restricted the field of study and the scope of questions asked. A paradigm was effectively the sum of the received wisdom and recognized practice of a professional community. To enter a profession, an apprentice would need to study, imbibe and take on the identity of the communal paradigm:

> The study of paradigms . . . is what mainly prepares the student for membership in the particular scientific community with which he will later practice . . . Because he there joins men who learned the bases of their field from the same concrete models, his subsequent practice will seldom evoke overt disagreement over fundamentals . . . [The] commitment and apparent consensus it produces are pre-requisites for normal science, i.e., for the genesis and continuation of a particular research tradition. (Kuhn 1996: 10–11)

In forwarding his argument Kuhn coined two key and related terms: 'normal science' and 'paradigm shift'. He understood normal science as research activity based upon and shaped by the recognized achievements and practice of the scientific community. Not surprisingly he observed that scientists expended most of their time and resources on normal science. The task was to build on their received understanding and to develop it further, filling in the gaps, solving problems and resolving hitherto unresolved ambiguities. Normal science was essentially a puzzle-solving activity. Scientists were thus expert puzzle-solvers driven on by the challenge of the unsolved puzzle. This led 'to a detail of information and to a precision of the observation-theory match that could be achieved in no other way' (Kuhn 1996: 65).

Kuhn recognized that no paradigm was a perfect fit for nature. Every paradigm co-exists with its own anomalies. A paradigm shift occurs when a community's shared understanding is overwhelmed by anomalies. After a period of flux the community releases the 'broken paradigm' and adopts another which is a better fit or representation of nature – a paradigm shift. Paradigm shifts mark the succession of one paradigm by another and the progress of science from less true representation of nature to more true. However, the succession is not necessarily smooth or cumulative. It may well be revolutionary – hence the title of Kuhn's work: a complete reconstruction of the discipline may be required. In the interim there may be significant areas of overlap, where the old and the new paradigms are both able to offer solutions to longstanding problems.

Whilst the community of natural scientists share an overall paradigm or set of paradigms, the individual natural sciences and the sub-specialisms within them are characterized by their own more closely defined paradigms. This means that when faced with a problem or puzzle, paradigm-shaped research does not begin with a stance open to all possibilities but constructs its approach in accordance with the predetermined disciplines of the sub-community and 'typically by reference to an earlier exemplar that the research was said to resemble' (Fuller 2000: 2).

Kuhn plotted the paradigm life cycle from genesis, to articulation, to orthodoxy; and from inconsistency, to challenge, to crisis, to revolution. He saw the communal mindset as a strength. It ensured that the paradigm would not be too easily surrendered. Communal resistance guaranteed that scientists would not be lightly distracted from their shared understanding of the world. However, anomalies that led to paradigm change will penetrate existing knowledge to the core (Kuhn 1996: 65).

When a paradigm begins to be questioned there may be competing claims for the succession. Comparisons will be made between alternative paradigms, nature and even philosophy. Fundamentals may no longer be accepted as fundamentals. The process of normal science becomes extraordinary science:

> Confronted with anomaly or with crisis, scientists take a different attitude toward existing paradigms, and the nature of their research changes accordingly. The proliferation of completing articulations, the willingness to try anything, the expression of explicit discontent, the recourse to philosophy and to debate over fundamentals, all these are symptoms of a transition from normal to extraordinary research. It is upon their existence more than upon that of revolutions that the notion of normal science depends. (Kuhn 1996: 91)

A paradigm shift within the scientific community would cause scientists to look at the world with new eyes and to engage with it differently. Even though the scientists after Copernicus were looking at the same objects through the same instruments they saw new things. It was the same world but different – in effect a different world – a different nature; 'after discovering oxygen Lavoisier worked in a different world' (Kuhn 1996: 118). Even those fragments of nature experimented upon with old instruments would appear to be different. Previously unexplored fragments of nature could be observed and measured with newly developed post-revolutionary instrumentation.

Of major concern for Kuhn was the apparent invisibility of scientific revolutions. He commented at length on the manner of pedagogical transference of scientific knowledge from one generation of the community to the next. He argued that the extensive use of standard textbooks, designed to give scientists a systematic grounding prior to practice, was a key issue. By their very nature, standard textbooks tend to present scientific development as a linear accumulation of knowledge. Every time there is a new discovery or development, existing textbooks are immediately out of date. 'In short they have to be rewritten in the aftermath of each scientific revolution, and, once rewritten, they inevitably disguise not only the role but the very existence of the revolutions that produce them' (Kuhn 1996: 137). Unlike 'Old Masters', old paradigm-based scientific textbooks are removed from circulation quickly, replaced by their new paradigm versions.

The shift begins when individual scientists focus on crisis-inducing anomalies. Kuhn considered that the scientists most likely to be involved would be the younger newer members of the community whose formation in the disciplines of the paradigm was less entrenched. And who were therefore most able to think the unthinkable. Possible replacement paradigms would be tested against each other, nature and for the allegiance of the community. Kuhn argued that paradigm shift was a matter of the survival of the fittest; weaker paradigm alternatives fall away in the debate and the strongest or perhaps the most strongly argued would survive:

> At the start a new candidate for paradigm may have few supporters, and on occasions the supporters' motives may be suspect. Nevertheless, if they are competent, they will improve it, explore its possibilities, and show what it would be like to belong to the community guided by it. And as that goes on, if the paradigm is one destined to win its fight, the number and strength of the persuasive arguments in its favour will increase. Most scientists will then be converted, and the exploration of the new paradigm will go on. Gradually the number of experiments, instruments, articles and books based upon the paradigm will multiply. Still more men, convinced of the new view's fruitfulness, will adopt the new mode of practicing normal science, until at last only a few elderly hold-outs remain. And even they, we cannot say, are wrong. (Kuhn 1996: 159)

Kuhn concluded that the existence of a science/academic discipline is dependent on a self-disciplining community which has a corporate ability to choose between paradigms; the strength of the community being very closely related to the strength of the boundaries they are able to create around their subject. He tentatively observed, from the practice of normal science, that scientific communities are marked by members who: have a concern to solve problems about the behaviour of nature; work on problems of detail within a global picture; propose solutions that are widely accepted; do not appeal to popular opinion for verification; and see their peers as the sole possessors of the 'rules of the game'. Such paradigm communities can clearly function outside the confines of traditional 'science'. Not least in the social sciences and the humanities.

- A paradigm is an understanding of reality shared by a community.
- The communal understanding shapes practice and values.
- The communal understanding limits the questions that may be asked.
- Practice in the present is informed by exemplars from the past.
- Existing members of the community enable new members to imbibe communal practice and values.
- Paradigms begin to break down when members of the community begin to ask new questions or find new answers to old anomalies.
- A paradigm shift takes place when the overwhelming majority of the community accept a revised understanding of reality.

Table 1: **Key features of Kuhnian paradigms**

Kirk in his review of theological education refers to 'the inadequacy of the existing paradigm' (1997: 60), while Heywood's sustained use of the concept of 'paradigm' in his article 'A New Paradigm for Theological Education?' confirms that it is an appropriate tool for the investigation of theological education. In his preliminary analysis of the tensions within Church of England theological education, Heywood develops contrasting 'academic' and 'vocational' paradigms. At first sight they resonate with 'Berlin' and 'Athens' respectively. Nonetheless, both 'Athens' and 'Berlin' contain elements of the academic and the vocational. For the purposes of this chapter it is important to note that Heywood includes a very helpful description of the 'academic' paradigm in action. The induction of the 'student' into the community paradigm is writ large:

> The student of theology comes to be initiated into the world of theology, to be become immersed in its characteristic methods and ways of thinking. She learns to read the Bible in its original languages, to apply the methods of biblical criticism recognized as valid by the academic community . . . The method of her initiation is to sit at the feet of established experts, either by hearing lectures or reading books and in this way soak up the required knowledge. Lectures are supplemented by seminars and discussions through which she learns the appropriate methods of debate and skills of criticism. (Heywood 2000: 20)

The discussion thus far observes that community is fundamental to Kuhn's concept of paradigm. On the one hand paradigm is a communal concept requiring the participation of at least two people. On the other, the shared beliefs, values and practices of the paradigm mark the very boundaries of the community – as exemplified by David Kelsey in his analysis of theological education.

David H. Kelsey: 'Athens' and 'Berlin'

In the early 1980s the Protestant theological community in the United States entered into an extensive debate about the nature of theological education. Kelsey mapped the debate in two key works: *To Understand God Truly: What's Theological About a Theological School?* (1992) and *Between Athens and Berlin: The Theological Education Debate* (1993). His distinctive contribution was to identify two educational paradigms at work within US theological education. He argued that they were present and deeply embedded in every theological institution and that most had negotiated 'some sort of more or less implicit truce' (Kelsey 1993: 8). Kelsey noted that the two paradigms were not only different but 'finally irreconcilable':

> For one type I shall suggest 'Athens' be the symbol, for the other 'Berlin' . . . Each type of excellent education has definite implications regarding a number of features of theological education, such as the relation between teachers and students, the characteristics looked for in an excellent teacher, what the education aims to do for the student, what the movement of the course of study should be, and the sort of community the school should be. (Kelsey 1993: 6)

Within an exclusively 'Athens' community, teachers and students would normally share a similar faith commitment. Regular attendance of community worship services would be expected of teaching staff and students alike, whilst 'spiritual' growth would be an explicit aspiration for both. Academic study is likely to be valued and undertaken with energy and commitment as an expression and outworking of the shared faith meta-narrative. Some aspects of the faith meta-narrative are likely to be deemed authoritative and beyond question. Part of the role of teaching staff is to offer spiritual support and to model a mature outworking of their own faith commitment.

Whilst within an exclusively 'Berlin' community, teachers and students may or may not uphold a personal faith commitment. Attendance of any acts of worship organized within or without the department or institution would be optional, and likely to be the object of rigorous and critical study. Where a 'Berlin' community was responsible for ministerial training, public worship and other aspects of Church life would be the source of theory used to inform professional practice. The key task of teachers would be to develop the critical scholarship of students – all aspects of faith would be subjected to rigorous questioning. Teachers' roles would be restricted to developing research/academic knowledge and skills.

'Athens'

The 'Athens' paradigm is rooted in the culture of ancient Greece where paideia was the communal process of 'culturing' the soul or forming of the whole person. Clement of Rome wrote to the Church in Corinth in AD 90, 'Christianity's not so alien; it's a paideia like yours, aiming at the same goal, but superior in the way it does so' (Kelsey 1993: 11). Theological education has been related to paidiea at various times in the history of the Church. As part of his contribution to the debate of the 1980s, Edward Farley proposed that his concept of *Theologica* 'purports to promote a Christian paideia' (Farley 1983: xi). Within paideia Kelsey observed four recurrent features from Plato onwards to create 'an ahistorical construct, a type of excellent education':

The **first** feature of paideia was the knowledge of the 'Good' itself – inquiry into a 'single, underlying principle of all virtues, their essence'.

The **second** feature was that the Good related to the highest principle of the universe – the divine. The goal of paideia was thus religious as well as moral.

The **third** goal was less about the transfer of information and more about knowledge of the Good through contemplation, leading to intuitive insight. Here teachers can only aid students indirectly by offering disciplines that may or may not be helpful in their expansion of insight.

The final and **fourth** feature of paideia involved a 'conversion', a turning around from preoccupation with outer appearances to focus on deeper reality – the Good. Such conversion was a slow process. It required the support and nurture of belonging to a community. 'Education as paideia is inherently communal and not solitary' (Kelsey 1993: 9).

Theological education is a movement from source to personal appropriation of the source, from revealed wisdom to the appropriation of revealed wisdom in a way that is identity forming and personally transforming . . . To be sure study focuses on various subject matters. However, this study is ordered to something more basic, the students' own personal appropriation of wisdom about God and about themselves in relation to God . . . The learning is in one way 'individualistic' . . . Yet by definition it cannot be solitary. Teachers and Learners together constitute a community sharing the common goal of personally appropriating revealed wisdom (summary of Kelsey 1993: 19).

- Theological education is about communal and personal ownership of revealed wisdom.
- This communally held wisdom shapes people's lives and values.
- Study covers a wide number of theological subjects.
- The main purpose of study is to feed an individual's relationship with God.
- Individual learning is supported by teachers who also seek to be shaped by the revealed wisdom.

Table 2: **Key features of the 'Athens' paradigm of theological education**

'Berlin'

In contrast with the ancient pedigree of the 'Athens' paradigm, the 'Berlin' paradigm belongs to the modern era. Kelsey roots it in the controversy about the establishment of a faculty of theology within the newly founded research University of Berlin in 1810. Theology was only included in the curriculum after an extended dialogue about the nature of research. The approach to research adopted by the new institution was Wissenschaft – orderly, disciplined and critical. Paideia was also recognized to be critical, in that 'it involved testing what was studied for clarity, logical validity, and coherence'. But the approach to research within the 'Berlin' paradigm was more fundamentally critical, testing all alleged bases of authority or truth. Declarations of revelation/divine inspiration could not be beyond critical inquiry. The 'Berlin' paradigm further understood inquiry to be disciplined and self-conscious of the methods used to establish 'truth'. The 'Berlin' paradigm thus constituted a fundamental challenge to the traditional status of theology:

> From the rise of the institution of the university in the Middle Ages onwards, because of its base in divine revelation, theology had been the highest and dominant faculty, superior to the faculties of arts and sciences and to the faculties of law and medicine, for theology was the 'queen of the sciences' whom all other inquiries ultimately served. (Kelsey 1993: 15)

But 'Berlin' did not recognize overarching authority from any quarter including that of theology. This was embedded in a culture of academic freedom. 'Freedom to learn' – *Lernfreiheit* – and 'Freedom to teach' – *Lehrfreheit* – were its mottos (Kelsey 1993: 15).

Schleiermacher proposed that theological education should be included in the new institution's provision because it constituted professional education. He argued that every human society had sets of practices dealing with physical health, social order and religious needs. Such practices were vital for the health and vitality of human society. Practitioners thus required properly trained and educated leadership. It was argued that because Christian theology was historically and philosophically based it could be subject to historical research and philosophical analysis. 'Historical theology' and 'philosophical theology' constituted legitimate Wissenschaft forms of critical inquiry, the results of which could determine the rules and practices of professional Christian ministry or 'practical theology' (Table 3).

Berlin is much less self-consciously 'community' orientated than Athens. Nonetheless, it is a community-held and self-reproducing paradigm. Indeed the development of future generations of research-orientated theologians is a highly regarded activity.

In the English and Welsh context, state-funded theological education, like all other academic disciplines, is subject to government policy. Not least policies related to 'quality' which are enforced by the Quality Assurance Agency (QAA). The key QAA document *Academic Standards: Theology and Religious*

Theological education is a movement from data to theory to application of theory to practice . . . Wissenschaft for critical rigour in theorizing; 'professional' education for rigorous study of the application of theory to practice . . . Critical inquiry focuses simultaneously on questions about the subject being researched and on questions about the methods of research . . . to discover as directly as possible the truth about the origin, effects, and essential nature of 'Christian' phenomena. [Teachers are appointed less for their] personal capacities to be midwife of others' coming to an understanding of God and of themselves in relation to God as . . . the ability to cultivate capacities for scholarly research in others (summary of Kelsey 1993: 22–25).

- Theological education is about critical study of the Faith phenomena.
- Where students are preparing for professional ministry it involves researching data to develop theory and application of theory to practice.
- Theological education is as much about developing the skills of rigorous scholarship as it is about the content of study.
- Teachers are appointed because of their ability to help others develop research skills.

Table 3: **Key features of the 'Berlin' paradigm of theological education**

Studies (2000) is firmly located in the 'Berlin' paradigm. It even acknowledges the role of the University of Berlin in the evolution of the discipline and its impact on theological education in Britain. The skills and 'qualities of mind that a competent student should acquire by studying Theology & Religious Studies' (QAA 2000: 5) clearly resonate with Kelsey's 'Berlin' paradigm with the purpose of forming the next generation of the community as committed, rigorous, and critical analysts of data. Within 'Berlin' the generic principles and practices of research orientated scholarship appear to take precedence over the subject matter:

> [T]he goal and focus of TRS programmes is to produce students capable of independently evaluating information and engaging in critical analysis and argument for themselves . . . It is important that students are inspired . . . to reach beyond the threshold. Excellent students transcend the tabulated learning outcomes and would display originality, insight and the ability to progress to research. (QAA 2000: 9)

Academic Standards is most consistent in the way it promulgates the orthodoxy of the 'Berlin' paradigm. The words critical/critico/criticism are mentioned some twenty-three times in the document including six times in the focal statements of achievement. With regard to the 'Athens' paradigm, there is just a single mention of the possibility that studying Theology and Religious Studies 'may foster a lifelong quest for wisdom' (QAA 2000: 3). In contrast to 'Berlin' this is possible or permitted, rather than an intended or planned outcome.

Given that the majority of Church training institutions work in partnership with Higher Education institutions they too are impacted upon by the QAA. At the same time they are also subject to the policy developments of their sources of funding – the Church(es). Within the Church of England this has been reinforced since 1987 by *ACCM22*, an occasional paper of the Advisory Council for the Churches Ministry (Church of England). This document expounded a consistent view of ministerial education, using similar language to Kelsey's description of the 'Athens' paradigm:

> It should be the fundamental aim of theological education to enable to grow in those personal qualities by which, with and through the corporate ministry of the Church. (ACCM 1987: 37 para 45)

> Clearly the main emphasis should be on the wisdom and godly habit of life . . . and how they are to be exercised. (ACCM 1987: 37 para 46)

> Theological education should therefore seek to form the ordinand in this wisdom and habit of life as a 'virtue' . . . It is a 'virtue' which requires personal discipline – intellectual, spiritual, moral and practical. But theological education will also be concerned with this virtue as corporate, as actively shared by staff and student. (ACCM 1987: 37/38 para 47)

> [S]tudents are apprenticed to tutors; – seeking thereby to know the God who presents himself in truth – and are concerned with learning to maintain the truth. They seek to do so with critical rigour and with the appropriate freedom, and should be provided with circumstances which permit careful thought and meditation. (ACCM 1987: 38 para 48)

ACCM22 promotes a very clear emphasis on wisdom, virtue and the corporate nature of learning. Whilst critical rigour is encouraged, it is closely related to 'maintaining the truth'. Thus even a preliminary analysis of *Academic Standards: Theology and Religious Studies* and *ACCM22* reveal that the 'Athens' and 'Berlin' paradigms can be readily identified in the English context. Not only do the paradigms exist, but each is promoted by a particular stakeholder.

I became interested in Kelsey's work when I was Director of Studies at my previous institution, Church Army's Wilson Carlile College in Sheffield, Yorkshire. There I was concerned by the emergence of a fault line within the theological education offered. Different parts of the curriculum were recognized and valued by different external bodies, e.g. church history, biblical studies and doctrine were university validated, whereas retreats, human relations training and communication in worship were in-house units approved by the Ministry Division of the Church of England. In response, students accorded different value to different parts of the curriculum. Prior to validation in 1995 the student body placed most emphasis on vocational and personal development. Whereas from 1995 onwards students tended to give increased attention to the credit-bearing university validated 'academic' modules. Amongst my colleagues there was ongoing and unresolved discussion about the balance of resources and status accorded to learning either side of the fault line. Kelsey's paradigms offered us a language and fresh insights into the tensions we were experiencing as a community. The 1995 university validation of the academic programme had shifted Wilson Carlile in the direction of the 'Berlin' paradigm. For some this was a significant gain; for others it was a significant loss. For staff whose own identity had been formed in the 'Athens' paradigm, the period of transition was bewildering and undermining. They also perceived and commented upon a diminution of community life.

Using 'Athens' and 'Berlin' to Reflect on the Communal and Identity Forming Aspects of Paradigms

Although Kelsey developed his typology specifically in relation to twentieth-century United States theological education, the origins of 'Athens' and 'Berlin' paradigms were much older and wider. 'Athens' was derived from a formational wisdom-based understanding of education in the ancient world. 'Berlin' drew upon the post-enlightenment research-based university established in Berlin during the early nineteenth century. By removing references to theological education in Kelsey it is possible to develop generic versions of the paradigms:

Education is a movement from source to personal appropriation of the source, from revealed wisdom to the appropriation of revealed wisdom in a way that is identity forming and personally transforming . . . To be sure study focuses on various subject matters. However, this study is ordered to something more basic, the students' own personal appropriation of wisdom and about themselves in relation to that wisdom . . . The learning is in one way 'individualistic' . . . Yet by definition it cannot be solitary. Teachers and Learners together constitute a community sharing the common goal of personally appropriating wisdom.

- Education is about communal and personal ownership of wisdom.
- This communally held wisdom shapes people's lives and values.
- Study covers a wide number of subjects.
- Individual learning is supported by teachers who also seek to be shaped by the wisdom.

Table 4: **Key features of a generic 'Athens' paradigm**

Such generic versions of 'Athens' and 'Berlin' offer the possibility of adopting a reflexive approach to Kuhn's work. The major thrust of the life of a Kuhnian type paradigm involves self-conscious and critical testing of theory against nature. As such, Kuhnian paradigms are firmly located within the 'Berlin' ethos. The text of *The Structure of Scientific Revolutions* abounds with references to problem solving, argument, counter argument, research, theory, experiment, data, facts and methods. However, Kuhn's major and perhaps most controversial contribution to knowledge was his recognition that a key part of the formation of the next generation of the community involved previously unrecognized and unacknowledged formational elements:

> Observation and experience can and must drastically restrict the range of admissible scientific belief, else there would be no science. But they cannot alone determine a particular body of such belief. An apparently arbitrary element, compounded of personal and historical accident, is always a formative ingredient of the beliefs espoused by a given scientific community at a given time. (Kuhn 1996: 4)

Kelsey would have identified such 'arbitrary elements' as belonging to 'Athens'. He would have also argued that they were intentional as much as they were the result of personal and historical accident. The 'Berlin' elements of a Kuhnian type paradigm suggest that all questions may be asked and investigated rigorously. However, Kuhn observed that members of the scientific community are so formed by the paradigm within which they work that normally they do not ask all possible questions. They tend to work systematically within the parameters of a sort of received wisdom that resonates with 'Athens'. Kuhn argued that whilst individuals may not be aware of such a shaping or forming of their practice, it was nonetheless a powerful factor within the overall development of modern science. He supported his view by noting:

> Almost always the men who achieve these fundamental inventions of a new paradigm have been either very young or very new to the field whose paradigm they change. And perhaps that point need not have been made explicit, for obviously these are the men who, being little committed by prior practice to the traditional rules of normal science, are particularly likely to see that those rules no longer define a playable game and to conceive another set that can replace them. (Kuhn 1996: 90)

Education is a movement from data to theory to application of theory to practice . . . Wissenschaft for critical rigour in theorizing; 'professional' education for rigorous study of the application of theory to practice . . . Critical inquiry focuses simultaneously on questions about the subject being researched and on questions about the methods of research . . . to discover as directly as possible the truth about the origin, effects, and essential nature of phenomena. [Teachers are appointed less for their] personal capacities to be midwife of others' wisdom and more for the ability to cultivate capacities for scholarly research in others:

- Education is about critical study of phenomena.
- Where students are preparing for a profession it involves researching data to develop theory and application of theory to practice.
- Education is as much about developing the skills of rigorous scholarship as it is about the content of study.
- Teachers are appointed because of their ability to help others develop research skills.

Table 5: **Key features of a generic 'Berlin' paradigm**

Newer members of the paradigm community were less constrained or formed by the received wisdom. And were more able to think 'outside of the box'. Kuhn further recognized that the process of paradigm shift might well involve an intuitive approach to knowledge that again Kelsey would identify as an expression of the 'Athens' typology:

> The man who embraces a new paradigm at an early stage must often do so in defiance of the evidence provided. He must, that is, have faith that the new paradigm will succeed with the many large problems that confront it, knowing only that the older paradigm has failed with a few. A decision of that kind can only be made on faith. (Kuhn 1996: 158)

The formation of 'scientists' meant that the majority of the community would hold to the existing tenets of the paradigm until they were overwhelmed by new evidence. For some, the scale of the new evidence would need to be disproportionately large. Conversely, the instigators of a paradigm shift needed to break free from the communal mindset and set the shift in motion while the weight of evidence still supported the existing paradigm.

Whilst it can be demonstrated that Kuhn's paradigm is an appropriate tool of categoriation and analysis of Kelsey's work, in turn generic versions of Kelsey's 'Athens' and 'Berlin' paradigms can be deployed to offer fresh insights into Kuhn's *Structure of Scientific Revolutions*. So, whilst 'Berlin' may be dominant, and Athens secondary, perhaps deep within the shadows of a scientific community both are useful tools for analysing implicit as well as explicit activity within the life cycle of a paradigm (see Figure 1). This discussion may catalyse further research.

Using Athens and Berlin to Reflect Further on the Communal and Identity within Contemporary Theological Education

In England theological education is offered within three distinct institutional settings:

- departments of Theology (and Religious Studies) in secular universities
- departments of Theology (and Religious Studies) in Church colleges/universities/institutions of higher education
- 'private'ordination or other Church training institutions.

Many in the secular universities would resist being classified in a single grouping. Some see themselves as 'ancient/historic' or 'red brick' or 'new' or 'post 1992'. Whilst the 'ancient'/'historic' institutions may have had the Church foundations, those established during the twentieth or late nineteenth centuries tend to be the products of civic pride or government policy. On the whole, the newer the institution, the more avowedly secular its stance. Indeed, the theology departments of the secular universities defend their secular status and maintain a cautious distance from 'church' influence – they are concerned to ensure that their scholarship is seen to be as independent and as rigorous as

Figure 1: **From Kuhn to Kelsey to Kuhn**

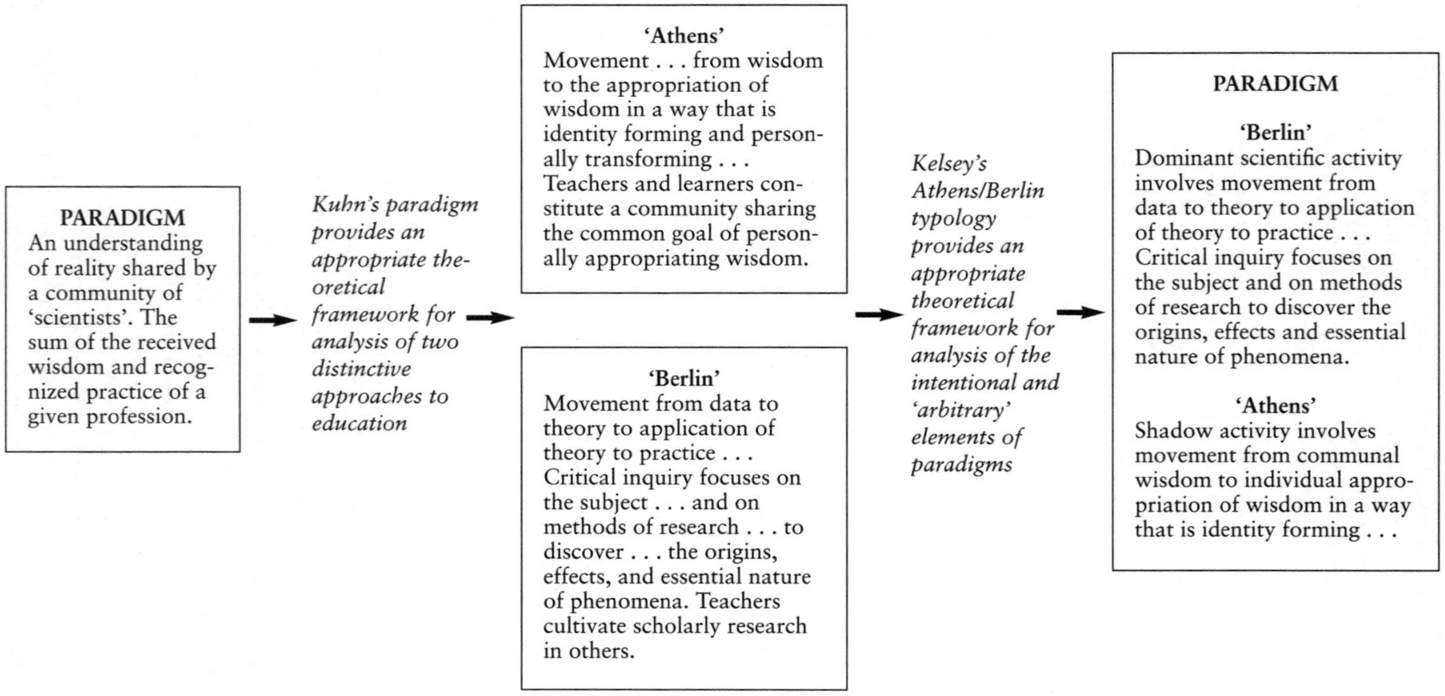

PARADIGM
An understanding of reality shared by a community of 'scientists'. The sum of the received wisdom and recognized practice of a given profession.

Kuhn's paradigm provides an appropriate theoretical framework for analysis of two distinctive approaches to education

'Athens'
Movement . . . from wisdom to the appropriation of wisdom in a way that is identity forming and personally transforming . . . Teachers and learners constitute a community sharing the common goal of personally appropriating wisdom.

'Berlin'
Movement from data to theory to application of theory to practice . . . Critical inquiry focuses on the subject . . . and on methods of research . . . to discover . . . the origins, effects, and essential nature of phenomena. Teachers cultivate scholarly research in others.

Kelsey's Athens/Berlin typology provides an appropriate theoretical framework for analysis of the intentional and 'arbitrary' elements of paradigms

PARADIGM

'Berlin'
Dominant scientific activity involves movement from data to theory to application of theory to practice . . . Critical inquiry focuses on the subject and on methods of research to discover the origins, effects and essential nature of phenomena.

'Athens'
Shadow activity involves movement from communal wisdom to individual appropriation of wisdom in a way that is identity forming . . .

any other academic discipline. The church colleges/universities/institutions of higher education usually acknowledge their church or Christian foundation, but rarely make claims to be exclusively or even primarily Christian communities today. Indeed, alongside their secular counterparts they are concerned to promote inclusivity and academic rigour. The ordination and other Church training institutions, however, do claim to be contemporary Christian communities which promote personal and spiritual development alongside the study of theology pursued with as much rigour as in the secular university and Church institutions of higher education. Not surprisingly distinctive institutional arrangements lead to distinctive communities of teachers and students.

The Theology and Religious Studies departments of the Secular Universities are powerfully shaped by the 'Berlin' paradigm. This is usually reinforced by the QAA and by the need to operate and be seen to operate by the same mores as other academic departments. Teaching staff are appointed exclusively for their 'scholarly ability and their ability to cultivate critical understanding'. The faith position or the ability to nurture faith in others is never asked of prospective colleagues. Students may recognize room within their community (department) for the exploration of faith and spiritual growth but see it as completely separate and incidental to official teaching and learning. Theology within a secular university is one arts or humanities subject amongst many others – a version of religious studies with the Christian tradition as the subject. Teachers thus see their role as educating and forming 'well-rounded arts students'. Those teachers who may be practising Christians would not express their practice within the official life of the community. It would be inconceivable for a lecture to begin with prayer. Matters of personal belief, spirituality and practice are reserved for church/faith settings. When interviewed, one member of teaching staff from a secular university spoke of a very strict personal distancing from the subject matter being 'trained-in' during his own post-graduate studies, 'Even though I have argued against it and don't believe it, it still seems to shape what you do' (Wilton 2005: 101).

Church Colleges of higher education/universities inhabit very similar institutional territory to secular universities. They are financed largely by the state and subject to the same oversight of the QAA. Consequently the 'Berlin' paradigm is the dominant shaper of the theological education offered and received. Critical research and scholarly collegiality are promoted; and with increasing emphasis where institutions have gained or are seeking university status. Teaching staff are appointed exclusively for their scholarly ability and their ability to cultivate critical understanding. Critical distance from the subject is the norm and the formation of arts graduates able to make independent and critical judgements is the goal. And despite the Church foundation, prayer, even at the beginning of lectures in Theology, would be discouraged. For the most part the 'theology' community in Church institutions of higher education would appear very similar to their secular counterparts.

However, Heads of Department are very aware of the Church link not least through regular meetings with their Church college/university peers. For some it may be only a potential revenue-raising opportunity. For most there appears to be a genuine desire to explore or develop areas of mutual interest with Church-based colleagues. This has been catalysed by the *Hind Report* (Hind 2002 and 2003). Some departments in Church institutions of higher education would see working more closely with the Church as part of their overall mission. Without compromising their essential 'Berlin' stance, some departments encourage individual members of staff to make their 'Athens' paradigm contributions away from the normal constrictions of institution, particularly in non-validated or Church settings. Here they may contribute to the formation of students who are able to move between engagement and detachment, but whose underlying motivation is from a committed faith perspective. Here teachers would be free to offer prayer at the beginning of sessions.

The development of Foundation Degrees in Theology and Ministry by various Church colleges/universities sits at the interface between engagement and detachment. It is also clearly a development designed to meet some of the training needs of the churches. Whilst teaching staff contributing to such programmes are appointed for 'scholarly ability and their ability to cultivate critical understanding', some are also required to understand or have experience of Christian ministry. This is a departure from the previous norm and may be significant for the development of theological education into the future. Thus far, curriculum development has occurred within safe 'Berlin' territory of applying theory to practice. Or more often, using theory to reflect upon practice. Students again are required to adopt a detached critical stance to reflect on their experience or the practice of others in relation to theory-based criteria. Intuitive elements of 'Athens'-based wisdom continue to sit uncomfortably with this approach. Even here students again continue to be shaped by the critical objectivity of the 'Berlin' paradigm.

The Church Training Institutions

The current generation of Church of England training institutions have been shaped by *ACCM22* (1987). As well as recognizing contributions from the 'Berlin' paradigm, this document very strongly supported an 'Athens'-based training. Here members of teaching staff are expected to share the faith tradition and to continue to be shaped by it. They are appointed to nurture faith as well as to develop critical skills. Critical skills and scholarship are important, but not an end in themselves. Teaching staff and students will at various times eat, learn, pray, worship and relax together. Teaching sessions will often begin with prayer. When interviewed, a member of teaching staff from one Church training institution saw community as an essential dynamic in theological education. This very clearly resonates with the 'Athens' paradigm. He also talked about community as an expression of 'church as a key controlling influence in the project of learning theology' (Wilton 2005: 92). Here we can see the Church as the guardian of knowledge rather than the university. He also went on to comment:

> The one word that sticks out for me is 'wisdom' – it seems to be a quite intuitive understanding of theological education; it seems to recognize

that it is about applying revealed truths to everyday life and learning how to do that. (Wilton 2005: 92)

Through teaching, community, prayer and worship, Church training institutions aim to form men and women for Christian service in the world. They value the critical approaches of the 'Berlin' paradigm and the possibilities of accreditation by the secular universities. At the same time they also wish to guard and promote a communally held, wisdom-based way of knowing which resonates with 'Athens' and which is outside of QAA 'Berlin'-derived approaches.

Concluding Comments

Whereas other chapters of this volume may look to more widely recognized theological, anthropological or sociological concepts of community, this chapter adopts a more epistemological approach. The generation, stewardship, dissemination and disintegration of knowledge were central to Kuhn's concept of paradigm. At the same time community and communal identity were intimately linked with the development of paradigm knowledge. For Kuhn, a paradigm both creates and is created by a community. The process of 'paradigm shift' tests, disturbs, destroys and (re)creates community. Paradigms include and exclude current and potential members. A paradigm shift potentially creates a very different community, with a very different way of understanding the world, and a very different way of behaving and understanding itself.

Arising from the great theological education debate during the 1980s, Kelsey observed that there were two mutually exclusive paradigms at work within US Protestantism: 'Athens' and 'Berlin'. Each had its own way of generating, stewarding and disseminating knowledge and each was expressed in a distinctive community with different categories of people included and excluded. He recognized that both paradigms of theological education were potentially excellent, and the probability that both were present in most theological establishments to a greater or lesser extent; with usually some degree of tension between the two. Analysis of key Church of England reports confirms that both paradigms are present in English theological education and that there are similar tensions here also. This enables me to understand some of the ill-ease I experienced when working in a Church training institution in South Yorkshire.

At the same time the generic versions of 'Athens' and 'Berlin' constitute a tool for further analysis of Kuhn's concept of 'paradigm'. In particular they promote further discussion of the formative and wisdom-based aspects of a scientific/academic community. This exploration of theological education in England demonstrates that the 'Athens' and 'Berlin' paradigms are useful tools of analysis – in particular giving voice to underlying tensions between more objective and wisdom-based approaches. The wisdom of 'Athens' is difficult to assess . . . yet is actually a vital and indeed a significant powerful element in the life of any paradigm community. It is present with Kuhn's work at a conceptual and theoretical level and clearly evident within real-life scenarios.

A community shaped by 'Athens' will feel very different to one shaped by 'Berlin' ways of knowing. There can even be a level of ill-ease or distrust between two such communities. Church training institutions tend to have a somewhat schizophrenic attitude to the universities and even the Church institutions of higher education. They greatly value the objective higher-education accreditation of their programmes, but prize even more their communally held wisdom. At the same time they often experience being at the end of the policy-development food-chain; Church training institutions can feel powerless in the face of ever constant policy changes, particularly in relation to quality assurance processes. Although the Church is undergoing unprecedented change, the pace of change in state-maintained higher education is even faster. Even when partnership is a key value and embedded in the language of validation relationships, Church training communities often find themselves 'running' to keep up with 'Berlin'-driven demands of their validating partners. Such demands can clash with their underlying 'Athens' motivation and even their very purpose.

References

ACCM (Advisory Council for the Churches Ministry) (1987), *Education for the Church's Ministry: The Report of theWorking Party on Assessment* (Occasional Paper 22; London: Church House Publishing).

Farley, E. (1983), *Theologica – The Fragmentation and Unity of Theological Education* (Philadelphia: Fortress Press).

Fuller, S. (2000), *Thomas Kuhn: A Philosophical History for Our Times* (Chicago: University of Chicago Press).

Groves, M. (2004), 'Locating Theology', *Journal of Adult Theological Education* 1.2 (December), pp. 147–59.

Heywood, D. (2000), 'A New Paradigm for Theological Education?' *Anvil* 17.1: 19–27.

Hind, J. (chair) (February 2002) *The Structure and Funding of Ordination Training.* The Interim Report (London: Ministry Division of the Archbishops' Council).

—— (November 2002) *Formation for Ministry within a Learning Church.* The draft final report of the working party on the structure and funding of ordination training (London: Ministry Division of the Archbishops' Council).

—— (April 2003) *Formation for Ministry within a Learning Church – The Structure and Funding of Ordination Training GS1496* (London: Church House Publishing).

Kelsey, D.H. (1992), *To Understand God Truly: What's Theological about a Theological School* (Louisville: Westminster/John Knox).

—— (1993), *Between Athens and Berlin: The Theological Education Debate* (Grand Rapids: Eerdmans).

Kirk, J.A. (1997), *The Mission of Theology and Theology as Mission* (Valley Forge, PA: Trinity).

Kuhn, T.S. (1996), *The Structure of Scientific Revolutions* (Chicago: University of Chicago Press, 3rd edn [1st edition 1962]).

McCarthy, J. (2004), 'Deepening Connections between the Church and the Theological School: Implications for Theological Education', *Journal of Adult Theological Education* 1.2 (December): 175–83.

Pears, A. (2004), 'The Study of Christian Theology in the British Academy: From Truth Giving to Critical Engagement', *Journal of Adult Theological Education* 1.2 (December), pp. 159–74.

QAA, (2000), *Academic Standards – Theology & Religious Studies* (London: QAA).

Wilton, G. (2005), 'Kuhn, Kelsey and the Hind Report: A Research Led Response to a Key Aspiration for Theological Education in the Church of England' (unpublished doctoral thesis, Nottingham University).

6

Differing Concepts of Community Identity: Debates over the 'Racial and Religious Hatred Bill'

Sebastian C. H. Kim

Introduction

Anthony Giddens discusses in his book, *Modernity and Self-Identity* (1991) the nature of the close interconnection between globalizing influences and personal dispositions, which has been caused by modernity. He characterizes the key aspect of the effect of modernity as the reorganization of time and space, which in turn transforms our daily social life and defines 'self-identity' as not something which is given, but 'something that has to be routinely created and sustained in the reflexive activities of the individual' (Giddens 1991: 52–53). While agreeing with this notion, I believe that in the modern and post-modern situation of a society like Britain, the question of identity has to be looked at in the context of various groups, including religious communities. Despite the predictions of sociologists and historians that religion would become far less significant in contemporary societies, the present context shows otherwise and the growth of religious fervour and the rise of fundamentalisms are apparent. Community identity formulated out of religious commitment tends to be far deeper and more consolidating than that from any other source. Their religion is, for many communities, a vital source of their identity. It is not difficult to understand the extent to which people of some traditions anchor their identity in religion and will maintain it at great cost. It is therefore vital for contemporary scholarship to examine the source and mechanisms of community identity, in a particular religious community, and its interaction with other communities, in order to understand how religious allegiance plays out in relation to the wide spectrum of individual and community life.

Though the diversity of religious traditions and their aspirations are welcomed, the interaction between different communities sometimes causes conflicts and misunderstanding and, in extreme cases, violence. One example of this is the verbal and physical attacks on the Muslim community after the terrorist attack in the USA and, as a response to the matter, a recent government proposal to introduce a Racial and Religious Hatred Bill. Examining this will give us some insights for our investigation of community identity in contemporary Britain, and furthermore, it is revealing because the arguments for and against are equally convincing depending on one's own understanding of religion, community and identity. I will examine the contents of the Bill, government documents and commission reports, the debates in the both Houses, articles appearing in the national media and documents produced by various groups. By way of conclusion, I shall discuss the differing concepts of the identity of secular and religious communities in contemporary Britain as revealed in the debates and shall suggest engagement in critical dialogue as a way forward for mutual understanding.

The 'Racial and Religious Hatred Bill': Government and Supporters' Positions

In the aftermath of 11 September 2001, the British government introduced the 'Anti-Terrorism, Crime and Security Bill' in November 2001 (House of Commons 2001), which includes a measure to deal with the problem of incitement to hatred on the grounds of religion in line with the law against 'racial hatred' in the Public Order Act 1986. This attempt initiated heated debates both in public and in Parliament, and the intended proposal was defeated in the House of the Lords in December 2001. In early 2005, the Home Office put forward the Racial and Religious Hatred Bill (Home Office 2005a) but it was again dropped due to opposition from the Lords, and also because of lack of time before the General Election. In their third attempt, the government presented the Bill again in June 2005 and this time the Bill completed its Commons stages in July. The House of the Lords passed its amendment on 25 October 2005 (House of Lords 2005) and, in spite of the government's attempt to have the amendment rejected, the government lost by a margin of one on 31 January 2006.[1]

In response to the Bill presented to the House of the Lords in 2001, the House launched a Select Committee on Religious Offences in England and Wales to 'consider and report on the law relating to religious offences' in May 2002 and the report was published in April 2003 (House of Lords 2003).[2] The questions addressed in the Committee were whether the 'Blasphemy Law' should be abolished and whether a new offence of incitement to religious hatred should be created and, if so, how. The Committee members, in their investigations, state that they particularly considered the role of religion in the twenty-first century and the large increase of the number of adherents to non-Christian religions. The Committee received over five hundred submissions, among which Christian churches and Muslim communities made significant contributions. The Muslim community particularly expressed their grievance that there was fear in relation to their own religious identity. For example:

> I would simply make the point that it is very difficult to encourage open and free dialogue, involving people of faith communities who may feel insecure and may actually have a sense of fear in relation to their own religious identity. Dialogue, and mutual understanding, can be developed much more successfully in a society where it is absolutely clear that people of different faiths have a legitimate place, that their place is respected, and that they will not be subject to ill treatment and abuse. (House of Lords 2003)

And similarly, the Commission for Racial Equality recognizes that for many minority ethnic communities there is a close relationship between race and religion and that identity through faith is as important as identity through racial origin (House of Lords 2003).

The Committee insists that the existing law breaches Article 9 combined with Article 14 of the European Convention on Human Rights[3] and, in this regard, many Muslims believe that the law treats them as second-class citizens of British society. The Committee concludes that there is an increasing role and multi-faith dimension of religion in the lives of people in Britain and, in this context, expressed agreement that there 'should be a degree of protection of faith', and 'in any further legislation the protection should be equally available to all faiths' and that there is 'a gap in the law as it stands' (House of Lords 2003).

The 2005 Bill was presented to 'make provision about offences involving stirring up hatred against persons on racial or religious ground', and for this purpose the offence is described as 'hatred against a group of persons defined by reference to religious belief or lack of religious belief' (Section 17A). And in Section 18(1):

> A person who uses threatening, abusive or insulting words or behaviour, or displays any written material which is threatening, abusive or insulting, is guilty of an offence if – (a) he intends thereby to stir up racial or religious hatred, or (b) having regard to all the circumstances the words, behaviours or material are (or is) likely to be heard or seen by any person in whom they are (or it is) likely to stir up racial or religious hatred. (Home Office 2005a)

If a person is found guilty, the punishment is up to seven years' imprisonment. In addition to the Bill, the Home Office prepared 'Explanatory Notes' insisting that the Bill is meant to protect 'all groups from having religious hatred stirred up against them, regardless of whether members of that group share a common ethnic background'; the Home Office does not define religion or religious beliefs but wishes the court to determine this; the term is meant to be a broad one, including people who hold Atheist and Humanist views. The offences are designed to include 'hatred against a group where the hatred is not based on the religious beliefs of the group or even on a lack of any religious belief, but based on the fact that the group do not share the particular religious beliefs of the perpetrator'. Furthermore 'what must be stirred up is hatred of a group of persons defined by their religious beliefs and not hatred of the religion itself' (Home Office 2005a).[4]

The debates were focused on the meaning of equal treatment of religious communities, the definitions of the terms for religious belief, the issue of freedom of speech and expression, and the ambiguity of the distinction between 'religious belief' and a 'religious person'. The Bill, as government and the supporters argue, may be necessary for affirming solidarity with particular religious communities suffering abuse from right-wing political groups, but it seems to have far-reaching implications for community life.

The supporters of the Bill include the Association of Chief Police Officers, the Crown Prosecution Services, the Commission for Racial Equality and Justice, some major church denominations and civil rights organizations, many minority religious groups and most Muslim organizations. The arguments of the government and supporters are: the necessity to protect all religious communities from aggressive attack by right-wing political groups; it is a preventive measure to warn those who abuse the loophole of the current law rather than actual implementation of new law; it is meant to protect religious communities and individual believers rather than belief itself since the latter is open to criticism and debate; as in the case of the law in relation to inciting racial hatred, freedom of speech and expression is not an absolute right and there must be limits to this fundamental right; and the new legislation will eventually become the accepted norm.

As the Government presented the Bill, it argued that

> It is widely accepted that individuals in our society are stirring up hatred against particular religious groups. This may take the form of publications distributed by extremist groups which equate a particular religion with mass murder or rape, or speeches at public meetings that use inflammatory language and exhort people to make life unbearable for those of a certain religion. (Home Office 2005b)[5]

And where this type of incitement to religious hatred exists, it has a 'disproportionate and corrosive effect on communities, creating barriers between different groups and encouraging mistrust and suspicion' (ibid.). The government also asserted that the legislation would have prevented the riots in Northern towns in 2001 (*The Times*, 9 June 2005). In addition it pointed out that the new legislation would not prevent people from criticizing the beliefs, teachings or practices of a religion or its followers, for example by claiming that they are false or harmful, propagating one's own religion or urging followers of a different religion to cease practising theirs. The government further argued that the Bill is rather for 'declaratory purpose and deterrent effect' (Home Office 2005b).

The Bill was very much promoted by the Muslim community along with other religious communities and this was well expressed in the extensive document presented by the Forum Against Islamophobia and Racism (FAIR) in October 2002 (FAIR 2002).[6] It included systematic discussion on the various laws relating to the 'incitement of religious hatred', such as the Criminal Libel Act 1819 and the Public Order Act 1986. The document insists that far-right groups in Britain 'deliberately incite hatred towards Islam and Muslims' (FAIR 2002: 13).

> It is our view that an offence of incitement to religious hatred is not only necessary to provide equality of protection from incitement across religious groups but critical to avoid 'the shifting focus of bigotry' we have witnessed in the UK from race to religion. In this shifting focus, the target remains the same, only the marker changes – 'not because he is

> Pakistani but because he is Muslim' or 'not because she is Chinese but because she is Buddhist'. Unless the new offence of incitement to religious hatred is introduced, in our view, it leaves a loophole in the law that could potentially make a mockery of the current offence of incitement to racial hatred. (FAIR 2002: 4)

In the Appendix, it gives various examples of aggressive slogans towards the Muslim community such as: 'Islam Out of Britain'; 'Islam a Threat to Us All'; 'The Truth about Islam: Intolerance; Slaughter; Looting; Arson; Molestation of Women'; 'Muslim Extremists Plan to Turn Britain into an Islamic Republic by 2025 . . . They Must be Stopped!'; 'An Islamic Britain: A Cross to Bear?'. The document convincingly argues that the British National Party is fully aware of the current loophole in legislative framework and calls for new legislation (FAIR 2002: 14). It further asserts that the legislation not only provides 'equality of protection from incitement across religious groups' but is also critical to avoid 'the shifting focus of bigotry' they have witnessed in the UK from race to religion (FAIR 2002: 5).

In support of the legislation, a joint statement was delivered by religious leaders in April 2004. It argues that 'there is significant overlap between racial and religious identity, with communities sometimes targeted on the basis of their religious, as much as any racial, identity' . . . that it is a 'highly desirable addition to the range of existing legal measures designed to ensure that our society is able peacefully to contain a wide range of strongly held beliefs and opinions'.[7]

Opposition to the Bill

Opposition to the Bill is from the media, both the Conservative Party and the Liberal Democratic Party, much of academia and some Christian groups.[8] The arguments include the following: the law will lead down the road to censorship; that though there are various safeguards for its implementation, it would have a great effect on people's expression of faith and practice; since religion is not clearly defined and cannot be defined, unlike race, it opens the way to the abuse of the law to justify any form of social practice and obtain protection from healthy criticism; it is open to religious extremists to use the law to silence any opposing opinions on their faith and practice; and that the present laws cover these problems and should be implemented strictly rather than creating new legislation.

Journalists and those who are in the public entertainment sector very much fear the restrictions on the freedom of speech the Bill is perceived to impose on them. The main objections are: that 'religious hated' is as subjective as 'religious belief itself', therefore it is impossible to discern what is 'likely to' stir up hatred from what is merely hostile anti-clericalism, and what is a simple joke at the expense of religion; a strong suspicion of politics behind the measure – as one commentator insists, a Bill put forward for 'such unprincipled [political] reasons, and built on such flimsy foundations, should not become law' (*Daily Telegraph*, 10 June 2005); that it is extremely difficult to create an adequate distinction between what would constitute legitimate criticism of faiths and what would constitute a 'stirring up' of 'religious hatred' without 'diminishing free speech' and therefore government is urged to 'greater focus on means to improve their [the Muslim community's] economic position' (*The Times*, 10 June 2005); that the Bill 'owes far more to politics than to justice . . . far from calming fears of prejudice, this law could actually exacerbate fear, as fundamentalists of all sorts demand police action against their critics' (*Independent*, 10 June 2005).

Some Christian groups are concerned with the implications of the law for preaching the Christian message.[9] The Lawyers' Christian Fellowship argues that it is *inappropriate* because: first, unlike race, a religious belief can be wrong and that it is 'in society's interests that such debates are as free as possible without fear of prosecution'; second, protecting a particular religious minority does not justify enforcing such a law at the expense of freedom of expression; third, it is almost impossible to separate vilification of a certain belief from vilification of the person who holds that particular belief and so it is inevitable that criticism of others' religious beliefs will be taken to be insulting. Furthermore, they argue that the legislation is *impractical* since the definitions of religion and incitement to religious hatred are too vague and open to misuse by various groups. They insist that 'the law would be punishing the most tolerant and protecting the least tolerant in society'. In addition, the legislation would be *counterproductive* because 'it could be abused to try and stifle the teaching of fundamental beliefs that go against the teaching of other religions' (thus curtailing freedom of religion), and also to 'stifle criticisms of other's beliefs and practices' (thus curtailing freedom of expression) (The Lawyers' Christian Fellowship 2005).

In similar vein, The Christian Institute argues that it would contravene both Article 9 (Freedom of Thought, Conscience and Religion) and Article 10 (Freedom of Expression) of the European Convention of Human Rights. It believes the government attempt to legislate would take the law into 'vast uncharted territory' and that 'in the name of protecting religion, the Attorney-General and the court would have unprecedented powers to adjudicate on Jewish and Sikh beliefs as well as all other beliefs . . . including . . . even Satanism'. It further argues that

> Religion is all about ideas, beliefs and philosophies. Religion (and irreligion) governs the choices people make between doctrinal, philosophical or moral alternatives. Race and national origin, on the other hand, are immutable characteristics. Arguments take place between people of different beliefs where people try to convince one another of their point of view. Attempts are made to convince people to change or abandon their religion. Such arguments are not possible over race – because no one can change their race. Bracketing together race and religion fundamentally misunderstands the difference between the two. (The Christian Institute 2001)

After extensive discussion, the House of the Lords amended the Bill to include:

> 29B: Use of words or behaviour or display of written material
> (1) A person who uses threatening words or behaviour, or displays any written material which is threatening, is guilty of an offence if he intends thereby to stir up religious hatred [omitting the words, 'abusive' or 'insulting' but keeping the word 'threatening'].
>
> 29J: Protection of freedom of expression
> Nothing in this Part shall be read or given effect in a way which prohibits or restricts discussion, criticism or expressions of antipathy, dislike, ridicule, insult or abuse of particular religions or the beliefs or practices of their adherents, or of any other belief system or the beliefs or practices of its adherents, or proselytizing or urging adherents of a different religion or belief system to cease practising their religion or belief system. (House of Lords 2005)

In this amendment, there is a considerable addition to the Bill to safeguard the freedom of expression.

Religion, Legislation and Identity

As we have heard from both sides of argument, I would now like to examine two areas which I believe are important to understanding the nature of the debates – one is the issue of the place of religion in contemporary society and the other is the understanding of the identity of a religious community.

Britain: Secular or Multi-religious Society?

In the course of the debates, there has been a strong argument against the Bill from the liberal sections of the media and academia, mainly on the basis of freedom of expression and also the anticipated misuse of the legislation by some fundamentalist groups. This is a valid caution, and there have already been some cases in Australia and in Pakistan, though the nature and context of their legislation is different from that in Britain, and a Christian group in Britain has recently declared that they will bring the Qur'an into the dock once the legislation is enacted. The underlying assumption of the opponents to the Bill is that Britain is a secular society and therefore should be treated as such. In particular, in her argument against the Bill, Polly Toynbee, expressing her dislike of anything religious, strongly asserts that 'this most secular state in the world, with fewest worshippers at any altars, should be a beacon of secularism in a world beset by religious bloodshed' (Toynbee 2005a). In this understanding, for the well-being of the society, religion should be regarded as a private matter and should not be on the agenda in the public sphere. This view is coupled with many sociologists' arguments that religion has become irrelevant in British society, which is perceived to be secular.

It is a commonly accepted view that Christianity in Britain has been experiencing rapid decline, and that this was most pronounced in the 1960s. Hugh

McLeod identifies this period as 'cultural revolution' and argues that the cause of this change was the search for greater individual freedom, which led to rejection of moral and doctrinal codes and authority. This was aggravated by social changes such as rapid decline in rural cultures, weakening of the sense of 'respectability', and loss of association of social identity with the church. As a result, 'religious community was ceasing to be a necessary source of identity and support' to the people of Western Europe (McLeod 1997: 141–43). This idea is taken further by Callum Brown, who insists that though Christianity had endured the challenge of the Enlightenment and modernity, the decisive decline in church attendance in the 1960s was because 'respectability' was supplanted by 'respect', and the traditional moral code was replaced by toleration and greater individual freedom (Brown 2001). In a similar argument, about the issue of the impact of modernity on religion in Britain, Steve Bruce observes that modernity changes the worldview of the people, bringing 'rationality' and 'subtly altering the way we think about the world so as to make religious beliefs and rituals ever more irrelevant' (Bruce 1995).

However, on the other hand, other religions in Britain have been gradually increasing since the 1960s, mainly through migration and natural growth of the members of religious communities and, as a result, Britain has become a multi-religious society. The report of the House of Lords' Select Committee on Religious Offences in England and Wales (2003) raised the question of whether religion still plays an important role in the formation of morals and values and whether this new phenomenon will lead to the transformation to a secular society. The Committee concluded that 'religious belief continues to be a significant component, or even determinant, of social values, and plays a major role in the lives of a large number of the population'. It emphatically states that 'beyond doubt Britain is a multi-faith society' and that 'The United Kingdom is not a secular state'. In fact, if we go further than looking at church attendance and the decline of church membership, we see a different picture from the notion of the sociologists above. The recent 2001 census shows that 77 per cent of respondents claim that they are part of 'Christian tradition and identity'.[10] Britain, in contrast to Toynbee's argument, has a distinctive combination of secularism and modernity on the one hand, and religion and spirituality on the other, each occupying different arenas of people's life in the society, and in this sense, using Grace Davie's terminology, Britain is an 'exceptional case' (Davie 2002: 2–8). In fact, one has to question Toynbee's perception of the reality of British society. Yes, British society cherishes and has been the beacon of secular and parliamentary democracy but not in the absence of religion. Yes, religions have been the cause of and factors in conflicts, but faiths in Britain have neither been simply pushed away by secularism nor have they ceased to contribute to the betterment of society.

In this context, the argument of the government is right that the state needs to protect vulnerable religious communities on equal terms without showing any impartiality. Secularism has two meanings – one has to do with the state keeping distance from religions, the other is to do with the state treating all religious groups equally. The government's intention, in this case, is to choose the latter option since the first option is not realistic in contemporary British society. In spite of the secularists' assertion and many sociologists' arguments that Britain is a secular society in the sense of the demise of religion in the public sphere, the debate has brought out the reality that Britain is a multi-religious society. Many religious communities are not embarrassed that their identity has a religious dimension.

During the course of debates on the Bill, the Muslim community has expressed that in their treatment not only by far-right groups but also by the general public their religious identity has been severally questioned as if the problem lies intrinsically in Islam as a faith. The Muslim community as a whole should not be judged by the actions of fundamentalist groups within them and they deserve protection from aggressive campaigns against their community and their faiths. This requires a sense of respect and appreciation of others' beliefs from the wider community since their faith is part and parcel of self and community identity. It is the strength of Britain that it has worked to maintain an open society where people are welcomed and share their values and aspirations. This effort has to be an ongoing one and should extend to the 'religious' dimensions of life as well as the cultural in order to create shared identities. This process requires the participation of both the majority community and the minority religious communities. Therefore, the protagonists of the Bill are seeking to demonstrate solidarity with vulnerable sections of society. This should be respected. However, whether enactment of legislation is the appropriate way to improve their situation is in question exactly because of the issue of the integrated identity of religious communities.

Religious Belief versus Religious Person: The Integral Identity of Religious Community

In response to opposition criticism that the legislation will infringe the freedom to healthy criticism of or jokes about religion, the government insists that the Bill is intended to protect religious people and not religious belief itself. However, the separation of religion and religious people is arbitrary if not impossible when it comes to many religions and religious communities. The identity of many religious people is drawn from their faith and this includes its doctrines, founders, particular religious practices and the religion as a whole. Therefore it is impossible to make a distinction and, in many cases, it is more insulting to criticize the religion or religious figure than the believers themselves. It is precisely because of this that some religious communities find it very hard to tolerate the insults of right-wing groups. Therefore, the new legislation will most likely be used by religious groups to defend their beliefs from being ridiculed or being criticized.

That religion is, for many communities, a vital source of their identity is often overlooked by those who oppose the Bill when they argue that there is an important distinction between race and religion: that is, one cannot criticize or ridicule someone on the basis of their race because this is an accident of birth whereas religion is a matter of choice. However, just because religion can be accepted by people of their own free will, this does not mean that all people of religion are so because of choice. For many their religion is determined by their origin and is central to their identity. Religion is not something you can change

– it is against the will of Allah for Muslims and against dharma for Hindus, for example. It is important to understand the extent to which people of some traditions anchor their identity in religion and will maintain it at great cost. This is why many religious traditions object to the notion of conversion. For them the freedom of religion is to do with freedom to keep and practise one's faith, whereas often in the West freedom of religion is understood as freedom to propagate one's religion or freedom to change one's religion. Because for many communities, religion is integral to identity, the Bill could eventually prevent any criticism of religious beliefs.

The question that then comes is whether we should criticize a religion that forms people's identity. Since many believers regard their religion as an integral part of their self-identity, should we not then treat religion as we treat race and bar it from criticism? On the contrary, we cannot treat religion as we treat race in this regard. The argument against racial abuse is correct: it is not acceptable to ridicule or make rude comments on the basis of skin colour or racial background and legislation should be enforced in the case of incitement of hatred towards an individual or a community on the basis of their race. However, though religion forms the core identity of many believers, religious ideas and faith have to be open to critique by both insiders and outsiders, otherwise a religious tradition or community can easily be corrupted and become dogmatic. We have seen this throughout the history of Western Christendom, Islamic fundamentalism and the Hindu nationalist movement in India. Religious beliefs as well as believers themselves need constantly to be reformed – and the only way to maintain this is by openness to criticism. Any aspect of religious faith – doctrines, rituals, authority, scriptures, institutions, religious leaders – should be open to scrutiny. It is vital for civil society that no individual, community, belief or ideology should stand above the criticism of the public, and religious belief is no exception to this principle.

In response to the criticism of the 'Racial and Religious Hatred Bill', the Home Secretary said that the legislation would be like a 'line in the sand', that it will be a warning to those who misuse the loopholes in the current law and will therefore contribute to the improvement of community relations (*The Times*, 9 June 2005). However, rather than promoting harmony between communities, it may be used to maintain boundaries, and therefore have the opposite effect. The grievance of the Muslim community is a reality and the aggression of far-right groups against this community would not seem to evaporate easily. The legislation may prevent verbal or written attacks on minority religious communities from hate campaigns, but the negative consequences seem to be far greater than the immediate protection of a religious group. It would be regrettable to find that by drawing a 'line in the sand' we end up digging a 'ha-ha' (sunken fence) that divides communities so that healthy interaction may no longer be possible and legal intervention the only recourse.

Differing Concept of Identity: In Need of Critical Dialogue

I have argued in the previous section that Britain is a multi-religious society *and* also a secular society, and that the value of each perception of society is hinged on the issue of identity. As I have discussed, the protagonists for and against the Bill were not simply religious groups versus secular groups but much more complex, and indeed we have witnessed the unusual alliance between some evangelical/fundamentalist Christian groups and secularists on this 'religious' issue, each asserting their own reasons for or against the Bill. Though I have argued against the Bill on the basis of healthy and open interaction of religious beliefs and communities with wider community, this does not mean that there are any single criteria for us to work with on disputes on religious matters. As we have witnessed the recent 'clash of culture' over the Danish cartoon issue, the secular assertion of freedom of expression irrespective of any religious sensitivity is rather exhibiting the attitude of ignorance and arrogance towards 'the otherness', though the Muslim reaction to the situation is equally unacceptable. And this situation is not necessarily conflict between Muslims and non-Muslims, but conflict between the fundamentalists, each claiming that they are representing the whole group.[11] This clash of secular and religious agendas is far more complex since it also relates to political and economic undercurrents between the Muslim and western world. The limits of the scope of this paper do not permit me to go further, but this illustrates the urgent need for open dialogue on religious issues and that neither the enforcement of law nor suppressing the issues will be the appropriate response to the problem. Meaningful dialogue between religious communities and secularists, and between various groups within communities, is urgently needed particularly on this issue of conflicting identities.

The Christian theology of dialogue, although its main concern has been between Christians and people of other faiths, may provide methodologies and working models for this complex situation of religious and secular conflict. Dialogue can be defined as commitment to one's faith and openness to that of others with genuine respect. Dialogue involves a desire to understand those of another faith better and learn from one another, an attitude that leads to an ongoing reflection on one's own faith and practice. It is also for mutual knowledge and friendship, which leads to the correction of prejudices toward one another. It is a relatively recent paradigm in the field of contemporary theology and has especially come to the fore as discussion on religious pluralism has developed.

Though the theoretical concept of dialogue has been developed in the field of systematic theology in the West, the philosophical and experimental experience of dialogue has been articulated most clearly among Indian theologians. Due to the vast diversity of religious and cultural communities, one of the most difficult public issues in India has been the problem of communal conflicts and, through these experiences, Indian theologians have developed a pragmatic approach of living together and a philosophical concept of finding truth and goodness in each other. They regard plurality as a blessing rather than an obstacle to harmony, and argue that active engagement in dialogue with others with respect is part and parcel of, if not essential to, any religious life. This was initially taken up by E. Stanley Jones, a well-known Methodist missionary to India, as he explored the idea of a 'round table conference' where people of different faiths could gather to share their own religious experiences without confronting each other or trying to persuade others to change their convictions (Jones 1925).

Stanley Samartha, who became the first director of the sub-unit on dialogue in the World Council of the Churches, articulated his theology of dialogue as an attempt to understand and express our own particularity not just in terms of our own heritage but also in relation to the spiritual heritage of our neighbours of our faiths (Samartha 1981). His theology is based on his understanding of God's covenant with his people and also Christ's incarnation, both of which demonstrate the dialogical relationship between God and his people. A natural expansion of this understanding is that the relationship between different religious communities should be a form of mutual dialogue, and not at all confrontational. Samartha draws his theology from the Indian multi-religious setting, from Indian philosophical approaches of finding truth by consensus, and from an attitude of acknowledging others as partners on the way rather than imposing one's own truth claims onto others. In his approach, mutual respect of one another's convictions is of crucial importance in dialogue and this should take place in community, creating a 'community of communities'. He saw dialogue among world religions as the demand of our age and an opportunity to work together to discover new dimensions of religious truths.

This idea of mutual search for the truth was taken up by the World Council of Churches and became a major plank of ecumenical theology, as explained in the document *Guidelines on Dialogue with People of Living Faiths and Ideologies* (WCC 1979). This document sets clear aims and objectives of dialogue and gives some practical guidelines for Christians who are engaging in a multi-religious situation. It states that dialogue is the responsibility of Christians and should be carried with the spirit of reconciliation and hope provided by Christ. It emphasizes the vital importance of acknowledging that all communities seek a secure sense of identity and realizing that in this process a religious community may often become exclusive and absolutize its own religious and cultural identity. It also asserts that dialogue should be based on mutual trust and respect for the integrity of others and therefore it is a vital part of Christian service in community as well as means of living one's faith in Christ. *Ecumenical Considerations for Dialogue and Relations with People of Other Religions* (WCC 2001) takes account of the recent development of fundamentalism and reflects the rising concern for the relevance of dialogue in this context. It insists that the role of dialogue is not only to reconcile conflict between communities but also to prevent religion becoming the source of tension between communities in the first place. It also adds the importance of mutual empowerment in the common pursuit of the betterment of society and encourages religious communities to critically examine their own conduct in relation to other communities.[12]

Taking this theological notion of dialogue between different religious communities, in the case of Britain, we find an urgent need for critical dialogue between religious and secular groups, accompanied by an attitude of 'commitment to one's conviction and openness to that of other's with genuine respect'. In the course of debate for or against the Racial and Religious Hatred Bill, British society has exhibited its mature attitude by conducting open and frank discussions in public and, as I see it, the end result of the Bill reflects both sides of the argument. This process should be a beacon of democratic society where both the secular and religious identities are respected and also critically assessed. By engaging in dialogue, we are able to question secularism that does not respect faith, which is part and parcel of the identity of many individuals and communities, and to challenge religion that sets itself against the wider interests of society, which often has been the most disturbing element undermining secular identity. The question of identity in a secular and multi-religious society lies in not whether one is right or not, nor who's holding the moral high ground, but it is rather an acknowledgement of differences and respect of each other's differing identities. The notion of dialogue encourages us to continue to engage in conversation with each other, to exchange our views for mutual inspiration, without holding an attitude of forcefully attempting to change others or ignoring other views as something irrelevant. Religious and secular communities need to listen to each other, and prepare to be shaped by each other's differing views. Both 'respect for faith' and 'freedom of expression' are core values to form the identity of both communities as they uphold them at a great cost. This, however, should not be regarded as the absolute value and needs to be negotiated in the context of contemporary society by engaging in open and critical dialogue.

Notes

1 See the 'Racial and Religious Hatred Act 2006', http://www.opsi.gov.uk/acts/acts2006/20060001.htm (accessed 4 February 2007).
2 See also the government reply to the Report from the Religious Offences Committee at http://www.archive2.official-documents.co.uk/document/cm60/6091/6091.pdf (accessed 31 October 2006).
3 See Article 9 (Freedom of Thought, Conscience and Religion): '1. Everyone has the right to freedom of thought, conscience and religion; this right includes freedom to change his religion or belief and freedom, either alone or in community with others and in public or private, to manifest his religion or belief, in worship, teaching, practice and Observance'; '2. Freedom to manifest one's religion or beliefs shall be subject only to such limitations as are prescribed by law and are necessary in a democratic society in the interests of public safety, for the protection of public order, health or morals, or for the protection of the rights and freedoms of others'. See also Article 14 (Prohibition of Discrimination): 'The enjoyment of the rights and freedoms set forth in this Convention shall be secured without discrimination on any ground such as sex, race, colour, language, religion, political or other opinion, national or social origin, association with a national minority, property, birth or other Status'.
4 See also http://www.homeoffice.gov.uk/comrace/faith/crime/frq.html (accessed 10 June 2005).
5 http://old.homeoffice.gov.uk/docs/racerel1.html (accessed 19 August 2005).
6 See also the statement from the Association of Muslim Lawyers (UK) at http://www.muslim-lawyers.net/news/index.php3?aktion=show&number=168 (accessed 31 August 2005).
7 http://www.ekklesia.co.uk/content/news_syndication/article_050118hatred.shtml (accessed 10 June 2005). It further argues that 'the hostility towards some religious communities will not easily be reduced while the international situation remains as

it is, particularly if the media continue to talk up terrorist threats and directly or indirectly relate them to these communities'.

8 See Neil Addison, 'Faith Doesn't Need a Bodyguard of Lawyers', *The Church Times*, 24 February 2006; Polly Toynbee, 'What's at Stake is the Right to Insult and Cause Offence', *Guardian*, 31 January 2006; Polly Toynbee, 'My Right to Offend a Fool', *Guardian*, 10 June 2005; Tania Branigan, 'New Hate Law "could have stopped riots"', *Guardian*, 10 June 2006; Joshua Rozenberg, 'Now You Face Jail for Being Nasty to Satanists', *Daily Telegraph*, 10 June 2005; Editorial, 'Religion and the Law', *The Times*, 10 June 2005.

9 BBC News, 'Black Churches Oppose Hatred Bill', http://news.bbc.co.uk/2/hi/uk_news/4671605.stm (accessed 18 August 2005).

10 http://www.statistics.gov.uk/CCI/nugget.asp?ID=460&Pos=1&ColRank=1&Rank=326 (accessed 20 October 2005).

11 See Timothy Garton Ash, 'Our Media Must Give Muslims the Chance to Debate with Each Other', *Guardian*, 9 February 2006; Fareena Alam, 'Why I Reject the Anarchists Who Claims to Speak for Islam', *Guardian*, 12 February 2006.

12 For Catholic discussion on dialogue, see Burrows 1993.

References

Articles and documents

'A Bill Built on Flimsy Foundations', *Daily Telegraph*, 10 June 2005.

'A Foolish and Unnecessary Bill', *Independent*, 10 June 2005.

'Racial and Religious Hatred Act 2006', http://www.opsi.gov.uk/acts/acts2006/20060001.htm (accessed 4 February 2007).

'Religion and the Law', *The Times*, 10 June 2005.

Association of Muslim Lawyers (UK) (2005), 'Statement', http://www.muslim-lawyers.net/news/index.php3?aktion=show&number=168 (accessed 31 August 2005).

The Christian Institute (2001), 'Why a Religious Hatred Law would Harm Religious Liberty and Freedom of Speech' (November 2001), http://www.christian.org.uk/incitement2005/incitement_aug05.pdf (accessed 31 October 2005).

European Convention on Human Rights (ECHR), http://www.echr.coe.int/NR/rdonlyres/D5CC24A7-DC13-4318-B457-5C9014916D7A/0/EnglishAnglais.pdf (accessed 3 November 2005).

Forum Against Islamophobia and Racism (FAIR) (2002), 'The Religious Offences Bill 2002: A Response' (October 2002).

Home Office (2005a), 'Racial and Religious Hatred Bill' (9 June 2005), http://www.publications.parliament.uk/pa/cm200506/cmbills/011/2006011.pdf (accessed 20 October 2005).

—— (2005b), Racial and Religious Hatred Bill – Frequently Asked Questions', http://www.publications.parliament.uk/pa/cm200506/cmbills/011/en/06011x--.htm (accessed 26 August 2005).

House of Commons (2001), 'Anti-Terrorism, Crime and Security Bill' (12 November 2001), http://www.publications.parliament.uk/pa/cm200102/cmbills/049/2002049.htm (accessed 18 August 2005).

House of Lords (2003), 'Religious Offences in England and Wales – First Report' (10 April 2003), http://www.publications.parliament.uk/pa/ld200203/ldselect/ldrelof/95/9501.htm (accessed 10 June 2005).

—— (2005), 'Racial and Religious Hatred Bill' (amendment: 20 October 2005), http://www.publications.parliament.uk/pa/ld200506/ldbills/015/amend/am015-e.htm (accessed 3 November 2005).

Lawyers' Christian Fellowship (2005), 'Incitement to Religious Hatred' (January 2005).

The Office for National Statistics, National Statistics, http://www.statistics.gov.uk/CCI/

nugget.asp?ID=460&Pos=1&ColRank=1&Rank=326 (accessed 20 October 2005).
'Public Order Act 1986', http://www.webtribe.net/~shg/Public%20Order%20Act%201986%20(1986%20c%2064)%20Sect%204A,%205,%206.htm
Secretary of State for the Home Department (2003), 'The Government Reply to the Report from the Religious Offences Committee' (December 2003), http://www.archive2.official-documents.co.uk/document/cm60/6091/6091.pdf (accessed 10 June 2005).

Books

Brown, C. (2001), *The Death of Christian Britain* (London and New York: Routledge).
Bruce, S. (1995), *Religion in Modern Britain* (Oxford: Oxford University Press).
Burrows, W. (ed.) (1993), *Redemption and Dialogue: Reading Redemptoris Mission and Dialogue and Proclamation* (Maryknoll: Orbis).
Davie, G. (2002), *Europe – The Exceptional Case: Parameters of Faith in the Modern World* (London: Darton, Longman & Todd).
Giddens, A. (1991), *Modernity and Self-Identity: Self and Society in the Late Modern Age* (Cambridge: Polity Press).
Jones, E.S. (1925), *The Christ of the Indian Road* (New York: Abingdon Press).
McLeod, H. (1997), *Religion and the People of Western Europe 1789–1989* (Oxford and New York: Oxford University Press).
Samartha, S. (1981), *Courage for Dialogue: Ecumenical Issues in Inter-Religious Relationships* (Geneva: WCC).
World Council of Churches (WCC) (1979), *Guidelines on Dialogue with People of Living Faiths and Ideologies* (Geneva: WCC).
—— (2001), *Ecumenical Considerations for Dialogue and Relations with People of Other Religions* (Geneva: WCC).

Part II

Community Identity in Local Contexts

7

Marian Shrines in Yorkshire and Roman Catholic Identity

Chris Maunder

Introduction

Shrines with a dedication to the Virgin Mary are commonplace throughout Roman Catholicism. They are often associated with miracles that led to their construction, such as a healing, rescue, finding of a statue, or vision, in which Mary is the central figure. Our Lady of the Pillar, in Zaragoza, Spain, claims to have the earliest foundation, with an unlikely vision of (the still living) Mary to St James in 40 CE. The founding stories for other early and famous Marian shrines, for example St Maria Maggiore in Rome and Le Puy in France, are dated more plausibly in the fourth century. These both comply with a formula that would become common: built on the site of an apparition, replacing a pagan goddess temple with a Christian basilica. Yet their origins are still uncertain. What can be stated with confidence, however, is that Marian devotion and places of pilgrimage have a long pedigree and go back at least as far as the establishment of Christianity across the Roman Empire in the fifth century.

Wherever Catholic Christianity was established, it was accompanied by the appearance of Marian shrines. Mediaeval England was described – possibly only by its own inhabitants – as 'Mary's dowry'. This ascription was due to the wealth of shrines dedicated to Mary in mediaeval England, in contrast to nations where other saints were prominent (for example, the Celtic countries are marked by shrines to nationally known saints, like Patrick in Ireland). Whilst England had its local saint cults too, including Cuthbert, Thomas Becket, Wilfrid, Alban, etc., it was particularly known for its Marian shrines. One could speak of a Marian 'geography' of England, which can be recovered in various books on the subject written from the nineteenth century onwards (Northcote 1868; Waterton 1879; Bridgett 1890; Gillett 1957; Vail 2004). This network was, and still is, centred on Walsingham in Norfolk, supposedly dating from the pre-Norman eleventh century and known across Europe. At Walsingham, a local nobleswoman's dream was said to have been the decisive factor in the decision to build an abbey at the site. The revelation/abbey pattern (not far from the European prototype at Zaragoza, Rome and Le Puy) is also found at the earliest of England's Marian shrines at Evesham in Worcestershire.

There, a supposed eighth-century vision to the swineherd Eoves resulted in his name being given to the town that grew up around the abbey.

Yorkshire is also home to this familiar Marian motif (see Figure 1). The monks at Kirkstall and Jervaulx (originally, Urevale) claimed that Marian visions were the original reason for their choosing the abbey site. Other important abbeys or priories with Marian shrines in mediaeval Yorkshire included Guisborough and Doncaster, and another was established a few miles from Doncaster, across the county boundary into Lincolnshire, at Melwood in the Isle of Axholme. Parish churches in Beverley and Pontefract boasted 'miraculous' statues of Mary and Child. York Minster, like all mediaeval cathedrals, had Marian chapels, which attracted pilgrims. Wakefield had a famous chapel of Mary on its bridge over the Calder (a feature known elsewhere in England, notably at Caversham on the Thames). Knaresborough featured an unusual Marian chapel carved into the sandstone crag during Henry IV's reign, licensed by a royal charter. Yorkshire also had many holy wells, in density rivalled only in England by Cornwall, several associated with Mary (Rattue 1995).

The Reformation saw an end to the network of Marian shrines. Knaresborough's chapel survived because of its cave construction, and even there the continued history of devotion is uncertain. Consequently, it was natural that, with the restoration in 1850 of the Roman Catholic priesthood and a renewed diocesan and parish structure, Catholics would seek to rediscover this heritage. One by one, the shrines returned: while the abbeys and priories were ruins, the devotion could be restored in the nearest parish church. In Doncaster, the building of a chapel as a renewal of Marian devotion, abandoned for three centuries, was completed as early as 1857. In the second half of the nineteenth century, when the restoration prompted Catholic hopes of a 're-conversion' of Britain to Catholicism, Roman Catholics published detailed material on the history of Marian shrines in Britain and Ireland (Northcote 1868; Waterton 1879; Bridgett 1890). This greatly encouraged the renewal process. In the twentieth century, the sites at Knaresborough (1915) and Osmotherley (1952) were purchased on behalf of Roman Catholic religious orders.

Today in Yorkshire (and just over into North Lincolnshire – see Figure 1), there are five sites which can be clearly designated Roman Catholic shrines of Mary. These are at Guisborough; Doncaster; Knaresborough; Osmotherley (being the restoration of the Lady Chapel of the ruined Carthusian priory of Mount Grace); and Crowle (commemorating Our Lady of Axholme, Melwood). A sixth could be added, as the nineteenth-century lady chapel of 'Our Lady of Mercy' in St Wilfrid's, York still exists, although it is no longer regarded as a shrine, and it has been overshadowed by the foundation of the shrine of St Margaret Clitherow in the parish. That is not the end of the story. The Church of England has restored the bridge chapel at Wakefield, which now belongs to the Cathedral.

Since the Reformation, the cult of Mary in Western Europe has been strongly linked to a sense of Roman Catholic identity, as it virtually disappeared in the Protestant churches. The one exception is the resurgence of the Catholic spirit in the Anglican Churches from the Anglo-Catholic revival in the 1830s. Anglo-Catholics were involved in a major restoration of Walsingham,

Figure 1: **Table of Yorkshire and North Lincolnshire shrines, giving foundation dates**

1. Shrine of Our Lady of Guisborough (1949 – Guisborough Priory 1119, ruin).
   Lady Chapel of parish church of St Paulinus, Guisborough.
2. Shrine of Our Lady of Mount Grace, Osmotherley (1956 – Mount Grace Priory 1398, ruin). Lady Chapel.
3. Jervaulx Abbey (1156, ruin).
4. Shrine Chapel of Our Lady of the Crag, Knaresborough (1408).
5. Shrine of Our Lady of Mercy (1884). Lady Chapel of parish church of St Wilfrid, York.
6. Kirkstall Abbey (1152, ruin).
7. St Mary's Church, Beverley (C of E – medieval statue, no shrine today).
8. Chantry Chapel of St Mary the Virgin, Wakefield (1356, restored 1847, C of E).
9. All Saints' Church, Pontefract (C of E – medieval statue, no shrine today).
10. Shrine of Our Lady of Doncaster (1857 – Doncaster Priory 1350, site only). Lady Chapel of parish church of St Peter's in Chains, Doncaster.
11. Shrine of Our Lady of Axholme (recent). Parish church of St Norbert, Crowle.
12. Site of Melwood Priory (1308), Isle of Axholme.

and they have also renewed other notable Marian shrines at Willesden in Greater London, Egmanton in Nottinghamshire, Glastonbury in Somerset and, in Scotland, Haddington in East Lothian.

This chapter seeks to establish the relationship between Marian shrines and Roman Catholic identity today, by focusing on the five principal sites in the Yorkshire and North Lincolnshire region: Axholme; Doncaster; Guisborough; Knaresborough; Osmotherley. To this end, I have visited pilgrimages and masses at the shrines, and interviewed people involved in looking after them, or visiting them. I myself have been for ten years the chair of the management group at the Roman Catholic shrine chapel of Our Lady of the Crag, Knaresborough, and so have a considerable amount of 'insider' experience of the activities and issues involved in the maintenance of a Marian shrine in England today. Finally, an understanding of this question cannot fail to take into account the watershed in Roman Catholicism that is the Second Vatican Council (known as Vatican II) of 1962–65. The dynamics of Roman Catholic identity in Britain in the twenty-first century stand in considerable contrast to the years between the restoration in 1850 and Vatican II.

Roman Catholic Identity in Britain before Vatican II

Adrian Hastings's history of twentieth-century English Christianity describes how the first half of the century for Roman Catholics in Britain could be categorized as being a movement from marginalization to strength (Hastings 1991: 131–55, 561–79). He outlines major features of the Roman Catholicism of this period. Although the Roman Catholic world was intellectually rigid, and remained anti-Protestant – despite some moves to ecumenism – and anti-secular, the period also saw social integration of Catholics in British society at large. The Catholic parishes were well attended, predominantly working class, and the clergy were given high status. This was the period of 'ultramontanism', which had originated in the first half of the nineteenth century, and became the dominant mode of Catholic self-understanding from the 1850s onward (see, e.g., McGrath 1997: 321–22). Ultramontanism – meaning, literally, rule from over the Alps, i.e. from Rome – was the movement in which the Pope was confirmed as 'infallible', and the Vatican given greater power over episcopal appointments, as well as styles of devotion and liturgy. Canon law was revised and re-enforced. Ultramontanism had been resisted in countries like France, but the weakness of national churches in the face of secularization and republicanism caused ecclesiastical power to be centralized in Rome. England's archbishops, as heads of a new ecclesial system, were staunch supporters of Roman dominance (Hastings 1991: 145–55, 488–90).

It is tempting to suppose that what could be called the 'cult' of the papacy – with the Pope supremely popular and regarded as the essence of all that is good about the tradition – has existed throughout the centuries without interruption. However, in the same way as the British monarch, the mid-nineteenth century marked a dramatic increase in the popularity of the Pope (McGrath 1997: 320), who later became something of a modern icon. The development of photography and film has contributed to this movement.

Sheridan Gilley lists a whole range of activities that characterize pre-Vatican II Catholic culture: prayer, worship, art, architecture, music, literature, custom, convention, sign, symbol, cycle of feasting and fasting, institutions and associations (1999: 29). Therefore, despite social integration in terms of holding senior posts in all aspects of British life, and participating in the war effort in both 1914–18 and 1939–45, Roman Catholics still maintained what could be called a separate cultural identity. Working-class devotional patterns included candles, statues of Our Lady, diocesan pilgrimages to Lourdes, and pictures of the Sacred Heart in the home (Hastings 1991: 136). Religious processions, including May devotions centred upon Mary, some at shrines, were used to reinforce this separate culture (Hornsby-Smith 2004: 44). Marian devotion in the 1950s was particularly intense and extravagant, and was characterized by the strength of the cult of Our Lady of Fatima, the Legion of Mary, Rosary crusades, and the papal definition of the Assumption of Mary in 1950. A cross-carrying pilgrimage to Walsingham began in 1948 as an attempt to evangelize lapsed Catholics, and it included the public wearing of religious habits, which had been avoided before the War (Hastings 1991: 480–82).

English Catholicism had survived, sometimes in exile, during the penal sixteenth, seventeenth and eighteenth centuries (Hastings 1991: 132). However, by far the greatest number of Roman Catholics in pre-Vatican II Britain consisted of immigrants, predominantly from Ireland. There has been debate as to the process by which the Irish were assimilated into the English Catholic culture in parish life. The process of assimilation is recorded by Michael Hornsby-Smith (2004: 48–51) and Hastings (1991: 134), but Mary Hickman (1999: 182–98) argues that these accounts do not take enough account of the politics of this, as Irish identity in the Church may have been maintained more robustly than is often observed, but in low profile. She points out that the apparent public loss of Irish Catholic identity occurred because the Church strengthened *Catholic* identity as generic and weakened *Irish* nationality, especially through the Catholic education system. It should be added that in Ireland, the tragedy of the Famine of the 1840s had *already* left Catholicism in its national form severely weakened, and at the mercy of two irresistible forces from without: (1) ultramontanism (O'Leary 1996: 183), and (2) the imposition of English as the national language, led by Archbishop Cullen of Dublin (Drumm 1996: 57–89). Irish Catholic identity was thereafter tied to fixed places, such as Croagh Patrick, Lough Derg and Knock, rather than transportable parish-based devotions.

Another important aspect of the immigration of Catholics into Britain was the influx of French and German religious orders due to late nineteenth-century anticlericalism in those countries. Added to the immigrant communities were also many converts to Catholicism, who seemed to like its inflexibility and authority (Hastings 1991: 487). Thus British (English, Scottish, Welsh), Irish and continental European backgrounds combined to form the Roman Catholic community in Britain, and before Vatican II, their allegiance to Roman Catholicism was a major factor in their self-identity, probably even greater than their sense of national origin.

Ultramontanism and Globalization

On the face of it, religious communities might be regarded as antipathetic to globalization; in particular, fundamentalism is seen as the extreme end of a spectrum of defensive reactions to globalizing tendencies (see, e.g., Robertson 2003: 110–23). In actual fact, religion is not hostile to globalization *per se* but only to its predominant contemporary manifestation in a liberal secular western form. The 'world religions' are precisely that: religions with a global influence. Of these, Christianity and Islam in particular, and to a lesser extent Buddhism, have promoted their own form of globalization in the past, accepting new adherents of every race and culture. Secular liberalism is their only serious rival in this respect. 'World religions' comprise networked institutions which downplay traditions and customs purely local in character; rather, they emphasize universal patterns of religiosity. Thus a Pakistani and Algerian Muslim may come together to the same British Mosque and both feel equally at home; they may both travel to Mecca on the *hajj*, and find promoted there a sense of global belonging and common, trans-national norms in belief and behaviour.

Of course, Christianity is made up of several denominations and sects, many of which are, and have been, rivals in the business of global proselytism. Of these, Roman Catholicism is the oldest of the 'globalizers'. The word 'catholic' itself arose in the second century, and means 'universal' in the sense of enforcing uniformity across a wide geographical area, which was Europe and North Africa in the early Church, but worldwide today. The aspects of the Catholic tradition in which convergence was most insisted upon were doctrine and morals. It was originally not so marked in the liturgy, which retained local forms (see, e.g., Jones *et al.* 1992); nevertheless, the universalizing tendency touched upon those parts of the liturgy regarded as the most focal, i.e. the canon of the Mass. Liturgical standardization did occur, however, although it took centuries, and the patterns of liturgical form were still relatively plural until the Council of Trent (1545–63). Trent's standardization of forms and processes in response to the Reformation took place at the same time as the beginning of the era of European colonialism. From the sixteenth to eighteenth centuries, these norms were urged upon Catholics worldwide, in particular by the Jesuits. The period between Trent and Vatican II in Catholicism is often regarded as one of centralized control over an increasingly global Church (see, e.g., McBrien 1994: 627–54). Vatican II attempted to relax the structure to some extent, by encouraging 'inculturation', i.e. the acceptance of local customs into the liturgy, while doctrine and morals remained dictated by the centre in Rome (Flannery 1996: 131–32). This situation has caused conflict where theologians, encouraged by the liberalizing tendency of Vatican II, have attempted to construct doctrinal or moral frameworks more pertinent to their local situation than the Vatican blueprint (see, e.g., Rowland 1999). To sum up, the pressure under which Catholicism has felt itself to be in the modern period, particularly from secularizing forces in various national contexts, has meant that Catholic resistance to the globalizing, universalizing tendency of Rome has been relatively weak. There has been a perception that a strong centre means a strong Church.

Shrines as an Expression of Pre-Vatican II Catholic Culture

Shrines, as manifestations of a religious tradition, are indicators of the current state of that tradition. Ultramontanism was a reinforcement of Papal power over national Catholic churches, but it needed doctrinal, political and devotional symbols as well as a change in ecclesiastical politics. Doctrinally, it was emphasized by the definition of the Immaculate Conception of Mary by Pius IX in 1854, and the proclamation of the Infallibility of the Pope at the First Vatican Council in 1870. Addressing the political sphere, the *Syllabus of Errors* in 1864 declared Pius IX's denunciation of modernizing tendencies such as liberalism and religious freedom, ironically embraced by Vatican II a century later (Bettenson and Maunder 1999: 286–89, 365–68). In devotional terms, the late nineteenth century saw a globalization of religious symbols, many of which originated in France, chosen as the front-line nation between Catholicism and secular modernizing tendencies (see, e.g., Pope 1985: 173–99). McSweeney argues that much Catholic piety in the nineteenth century, including the construction of shrines, was part of a Roman strategy (1980: 38–47).

The system of shrines in modern Roman Catholicism reflects the ultramontane tendency. It accords with the principle of central control in that one shrine has been chosen to be exalted above all the rest as an icon of the essence of the spirituality of Catholic pilgrimage. This shrine is Lourdes (see, e.g., Harris 1999). The image of Bernadette kneeling before her vision of the Virgin Mary in the French Pyrenean grotto has been exported across the world. Its best-known manifestation is in small shrines: many parish churches have their Lourdes grotto, and they are also built at holy wells. The image of the Virgin Mary wearing the white gown and blue sash of Lourdes, holding her hands in prayer as in the visions, is also an extremely common one in statues and pictures.

The reason that Lourdes has acquired this iconic status may be partly due to the qualities of the visions themselves: the discovery of the mountain spring which came to be visited by millions, especially the sick and disabled, for its healing properties; the strong charismatic personality of the visionary, Bernadette Soubirous (later Sister Marie Bernarde); the beauty of the surrounding area, and its comparative remoteness from large urban centres; the topographical features, a grotto at the base of the mountains next to a river valley. Its popularity was helped by the building of the railways, the usual mode of travel for the late nineteenth-century pilgrim. However, from the point of view of ecclesiastical politics, the case had three very important aspects:

(a) Bernadette's visionary messages included no political content; they were short, simple and restricted to sixteen visions over five months.
(b) Bernadette reported that the vision had identified herself as 'the Immaculate Conception', only four years after the Pope declared the Immaculate Conception of Mary as a binding dogma.
(c) The date of the visions (1858) coincides with the victory of the ultramontane party during the papacy of Pius IX.

In contrast to Lourdes, locally based cults of saints or Mary diminished in importance by comparison. It is true that some other new shrines like La Salette in France (1846) also enjoyed international interest. Other devotions 'exported' in this way to become prominent in local parishes included the Miraculous Medal; the Sacred Heart (France) and, to a lesser extent, Our Lady of Perpetual Succour (Italy). From the middle of the twentieth century, the cult of Our Lady of Fatima (Portugal) achieved prominence.

Therefore, it is not surprising that British Catholicism, since the restoration of 1850, has established shrines and pilgrimage with a notably European flavour. As the majority of Catholics in Britain during this period have had Irish descent, this is reinforced by the fact that the same situation pertains in Ireland, which has an even greater number of Lourdes grottos. This point is illustrated by the fact that the Marian shrines most associated with Irish immigration, having been built by Irish workers, are Lourdes grottos at Carfin (near Motherwell, Scotland), Cleator (Cumbria, England) and Abercynon (South Wales). At English Catholic shrines, there is virtually no trace of Irish tradition. The only shrine which especially marks Irish history, with a recently built memorial of the Famine, is Carfin, but there one can find testimonials to other Catholic immigrant communities from Eastern Europe.

It is reasonable to suggest that, as far as British Marian shrines are concerned (and they do act as a barometer for more general features), Irish identity is not maintained and supported, despite the fact that so many British Roman Catholics have Irish descent. This owes a great deal to the ultramontane tendency of modern Roman Catholicism. One could say much the same for British Catholic identity, whether Scottish, Welsh or English, although here the situation is more complex, due to the fact that many pre-Reformation British Marian shrines were restored and their mediaeval histories retold (there are also a few examples of this in Ireland, such as Trim and Limerick).

The exporting of European traditions can be illustrated at York, in the purchase of a famous Belgian statue (stolen in the 1980s) to serve as the centrepiece of the shrine, which had been smuggled out in the anti-Catholic days of the French Revolution. Later, the shrine of Our Lady of Mount Grace at Osmotherley and the lady chapel at Ampleforth Abbey were also to feature comparatively old European statues; indeed, anyone establishing a shrine and desiring a statue older than the nineteenth century had to look outside Britain and Ireland.

Roman Catholic Identity since Vatican II

There is a common Roman Catholic view that since the Second Vatican Council, there has been a collapse of the older devotional system, with its emphasis on Mary and the saints (see, e.g., Hebblethwaite 1991: 240–45). Gilley points out that, ironically, a Church which has become generally more lay-oriented has apparently minimized lay devotions (the 'sacramentals'), and retained those which are priest-led (the 'sacraments') (1999: 31). His other irony is that the Church also seemed to abandon non-verbal symbols when anthropologists were discovering them (1999: 33).

As Hornsby-Smith says, Mary Douglas singles out the removal of Friday abstinence among a range of abandoned practices, all of which served to reinforce the sense of Catholic identity (1999: 294), much as Ramadan is a strong marker of Muslim identity. Other strong Roman Catholic markers which were removed included the Latin Mass and distinctive clerical and religious dress. After Vatican II, liturgical development based on historical research tended to the more strictly christocentric (Christ-centred), and paralleled developments in other churches, which meant that 'the obvious and overwhelming contrast between the eucharistic practice of Catholics and of the other Christians had gone for good' (Hastings 1991: 567). Thus important signifiers of Catholic identity were weakened. At Knaresborough, parishioners mention the loss of the annual procession in May in honour of Our Lady; they remember conflict between Catholic and other local schoolchildren in the 1950s and 1960s which is not occurring now, as the Catholic minority is not clearly distinguished from the rest of the community.

Many Roman Catholics have observed a modern decline in devotion to Mary, with its pilgrimages, May processions, rosaries, singing of the *Salve*

Regina, etc. Marian devotion was one of the most important signs that once distinguished Catholic Christianity, but Vatican II emphasized what is called the *ecclesiotypical* tendency in Mariology (Mary is the symbol and forerunner of the Church) as opposed to the *christotypical* one (Mary is due high honours, and is more like Christ than the rest of the human race). The Council documents also distanced the hierarchy from Marian fervour which saw her as one who bestowed mercy, and stressed that she guided people, not to herself, but to her Son (Flannery 1996: 80–95). In many ways, Vatican II moved Roman Catholicism towards the *solus Christus* and *sola scriptura* of the Reformation; while tradition remained, it now had to have firm biblical and christocentric anchoring. Thus much of Marian doctrine, being non-biblical, was qualified; while Vatican II did not revoke beliefs in the Immaculate Conception and Assumption of Mary, its general tenor put them in doubt, at least in some liberal interpretations. A few years later, Paul VI forbade the saying of rosaries during Mass (Paul VI 1974). The Marian movement saw a resurgence with the accession of John Paul II, with his Polish background, but more common among the local clergy, in Britain at least, was a downplaying of Marian devotions. The liberal view which distanced itself from Mary is criticized by Charlene Spretnak, herself a liberal, but one who regarded the loss of Marian devotion to be an unnecessary and tragic development (2004).

Even with Vatican II's promotion of the sacraments, there has nevertheless been a widespread drop in Mass attendance, and a weakening of knowledge of Roman Catholic theological doctrine (Hornsby-Smith 1999: 300). Whereas Protestantism or continental Catholicism had already seen a marked decline in commitment before the 1960s, this was not true of British or Irish Roman Catholicism, and so in Britain, this is often blamed on Vatican II. The 1970s saw many local closures of institutions, a marked decline in people seeking admission to the priesthood and religious orders, and a corresponding and necessary promotion of the laity to key posts (e.g. heads of schools, members of parish councils, counsellors, organizers of liturgy). In some quarters, there has also been a decline of respect for papal authority, which was provoked by the conservative tone of encyclicals such as *Humanae Vitae* (1968), which ignored the findings of the Vatican's own commission in reaffirming the ban on artificial contraception (Hastings 1991: 575–77, 630–48).

Commentators on the nature of identity today agree that, while religion helps to form a sense of identity and belonging, this cannot be separated from other forms of personal and social identity (Coleman and Collins 2004: 21–22). In other words, people have multiple identities which inter-relate (Bauman 2004: 13). One identifies oneself as 'Catholic' but also as 'English' or 'British', as being from Yorkshire, as belonging to a gender, class, occupation, interest group, etc. Thus there is a process in modern society whereby religious identity has the tendency to become diluted as other forms of belonging compete for priority. In Roman Catholicism, the process by which 'Catholic' identity has less of a hold on the whole commitment of a person has accelerated during the period after Vatican II; whether Vatican II aggravated this tendency, or simply marked something which was inevitable anyway, is difficult to decide.

Sociological commentators like Giddens, who argue that religious authority is only now part of a pluralism of expertise, and therefore no longer absolute (1991: 195), concur with observers of Roman Catholicism like McSweeney who, even by 1980, remarked on the theological individualism in the Catholic Church today (1980: 239). In Hornsby-Smith's view, there was a post-Vatican II shift from communal to individual paradigms of self-understanding, moral decision-making, belonging and understanding of authority. The most obvious example of non-observance of moral teaching is the use of contraceptives (Hornsby-Smith 1999: 303; 2004: 42–56). Fulton's study of young Catholics adds further detail to this thesis: the shift to prioritizing experience over precepts, meaningfulness and participation over observation of rules, and belonging over agreement with leadership (Fulton 1999: 180). One important factor in the weakening of a strong sense of Roman Catholic identity in post-1960s Britain has been the growth in marriage to non-Catholics, arguably both a cause and effect of change (Hastings 1991: 636).

Hornsby-Smith's observations of changes in Roman Catholicism in today's Britain leads him to suggest that social identities are less inherited than they once were and more constructed (2004: 54). The whole process of construction therefore demands energy and commitment; without this, the Catholic is likely to allow other priorities to become dominant. For contemporary Catholics, the now *voluntary* and *individual* Catholic identity competes with other leisure-time pursuits (Hornsby-Smith 1999: 293).

Two qualifications can be made to the generally true thesis that Catholic identity has been diluted in the last forty years. First, there are of course very influential sub-groups which do not follow the rule. Hastings identified three separate camps in English Roman Catholicism from the 1970s (1991: 636–40): the traditionalist right, which resists the trend of the undermining of authority; the progressive left which embraces it; and the charismatic movement, which is more comfortable with liberal tendencies such as female (non-ordained) leadership and ecumenism, but is otherwise theologically conservative – these characteristics can be seen in the charismatic movement's adoption of the pre-Reformation Marian shrine at Liskeard in Cornwall (Riche 2002; Maunder 2003b: 196–201). Of these three tendencies, the first reinforces Catholic identity, and the third does to a lesser extent.

Second, there are still signs that even liberal young Catholics continue to preserve or, at least, reformulate older traditions. Interestingly, Fulton's interviews with young Catholic women emphasized the Marian dimension. He found that they were active in Lourdes pilgrimages and frequent retreats, and regarded silent worship and Marian devotion as important. As well as the community celebration of the Mass, sacred spaces include the Lourdes grotto and quiet chapels (Fulton 1999: 173–74).

The counter-tendency to general change, in the holding to a strong sense of identity coupled with a conservative view of papal authority, corroborates the view of sociologists in the tradition of Hans Mol, that religious identity is fundamentally conservative in nature (1976). Bauman points out how communities seem to provide a shelter against globalization, and also familiarity within boundaries: chaos is outside, security inside. However, the question of preserving 'identity' may well, as Bauman notes, only become important when religious belonging ceases to be automatic, as in modern western societies or those faced with their incursion (2004: 11–12). Since Vatican II, Irish immigration has been greatly reduced. European immigration continues, and Catholic immigration from Europe might see an increase with the extension of the European Community into Eastern Europe's Catholic countries, such as Poland, the Czech Republic and Hungary. However, another notable contingent of new Catholic communities in Britain in recent years is from other continents: parts of Africa, Goa, the Philippines. These communities are particularly prominent in urban parishes. They bring their own styles and customs into Catholic parish life, its liturgy and devotions and, generally, they have a strong Marian piety.

The Value of Shrines in the Present-day Context

Bauman argues that, in general, people are not atheists today; rather, it is that there is no perceived use for eternal discourses in dealing with everyday life; the emphasis is on practical ones (2004: 70–75). This will mean that, for many people not committed to a religious practice, religion will be of the 'gaps'; in other words, religious activities will help where practical discourses break down or where one needs relief from the multi-tasking stresses of the workplace, home and local community. The evidence suggests that Roman Catholics with responsibility for shrines which are publicly accessible are very much aware of their possible social function in this respect. Thus Catholics at Knaresborough (Our Lady of the Crag) and Osmotherley (Our Lady of Mount Grace), both chapels in places of natural beauty, were very keen to state that the shrines were holy places owned by and available to the whole community, that is people of all faiths and none. Understandably, this sentiment is less marked where the shrine is within the Roman Catholic parish church itself. Yet, even in those places, most people agreed that everyone should be welcome, 'including those who come for historical interest only'.

The belief of Catholics at Osmotherley and Knaresborough that their shrines had widespread value was expressed in such terms as 'a reminder of our final destiny'; a 'place to be refreshed'; a 'temporary haven'; 'within Babylon it's nice to have a piece of the new Jerusalem'; 'a place of peace and tranquillity away from a hectic world'; '[they] enable others – of any faith or none – to have the opportunity to visit'; 'visitors are drawn to the shrine if sad or lonely'; 'I have seen the relief on the faces of some people after spending just a few minutes alone in our shrine'; 'people of all faiths should be encouraged to visit a shrine at least once in their lives'. The fact that the shrines were not in churches was an advantage: 'some find it easier to pray at the shrine rather than in church'.

At Doncaster, Guisborough and Crowle, where the shrines are in parish churches, there is a very strong sense of the importance of local Catholic history. This is because the shrines are related to nearby religious houses with Marian shrines that were destroyed during the Reformation. There has been a recent revival of interest in these shrines. While Our Lady of Doncaster's modern shrine dates from 1857, there has been a movement of renovation and refurbishment since 2003, with a strong accent on motifs from local history. As the pre-Reformation religious house which housed the shrine was Carmelite, members of this order have a particular interest, with members visiting Doncaster from other regions. Our Lady of Guisborough's shrine was set up in the parish church in 1949. In Crowle (Our Lady of Axholme), the link to Catholic history has a special intensity, because of the memory of the Carthusian prior of Melwood, Augustine Webster, executed during the Pilgrimage of Grace in the sixteenth century. There has been a renewal of interest in these events, with the recent commissioning of a statue of Webster in his death agony. This and a moveable altar are taken to the site of Melwood Priory, in the Isle of Axholme a few miles from Crowle, for a commemorative pilgrimage and Mass at the end of May each year. Interestingly, in the neighbouring Middlesbrough Diocese, a recent evangelization effort was named the 'Pilgrimage of Grace'. While at both Knaresborough and Osmotherley, there are also ruined abbeys or priories, the history of the Reformation seems much less emphasized there.

The renewal of commitment to shrines associated with the Reformation's suppression of both religious orders and Marian devotion may seem to reinforce Catholic identity. However, it does so in a way that provides a counterweight to the prevailing ultramontanism of nineteenth- and twentieth-century Roman Catholicism, in emphasizing local traditions and not only those derived from continental Europe and encouraged by Rome. At Doncaster, there was a reference to the recent renovation of the shrine giving people 'a sense of local identity'. The greater majority of respondents agreed that the history 'was integral to the meaning of the shrine today' (as opposed to 'to some extent' or 'not very much').

Furthermore, a greater majority agreed that the Marian symbolism of the shrines was also very important; it was not incidental. At Knaresborough, it was believed that the maternal dimension encapsulated in a Marian shrine was important for everyone, especially mothers. The maternal, Marian, aspect was more important than the Catholic heritage of the shrine. The shrine, being separate from the church, was perhaps less threatening for non-Catholics or occasional attenders than the parish Mass with its christocentric basis. However, there was a view at Osmotherley that the overriding feature of the shrines was that the hill provided a 'sacred space', and that Mary was only 'the icing on the cake'.

As Coleman and Elsner put it, 'the landscape of any pilgrimage site consists not only of a physical terrain and architecture, but also of the myths, traditions and narratives associated with natural and manmade features' (1995: 212). Another interesting idea that emerged from discussion at Osmotherley and Knaresborough was the integration of the shrine with the local environment. As the lady chapel at Osmotherley is in the Cleveland Hills, it is a natural place for hill walkers, and so people can 'just wander in'. For those who come deliberately on pilgrimage, 'walking up the hill was part of the experience'. So the shrine belongs to its natural habitat. This is also in evidence at Knaresborough, where visitors to the crag chapel are told its founding legend: that a master mason hewed it out of the rock in thanksgiving for the saving of his son from a falling boulder. In modern Knaresborough, the Nidd river gorge is replete with signs warning visitors to beware of falling rocks and not to climb on the unsafe sandstone crag. Thus the shrine legend has a meaning within the local environment that links the fifteenth-century builders to twenty-first-century visitors. Knaresborough's shrine has also received funding for work that combines local heritage, art, education and environmental awareness.

Therefore, the most prominent themes that emerged from people at the shrines, when asked to comment on the meaning of the shrines for today, were:

(a) The importance of local Catholic history.
(b) The importance of maintaining the Marian dimension of the Christian faith and teaching people about it.

For Osmotherley and Knaresborough, with their chapels in places of beauty, these themes would be added:

(c) The necessity of providing local holy places for people of all faiths and none, for spiritual refreshment and a break from the stresses of modern life.
(d) The local environment.

These themes are common elsewhere in Europe. (a) The importance of local history and heritage, with its Catholic and non-Catholic elements, is high on the priority list for national and local government commitment. All shrines distribute stories of their history. (b) Marian shrines have a catechetical function; symbols and materials are used which teach visitors about the Christian faith, particularly its Marian dimension. (c) Shrines are places that, usually today, provide opportunities for retreat centres, healing centres and quiet meditation. Beauty spots such as Pennant Melangell, an Anglican shrine of St Melangell in the Welsh mountains west of Shrewsbury, with its healing centre for cancer sufferers, are obvious locations for spiritual refreshment. (d) Many founding stories have local connections, for example the legend of the finding of a miraculous statue by cows at Notre Dame d'Estours in the Auvergne in France emerged in a locality where the keeping of cows is important. Environmental preservation is a growing issue at shrines in places of beauty. A good example is the hill shrine of Notre Dame de Sion, in Lorraine, France, which has been purchased by the regional council and utilized for environmental awareness without diminishing its Catholic character.

Two themes that are not a feature of Yorkshire shrines, but which can be found at many places elsewhere in Europe, are (e) expectations of miraculous healing (as at Lourdes), and (f) apocalyptic scenarios involving the shrine (as, notably, at Garabandal, Spain; Medjugorje, Bosnia-Hercegovina). Britain has not seen the explosion of nineteenth- and twentieth-century apparitions and miracles that have been commonplace in countries like France, Portugal, Spain, Belgium, Holland, Germany, Poland, the states of the former Yugoslavia and Ireland (see, e.g., Maunder 1991; 2000: 69–85; 2003a: 239–54; Matter 2001: 125–53). These are all countries with large homogeneous Catholic populations, whereas Catholic minorities in predominantly Protestant states do not appear to have experienced sensational miracles with any regularity. As claims of supernatural interventions are nurtured in local Catholic contexts, and then encouraged and promoted by ecclesiastical authorities, it might not be surprising to note that this is less likely to happen where the Catholics are in the minority, and the national Church is concerned about its respectability in the nation as a whole.

Conclusions

The thesis that there has been a tendency to a weaker sense of identity among British Roman Catholics since Vatican II is generally true, but there are counter-currents: continued immigration from countries where there is a stronger sense of Catholic community; groups formed to protect the hierarchical and didactic nature of the Church, such as *Opus Dei*. Views on the importance of maintaining Catholic identity thus form a spectrum. On the one side, there is a strong sense of obedience to the Church hierarchy on matters of doctrine and morals, a connection that Catholic traditions need preserving. However, a strong sense of difference is undermined to some extent by the decline of older traditions that marked Catholics out: processions, lay devotions such as the rosary, fasting on Fridays and before Mass. The main factor that might still demarcate people, other than observance of the Church services, is attendance at Catholic schools. At the other end of the spectrum, liberal Catholics do not regard priestly authority as absolute, and are prepared to come to individual judgements on moral issues. They encourage ecumenical initiatives, and may not accept all of the traditional Catholic doctrine; in particular, they may doubt those parts of Marian doctrine which are outside the Bible. In some ways, it is becoming more difficult to distinguish them from Protestants, and there are examples of people transferring into Protestant churches.

It would be expected, then, that shrines will reflect that range of views. As we have seen, some Catholics regard shrines as important for the whole community; the sense of Catholic identity is not as important in these cases. These shrines are places of local heritage and natural beauty. Other shrines, being located in parish churches near to the sites of pre-Reformation religious houses, are more linked into Catholic history because of their situation. A possible way forward at Doncaster and Guisborough would be the placement, in a public place outside the parish church, of a plaque commemorating the Marian shrine as part of the town's heritage. There could be an associated image of Madonna and Child, as can be found in Ipswich and Coventry.

In all cases, local history is important, and to some extent, this does work against the ultramontane globalizing tendency of modern Catholicism. Vatican II itself called for *inculturation*, that is, the integrating of local customs and heritage with the universal canons of liturgy and doctrine, and so there is nothing unorthodox about it. Nevertheless, it will help to break down any rigid views of Catholic separatism, as local history is clearly something that Catholics have in common with their neighbours of all Christian denominations. What remains at issue is the weight put on denominational conflict and division arising from the Reformation, on the one hand, and a shared history in the mediaeval period, on the other.

The international network of Marian shrines visited by great numbers of people coming from a wide range of countries and regions might be a sign of the continued vitality in Marian pilgrimage; it could also, as an Irish priest once remarked to me, be a sign of the decline in *local* devotions (Maunder 2003a: 242). In other words, you have to travel to take part; elsewhere I have remarked on the networks needed to sustain shrines, with the use of electronic communications by people spread over a wide area who come together from time to time (Maunder 2003b: 196–201). There is a role for the diocesan shrine, a smaller-scale gathering place; Osmotherley functions as one for the Middlesbrough diocese. Probably, however, the best way forward for most small local shrines is an emphasis on ecumenism, inter-faith hospitality, local community projects, heritage and the environment. It is not possible to foresee the future of Marian shrines in Yorkshire or anywhere else, but what is certain is that the technological and demographical changes of the world of the twenty-first century will shape that future, and the development of Marian devotion will never occur in the cultural equivalent of a walled garden. Thus Roman Catholic identity, as it is refracted through the lens of Marian shrines and pilgrimages, will evolve organically, in response to the social and cultural milieu in which it is expressed.

References

Bauman, Z. (2004), *Identity: Conversations with Benedetto Vecchi* (Cambridge: Polity Press).

Bettenson, H. and C. Maunder (1999), *Documents of the Christian Church* (Oxford: Oxford University Press, 3rd edn).

Bridgett, T.E. (1890), *Our Lady's Dowry: How England Gained that Title* (London: Burns & Oates, 3rd edn).

Coleman, S. and P. Collins (2004), 'Introduction: Ambiguous Attachments', in S. Coleman and P. Collins (eds), *Religion, Identity and Change: Perspectives on Global Transformations* (Aldershot: Ashgate), pp. 1–25.

Coleman, S. and J. Elsner (1995), *Pilgrimage: Past and Present in the World Religions* (Cambridge, MA: Harvard University Press).

Drumm, M. (1996), 'Irish Catholics: A People Formed by Ritual', in E.G. Cassidy (ed.), *Faith and Culture in the Irish Context* (Dublin: Veritas), pp. 57–89.

Flannery, A. OP (ed.) (1996), *Vatican Council II: Constitutions, Decrees, Declarations* (Dublin: Dominican Publications).

Fulton, J. (1999), 'Young Adult Core Catholics', in Michael P. Hornsby-Smith (ed.), *Catholics in England 1950–2000: Historical and Sociological Perspectives* (London: Cassell), pp. 161–81.

Giddens, A. (1991), *Modernity and Self-Identity: Self and Society in the Late Modern Age* (Cambridge: Polity Press).

Gillett, H.M. (1957), *Shrines of Our Lady in England and Wales* (London: Samuel Walker).

Gilley, S. (1999), 'A Tradition and Culture Lost, to be Regained?' in M.P. Hornsby-Smith (ed.), *Catholics in England 1950–2000: Historical and Sociological Perspectives* (London: Cassell), pp. 29–45.

Harris, R. (1999), *Lourdes: Body and Spirit in a Secular Age* (London: Allen Lane/Penguin).
Hastings, A. (1991), *A History of English Christianity 1920–1990* (London: SCM Press, 3rd edn).
Hebblethwaite, M. (1991), 'Aspects of Church Life since the Council: Devotion', in Adrian Hastings (ed.), *Modern Catholicism: Vatican II and After* (London: SPCK), pp. 240–45.
Hickman, Mary J. (1999), 'The Religio-ethnic Identities of Teenagers of Irish Descent', in Michael P. Hornsby-Smith (ed.), *Catholics in England 1950–2000: Historical and Sociological Perspectives* (London: Cassell), pp. 182–98.
Hornsby-Smith, M.P. (1999), 'English Catholics at the New Millennium', in M.P. Hornsby-Smith (ed.), *Catholics in England 1950–2000: Historical and Sociological Perspectives* (London: Cassell), pp. 291–306.
—— (2004), 'The Changing Identity of Catholics in England', in S. Coleman and P. Collins (eds), *Religion, Identity and Change: Perspectives on Global Transformations* (Aldershot: Ashgate), pp. 42–56.
Jones, C., G. Wainwright, E. Yarnold SJ, and P. Bradshaw (eds) (1992), *The Study of Liturgy* (London: SPCK, rev. edn).
Matter, E.A. (2001), 'Apparitions of the Virgin Mary in the Late Twentieth Century: Apocalyptic, Representation, Politics', *Religion* 31: 125–53.
Maunder, C. (1991), 'Apparitions of the Virgin Mary in Modern European Roman Catholicism (from 1830)' (unpublished PhD thesis, available at the University of Leeds Library and British Library).
—— (2000), 'Apparitions in Late Twentieth Century Ireland – Visions and Reflections: Part I', *Maria* 1: 69–85.
—— (2003a) Apparitions in Late Twentieth Century Ireland – Visions and Reflections: Part II', *Maria* 3.2: 239–54.
—— (2003b), 'Popular Devotion in a New Age', *Priests and People* 17.5: 196–201.
McBrien, R. (1994), *Catholicism* (London: Geoffrey Chapman, 3rd edn).
McGrath, A.E. (1997), *An Introduction to Christianity* (Oxford: Blackwell).
McSweeney, B. (1980), *Roman Catholicism: The Search for Relevance* (Oxford: Basil Blackwell).
Mol, H. (1976), *Identity and the Sacred: a Sketch for a New Social-Scientific Theory of Religion* (Oxford: Blackwell).
Northcote, J.S. (1868), *Celebrated Sanctuaries of the Madonna* (London: Longman, Green & Co).
O'Leary, P. (1996), 'From the Cradle to the Grave: Popular Catholicism among the Irish in Wales', in P. O'Sullivan (ed.), *The Irish World Wide: History, Heritage and Identity. Vol. V: Religion and Identity* (London: Leicester University Press), pp. 183–95.
Paul VI (1974), *Marialis Cultus (To Honour Mary)* (London: Catholic Truth Society).
Pope, B.C. (1985), 'Immaculate and Powerful: The Marian Revival in the Nineteenth Century', in C.W. Atkinson, C.H. Buchanan and M.R. Miles (eds), *Immaculate and Powerful: The Feminine in Sacred Image and Social Reality* (Boston, MA: Beacon Press), pp. 173–99.
Rattue, J. (1995), *The Living Stream: Holy Wells in Historical Context* (Woodbridge: Boydell).
Riche, C. (2002), *The Lost Shrine of Liskeard* (London: Saint Austin).
Robertson, R. (2003), 'Antiglobal Religion', in Mark Juergensmeyer (ed.), *Global Religions: An Introduction* (Oxford: Oxford University Press), pp. 110–23.
Rowland, C. (ed.) (1999), *The Cambridge Companion to Liberation Theology* (Cambridge: Cambridge University Press).

Spretnak, C. (2004), *Missing Mary: the Queen of Heaven and Her Re-Emergence in the Modern Church* (London: Palgrave Macmillan).
Vail, A. (2004), *Shrines of Our Lady in England* (Leominster: Gracewing).
Waterton, E. (1879), *Pietas Mariana Britannica* (London: St Joseph's Library).

8

Moving Mountains: The Carmelite Community's Development of an Identity in York

Johan Bergström-Allen and Antony Lester

Introduction

The religious community within the Roman Catholic Church known today as the Carmelite Family emerged in the Holy Land sometime in the first decade of the thirteenth century when a group of Christian hermits living on Mount Carmel requested the Patriarch of Jerusalem approve a document outlining their way of life. Eight hundred years later, in 2007, the Patriarch's successor commemorated the giving of this *Carmelite Rule* at the Minster in the northern English city of York.

This chapter looks at how the identity of the Carmelite Family – a *community of communities* – transferred from mediaeval Palestine to modern-day York and beyond. It addresses how the Carmelite Family has developed a sense of corporate identity, and how it interacts with other communities in York today. The chapter begins by briefly outlining some major historical events in the Carmelite Family's global quest to construct an identity of 'self', before looking more discursively at its contemporary ministry in the city of York, and concluding with an overview of documentation regarding Carmelite community identity in the years following the Second Vatican Council.

The Foundations of Carmelite Identity in the *Rule of Saint Albert*

Much of Carmelite spirituality and heritage (often known simply as 'Carmel') is concerned with the building of communal identity.[1] Community is at the heart of Carmelite identity because communal living is where relationships are developed between people and also between people and God. 'Carmel' stands for the intimate encounter which people of faith maintain God brings about between the person and God in the midst of all that is most ordinary in life. Carmelite preoccupation with communal identity is witnessed to by the movement's foundational text, the *Way of Life* approved by Saint Albert Avogadro (d. 1215), Patriarch of Jerusalem. This document, one of the shortest such quasi-monastic texts of the period and papally sanctioned as a *Rule* in 1247, outlined the way that the hermits living by the Spring of Elijah on Mount Carmel were to live 'in allegiance to Jesus Christ' (ch. 2) by combining solitary meditation with communal living.[2] The whole purpose of the *Carmelite Rule* is to establish a paradigm of community living for men who were otherwise solitaries, a paradigm consciously modelled on the early Jerusalem community as described in *Acts of the Apostles*. Albert's first requirement is the election of a Prior from within the community (ch. 4) to whom the brothers must promise obedience. In matters regarding the community the *Rule* stresses the importance of consensus and collegiality and that the Prior's authority must follow the dictate of Christ that 'whoever wishes to be greater among you shall be your servant' (ch. 22). In return the brothers must hold the Prior in humble reverence and 'rather than thinking about him you are to look to Christ who set him as head over you' (ch. 23). The Prior's cell is to stand near the entrance to the community (ch. 9) for the purposes of protection and hospitality. The cells of the other brothers are to be allocated by the Prior and senior brothers (ch. 6) and in which each hermit should stay 'meditating day and night on the law of the Lord and being vigilant in prayers, unless otherwise lawfully occupied' (ch. 10). The Carmelite attitude towards property is communal: 'None of the brothers is to claim something as his own; everything is to be in common' (ch. 12). The community also has a duty of care for its brethren, since 'On Sundays . . . you shall discuss the welfare of the group' (ch. 15). The brothers are also to gather for corporate prayer, namely daily Eucharist (ch. 14) and the Divine Office (ch. 11). Eventually they did so in a chapel dedicated to the Virgin Mary, the ruins of which still stand on the mountain range of Carmel.

The Carmelite way of life as set out in the *Rule of Saint Albert* is one of contemplation, rooted in prayer, communal living and service. Consisting largely of quotations from Scripture, the *Rule* echoes the teaching of St Paul that each brother should give himself to work of some kind (ch. 20). Contemporary records inform us that part of this work included ministering to pilgrims passing by Mount Carmel, and we also know that the hermits celebrated the sacraments for and with the nearby community of Knights Templar (Barber 1994: 198). Since its earliest days, therefore, the Carmelite sense of corporate identity has spurred it to reach out to other communities. The significance of communal living does not lie simply in the hope that Carmelites can do more work as a group than they could as separate individuals; rather, living together is seen as responding to the mandate of Jesus that his followers should love one another as he has loved them (Jn 13:34; 15:12).

The end of the *Rule* speaks of *discretione que virtutum est moderatrix* (discernment the guide of the virtues). The notion of discernment, especially discovering the will of God, is key to Carmelite spirituality, which emphasizes that such listening and decision-making are best done in the context of a wise community. The Carmelite experience is that God's will is not usually manifested in apparitions or mystical phenomena; rather, the human discovers what God wants for him or her in very human ways, especially through contact with other persons who are manifestations of the presence of God. Living together as a community therefore provides – according to Carmelite belief – a witness to the presence of God in the world.

A Fractured Identity: The Carmelite Migration to Europe

Though the *Rule* hints towards the existence of strong intra-communal relations in the first Carmelite community, sadly the rapport between the Christian and Muslim communities was not so convivial in the Holy Land during the Middle Ages. By the 1230s the Carmelite hermits had begun to flee Mount Carmel. It is probable that some were former Crusaders, and they returned to Europe in the company of knights who gave them land for hermitages in Cyprus, Sicily, France and England, where the Carmelites arrived in 1242.[3]

Most religious orders take their identity from a founder such as Benedict, Francis or Dominic. In the case of the Carmelites, communal identity derived from a place. The break with their site of origin and dispersal across Europe caused the hermits to reassess their understanding of community. The situation in western Europe was not so conducive to the eremitical (hermit) way of life. Hence at a general chapter meeting held in 1247 at Aylesford in Kent the hermits decided to petition the Pope for a mitigation of Albert's *Rule*, granting them permission to make urban as well as rural settlements. The growing towns and cities of mediaeval Europe were the best places for the Carmelites to earn an income from alms-giving and to attract recruits into the novitiate. The hermits thus gradually changed from leading an eremitic lifestyle to that of the mendicant (begging) friars. Like the Dominican and Franciscan Orders, the Carmelites quickly perceived that there was a need in the centre of major towns across the continent for the service of 'religious' as teachers, preachers, confessors, administrators, and in a wide variety of public services. As a result the identity of the Order became increasingly clerical, with a growing hierarchy distinguishing the ordained from the un-ordained brothers.

This change towards the mendicant lifestyle and identity was not universally embraced within the Order. One of the earliest surviving documents regarding Carmelite identity after the *Rule* is a text written in the form of a letter by the Prior General (the Order's senior brother) Nicholas the Frenchman, in which he castigates his brethren for the lifestyle they have adopted in the cities. Entitled *Ignea Sagitta* (*The Flaming Arrow*)[4] the letter accuses the Carmelites of having lost their contemplative identity by taking up apostolates for which they are not qualified. According to Nicholas, by becoming city-dwellers the Carmelite sense of community has become deformed:

> What is this new Order that has appeared in the cities, tell me? Answer me – though you must surely blush as you do so – in what useful occupation are you engaged there? I will spare you the embarrassment of telling the truth, and will answer more truthfully than you would yourselves. Two by two you roam the streets of the city, from morning to night you scurry hither and thither; and your master is he who 'prowls like a roaring lion seeking someone to devour'. Thus, in you, to your utter disgrace, is this prophecy truly fulfilled: 'On every side the wicked prowl'. For your correction I must rebuke you. Let me draw back the cloak a little, and lay bare the true reason for these perambulations of yours,

> these rovings which are so frequent. The main reason for your wanderings is to visit not orphans but young women, not widows in their adversity but silly girls in dalliance, beguines, nuns, and highborn ladies. (Chapter 5)

Though perhaps written in 1271, *The Flaming Arrow* seems not to have circulated widely within the Carmelite Order until the early fifteenth century, possibly due to the death of its author shortly after composition. However, it tells us much about the struggle within some sections of Carmel regarding corporate identity and sense of direction, at a time when the wider church was also pondering the role of new religious orders; an issue which would come to a head three years later at the Second Council of Lyons in 1274. Despite its impassioned rhetoric *The Flaming Arrow* had no quantifiable impact upon the identity of the brethren at the time it was written, and the majority of Carmelites continued to regard themselves as 'contemplatives' as well as pastors. A more significant self-expression of collective Carmelite conformity from the period is a text known as the *Rubrica Prima*. This was the opening rubric of the *Constitutions* amplifying the *Rule of Saint Albert* drawn up by the Carmelites in a general chapter held in London in 1281:

> Since some young brothers in the Order do not know how to reply truthfully to those who wish to know how and in what way our Order had its beginning, we want to provide them with a written account of how to respond to such demands. We say that, on the evidence of trustworthy witnesses, that from the time of the prophets Elijah and Elisha, the holy fathers of both the Old and New Testaments have lived devotedly on Mount Carmel, true lovers of the solitude of that mountain for the contemplation of heavenly things. There, near the fountain of Saint Elijah, without any doubt, they lived praiseworthy lives, and their successors continually thereafter.[5]

The *Rubrica Prima* is the earliest known formulation of Carmelite identity linked to Elijah and Elisha, the Old Testament prophets associated with Mount Carmel.[6] Thus by the end of the thirteenth century, Carmelite characteristics were focused not only on a place but also upon a mythical affiliation with the saints associated with that place.

Consolidating Carmelite Identity in Mediaeval Europe

By professing to descend – at least spiritually – from the prophet Elijah and his followers, the Carmelites were able to claim the status of the oldest religious order in Christendom, predating even Christ himself. The Carmelite Order – whose full title was *The Brothers of the Blessed Virgin of Mount Carmel* – also claimed to enjoy a special kinship with Mary the Mother of God, in whose honour, its members claimed, the Order flourished.[7] These privileged relationships, Carmelites argued, gave their community pre-eminence amongst religious, an idiosyncrasy that did not endear them to other mendicants and monks, though such external opposition was itself a catalyst for bonding communal feeling. The arrival of Carmelites in western society was not universally welcomed by diocesan clergy either, who resented the fact that their parishioners were being ministered to by the 'Whitefriars'.[8] This nomenclature derived from their white cloaks, and the habit of the friars became another important distinguisher of corporate designation.

The outlandish claims from which Carmelite communal identity was forged were reinforced by a succession of papal decrees in favour of the Whitefriars, coupled with royal patronage and other benefactions. The Carmelites propagated their pretensions to antique identity in the *Constitutions* governing the Order; they defended their claims in major university debates (thanks to their growing identity as an academic as well as contemplative-pastoral order); and they disseminated their corporate image in works of 'history' such as *The Ten Books on the Way of Life and Great Deeds of the Carmelites* in which the fraternity was portrayed as descending from the 'brotherhood of prophets' mentioned in 2 Kings 2:3.[9] The Order's construction of a communal identity from legendary sources in the Middle Ages was a tactic both successful and self-defeating: the friars made grandiose claims to support the antiquity and prestige of their Order which simultaneously served to undermine the credibility of their communal identity.[10]

The Establishment and Destruction of Carmelite Identity in Pre-modern York

Regardless of the veracity of Carmelite claims in this period, a consistent and collective sense of identity helped the friars to spread rapidly. Within two hundred years of their arrival in Britain in 1242 the Order had approximately seventy-five communities of friars spread across England, Scotland, Wales and Ireland.[11]

The Carmelites came to York around the year 1250 and quickly established a community at the heart of one of England's most important civil and ecclesiastical centres. The first Carmelite friary in York was at the Horsefair, but this was later abandoned in favour of a more central site by the River Foss. The York community was a regional focus for Whitefriars, serving as the northern study house of the English Province. The Carmelites exercised a sacramental ministry to the local populace, and were deeply involved in civic affairs. Of particular interest is the role played by the York friars in extending Carmelite identity to incorporate local laity, particularly anchorites and members of city guilds, by providing hospitality, spiritual guidance and letters of confraternity granting honorary membership of the Order.[12]

Carmelites in York shared the interests and activities of their confreres in the wider Province. Such deeds helped to define the identity of the Order. For example, York Carmelites – like their brethren in nearby Doncaster – encouraged popular piety and pilgrimage.[13] They were also involved in the intellectual life of the city, and the Order as a whole was instrumental in policing the orthodox identity of the wider church by combating Lollardy.[14]

The communal identity of the Carmelites suffered the same fate as the other mendicant and monastic orders at the Reformation. After the suppression of the York friary in 1538, individual Carmelites continued to minister to the people of the city, but the community was disbanded.[15] It was in York Castle that the last known active Whitefriar of mediaeval England, George Rayner, was imprisoned and possibly died.[16]

The Renaissance Reinvention of Carmelite Identity

At the same time as Carmelite identity was being destroyed in York, elsewhere in Europe it was being reinvented and reinvigorated. An increasingly important feature of the Order's identity in the fifteenth and sixteenth centuries was the role of Carmelites who were not friars. Although these had been an important part of Carmelite life since the days of the Mount Carmel community, it was not until 1452 with the papal bull *Cum Nulla* that official recognition was given to Carmelite lay people, especially women. This document paved the way for communities of Carmelite nuns.[17]

The nuns played an important role in the reform movements that helped to refashion Carmelite communal identity. In the 1400s a number of reforms developed within the Order, such as the congregations of Mantua and Albi, which sought to reinvigorate Carmelite identity by addressing various aspects of community life.

Probably the greatest reformers and best-known exponents of Carmelite spirituality emerged in the mid-sixteenth century, namely Saint Teresa of Jesus (of Avila) and her companion Saint John of the Cross. These two Spanish Carmelites initiated a reform movement within the Carmelite Order known as the 'Teresian' or 'Discalced' (shoeless) observance. Their vision of religious life provoked a massive shift of self-designation within Carmel. Whilst other reform movements had remained within the wider Carmelite Order, an eventual split between the Carmelites and Discalced Carmelites was prompted by disputes between internal and external authorities (the Spanish crown, the Papacy, local priors provincial, the papal nuncio, the prior general, community visitators, priors of the reform, and others). As the direction and governance of the Carmelite Family splintered into two separate religious orders – the Carmelites (O.Carm.) and Discalced Carmelites (O.C.D.)[18] – the seeds were sown for centuries of animosity and divided opinions about the very nature of communal identity (as had previously happened in several other religious orders).

Through her reform Teresa had sought to maintain rather than fracture the integrity of the Carmelite Order. Looking to the early eremitical form of Carmelite life and the *Rule of Saint Albert*, she had encouraged Carmelites to radically rethink their communal identity in the context of the Counter-Reformation. She and John wrote a number of poetic and prose works on the nature of prayer and contemplative living which have been hugely influential in the realms of Christian self-knowledge and communal discernment, and which have indelibly changed the collective self-image of both Carmelites and Discalced Carmelites.[19]

Carmelite Community Identity Revived in York

Despite the split within the Carmelite Family in the sixteenth century, and the contemporary divisions within England between Catholics and Protestants, there were various attempts in the modern era to (re-)establish a presence in Britain by both the Carmelites and the Discalced Carmelites. The Carmelite Order finally returned to England in the early twentieth century.

At the start of the twenty-first century, York is something of a microcosm of the Carmelite Family, being home to at least four different expressions of Carmelite identity. The city witnessed the return of a Carmelite presence in 1955 with the arrival of Discalced Carmelite nuns at Thicket Priory near Thorganby.[20] The enclosed nuns were followed forty years later by the return of friars of the Carmelite Order who had been at the nearby retreat centre in Hazlewood Castle in Leeds Diocese for the previous twenty-six years.[21] Shortly after them the Corpus Christi Carmelites, a congregation of active sisters affiliated to the Carmelite Order, were established on Lawrence Street.[22] Finally, in 2006 a Carmelite Spirituality Group began meeting in York as a way of nurturing a community of lay people inspired by the Carmelite Family's spiritual patrimony. We turn now to address the contemporary witness and mission of these various Carmelite communities in York.

Carmelite Communities of Women in York Today

The longest-established Carmelite community in present-day York is the monastery of Discalced Carmelite nuns at Thicket Priory. Thanks to the impact of Saint Teresa it is the nuns who are the best-known contingent of the Carmelite Family, though one of the later to develop. Outside observers might consider that the nuns form the Carmelite community which has the least impact and interaction with other communities in the city and region, given the enclosed nature of the nuns' lifestyle. It is true that as a general rule the nuns do not leave their cloister, spending much of the day in prayer and manual labour. However, their relative isolation from the world has not prevented the community from playing an important if largely hidden role in York society, and for many people Thicket is the place where they engage with Christianity on a regular basis. It is the community's belief – and one backed-up by Roman Catholic tradition – that its life of prayer is not for the nuns' personal benefit but rather for the good of society at large. The dozen-or-so sisters contend that their presence is a constant witness to the values of the Christian Gospel, and to the opportunities and challenges of living together in imitation of the first Christian community.

The Discalced Carmelite nuns intend that their communities should reflect the size and lifestyle of a small family. Teresa of Jesus specified that in these communities 'all must be friends, all must be loved, all must be held dear, all must be helped'.[23] This is a highly attractive model of community life, and thus Thicket monastery attracts visitors from across the region and across denominational divides, giving it an important ecumenical role in the county.

The role in society of the Corpus Christi Carmelite community is perhaps more obvious to the casual observer than that of the nuns at Thicket, despite the small size of the sisterhood in York (three in 2006).[24] The main apostolates undertaken by the community are parish ministry, catechesis, prison chaplaincy and fundraising for a Carmelite mission in Liberia. The community at Lawrence Street reflects the international nature of Catholic religious life, bringing together sisters from England, North America and the Caribbean (where the Generalate of the congregation is located). This embodiment of cross-cultural living may be small in scale but undoubtedly impacts upon the consciousness of local parishioners in a city with a dominant Anglo-Saxon/Viking demographic.

The Community of Carmelite Friars in York Today

The community of Carmelite friars is perhaps the Carmelite Family group which most actively interacts with other communities in the city and district of York because of the diverse ministries of its members (four in 2006). The vocation of the friar is to be 'in the midst of the people' and to respond to the needs of society in each time and place. Hence there is practically no limit on the type of ministry in which friars might engage themselves.

Since its return to York in 1995 the main ministry of the friar community in York has been the chaplaincy (established 1964) at the University of York's campus in the village of Heslington. The community is resident in More House, the chaplaincy building owned by the Roman Catholic Diocese of Middlesbrough. Two friars from the More House community work as full-time chaplains with Anglican and Methodist colleagues bound together by an ecumenical covenant established between the denominations in 1998.[25] The full-time staff work closely with a wider network of part-time chaplains representing different Christian churches and other faiths. The chaplaincy is therefore itself an ecumenical community with significant Carmelite input, not only through the chaplain himself but also through Carmelite representation on the Chaplaincy Support Group. Anecdotal evidence suggests that the fact that the Roman Catholic chaplain is a member of a religious community and an ecumenical partnership is significant to the students he ministers to. Most students seem to find some affinity with the chaplain in that he – like them – lives with a community of people that he has not 'chosen' but with whom he throws in his lot. A vocations promotion booklet produced by the British Province of Carmelites in the early 1990s humorously captures the possible tensions and opportunities such a community experience affords:

> It has been said that whenever you get two Carmelites together, you will get at least three strongly held positions on even the simplest of matters! Should you have a cup of tea? What, and exploit the plantation workers of Sri Lanka! But this tea is not from a multi-national. Have you considered the health risk from addictive drugs like caffeine? I suppose you want coffee thus demonstrating your social superiority. Strong or weak, warm the pot or not, tea bags or tea leaves? For heaven's sake, it is only tea! Imagine then the anguish over values which touch you deeply.[26]

There are more affinities between the joys and pressures of living communally as students and as religious than some might think! As brothers the friars are expected to grow in the communal spirit of religious life, sharing all things in common, being accountable for community goods, responsible for the growth and spirit of community life. The Carmelite friar is expected to give of himself and share his talents by participating in the various aspects of community living such as prayer, study, house jobs and relaxation together. Communal sharing involves even the very core of one's personality. This involves learning to maintain a healthy balance of prayer, study, work and being with the community. This 'holistic' way of life is a valuable witness to the students at the universities where Carmelites are present.

As well as working ecumenically, an important aspect of the university chaplaincy's ministry in York has been interfaith dialogue. In particular, the chaplaincy has supported the interaction of Christian, Jewish and Muslim students. This has taken place at every level of university life, from football matches played between different religious societies on campus, to organizing the annual Heslington Lecture on religion in the modern world and negotiating with the university authorities on behalf of Muslim students seeking a Prayer Room during Ramadan (now a permanent venue for Islamic prayer). In this atmosphere of interfaith cooperation, nurtured by Carmelites, the university's Jewish Society regularly celebrated Purim in More House, and invited Catholics to events in their own Hillel House. The Carmelite motivation for interfaith projects comes partially from the fact that the founding inspiration of Carmel, the prophet Elijah, is revered by the three great Abrahamic and monotheistic faiths: Judaism, Christianity and Islam.[27]

As well as engaging with other faiths, the Carmelite community in More House has found it necessary to reach out to groups that were initially hostile to it. Any community which preaches and indeed embodies the values of a particular faith-system will come under scrutiny and criticism from those who feel threatened by those values. When the Carmelite friar community initially moved to More House there was considerable opposition from a small minority of Evangelical Christians on the university campus. This is not surprising given that some sections of Protestantism from before the time of Wycliffe have been opposed to monastic and para-monastic ways of life. Some members of the University of York Christian Union refused to enter the Catholic chaplaincy after the arrival of a permanent religious community (previous chaplains had either been solitary occupants or non-resident, and until 1995 More House had predominantly housed students). The reaction of the chaplain and community was to make it clear that all were welcome in the chaplaincy, regardless of their theological background. Through small but significant projects which built links between the communities on a 'human' rather than theological level (such as film-showings and sports) the barriers began to be lowered. Eventually the Christian Union Alpha (Christian introduction) Course began meeting in More House. Another religious grouping which did not expect support from the Carmelite community was the university Pagan Society, but after conversation the facilities of More House were made available for the Pagans' summer picnic. Likewise the Carmelite community was initially greeted with suspicion by some of the lesbian, gay, bisexual and transgender (LGBT) community on the university campus who feared that the friars would not minister to those of non-heterosexual orientation. Again, the policy of the community was to be an open house for all, and York Pride (the university society for the LGBT community) began to hold events at the chaplaincy.

Throughout the last decade of the second millennium the open-door policy of More House grew, with its facilities available to students, staff and local residents. Today it is also used by counselling, therapy and peer-support groups from outside the university. In an age when religion is seen as a potential source of extremism and violence or at least small-mindedness, the Carmelite community has sought – with the blessing of the Bishop of Middlesbrough – to use More House as a venue for countering narrow ideologies by introducing the Catholic Student Society (CASSOC) to a wide range of speakers who both support and challenge traditional Catholicism. In the years between 1995–2005 over a hundred speakers from both within and outside the university have addressed students on topics as diverse as how to read the Bible, economic development, Islamic law, sacramental theology, Orthodox Christianity, pacifism, homelessness, apparitions of the Virgin Mary, schizophrenia, the United Reform Church, Belgian beer, the rosary, missionary activity, contraception, care for the elderly, local history, medical ethics, journalism, parliamentary lobbying and so on.

When confronted by churchgoers who disapprove of offering hospitality to groups they deem to be at odds with Christian values, the Carmelite community's explanation has been that their tradition encourages dialogue and listening in the modern world. Crucial to the Carmelite sense of self, both individual and corporate, is a notion which is given the Latin title of *vacare Deo*. Meaning 'space for' or 'openness to' God, *vacare Deo* describes an attitude of heart through which the Carmelite seeks to be open to the voice and presence of God in the most unlikely circumstances, and through even the most socially ostracized people.[28]

Carmelites regard such openness and prayer as the glue which holds a community together. The Carmelite fraternity in More House offers its visitors an experience of prayer in the Carmelite tradition, with the Divine Office and Eucharist prayed there daily. Additionally the Carmelites in the chaplaincy have helped develop a strong spiritual programme for students and staff. As well as organizing (in conjunction with student societies) a full programme of talks, social events, Christian initiation classes, retreats, and so on, the Carmelite chaplains have been involved in the establishment of The Quiet Place on campus. This is a building renovated by the Society of Friends (Quakers) and administered by the chaplaincy for any person seeking a place for silent reflection.

In keeping with the *Rule of Saint Albert*, the Carmelite way of life emphasizes active service as well as prayer and silent reflection. To this end the Carmelite chaplains have encouraged students to become involved in community social action projects both on and off campus. This has involved students in visiting patients at the nearby Retreat Hospital, and becoming involved in fundraising for justice and peace projects. Being part of a worldwide 'community of communities'[29] (a term employed in the 2002 *Acts of the Twelfth Provincial Chapter of the British Province of Carmelites*) means that the Carmelites in York are themselves supportive of wider Carmelite social efforts, including the work of the Carmelite Non-Governmental Organization (NGO) at the United Nations.

The first community of Carmelites in More House consisted of five friars. Since then there has been the usual coming-and-going of individual brothers which is typical of modern mendicant life, and apart from the university chaplaincy the ministries undertaken by the community have varied with the talents and interests of the men living in the friary, and the needs of the local church. The apostolates have included retreat-ministry, school chaplaincy (All Saints School), prison chaplaincy (HMP Full Sutton), hospital chaplaincy (York District Hospital) and ministering to the nuns at Thicket Priory. Administration is another apostolate undertaken by the community, and since 2002 the friary at More House has hosted the office of the Prior Provincial of the British Province of Carmelites, which numbers some forty friars in six communities.

In 2003 a new Carmelite ministry began in More House alongside that of the friars, when a former student of the University of York was employed in the newly formed Carmelite Projects and Publications Office. The main apostolate of this office is the printing of devotional and academic books on the history and spirituality of the Carmelite Family, as well as promoting Carmelite involvement in cultural, heritage and faith-related projects. A major aspect of the Office's work is developing communication within the Province, communication being an essential dynamic in building community.[30] The internal sense of community within the Carmelite Family in Britain is enhanced by communication projects such as regional and national gatherings, chapters, formation programmes, forum discussion days, vision statements, websites, newsletters, bulletins and so on. Communicating the values of the Carmelite Family is a shared responsibility and a challenge in a society sometimes hostile to organized religion. This is where the establishment of the Carmelite Projects and Publications Office is significant since its work enhances not only the Carmelite community's appreciation of its own identity but also extends – through a model of collaborative ministry – the Carmelite Family's involvement in the activities of the citizens of York.

Carmelite Involvement in the Ecclesiastical and Civil Communities of Present-day York

Together the community of Carmelite friars and its Projects and Publications Office have been involved in a number of ecumenical projects in addition to those at the University of York. One such example is the Carmelite community's collaboration in *The Holy Trinity Project*. In 2003 the Archdeacon of York invited the Carmelites to partake in discussions about the development of Holy Trinity Priory Church on Micklegate. Since the Priory Church was a former monastic (Benedictine) building, the Archdeacon wondered whether it could be used as an ecumenical centre for explaining and promoting religious community life, whilst still functioning as a parish church. This project led to a collaboration between the parish community of Holy Trinity, the various communities of the Carmelite Family in York, and other religious communities in the vicinity including the Congregation of Jesus at the Bar Convent, the Community of the Resurrection at Mirfield, the Benedictines at Ampleforth Abbey and the Order of the Holy Paraclete at Whitby. In 2004–2005 these communities put on a programme of events to facilitate contact between religious communities and members of the public. A series of encounter days entitled *Meet the Monks* took place in the Priory Church, and members of religious communities animated a series of *Lectio Divina* prayer sessions over a three-month period.[31] In consultation with the Parochial Church Council, the religious communities in The Holy Trinity Project decided to erect a display within the Priory Church explaining the history, social contribution and contemporary relevance of community religious life, and with significant backing from the Heritage Lottery Fund the *Monks of Micklegate* exhibition was launched in 2007.

Another fruitful ecumenical collaboration involving the Carmelite community has been the establishment of the Chair in Theology and Public Life at York St John University, jointly sponsored by the British Province of Carmelites, the York Institute for Community Theology and the Methodist Church. In conjunction with this, a series of public talks, the *Ebor Lectures on Theology and Public Life*, began in 2006 with the collaboration of the Carmelites, York St John University, the York Institute for Community Theology, the Churches Regional Commission for Yorkshire and the Humber, and York Minster. The Carmelites' interaction with the latter has been particularly fruitful, with a succession of Carmelite events held at the Minster, including chaplaincy celebrations of the Eucharist, major liturgies marking Carmelite anniversaries (in 2003 and 2007) and the sharing of various resources between the Carmelite Projects and Publications Office and the Minster Collections (particularly the Library). The Carmelites and the Minster have also been partners in supporting the *Christianity and Culture* project operated from St John's Theological College in Nottingham and the University of York's Centre for Medieval Studies. By collaborating with a diverse array of civil and ecclesiastical institutions the Carmelite Family has sought to involve itself in a new way in the life and well-being of York's citizens.

The interaction between the Carmelite communities and the people of York and Yorkshire developed further in 2006 with the advent of a Carmelite Spirituality Group in the city. For many people the traditions and insights of a religious community are simultaneously attractive and dauntingly 'specialized', and the purpose of the Spirituality Group was to allow members of the general public to learn about and share something of the Carmelite perspective on the Christian story. Each month the Group (which numbered some twenty people at the close of its first year) meets to discuss an aspect of the Carmelite charism, to pray together using the Bible, and to share time socially as a community. The meetings bring together a variety of people from across and beyond the Carmelite Family: friars, nuns, sisters and lay people. These people of different ages, sexes and social backgrounds all draw inspiration in some way from the

Rule of Saint Albert and subsequent Carmelite writings and figures. The Group has also deepened the already strong bonds between the different Carmelite communities in York: the nuns, the sisters, the friars and lay Carmelites.

Carmelite Identity in Documents Following Vatican II

Having looked at the various ways in which Carmelites form communities in York, and the manner in which those interact with other communities, it is worth reviewing the theories and beliefs which underpin Carmelite communal identity globally, as expressed in recent documents of the Carmelite Family. Of course no documentation will ever adequately express the experience of living in a religious community, but it can give some insight into the motivations.

The Second Vatican Council (1962–65) had massive implications for the Christian – and indeed Carmelite – understanding of community.[32] It encouraged the faithful to regard the Church not as an exclusive club at variance with the modern world, but rather sought to engage with contemporary hopes and concerns in the modern world. Theologians such as Karl Rahner, Yves Conger and Joseph Ratzinger (now Pope Benedict XVI) sought to integrate Christian dogma with the common experience of humanity so as to proclaim the Gospel in a relevant and engaging way. To do this the Council looked to the timeless wisdom of Scripture and the early Church Fathers and Mothers. In the 1965 decree *Perfectae Caritatis*, religious orders were similarly asked to return to the sources of their wisdom and to share them with the modern world in a reinvigorated way.[33] This invitation led institutions of religious life, including the Carmelite and Discalced Carmelite Orders, to engage ever more deeply in an academic and pastoral revisiting of their origins. In such institutions *Constitutions* seek to interpret and articulate for the present day the community's founding spirit. The general thrust of Vatican II therefore led to the revision of legislation and communal self-expression across the Carmelite Family.

The *Constitutions* of the Discalced Carmelite nuns, approved by the Apostolic See in 1991, looked back to venerable sources – primarily the Bible, the *Rule of Saint Albert* and the example of Saint Teresa – for an authentic vision of enclosed community life:

> Community life, as set forth in the *Rule of Carmel* and renewed by Saint Teresa, follows the example of the primitive Church. It requires that the sisters who have been called to form the little 'College of Christ' should help one another advance toward sanctity. Their supreme law must be the love which the Master enjoined on his disciples, the very love which he proved in giving his life for us (cf. John 15:12–13). When this mutual love is put into practice, it is a proof of the authenticity of their life of prayer. It ensures for them the presence of the Lord in the midst of the community. It maintains peace and concord. This love should make every monastery an example of mutual concern, a witness to unity, a sign of universal reconciliation in Christ, and a beacon of the Gospel of justice and peace.[34]

Twenty years earlier, in 1971, the Carmelite friars also published new *Constitutions* following the promptings of the Second Vatican Council. It became clear, in revising the *Constitutions*, that the Carmelite vision of community shares much with that of other religious institutions and congregations within Roman Catholic Christianity, yet it also articulated in a distinctive way how the *charism* of the Carmelites (the Order's unique gift from God for the benefit of the church and the world) developed in particular circumstances and how it is expressed in singular ways.

Another factor which influenced Carmelite understanding of community following the Council was the regular meetings of friars known as the Councils of Provinces which took place during the six-year intervals between General Chapters.[35] According to a recent observer:

> The topic which seems to have occupied the greater part of all the meetings was that of brotherhood and fraternity. An important time were the years from 1968 to the first Council of Provinces [1972] in which fraternity was brought to the forefront of people's thinking following the Conference of Latin American Bishops which met in 1968 at Medellín. At this council liberation theology was given its first public airing, and one of the key points of this school of thought was the notion of universal brotherhood and standing in solidarity with our fellow men and women. This time also saw the demonstrations and rallies in the United States against the war in Vietnam. Here again brotherhood and solidarity were key points. For this reason brotherhood and fraternity became a very important issue for the Order and the focus of so many of the Councils of Provinces.[36]

The titles of these Carmelite meetings reveal this 'horizontal' theological shift, that is to say a focus on communal relationships between Carmelites and how this impacts on the 'vertical theology' of relating to God and God's kingdom:

- First Council of Provinces – Spain (1972): 'Pledged to the service of brotherhood'
- Third Council of Provinces – Ireland (1975): 'In the midst of the people'
- Sixth Council of Provinces – The Netherlands (1981): 'Growing in brotherhood'
- Ninth Council of Provinces – Portugal (1985): 'Our international dimension'
- Tenth Council of Provinces – The Philippines (1987): 'Justice and peace'
- Eleventh Council of Provinces – Ireland (1988): 'Brotherhood'
- Thirteenth Council of Provinces – France (1994): 'The Carmelite Family'

The choice of venues for these Councils of Provinces also betrays a shift in Carmelite thinking post-Vatican II from regarding Rome as the focus of Catholic and hence Carmelite community towards a broader awareness of the Church as an international reality.

The deliberations of the Councils of Provinces, coupled with developments within the Church and the Order following the Second Vatican Council (such as the increased role of the laity, the growing ties with the Discalced Carmelites, and the promulgation of a new *Code of Canon Law* in 1983) required the 1971 *Constitutions* to be revised yet further. The result was the approval of new *Constitutions* at the 1995 General Chapter of the Order.[37] The opening paragraphs of the first section (The Gift and Charism of the Carmelite Order and its Basic Characteristics) place community at the heart of Carmel's mission:

> Through Jesus Christ, Son of the Father and 'firstborn of all creation', we live in union with God and with our neighbours in a new way . . . we seek to live together in mutual service of one another and of all people. In this way, we co-operate in God's plan to gather all men and women into one Holy People. (Part 1, §1 and 2)

The 1995 *Constitutions* go further in explicitly mentioning 'community' as one of the three primary features of the Carmelite charism, alongside prayer and service. The document addresses both the community of the Carmelite fraternity and the community of the people in which the Order is called to serve:

> Carmelites live their life of allegiance to Christ through a commitment to seek the face of the living God (the contemplative dimension of life), through fraternity, and through service (*diakonia*) in the midst of the people. The spiritual tradition of the Order has stressed that these three fundamental elements of the charism are not distinct and unrelated values but closely interwoven. (Part 1, §14 and 15)

The Carmelite attitude towards community, concretized in the 1995 *Constitutions*, is rooted in the Order's understanding of the 'contemplative attitude' at the heart of Carmelite life:

> A contemplative attitude towards the world around us allows us to discover the presence of God in the events of ordinary daily life and especially to see him in our brothers and sisters. Thus we are led to appreciate the mystery of those with whom we share our lives. Our *Rule* requires us to be essentially 'brothers' and reminds us that the quality of interpersonal relationships within the Carmelite community needs to be constantly developed and enhanced, following the inspiring example of the first community in Jerusalem. For us to be brothers means to grow in communion and in unity, overcoming privileges and distinctions, in a spirit of participation and co-responsibility, in sharing material possessions, a common programme of life, and personal charisms; to be brothers also means to care for one another's spiritual and psychological well-being, through walking in the way of dialogue and reconciliation. (Part 1, §19)

The Carmelite sense of community – according to the *Constitutions* – is rooted in the sense of belonging to a wider community, that of the praying people of God:

> These fraternal values find expression and nourishment in the Word, in the Eucharist, and in prayer . . . Every day, if possible, the brothers are called, from solitude and from their apostolic work, to the Eucharist – source and culmination of their lives – so that, gathered together around the Lord's table, they may be 'united, heart and soul', living true, fraternal *koinonia* in unselfishness, in mutual service, in faithfulness to a common goal and in a spirit of reconciliation inspired by Christ's love. (Part 1, §20)

The second section of the friars' *Constitutions* – entitled 'Our Life Together' – elaborates on how the communal dimension of the Carmelite vocation impinges on every aspect of life, addressing such topics as 'life in community', 'evangelical counsels and vows', 'apostolic mission', 'the local church' and 'promotion of justice and peace'.[38]

The Notion of *Carmelite Family*

Particularly important to the Carmelite sense of communal identity since Vatican II is the notion of 'family'. An almost unparalleled feature amongst religious congregations in the Roman Catholic Church is the Carmelite Order's sense of extended membership, expressed in the 1995 *Constitutions*:

> The many and various embodiments of the Carmelite charism are for us a source of joy; they confirm the rich and creative fruitfulness of our charism, lived under the inspiration of the Holy Spirit – a fruitfulness to be welcomed with gratitude and discernment. All individuals and groups, whether institutional or not, which draw their inspiration from the *Rule of Saint Albert*, from its tradition and from the values expressed in Carmelite spirituality, constitute the Carmelite Family within the Church today. This Family includes ourselves and our brothers of the Teresian Reform; the women religious of both branches; affiliated religious congregations; the Third Orders Secular; secular institutes; individuals affiliated with the Order through the sacred scapular; and those who by whatever title or bond are affiliated with the Order; those movements which, though juridically not part of the Order, seek inspiration and support from its spirituality; and any man or woman who is drawn to the values of Carmel. (1995 *Constitutions*, §28)

This wide-embracing sense of collective identity did not emerge overnight; it required community self-reflection and dialogue between different branches of the Carmelite Family for centuries of division to be overcome, but this ongoing process is itself a powerful witness to the possibility of reconciliation in the wider human family. Despite the inevitable pain engendered by the split between the Carmelites and Discalced Carmelites, the partition is today regarded as having prompted creative exploration into the very nature of what it is to be a community. Increasing collaboration between the two orders – such as the joint meetings between the governing councils of both traditions at international and provincial levels – has also helped further the collective understanding of Carmelite identity.[39] The question of communal identity is continually revisited as new movements develop within the Carmelite Family (such as the Carmelites of Mary Immaculate in India).

The term Carmelite Family came into common usage in the last quarter of the twentieth century, particularly promoted by the Prior General (1983–95) John Malley.[40] By using this nomenclature the various diverse expressions of Carmel throughout the world recognize that Carmelite identity is not something to be possessed in a selfish and exclusive manner. Rather, the Order accepts that, in the words of its ninety-fourth Prior General:

> A charism is a gift of God to the Church for the world. Since no one can exhaust the riches of Christ who is the perfect image of God (2 Corinthians 4:4) each of the different charisms which exist within the Church express some aspect of Christ's mission to proclaim the Good News and through his death and resurrection to reconcile the whole of humanity to God. The Carmelite charism does not belong to the Carmelite Family; we are the stewards and we have the sacred duty to pass it on to future generations and to share it with the people among whom we live.[41]

It is this desire to share Carmelite identity with others, as well as recognition of it outside formal bonds, that has led the Carmelite Family to share its message and spirituality – including its vision of community life – with lay people from the earliest days right up to the formation of spirituality groups in the present.[42]

One such community, the York Carmelite Spirituality Group, consists largely of lay people who have committed to the Carmelite way of life by making profession as members of the so-called 'Third Order Secular'. The 2003 *Rule for the Third Order of Carmelites*,[43] which functions in a way similar to the *Constitutions* of religious, realizes that most lay people already live in some form of community in which they are asked to share the Carmelite vision:

> Lay Carmelites can create community in various ways: in their own families, where the domestic church is to be found; in their local parish, where they worship God with their fellow parishioners and take a full part in the community activities; in their lay Carmelite community in which they find support for the spiritual journey; in their workplace and where they live. (§42)

The document also regards communal living as a witness to the kingdom of heaven which is to be built on earth:

> Every lay Carmelite is like a spark of love thrown into the forest of life: they must be able to enflame anyone who approaches them. Family life,

> the workplace, professional and Church areas where lay Carmelites are found will all receive from them some warmth from their contemplative hearts which can see the image of God in others. The lay Carmelite community becomes a centre for life which is authentically human because it is authentically Christian. From the experience of recognizing each other as brothers and sisters comes the need to involve others in that fascinating human and divine undertaking which is the construction of God's Kingdom. (§44)

Paradigms for Communal Identity in the Carmelite Tradition

In its *Constitutions* and developing tradition the Carmelite Family upholds particular models for building fraternity. The primary influence is the Christian understanding of God's own self, the Trinity of three persons in one God. The relationships between Father, Son and Holy Spirit show Carmelites how communal relationships founded on love allow for both unity and diversity: 'the Holy Trinity, source and model of the Church, is also the source and model of our life as brothers' (1995 *Constitutions*, §29). Amongst the many Carmelite saints whose lives are upheld as examples in the arena of building community, first place is always accorded to Elijah and the Blessed Virgin Mary. According to the 1995 *Constitutions* Elijah was the prophet who 'became involved in the lives of the people . . . who was in solidarity with the poor and the forgotten' (§26). In Mary the Carmelites find solidarity with a woman who was immersed in the community of her son's followers and beyond, 'walking with the disciples, sharing their demanding and wearisome journey – a journey which required, above all, fraternal love and mutual service . . . She is the woman who built relationships not only within the inner circle of Jesus' disciples, but beyond that, with the people: with Elizabeth, with the bride and bridegroom in Cana, with the other women, and with Jesus' "brothers"' (§27).

Another important model for fashioning the Carmelite community is the example of the early Christian community in Jerusalem which came together for prayer and mutual support, as described in the Acts of the Apostles. According to the latest Carmelite *Constitutions* this is the prototype for all Christian communities, and its spirit is reflected in the *Rule of Saint Albert*:

> Our *Rule* requires us to be essentially 'brothers', and reminds us that the quality of interpersonal relationships within the Carmelite community needs to be constantly developed and enhanced, following the inspiring example of the first community in Jerusalem . . . Fraternal life modelled on the Jerusalem community is an incarnation of God's gratuitous love, internalized through an ongoing process by which we empty ourselves of all egocentricity – which can affect groups as much as individuals – as we move towards authentic centering in God. (1995 *Constitutions*, §19 and 30; see also §8)

Looking to the early Jerusalem church as a model of building community speaks to Carmelites not only of the Family's origins in the Holy Land but also has an eschatological dimension.

Carmelite Identity in the Future

It is this question of looking to the future whilst being faithful to its past that exercises the Carmelite Family today, as it has done in every age. Further research – both theoretical and empirical – on the Carmelite sense of communal identity is needed from a variety of approaches, including sociology, anthropology, theology, psychology, history, gender and cultural studies.[44]

In many parts of Carmel new forms of community are evolving. In the Netherlands gender barriers are breaking down as Carmelite men and women experiment with shared living. In Italy the barriers between 'religious' and 'lay people' are becoming increasingly blurred as multigenerational communities are assembled from the ranks of friars and lay Carmelite families. In York different expressions of the Carmelite Family interact with each other and with the surrounding society. New expressions of Carmelite community are progressing around the globe and reveal an openness among many (though not all) Carmelites to evolving new models of living, praying and serving together. Despite the criticism of Nicholas the Frenchman in the thirteenth century the community of communities that is Carmel has adapted remarkably to the needs of the Church and the world in the modern and post-modern era. The mountain has been moved, and it keeps on moving.

Notes

1 For an introduction to Carmelite spirituality see: Welch (1996); Slattery (2000) [1991]; McGinn (2000: 25–50); Egan (1987: 50–62); McGreal (1999); Louth (2003 [1991]: 84-103); Obbard (1999); Paul-Marie of the Cross (1997); Chalmers (1999; 2001).

2 The Latin text is printed in Clarke and Edwards (1973). A translation is available online at: http://www.ocarm.org/. The translation quoted in this chapter is that of Christopher O'Donnell from Griffin (2004), and chapter numbering follows that agreed by the Superiors General of the Carmelite and Discalced Carmelite Orders in 1999. Recent commentaries on the *Rule* include: Cicconetti (1984); Mulhall (1989); Waaijman (1999; 2000).

3 On the historical development of the Carmelites in Europe, see Smet (1988); Copsey (2004); Andrews (2006); Lawrence (1994).

4 The original Latin text is edited by Staring (1962: 237–307). The translation by Bede Edwards has been included in the forthcoming collection of *Early Carmelite Documents* edited by Richard Copsey. On the circulation and impact of the text, see Copsey, *The Ignea Sagitta* and its readership: a re-evaluation (2004: 17–28).

5 Translated by Richard Copsey from Saggi (1950: 203–45).

6 As documented in the Bible's *Books of the Kings*.

7 On Carmelite devotion to Mary see Boaga (2001) and (2000).

8 For an illustration of the antagonism see Greatrex (1999: 69–73).

9 On the early *Constitutions* see Copsey (forthcoming). On the famous debate regarding Carmelite claims at the University of Cambridge in 1375 see Clark (1992). On *The Ten Books* (better known as *The Institution of the First Monks*) by Felip Ribot, see the translation by Copsey (Ribot 2005).

10 On this theme see: Jotischky (2002) and Copsey (2004: 1–15).

11 On the growth and dispersal of the Order see the articles by Keith Egan in Fitzgerald-Lombard (1992).

12 For further information on the mediaeval friary see Bergström-Allen, J. (2005 and forthcoming); Dobson (1984: 109–122).

13 On the Carmelite shrine at Doncaster, recently revived, see the chapter in this volume by Chris Maunder, and Whitman and Bergström-Allen (2005: 21–25).
14 On the Carmelites and Lollardy see Bergström-Allen and Copsey (forthcoming).
15 On the suppression and subsequent activities of the York friars see Cross (forthcoming).
16 See Alban (1999: 128-37), available online at: http://www.carmelite.org/chronology/rayner.htm.
17 For a brief history of the nuns see Smet (1986).
18 To distinguish it from the Discalced or Teresian Carmelite Order, the Carmelite Order has sometimes been known as the 'calced', 'mitigated' or 'ancient' observance; however, since these titles are only applied retrospectively they are not widely used within the Order itself.
19 For further information on Teresa and John see: Teresa of Jesus (1976–85); Williams (1991); John of the Cross (1991); Matthew (1995); Kavanaugh (1999).
20 On the establishment of the Carmelite nuns at Thicket, see Litchfield (1997).
21 On the re-establishment of the Carmelite friars in England, particularly Aylesford Priory, see Fielding (1968).
22 On the history of the Corpus Christi Carmelites, see (1990) [1944].
23 Teresa of Jesus (2000: 67).
24 There are very few written records in the public domain regarding the establishment of the friar community in York in the 1990s. Information in this section of the article is drawn from personal reminiscences and interviews with members of the community since its arrival, as well as the brief summaries of communal activities in the British Province's quarterly *Bulletin*. Some insight into Carmelite communal life in York is also offered by the interviews with friars in various issues of *Christis*, the Christian magazine of the University of York. After the usual period of reservation elapses, historians in the future may find useful material in the Provincial Archives of the Order such as the reports from the house in preparation for Provincial Chapters.
25 http://www.york.ac.uk/univ/chap/covenant.html
26 Grady (1993).
27 On the Carmelite Family's relationship with the prophet Elijah, see Ackerman (2003).
28 On *vacare Deo* and related Carmelite images associated with contemplation, see the friars' formation document (Carmelite General Curia 2000), *Ratio Institutionis Vitæ Carmelitanæ*, §27, available online at http:// www.carmelite.org/heart.htm.
29 A term employed in the *Acts of the Twelfth Provincial Chapter of the British Province of Carmelites*, Aylesford 2002. The 'Province Vision' is of 'a community of praying communities' (p. 33).
30 On the importance of communication for building Carmelite identity see Lucas (2006a: 313–21); Davis (2002).
31 *The Holy Trinity Project*'s early activities were reported in: *Building Faith in our Future: A Statement on Behalf of the Church of England by the Church Heritage Forum* (London: Church House Publishing, 2004), p. 42; 'Focus on Religious Life', York's *Evening Press*, 27 May 2004, p. 14.
32 There are many translations and commentaries on the Council documents, which are available online at http://www.vatican.va/. For the effect of the Council on religious communities see the entry on 'Religious Life' in a theological encyclopaedia of the Church edited by a Carmelite, Christopher O'Donnell (1996: 406–409).
33 *Perfectae Caritatis* (Decree on the Adaptation and Renewal of Religious Life), proclaimed by Pope Paul VI on 28 October 1965. See also the post-Conciliar Apostolic Exhortation on the Renewal of Religious Life, *Evangelica testificatio*.
34 Discalced Carmelite Generalate (1991, §87).
35 For the proceedings of some of these Councils of Provinces see Carmelite Order (1984).

36 Breen (2006), http://www.cibi.ie.
37 Carmelite Order (1995). Part I is available online at: http://www.carmelite.org/heart.htm. On the development of the *Constitutions* see also O'Donnell (1997: 61–71).
38 For a further reflection on these themes, see the text written by the Carmelite Community of Pozzo di Gotto (1999).
39 See Malley, Maccise and Chalmers (2003).
40 See Carmelite Order (1994); Malley (2004: 186–98; 2006: 63–78).
41 Chalmers (2001: 2).
42 For an analysis of Carmelite notions of community from a lay perspective see Lucas (2006b: 3–19). For a history of the Third Order Secular, see Motta-Navarro (1960).
43 Carmelite Order (2003). Available online at: http://www.ocarm.org/eng/articles/rtoc-eng.htm.
44 Carmelites are pioneering methodologies for the systematic study of spirituality and communal religious life; see, for example, the work of Waaijman (2002; 2005: 169–83). One of the difficulties facing researchers of Carmelite history is access to relevant publications. It is worth noting that some of the Carmelite libraries and archives in Britain and Ireland are substantial and very accommodating to scholars, particularly the priories at Aylesford in Kent, and Gort Muire in Dublin.

References

Ackerman, J. (2003), *Elijah: Prophet of Carmel* (Washington DC: ICS Publications).

Alban, K.J. (1999), 'George Rayner – An Elizabethan Carmelite', *Carmelus* 46: 128–37.

Andrews, F. (2006), *The Other Friars: The Carmelite, Augustinian, Sack and Pied Friars in the Middle Ages* (Woodbridge: The Boydell Press).

Barber, M. (1994), *The New Knighthood: A History of the Order of the Temple* (Cambridge: Cambridge University Press).

Bergström-Allen, J. (2005), 'The Whitefriars Return to Carmel', in L. Herbert McAvoy and M. Hughes-Edwards (eds), *Anchorites, Wombs and Tombs: Intersections of Gender and Enclosure in the Middle Ages* (Cardiff: University of Wales Press), pp. 77–91.

—— (forthcoming) 'Carmelites and Lay Piety in Medieval York Prior to the Papal Bull *Cum Nulla*', in *Carmel in Britain 5* (Faversham: Saint Albert's Press).

Bergström-Allen, J., and Copsey, R. (eds) (forthcoming), *Carmel in Britain 4: Thomas Netter of Walden – Carmelite, Diplomat and Theologian (c. 1372–1430)* (Faversham: Saint Albert's Press).

Boaga, E. (2000), *Con Maria sulle vie di Dio: Antologia della marianità Carmelitana* (Rome: Edizioni Carmelitane).

—— (2001), *Lady of the Place: Mary in the History and in the Life of Carmel* (Rome: Edizioni Carmelitane).

Breen, P. J. (2006), *The Order of Carmelites: Charism in the Twentieth Century*, Unit 3 of the *Adult Education Diploma in Carmelite Studies* offered by the Carmelite Institute of Britain & Ireland: www.cibi.ie.

Carmelite Community of Pozzo di Gotto (1999), *Growing as Brothers* [vol. 9 of the *Horizons* Carmelite Spiritual Directory project] (Middle Park, Victoria, Carmelite Communications).

Carmelite General Curia (2000), *Ratio Institutionis Vitæ Carmelitanæ* (Rome: General Curia of the Carmelite Order).

Carmelite Order (1984), *Towards a Prophetic Brotherhood: Documents of the Carmelite Order 1972–1982* (Melbourne: The Carmelite Centre).

—— (1994), *The Carmelite Family – Documents of the XIII Council of Provinces* (Melbourne: Carmelite Communications).

—— (1995), *Carmelite Constitutions* (Middle Park, Victoria: Carmelite Communications).

—— (2003), *Living the Carmelite Way: The Rule for the Third Order of Carmel* (Rome: Edizioni Carmelitane).
Chalmers, J. (1999), *In Allegiance to Jesus Christ* (Rome: Edizioni Carmelitane).
——(2001) *Mary the Contemplative* (Rome: Edizioni Carmelitane).
——(2001), 'Presentation of the Carmelite Charism', in *The Carmelites* (Rome: General Curia of the Carmelite Order).
Cicconetti, C. (1984), *The Rule of Carmel* (ed. and abridged P. Hoban; Darien: Carmelite Spiritual Center).
Clark, J.P.H. (1992), 'A Defence of the Carmelite Order by John Hornby', in P. Fitzgerald-Lombard (ed.), *Carmel in Britain 2: Theology and Writing* (Rome: Institutum Carmelitanum).
Clarke, H., and Edwards, B. (eds) (1973), *The Rule of Saint Albert* [Vinea Carmeli 1] (Aylesford and Kensington: Carmelite Press).
Copsey, R. (2004), *Carmel in Britain 3: The Hermits from Mount Carmel* (Faversham: Saint Albert's Press).
Copsey, R. (ed.) (forthcoming) *Early Carmelite Documents* (Faversham: Saint Albert's Press).
Corpus Christi Carmelites (1944), *A Great Adventure: The Story of Corpus Christi Carmel* (Tunapuna: Corpus Christi Carmelites).
Cross, C. (forthcoming) 'Carmelite Friars in the Diocese of York in the Early Sixteenth Century', in *Carmel in Britain 5* (Faversham: Saint Albert's Press).
Davis, M. (2002), *Walking on the Shore: A Way of Sharing Faith in Groups* (Chelmsford: Matthew James Publishing).
Discalced Carmelite Generalate (1991), *Constitutions of the Discalced Nuns of the Order of the Blessed Virgin Mary of Mount Carmel* (Rome: Discalced Generalate House).
Dobson, B. (1984), 'Mendicant Ideal and Practice in Late Medieval York', in P.V. Addyman and V.E. Black (eds), *Archaeological Papers from York Presented to M. W. Barley* (York: York Archaeological Trust), pp. 109–122.
Egan, K.J. (1987), 'The Spirituality of the Carmelites', in J. Raitt (ed.), *Christian Spirituality: High Middle Ages and Reformation* (London: Routledge & Kegan Paul), pp. 50–62.
Fielding, E. (1968), *Courage to Build Anew* (London: Burns & Oates).
Fitzgerald-Lombard, P. (ed.) (1992), *Carmel in Britain 1: People and Places* (Rome: Institutum Carmelitanum).
Grady, B. (ed.) (1993), *Carmelite Friars: Praying Communities Serving God's People* (British Province of Carmelites, private printing).
Greatrex, J. (1999), 'The Dispute between the Carmelite Friars and the Rector of St Crux, York, 1350', in D.M. Smith (ed.), *The Church in Medieval York: Records Edited in Honour of Professor Barrie Dobson* [Borthwick Institute of Historical Research, Borthwick Texts and Calendars 24] (York: University of York), pp. 69–73.
Griffin, E. (ed.) (2004), *Ascending the Mountain: The Carmelite Rule Today* (Dublin: The Columba Press).
John of the Cross (1991), *The Collected Works of St. John of the Cross* (Washington DC: ICS Publications).
Jotischky, A. (2002), *The Carmelites and Antiquity: Mendicants and their Pasts in the Middle Ages* (Oxford: Oxford University Press).
Kavanaugh, K. (1999), *John of the Cross: Doctor of Light and Love* (New York: Crossroad).
Lawrence, C.H. (1994), *The Friars: the Impact of the Early Mendicant Movement on Western Society* (London: Longman).
Litchfield, M.T. (1997), *Countryside and Cloister: Reminiscences of a Carmelite Nun* (Oxford: Family Publications).
Louth, A. (2003) [1991], 'Mount Carmel and St John of the Cross', in *The Wilderness of God* (London: Darton, Longman and Todd), pp. 84–103.

Lucas, S. (2006a), 'The Challenge of Communication', in *Formation and Communication at the Service of the Community* [Proceedings of the 2006 International Congress of Lay Carmelites] (Rome: Carmelite General Curia), pp. 313–21.

—— (2006b), 'Community', *Assumpta* 49.5 (April): 3–19.

Malley, J. (2004), 'The Carmelite Family', *The Sword: A Journal of Historical, Spiritual and Contemporary Carmelite Issues* 64.1 & 2 (Fall), pp. 186–98.

—— (2006), 'Fundamental Values of Carmelite Spirituality', in *Formation and Communication at the Service of the Community* [Proceedings of the 2006 International Congress of Lay Carmelites] (Rome: Carmelite General Curia), pp. 63–78.

Malley, J., Maccise, C. and Chalmers, J. (2003), *In Obsequio Jesu Christi: The Letters of the Superiors General OCarm and OCD 1992–2002* (Rome: Edizioni OCD).

Matthew, I. (1995), *The Impact of God: Soundings from St. John of the Cross* (London: Hodder and Stoughton).

McGinn, B. (2000), 'The Role of the Carmelites in the History of Western Mysticism', in K. Culligan and R. Jordan (eds), *Carmel and Contemplation: Transforming Human Consciousness* [Carmelite Studies 8] (Washington, DC: ICS Publications), pp. 25–50.

McGreal, W. (1999), *At the Fountain of Elijah – The Carmelite Tradition* [Traditions of Christian Spirituality Series] (London: Darton, Longman & Todd).

Motta-Navarro, T. (1960), *Tertii carmelitici saecularis Ordinis historicojuridica evolution* (Rome: Institutum Carmelitanum).

Mulhall, M. (ed.) (1989), *Albert's Way: The First North American Congress on the Carmelite Rule* (Rome and Barrington: Institutum Carmelitanum & The Province of the Most Pure Heart of Mary).

Obbard, E.R. (1999), *Land of Carmel: The Origins and Spirituality of the Carmelite Order* (Leominster: Gracewing).

O'Donnell, C. (1996). *Ecclesia: A Theological Encyclopaedia of the Church* (Collegeville: The Liturgical Press).

—— (1997), 'Modern Carmelite Legislation, 1971–1995', in K. Alban (ed.), *Journeying with Carmel: Extracts from the 1995 Carmelite Constitutions* (Middle Park, Victoria: Carmelite Communications), pp. 61–71.

Paul-Marie of the Cross (1997), *Carmelite Spirituality in the Teresian Tradition* (Washington DC: ICS Publications, rev. edn).

Ribot, F. (2005) [c.1385], *The Ten Books on the Way of Life and Great Deeds of the Carmelites* (trans. R. Copsey; Faversham: Saint Albert's Press).

Saggi, L. (ed.) (1950), 'Constitutiones Capituli Londinensis', *Analecta Ordinis Carmelitarum* 15: 203–45.

Slattery, P. [1991] (2000), *The Springs of Carmel: An Introduction to Carmelite Spirituality* (New York: Alba House).

Smet, J. (1986), *Cloistered Carmel* (Rome: Institutum Carmelitanum).

—— (1988), *The Carmelites – A History of the Brothers of Our Lady of Mount Carmel* (4 vols in 5 parts; Rome: Institutum Carmelitanum, rev. edn).

Staring, A. (1962), 'Nicolai Prioris Generalis Carmelitarum Ignea Sagitta', *Carmelus* 9: 237–307.

Teresa of Jesus (1976–85), *The Collected Works of St Teresa of Avila* (3 vols; Washington DC: ICS Publications).

—— (2000), *The Way of Perfection: Study Edition* (ed. K. Kavanaugh; Washington DC: ICS Publications).

Waaijman, K. (1999), *The Mystical Space of Carmel: A Commentary on the Carmelite Rule* [The Fiery Arrow Collection] (trans. J. Vriend; Leuven: Peeters).

—— (2000), *The Rule of Carmel: New Horizons* (Rome: Il Calamo).

—— (2002), *Spirituality: Forms, Foundations, Methods* [Studies in Spirituality Supplement 8] (Leuven: Peeters).

—— (2005), 'The Riches of Religious Community Life', *Studies in Spirituality* 15: 169–83.

Welch, J. (1996), *The Carmelite Way: An Ancient Path for Today's Pilgrim* (Leominster: Gracewing).
Whitman, W.B. and Bergström-Allen, J. (2005), 'Carmelites at the Shrine of Our Lady of Doncaster', *Assumpta* (magazine of the Carmelite Third Order, British Province), 48.7/8 (July–August), pp. 21–25.
Williams, R. (1991), *Teresa of Avila* (London: Geoffrey Chapman).

9

Contemporary Anglican York: Denominational Identity, Association and Affiliation

Greg Hoyland

Introduction

'It was at Rome, on 15th October 1764, as I sat musing amidst the ruins . . . that the idea of writing the decline and fall of that city first started on my mind' (Edward Gibbon). For the next two hundred years Gibbon's *Decline and Fall of the Roman Empire* shaped the West's understanding, vocabulary and perception of 'what happened to the Roman Empire'. Words such as 'crisis', 'disaster', 'collapse' and 'death' characterized the narrative of the Empire's fate. More recently these have been replaced by a different vocabulary – words such as 'transformation', 'assimilation' and 'adaptation' now characterize the narrative, representing a shift in understanding which argues that whilst certain aspects of the Roman Empire terminated suddenly and catastrophically, other changes were much more gradual – even evolutionary.

The story of Christianity in Britain is subject to a similar semantic shift. As the twentieth century passed middle age and headed to its conclusion, the narrative confidently predicted the decline (and in some cases the complete demise) of Christianity as a public, powerful force, certainly in Western society. Secularization theorists, whether tracing the origins of that phenomenon to the Enlightenment, subsequent scientific advances or the cultural revolution of the 1960s, charted the steady and apparently irresistible weakening of Christianity in the West.The opening of the twenty-first century has therefore come as a shock. As Callum Brown cryptically comments, following 9/11, 'Religion is back on the agenda' (Brown 2006: xv) and the language of the studies of contemporary Christianity is changing to reflect this. We are no longer looking at 'decline and fall'; we are exploring how and in what form Christianity has survived. That survival – and in some senses *revival* – poses important and interesting questions and the situation is complex. Brown (2006) goes on to suggest that we need to explore three areas: the nature and extent of secularization or, as he prefers, 'de-Christianization' (an almost entirely Western phenomenon); the rise of religious militancy world wide; and what Heelas *et al.* (2004) call the 'spiritual revolution' – 'the refashioning of religion as a spiritual experience devoid of central authority' (Brown 2006: xv).

With regard to 'de-Christianization' a lot of the research in recent years has focused primarily on issues such as church membership, attendance figures, church finance, numbers going forward for ordination and the involvement of the church in public life. Bruce (2000; 2002), Davie (2000), Davie and Martin (1994), Davie and Woodhead (2003), and Heelas *et al.* (2004), among many others, are engaged in studying the nature and practice of Christianity in this way. The evidence from such studies suggests that the church is indeed in decline and, as already noted, some writers even make predictions about its ultimate demise. Others suggest that the traditional denominations of the church are being replaced by new types of church, e.g. Miller's 'new paradigm churches' (Miller 1997) or Heelas's 'holistic churches' (Heelas *et al.* 2004) and yet others explore the idea that Christian *belief* is continuing, but the role and nature of belonging to the church is shifting. Such studies are valuable and necessary if we are to understand our contemporary religious world more fully.

A number of these scholars, along with other researchers, take a different line. Davie and Martin (1994), Martin (2005), Richter and Francis (1998), Jamieson (2002), Avis (2003) and Chambers (2005) have all undertaken studies of Christian belief in diverse contexts. Here the emphasis is more on the *nature* of believing and the content of belief and they explore the 'believing without belonging' approach. This kind of study is becoming increasingly important as we seek to understand the form in which Christianity has survived. There is yet a third area to be looked at and that is to get inside the mainstream denominations and explore what is going on there. To put it simply, if the argument for decline is correct – and it is difficult to resist some of that evidence – why and how do people stay in the mainstream churches? How is Anglicanism faring in York today and is there anything inherent in Anglican 'identity' of particular significance in the contemporary Christian scene?

Anglican York: Yesterday and Today

The evaluation of the state of the Anglican Church in York today depends in part on how its past is viewed. I therefore want to begin with a brief look at the history of York's Anglican heritage and argue that that history has resulted in a perception of the contemporary scene which may need to be challenged.

York has a particular history, demography and character and many of its Anglican churches are part of its heritage landscape. They are seen as a valuable asset for the tourist industry and feature prominently in the marketing of the city. Advantageous as this might be for the local economy it can give rise to unintended misconceptions. It can give the impression, for instance, that York had a glorious Christian past – it must surely have been packed with believers to need *so* many churches! The fact that churches were often built with more of an eye to the reputation of the benefactor than to house a growing number of worshippers is lost in the story. Few churches were full every Sunday. Moreover it can insinuate that Christianity is something to do with the past – mediaeval walls and castles are remnants of the past and are now redundant. Church buildings, of a similar date and architectural style, clearly fall into the same category, a view reinforced by a number of church buildings being given over today to other (secular) uses. These perceptions, when placed alongside the oft-repeated statistical evidence relating to declining church attendance and membership, create a particular prevailing discourse. The result is what investigators of social language refer to as 'compacted information' and 'nominalization' (e.g. Gee 1999: 31).

> Nominalizations . . . allow one to take a lot of information – indeed a whole sentence's worth of information – and compact it into a compound word or phrase. (ibid.)

The 'compacted' language of the media and the press relating to contemporary Christianity in Britain is that the church is in decline and its members in despair. It is so often repeated that it is accepted without question; but that discourse needs more careful interrogation. Did York ever have a 'glorious' Christian past in quite the way it is assumed, with all its churches vibrant and full?

By the time of the Reformation the Western (Roman) church had been the major religious influence for almost a thousand years, its theological, liturgical and political power having done much to influence the life of the state as well as the church in Britain. The building of churches, the provision of chantry chapels and the religious philanthropy displayed in the founding and maintaining of monastic institutions were simply visible, physical reminders of the centrality of the church in the life of the nation. This often masked the fact that the relationship between church and state and between church and people was not always easy or comfortable, and the European Reformations of the sixteenth century at least in part represent a boiling over of some of the political frustrations and aspirations of the emerging nation states.

The Reformation was the watershed for the English Church but the break with Rome was not a clean, clear-cut beginning of something new. We only have to take a cursory look at the centuries following Henry VIII's 1534 Act of Supremacy to see that in each of them the pendulum of power between Catholicism and Protestantism was in constant motion. That break with Rome by its very nature set a precedent which endorsed the idea of dissent. Quick on the heels of the new Church of England came 'dissenters' of various kinds, from recusants to Brownists, Puritans to Presbyterians. The Quakers arrived in York in the 1650s, for example, and they were soon joined by Congregationalists (Independents), Presbyterians and Methodists (who in turn split into Primitive, Wesleyan, Wesleyan Reform, Countess of Huntingdon's Connection, etc.) as well as Roman Catholics returning from exile or emerging from hiding. The fragmentation continued so that, whilst the Anglican Church gradually clawed its way to primacy of place as the established and state-endorsed church it was one among many. *The* church was replaced by the *churches*. The already large number of mediaeval churches was augmented by the building of chapels and meeting houses, mission huts and new churches and the worshipping congregations were shared among a growing number of options.

Attendance figures do suggest a high level of church going (see, for example, Elliott-Binns 2002) but, again, we need to be careful with these and interpret them with caution. By the Victorian period there were many people who used the Anglican Church for social and economic benefits. The poor attended to gain goods such as clothes and food; the respectable working class attended to ensure promotion. Children attended Sunday Schools for several weeks before the annual outings to ensure they had sufficient marks on their attendance card to secure a place. Primitive Methodists (among others) displayed an apparently superstitious mindset by attending the Anglican Church for Rites of Passage as these were deemed more 'advantageous' or of more intrinsic value if performed by a Church of England clergyman. Such aspects of church attendance, particularly in the Victorian era, may well mean that the statistics are skewed and that we cannot be certain that we are comparing like with like when placing today's figures alongside those of the past.

The point of this brief and highly selective historical overview is to challenge the prevailing narratives concerning contemporary Anglicanism in York as an institution in terminal decline. There are three issues to highlight. The first is to challenge the myth that the Anglican Church in York was once numerically strong, confident, untroubled and unchallenged. Its history demonstrates that, whilst it undoubtedly was once more numerous and powerful, many of the questions, uncertainties and dilemmas it faces in the twenty-first century are not dissimilar to those it has had to tackle in the past. It is, as White comments, 'a recurring vanity of every age to think it is suffering radically new experiences' (2002: 3). Since its inception the Anglican Church has had to face crises from within and without and its demise was more than once a serious possibility. The second is to argue that Anglicanism's history suggests a resilience and tenacity born of a pragmatic, evolutionary approach to theology. 'To live is to change', according to Newman, 'and to be perfect is to change often' (*On the Development of Christian Doctrine* 1848) which, in the case of Anglicanism, might be rendered 'To live is to change and to survive is to change often'. St Benedict articulates the paradox that lies at the heart of this in his monastic vows: 'Stability' is balanced with 'Conversion' – things remain the same whilst ever changing. That tenacity might in part be the innate conservatism of institutions or their stubborn refusal to know when to quit, but it might also be because there is something inherently adaptable about Anglicanism. Third, the Christian church in York has constantly witnessed the arrival of competition in the form of new denominations, new expressions of church, revivals and new movements. Being a Metropolitan See is to be 'high profile' and to attract considerable attention and York was a strategic target for such enterprises. So again, the arrival of different expressions of Christianity, particularly 'experiential' forms, is not a new phenomenon.

The situation facing the Anglican Church in York at the beginning of the twenty-first century is complex. Its historical legacy has left it with a considerable 'residual' strength which, though it may be declining, appears to have a long way to go before it disappears. That legacy has also left York with an ethnic and religious profile different from many of its neighbouring Yorkshire cities although this may be changing. The agenda for the Anglican Diocese of York is therefore very mixed and many of the social, religious and cultural issues which deeply affect certain areas have less impact on York itself.

Identity, Association and Affiliation

> One thinks of identity whenever one is not sure of where one belongs . . . [It is] a name given to [the] escape from uncertainty. Hence 'identity', though ostensibly a noun behaves like a verb, albeit a strange one to be sure: it appears only in the future tense. (Bauman 1996: 19)

Identity is used in relation to individuals, institutions, groups – nations even. It is a question which exercises the English in particular at a personal and a collective level: what is 'English'? In terms of Anglicanism the question of identity is particularly complex. We shall explore the idea, first at the level of the person and then collectively of the institution.

Words such as 'identity', 'self', 'personhood' and 'individuality' are sometimes used interchangeably and sometimes used very precisely in different discipline discourses. Self is a central, classic concept in psychology, though it has long remained a difficult and much debated issue. The view that there was some kind of 'pre-existent' self, objective, observable and measurable, was replaced by a conceptual view of a self created by retrospection and reflection. This led to a growing interest in what has become known as a transactional self, which is, according to Bruner, writing from the perspective of a narrative psychologist:

> a way of framing one's consciousness, one's position, one's identity, one's commitment with respect to another. Self in this dispensation becomes 'dialogue dependent', designed as much for the recipient of our discourse as for intrapsychic purposes. (Bruner 1990: 101)

The Lebanese writer Amin Maalouf argues that, 'Every individual is a meeting ground for many different allegiances' of varying degrees of importance and power to me (Maalouf 2000: 10). Identity is something to do with that mix of 'differing allegiances', experiences, genetic and biological inheritances and many more factors besides, all or many of which are shared by many others. But what makes me 'me' is the unique mix and interaction of them which, again to use Maalouf's words, 'prevents me from being identical to anyone else' (Maalouf 2000: 10). An equally powerful driving force is the desire to be 'normal' and normality is best measured against the surrounding community. I conform to the groups significant to me in order to belong.

> Persons have to be understood in social terms. Individuality, personhood and selfhood do not refer to some internal and independent source of identity, but to the way one is and has been in relation [to others]. (McFadyen 1990: 18)

Goffman's (1959: 2) early view that 'the "true" or "real" [self]' in the form of 'attitudes, beliefs and emotions of the individual can be ascertained only indirectly through his avowals or through what appears to be involuntary expressive behaviour' suggests a view of identity as something rather static and buried.

Lejeune (1989: 132), on the other hand, implies a more dynamic, provisional notion of identity as a process in which each individual forms 'a rough draft, perpetually reshaped, of the story of his life'.

> [T]he individual does not in fact begin his quest for knowledge *de novo*, as if he were an isolated individual abstracted from history and society. A shared public world pre-exists both him and his own thinking. The public world shapes his thoughts in such a way that it not only transmits shared resources of knowledge, but also shapes the terms on which he examines and tests that knowledge. (Thistleton 1981: 47)

For the researcher this gives rise to the fundamental question of where identity in the individual is located. But if identity is more process than product a better question is how identity is manifested. In this respect Goffman (1959) is right to suggest that identity is often betrayed involuntarily. It appears in behaviours, habits and language both consciously and unconsciously so the research methodology employed in identifying identity has to be both direct and indirect. Furthermore, associations and affiliations give clues to an individual's sense of identity. We define ourselves in part by the relationships we choose, the groups we belong to, the people we associate with.

I want to distinguish these terms at this point to signify different levels of belonging. Etymologically, association has the sense of *connecting* whilst affiliation has the sense of *relating*. Pressing this further, association suggests a 'mechanical' relationship whereas affiliation conjures up blood ties and familial relationship. I will argue later in the chapter that there has been a significant shift in recent years away from affiliation and towards association with regard to denominational 'belonging'.

So far we have been speaking of individual identity. But what of organizations, groups and communities: can a nation, an institution or a denomination be said to have an identity in the same way as an individual? Corporate, class, institutional, or national identity tends to be assumed rather than argued, but it seems a reasonable assumption. Characteristics emerge which identify certain social groupings and mark them out as distinct from others. In this sense the term 'identity' describes both uniformity and difference, inclusion and exclusion. Groups create 'markers' of identity which operate for those within the group and those outside it. Language (particularly vocabulary), dress, practices (ways of doing things) and stories all act as markers in this way.

What is more complex is the dynamic process which creates identity. Schreiter suggests, 'Traditions have beginnings, but not manufactured ones' (Schreiter 1985: 108). 'They begin', he continues, 'in revelations, in unexpected insights, in the charisma of leaders.' The Conseil de l'Europe identified seven features which create national identity, including an historic homeland or territory, a common language and a common popular culture. However, it suggests that the most powerful among them are common myths and shared memories. These shared experiences, recounted verbally in oral cultures, reflected upon, elaborated and expounded, are what bond people together. The experience alone is insufficient; it is the group reflection and exploration of the *meaning* of the event, encapsulated in story, which creates or strengthens the bond between people.

So is there such a thing as Anglican identity and, if there is, how is it constructed and where can it be located? Rowan Williams argues that Anglicanism

> has tried to find a way of being a Church that is neither tightly centralized nor just a loose federation of essentially independent bodies – a Church that is seeking to be a coherent family of communities meeting to hear the Bible read, to break bread and share wine as guests of Jesus Christ, and to celebrate a unity in worldwide mission and ministry. (Williams 2006)

Therein lies either the genius or the tragedy of Anglicanism, depending on your point of view.[1] Richard Hooker, in articulating what became 'Anglicanism', tried to balance catholic traditions with the insights of reformers, episcopal authority with the responsibilities of councils and an incarnated, national church with an ecumenical openness. His pragmatic approach was to state that neither 'Rome' nor 'Geneva' had it all right or all wrong: there must be a *via media* which embraced the good from both. Originally this comprehensiveness was a costly (even radical) idea, not an attempt at appeasement: moderation was not a euphemism for blandness. But trying to embrace the good from two opposing sides is to court dissatisfaction and Anglicanism's fate has been seen as unclear in its theology, too broad in its ecclesiology and too accommodating to be strong. Comprehensiveness is too easily seen as compromise.

What, then, is Anglican ecclesiology or *ecclesiality* as Volf (1998: 127) prefers? Does the Anglican Church have a recognizable identity? I have already quoted in this chapter people such as Rowan Williams and Paul Avis. Their writings along with the positions they hold in the Anglican Church mean that their pronouncements have weight, authority, knowledge and understanding and, whilst undoubtedly containing personal opinion, could be taken as giving an 'official' line on this question. I want to explore some of these 'official' perspectives. But there is now an established viewpoint which argues that studying the Church must include data on 'the views from the pews' (e.g. Grundy 1998; Stringer 1999; Guest *et al.* 2004; see also Friend in this volume). To adapt Stringer's contention regarding meaning in worship, Anglican identity 'must lie somewhere between the text and the minds of the worshippers who use the text' (Stringer 1999: 2). The official pronouncements are not the whole story. There are a number of ways of understanding 'church'. The first is to see the church as made up of those united with Christ. This argues that those who have a personal faith – 'the saved' as opposed to 'the unsaved' – are automatically members of the church. In this view the church is the totality of all Christian believers. As a theology it therefore prioritizes the personal over the collective. 'Church' is an unseen and unseeable entity, to be revealed only at the *parousia*. And being a member of the church is only defined accidentally by adherence to a local group of Christians: the fundamental definition is experiential. The weakness of this position is that, by implication, 'church' is 'desirable' rather than 'essential' in Christian identity. Whether or not one identifies with, partakes in or contributes to the life of the local church is not ultimately important. Local expressions of church appear to be arbitrary. It also has the added problem that defining 'Christian believer' is not a straightforward matter. It appears to champion an experiential, individualistic model: the 'union' is 'with Christ' (e.g. 1 Cor. 6:15ff.) rather than with Christians. The place, role and theology of the local church is not addressed. As I will argue later, this represents an 'associational' model which is an increasingly common view of church.

Another view focuses on *ecclesia* stressing the idea of being gathered 'around' Christ rather than 'in' Christ: church exists when gathering happens. Though this approach does not address the question of what it means to be a Christian it implies a more 'mechanical' model, that is, the baptized. I use 'mechanical' here, not in a pejorative sense (a reductionist view of *ex opere operato*) but in terms of behaviours, rituals and practices which carry meaning for particular groups. Beliefs are constructed and communicated in part by the performance of 'storied' theologies – narratives of faith carried in the practices of the faith community. In this sense 'mechanical' refers to the externalization of the personal experience so that it is expressed in a recognized ritual shared by the particular faith community.

'Gathered' is an idea of church in line with a Narrative Theology approach and emphasizes 'belonging' rather than 'believing'. Narrative Theology is a slippery term and gets used in a variety of ways but one understanding of it at least is that it places story at the heart of faith. Its advantage over a dogmatic approach is that it validates each individual's and community's experience and communicates in language which is readily understandable. It begins where people are, rather than where they could, should, might or ought to be. It respects the freedom of both God and humanity. The call of the Gospel is that we move into a creative dialogue with God, fusing our story with God's, interpreting God's story through ours and *vice versa*. The *ecclesia* is those gathered around Christ, looking to the same story and sharing their perspectives on it. Orthodoxy thus emerges from that sharing, rather than being extrapolated from a written text. This model of church moves towards affiliation rather than association.

Yet another is to take a social approach to the doctrine of the Trinity as the model for understanding church. It is about *koinonia* rather than *ecclesia*. If personhood is relational, based on a Trinitarian understanding of God's relationality as the 'image' in which humanity is created, then the church demonstrates the nature and character of God by being a community which allows and enables individuals to be persons-in-relationship. Our twin fears, according to Williams (1965: 112ff.), and following Sartre, Tillich and Buber *et al.*, are of total isolation or total absorption. I do not want to lose my identity by being exactly the same as everyone else, but nor do I want to be so different that I am cut off from everyone else. I need to be me and I need to belong. 'Church' in this approach is more than simply an organization or institution. It is a way of being which is central to the Gospel message and inherent in it. If the previous models are about 'believing' and 'belonging', this is about 'being'. It is the strongest expression of affiliation. These models are rarely mutually exclusive. Rather, we can see tendencies to prioritize one or another whilst incorporating aspects of another.

Turning our attention to more specifically Anglican understandings two contemporary theologians stand out – Paul Avis and Stephen Sykes. Both place understandings of church at the centre of current theological debate – Avis as an ecumenist and expert on church unity and Sykes as an Evangelical.

According to Avis the Church is the baptized, 'a mystical, certainly intuitive, perception of that fundamental ecclesial reality' (Avis 2002: 354). Local church, denominational church, world-wide church and eschatological church are constituted by those baptized into Christ and each should recognize the other in mutual acknowledgement of different traditions within the Body of Christ. He rejects the idea of Erastianism and is wary of a Tractarian approach which focuses too much on Apostolicity. A view of church which places priesthood at the centre tends to narrow the understanding of church.

Instead he suggests that a baptismal paradigm lies at the heart of the Anglican understanding of church as it is the fundamental sacrament.

> Baptism presupposes the faith of the Church and is accompanied by a creedal profession of faith. Confirmation appropriates baptism. The Eucharist presupposes it. Ordination authorises and empowers the representative expression of the royal priesthood of Christ into which all the baptised are incorporated . . . Baptism constitutes the primary ground of our unity. (Avis 2002: 348)

Stephen Sykes makes a passionate plea to those from a 'lower' church, Evangelical tradition to engage with ecclesiology and regain what he sees as lost confidence in Anglicanism. The Reformation was not a mistake – an aberration on the part of some sixteenth-century churchmen – but a vital recovery of lost truths resulting in a church with a distinctive theology.

He puts forward three foundations for an Anglican ecclesiology. The church is an 'instrumental' sign – 'the necessary appearance in history of its beyond-historical character, to which it points' (Sykes 1995: 126). In this sense it proclaims and points to that which is greater than itself, which is both the eschatological reality of 'church' (a rather Platonic concept) and the 'Gospel' of God's love incarnate.

The church is also a redeemed community of *sinners* and therefore cannot be triumphalistic. It has shortcomings, failings and weaknesses which it must honestly own, but this in turn is a sign that God came not to seek the righteous but to call sinners to repentance (Lk. 5:32). If his first foundation is the 'instrumental' sign the second could be called the 'incarnational' sign. In these first two foundations Sykes shows a different starting point to Avis. Whereas Avis looks to history, Sykes locates his thinking in the biblical corpus. Where they come together is in Sykes's third foundation which is baptism, though differently nuanced from Avis.

Baptism for Sykes expresses the totality of the Gospel. It is all there in that one sacrament. And therefore to be baptized is to enter into the totality of the church, not just a part of it. As with Avis this is no 'mechanistic' or reductionist understanding – the rite without faith is meaningless – but it marks the church out as the community of baptized believers.

Sykes champions the use of 'sign' imagery on the grounds that it is a key New Testament concept, particularly in the Fourth Gospel. In so doing he perhaps limits his argument somewhat. 'Symbol' has added meaning which might be useful in his argument in that the essence of a symbol is that it 'evokes' more than it 'points'. That is, there is something of the thing symbolized in the symbol itself. It has useful links to the Hebrew idea of 'remembering' which is considerably richer in meaning than mere nostalgia. To remember is 'to make present' and symbols are called upon with that intention. The bread and wine of the Eucharist have in them something of that which they symbolize. It seems to me both Avis and Sykes are arguing for an affiliation rather than an association model. Membership of the church in the Anglican view is (or should be) what we 'are' rather than what we 'do'. For both of them denomination in this sense is central not arbitrary because denomination is an embodiment of a particular understanding of the totality of the Gospel. It is not simply a matter of 'we do things differently': the theological identity of a church – its self-understanding – is carried in its liturgy and practice. But that is to state, if you like, the 'official line'. It is couched in the language of the theologian, church official or council. What happens when we look at understandings of church at the grass roots? To what extent do those views match the official line? In order to get at that we need to understand something of how people in the Anglican Church understand the notion of being Christian, though that can be difficult. Frances Ward warns us that 'ethnography is a messy business' (Guest *et al.* 2004: 125). From research carried out in York three initial reasons surfaced explaining why people attended a specific denominational – in this case Anglican – church. There are 'cradle' Anglicans, born into and nurtured in the tradition, for whom it is so much a part of their personal life history that they could not imagine belonging anywhere else. There are 'conviction' Anglicans who make a conscious decision to belong to either the Anglican Church as denomination or to a particular local Anglican church. Of these there are those whose decision is guided primarily by an intellectual choice and those informed by what might be described as a more emotional choice. In other words, some prefer the theology of Anglicanism or the theology preached in a particular local church, whereas others are motivated more by the 'feel' of Anglicanism – liturgical, sacramental, parochial.

A third group have a more straightforward, pragmatic motive – that of convenience, in rural areas for instance, where there is only one church. Developing this further it seems that we can identify a more significant taxonomy based around four approaches to Anglican identity which inform and underpin those mentioned above. Again, these are not exclusive and they merge and overlap both conceptually and in the understandings of individuals. Denominationalists are those with a clearly articulated commitment to a particular church tradition. They are probably in a minority – and possibly a shrinking minority at that. More research is needed to confirm this but it is possible to suggest that combining some of the statistical evidence around Christian belief and practice would support this view.

If we look at those attending churches (e.g. Sunday worship figures) and those becoming members (e.g. electoral roll numbers) we note the latter falling more quickly than the former. One reading of this is to suggest a more fluid or transient church population, less keen on commitment to a specific church. But there are still a significant number who are drawn to the Anglican Church (and other denominations) because of what they believe it stands for. Liturgical worship and parochial structure are the most often-cited reasons for belonging to an Anglican church but there appears to be an emerging issue more related to the contemporary milieu of Western society. I have already cited Rowan Williams's comment that Anglicanism tries 'to find a way of being a Church that is neither tightly centralized nor just a loose federation of essentially independent bodies' (Williams 2006). Williams was addressing the issue contemporary Anglicanism faces in trying to keep a world-wide communion united whilst beset with major moral, ecclesiological, theological and cultural differences. But his description of what Anglicanism is at a global level works equally well at a local, individual level. Anglicanism appears to have a particular genius for encouraging people both to belong and to 'work out their own salvation'. Dormor, McDonald and Caddick go so far as to suggest that Anglicanism is, in this sense among others, 'the answer to modernity' (Dormor *et al.* 2003).

Communalists follow on as the second group and here the emphasis is on locality and identity. Community is a difficult word to pin down. It is used in diverse and sometimes conflicting ways but three 'layers' of the word – family, friends and neighbours – are still of significance in a world of instability, mobility and change. It is not that 'community' no longer exists: it is simply that we do it differently. Issues of continuity and stability feature strongly in this form of belonging. The (apparent) increasing 'anonymization' of society coupled with the rapidity of technological and social changes seems to lead some to see Anglicanism as a balance between the new and the old. Contemporary expressions of worship – modern music, liturgical experimentation, a democritization of leadership – are carried out in the context of a church rooted in a local community. The physical presence of the building with its sense of 'belonging' to the local community seems to nurture a sense of security. An interesting feature of this approach is the rather old-fashioned idea of 'neighbouring'; people go to church because their neighbours go (see Furlong 2006). There has long been an acceptance that few people will start attending church from cold and that personal invitations and contacts are the most fruitful means of communication. Conversionists represent an interesting approach. These are strongly of the 'union' variety with its emphasis on personal faith. Union is the way of describing being Christian and it is union 'with Christ' first and foremost. Which church is attended is a matter of personal guidance from God for the individual: denomination is largely if not totally irrelevant. Those driven by this approach tend to have a very strong mission/evangelization agenda, often believing they had been 'sent' by God to 'save' or 'minister' to a local church. There is some evidence, however, of a process of what might be termed domestication which goes on over time.

Take the case, for example, of one particular church where a married couple who had previously travelled to another church (one of what Donald Miller refers to as 'new paradigm' churches) had felt 'led' by God to switch to their local Anglican Church. Over a period of nearly two years they demonstrated a significant shift in approach. Though still of the opinion that personal conversion was necessary for a 'true' faith they had softened their position on this matter considerably, recognizing that some of their fellow congregants, whilst having had no conversion experience, none the less had a vibrant 'living' faith. Undoubtedly the arrival of a couple such as this in a relatively small church had a profound effect on the group dynamics. But the traffic was not one way: whilst the existing members had shifted their opinions on a number of issues so too had the couple. This process of 'socialization' is complex to observe but is significant. Others convert to Anglicanism as a result of a process of intellectual searching or disaffection with an existing tradition. For example, a former elder at a new paradigm church who had left to join an Anglican church where there was a greater sense of 'church'. His argument was that his former church, though claiming to be *denominationless*, was turning into a denomination, probably through the presence of second-generation church members. His choice of Anglicanism revolved around it having a sense of tradition and continuity whilst free of (as he saw it) the centralized nature of Roman Catholicism. Sacramentalists form the last group and come closest to Sykes's and Avis's baptismal paradigms. For these people the objective aspect of baptism and confirmation balances their subjective allegiance to the church and the regular participation in Holy Communion feeds that sense of belonging to the wider church, the church triumphant and the local church. Such people appear to have a much more clearly thought-out idea of the church as sacrament and the canonical sacraments as epitomizing all that the church stands for. If we think of church in terms of 'church universal' (across time and space) and 'the local church' this group see their primary belonging as to the former, expressed ('incarnated') by membership of the latter. In answer to why they belong to the Anglican Church (given that other denominations recognize sacraments) the reasons are many. As mentioned above, none of the foregoing categories is exclusive so some Sacramentalists were Communalists, some Denominationalists. But there is evidence to suggest that vestiges of Hooker's pragmatic theology can be detected in such people. 'Rome's' more mystical approach and 'Geneva's' more earthy approach to sacraments lead some to seek the middle way of Anglicanism, not as compromise but as more balanced.

Conclusion

Various theologians tell us where Christian Theology must begin – with the Resurrection (Michael Ramsay), with Christology (Karl Barth), with God (Thomas F. Torrance). Stanley Hauerwas suggests that 'all theology must begin and end with ecclesiology' (Hauerwas 1997: 58). In a sense he is playing the trump card insisting that all these doctrines are contained in and expressed by the church. As the fellowship of the redeemed, the Body of Christ, the New Israel, the communion of saints, the Church sums up the Gospel. To close this chapter therefore we need to address the question of Anglican identity again and where this ongoing study might lead us. I want to make four brief comments.

The first concerns the questions we are asking. Timothy Jenkins and his co-authors, writing in *Anglicanism: The Answer to Modernity* (2003), offer a robust defence of the spirit of Anglicanism modelled on two illustrious predecessors – *Essays and Reviews* (1860) and *Soundings* (1962). Jenkins poses the question 'How might we set about articulating the Anglican vision?' (Dormor *et al.* 2003: 196). In this study I am asking a slightly different question: *where* is this 'Spirit of Anglicanism' located? My contention is that we need to interrogate both the theological pronouncements of the church or 'academy' and the public understandings in the 'pews'. The two are related but precisely *how* they are related is my question. Further to this is an often neglected question. 'Leavers' leave for a variety of reasons, some completely and some to other destinations; 'joiners' come from a variety of backgrounds – returners, new converts, occasional/casual attenders, transfers. All of these receive quite a lot of academic attention. But what of the 'stayers'? Why do they stay/why don't they leave? How do they 'believe'? What do they believe? Even if the prevailing narrative is correct (and I have argued above that we need to be cautious about this) and the church is declining, why do those who remain stay and how do they maintain their faith? There would appear to be three broad options for those who stay in the church: relocate to a more 'secure', 'thriving' church; adopt a 'remnant' mentality (theology) and wait for the good times to return; believe 'differently'. I suspect it is more complex than this and we need to explore the faith of such people. The second comment relates to the study of 'identity'. Identity has something to do with allegiance *extended through time*. This means we need a diachronic approach to the study of identity in an arguably synchronic generation. Whilst academic theologians cannot 'fiddle while Rome burns' they must none the less take a longer view of the situation than is popular today. The question of identity is centre stage at present and has considerable complexities. 'Englishness', 'Britishness' and Anglican identity are interwoven to some degree and understanding this is an ongoing process.

The third relates to what is happening in the Anglican Church. (The same may be true of other mainstream denominations but that is beyond the scope of this paper.) There is a glut of books on 'new ways of being church' (e.g. *Liquid Church* by Pete Ward 2002; *Emerging Churches* by Gibbs and Bolger 2006; *Mission Shaped Church* by the Church of England's Mission and Public Affairs Council 2004; *Organic Church* by Cole 2005). They represent attempts to grapple with changes in society, attitudes, technologies and lifestyles and to make the Church relevant. Alongside these are the 'new' churches – so-called post-denominational churches. York has its fair share of these. (Few of the city's schools do not host one or another form of such church Sunday by Sunday.) The response to this by the mainstream churches is unfolding, and Figure 1 is a suggestion of the options for a new 'settlement' in the twenty-first century. The 'new paradigm churches' are moving into second-generation issues and face interesting evolutionary changes. The 'hybrid' churches are those of the mainstream who adopt the approaches and methods of the new paradigm churches. The traditional are the mainstream denominations. What are their future prospects?

Figure 1: **Future prospects for existing forms of church**

New paradigm → Continue differently
New paradigm → Status quo
New paradigm → 'Denominationalize' (Miller's 'routinization')
New paradigm → Fade

Traditional → Hybridize or become New Paradigm
Traditional → Status quo
Traditional → Disappear
Traditional → Reverse the trend

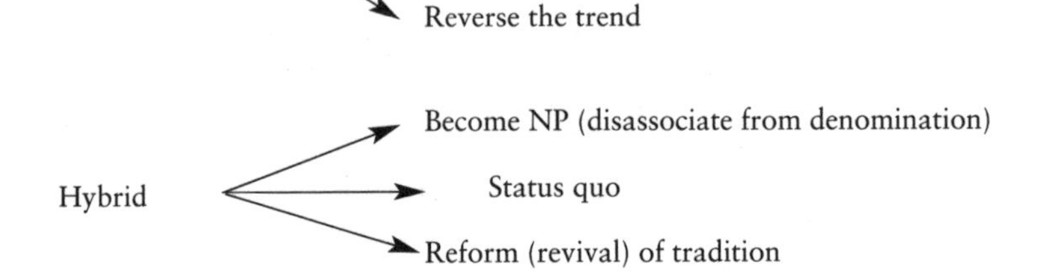

This suggests two issues need consideration. First, the dynamic between 'church' and 'believer' appears to be changing: 'I belong to it' is shifting to 'It belongs to me'. Second, though often described as 'new ways of being church', many of these are 'new ways of *doing* church'. That is, they are activity rather than concept based. There is an urgent need to look afresh at the nature and purpose of the church. Is a 'looser' association replacing a former affiliation, and what are the repercussions of this for the Anglican Church?

When Brown (2006) talks about the return of religion in the twenty-first century he rightly points out that it is in a different guise: the emphasis is much more on personal religious experience. In the past (as we have seen in identifying 'union' ecclesiologies) personal experience has always been a feature of mainstream denominations, particularly in the evangelical wing of the church. But what we see happening now is that the personal is becoming much more prevalent – religion is being privatized, even mainstream denominational religion. And that raises a number of important questions. It has always been the case that people conform to a faith more closely in public than they do in private. Whilst endorsing the mainstream teachings of a faith in public, people keep more hidden their private understandings, doubts or questions which might be at variance with that 'orthodox' expression. That 'gap' is significant and a number of research questions present themselves: Why do those gaps emerge? How are such gaps negotiated? What happens if the public and the private come under stress and the gap begins to grow? Is 'gap' the right model to use? Understanding this interface between a private and a public faith has obvious implications for institutional religion as issues such as radicalization and fundamentalism in religion are currently under scrutiny, and the link between what Christianity stands for and how that relates to individuals who act in its name needs serious interrogation. Institutions cannot survive without members and the danger for the church is that the dominance of the kind of personal religion I have been describing is more 'associational' and less dependent on the institution. Christian identity appears to be having less and less to do with denominational identity. The fourth comment relates to the future. A number of recent books on Anglicanism already quoted here (Dormor *et al.* 2003; Avis 2002; 2003) share a similar ending. They finish by looking at the 'vision' of Anglicanism, the 'vocation' of Anglicanism, the 'spirit' of Anglicanism. Such language suggests some degree of optimism in the face of the prevailing discourse outlined in the introduction. Is such optimism warranted? Colin Podmore writes:

> Ecclesiology tends to be written by theologians, ecumenists and canon lawyers. When written by exponents of one of these disciplines without regard to the others it can be unsatisfactory. (Podmore 2005: 160)

I would add that ecclesiology done without the laity is equally unsatisfactory. It is there that this study has found the most optimism. Anglicanism has much to offer by way of a particular Christian identity in contemporary Britain if it pays attention, not to its past, but to its inherent genius. In allowing a looser form of affiliation – but affiliation none the less – Anglicanism may still have something significant to offer contemporary society, if only it doesn't tear itself apart over the variety it seeks to embrace.

Note

1 For a succinct study of the origins of the words 'Anglican' and 'Anglicanism' see Avis in Sykes *et al.* (1998: 460).

References

Avis, P. (2002), *Anglicanism and the Christian Church* (Edinburgh: T&T Clark).
—— (2003), *Public Faith?* (London: SPCK).
Bauman, Z. (1996), 'From Pilgrim to Tourist', in S. Hall and P. du Gay (eds), *Questions of Cultural Identity* (London: Sage), pp. 18–36.
—— (2006), *Religion and Society in Twentieth Century Britain* (London: Pearson).
Bruce, S. (2000), *Religion in the Modern World* (Oxford: Oxford University Press).
—— (2002), *God is Dead* (Oxford: Blackwell).
Bruner, J. (1990), *Acts of Meaning* (Cambridge, MA: Harvard University Press).
Chambers, P. (2005) *Religion, Secularization and Social Change in Wales* (Cardiff: University of Wales Press).
Church of England's Mission and Public Affairs Council (2004), *Mission Shaped Church* (London: Church House Publishing).
Cole, N. (2005), *Organic Church* (San Francisco: Jossey-Bass).
Davie, G. (2000), *Religion in Modern Europe: A Memory Mutates* (Oxford: Oxford University Press).

Davie, G., P. Heelas and L. Woodhead (eds) (2003), *Predicting Religion* (Aldershot: Ashgate).
Davie, G., and D. Martin (1994), *Religion in Britain Since 1945: Believing Without Belonging (Making Contemporary Britain)* (Oxford: Blackwell).
Dormor, D., J. McDonald and J. Caddick (eds) (2003), *Anglicanism: The Answer to Modernity* (London: Continuum).
Elliott-Binns, L. (2002), *Religion in the Victorian Era* (Cambridge: James Clarke & Co).
Furlong, M. (2006), *The C of E: The State it's In* (London: SPCK).
Gee, J.P. (1999), *Social Linguistics and Literacies* (London: Routledge-Falmer).
Gibbon, E. (1910), *Decline and Fall of the Roman Empire* (London: Everyman's Library, Dent).
Gibbs, E., and R.K. Bolger (2006), *Emerging Churches* (London: SPCK).
Goffman, E. (1959), *The Presentation of Self in Everyday Life* (New York: Doubleday).
Grundy, M. (1998), *Understanding Congregations* (London: Mowbray).
Guest, M., K. Tusting and L. Woodhead (2004), *Congregational Studies in the UK* (Aldershot: Ashgate).
Hauerwas, S. (1997), *In Good Company: Church as Polis* (Notre Dame: Notre DamePress).
Heelas, P., L. Woodhead, B. Seel and K. Tusting (2004), *The Spiritual Revolution* (Oxford: Blackwell).
Jamieson, A. (2002), *A Churchless Faith* (London: SPCK).
Jenkins, T. (2003), 'Anglicanism: The Only Answer to Modernity', in D. Dormor, J. McDonald and J. Caddick (eds), *Anglicanism: The Answer to Modernity* (London: Continuum), pp. 186–205.
Lejeune, P. (1989), *On Autobiography* (Minneapolis: University of Minnesota Press).
Maalouf, A. (2000), *On Identity* (London: Harvill Press).
Martin, D. (2005), *On Secularization* (Aldershot: Ashgate).
McFadyen, A.I. (1990), *The Call to Personhood* (Cambridge: Cambridge University Press).
Miller, D.E. (1997), *Reinventing American Protestantism* (London: University of California Press).
Newman, J.H. (1848), *An Essay on the Development of Christian Doctrine* (Notre Dame: Notre Dame Press, 6th edn, 1990).
Podmore, C. (2005), *Aspects of Anglican Identity* (London: Church House Publishing).
Richter, P., and L. Francis (1998), *Gone But Not Forgotten* (London: Darton, Longman and Todd).
Schreiter, R.J. (1985), *Constructing Local Theologies* (London: SCM).
Stringer, M.D. (1999), *On the Perception of Worship* (Birmingham: University of Birmingham Press).
Sykes, S. (1995), *Unashamed Anglicanism* (London: Darton, Longman and Todd).
Sykes, S., J. Booty and J. Knight (eds) (1998), *The Study of Anglicanism* (London: SPCK).
Thistleton, A. (1981), 'Knowledge, Myth and Corporate Memory', in *Believing in the Church*. Report for the Doctrine Commission of the Church of England (London: SPCK).
Volf, M. (1998), *After Our Likeness: The Church as the Image of the Trinity* (Grand Rapids: Eerdmans).
Ward, P. (2002) *Liquid Church* (Carlisle: Paternoster Press).
White, V. (2002), *Identity* (London: SCM).
Williams, H.A. (1965), *The True Wilderness* (Harmondsworth: Penguin).
Williams, R. (2006) 'The Challenge and Hope of Being an Anglican Today: A Reflection for the Bishops, Clergy and Faithful of the Anglican Communion', 7 June, http://www.archbishopofcanterbury.org/.

10

York's Evangelicals and Charismatics: An Emergent Free Market in Voluntarist Religious Identities

Rob Warner

Introduction

This chapter will examine the shifting centre of gravity of York's evangelicals and charismatics. It represents a preliminary enquiry into the rise of a voluntarist coalition among evangelicals in York, which we have found to be centred upon Anglican charismatics and neo-Pentecostals. Empirical data and semi-structured interviews with clergy and other senior leaders are employed to construct an account of current church life and its future trends. This will be tested against the classical accounts of pluralism and secularization (Wilson 1966; Bruce 1996; 2002), free-market theories of the rise of voluntarist religion (Stark and Bainbridge 1985, 1987; Finke and Stark 1992), and debates concerning why conservative religion endures (Kelley 1972; Hunter 1983; 1987; Smith 1998; 2000) and what forms of religion seem most adept at cultural adaptation and survival (Heelas, Martin *et al.* 1998; Tamney 2002; Heelas, Woodhead *et al.* 2005).

The Empirical Opportunity

Robin Gill noted, 'Of all the cities and large towns in England, York provides some of the most complete churchgoing data' (Gill 2003: 169). He utilized the data to confirm his thesis that the over-provision of church capacity in the mid- to late nineteenth century served to exaggerate the subsequent degree of decline in actual church attendance. For example, Methodist over-expansion in York and their inability to fill the additional capacity and subsequent decline correspond with the general pattern of that denomination. Gill identified two specific characteristics of York. First, the Anglican city centre parishes have provided long-term excess capacity. As a result, their recruitment has reached beyond their parish boundaries and it has never been possible for all to enjoy simultaneous, large congregations. Second, he describes York, and more particularly St Michael le Belfrey, as 'the *locus classicus* of recent evangelical Anglican revival' (Gill 2003: 169). St Michael's impact upon other churches, through its own meteoric growth and subsequent plateau, is highly significant over the past thirty-five years. Gill further argues that the Free Churches in

York, after growing substantially in the period 1764–1837, have suffered continuing decline. As a result, Gill concludes that the historic Free Churches have become numerically marginal in the city. This echoes the conclusion of Grace Davie that in an era of 'believing without belonging' only the state church retains a repository of half-remembered faith (Davie 1994, 2002). Similarly, David Martin concluded that northern Europe is essentially post-Protestant (Martin 2002, 2005), and concluded that Pentecostalism, notwithstanding its global impact, showed little capacity or evidence of taking root in secular Europe (Martin 2002). Pentecostalism had failed therefore to amend Martin's earlier conclusion that the degree of secularization in a nation was closely correlated with the closeness of the official religion to the power of the state (Martin 1978).

St Michael le Belfrey: The Late Twentieth-century Market Leader

In the 1970s, under David Watson's leadership, St Michael le Belfrey achieved market dominance in York and international prominence (Watson 1983). Watson had arrived in York in 1965 as the curate in charge of St Cuthbert's, a parish church on the edge of the city centre with a congregation of half a dozen. Although the church was expected to become redundant after 12 months, rapid growth over the coming years resulted in services being relayed to other buildings. In 1973 the church moved to St Michael le Belfrey, another near empty church, but with a much larger seating capacity and a highly prominent location directly adjacent to York Minster. Watson moved to London in 1982 to develop his itinerant ministry as an evangelist and advocate for moderate charismatic renewal. He died of cancer in 1984.

St Michael's burgeoning congregation received criticism from the *Yorkshire Evening Press* (19 September 1978) that the congregation drained middle-class people away from other parishes. External Anglican advisers at that time recommended to Watson that St Michael's needed to strengthen its Anglican identity – as a result the Magnificat and Song of Simeon were restored to weekly use, albeit in contemporary settings, in the slimmed-down liturgy Watson had adapted from CPAS (Church Pastoral Aid Society – a broadly based evangelical Anglican agency) resources. They also noted that St Michael's conversion growth appeared to have diminished so that many in the regular congregation rarely brought friends and neighbours to the evangelistic guest services held at St Michael's and the Festivals of Praise for which the church used the Minster. When St Michael's was at its fullest, most enquirers were brought by people from other churches, making use of the city centre church as a mission resource.

In this period, the vast majority of evangelical students at the University of York attended St Michael's. In 1977, when I was an undergraduate in York, the evangelical Christian Union comprised around 150 students and was the largest student organization: one attended Elim, one attended the Salvation Army, less than half a dozen attended the Calvinistic and strictly non-charismatic Priory Street Baptist, a dozen or so attended Heslington Parish

Church, and almost all the others attended St Michael's. Indeed, many who attended other churches in the morning, migrated to St Michael's for the evening service. Just as the church was dominant in the student market, its prominence created a near evangelical-charismatic monopoly among the adult laity. When David Watson was writing *I Believe in the Church* (Watson 1978), he preached a series of sermons on biblical metaphors for the church; the sermon on 'light' included an excursus on concerns expressed by a minority about candles on the altar for the Eucharist. Watson's view was that the candles were unimportant and should therefore stay in use without any need for contention. This was an early, public indication of the presence of low or Free Church charismatics who were fellow travellers with Watson's Anglican renewal, but would subsequently form a church of their own. This incident is illustrative of one significant reason why new churches emerged late in York: neither the Bradford network, geographically proximate, nor the southern networks of Ichthus and Pioneer, socio-economically proximate to the middle classes of York, were able to secure an effective foothold in a city where a single church had secured market dominance.

Watson was a precursor of Alpha – indeed Sandy Millar's predecessor as vicar of Holy Trinity Brompton, the originator church of Alpha, was John Collins, who had been Watson's vicar during his curacy at St Mark's Gillingham. Like Alpha, Watson combined the conventional conservative apologetic and evangelistic fervour of the Bash camps[1] with a non-Pentecostal form of charismatic renewal, in which continuing experiential encounters with the Holy Spirit were severed from any mandatory linkage with the gift of tongues. Watson's *One in the Spirit* (1973) articulated an extremely moderate form of charismatic theology and he had intended it to be published by InterVarsity Press, the leading conservative evangelical publishing house of the day. Eventually he lost patience with the cavils of their editorial committee and the manuscript was accepted for publication without further amendment by Hodder & Stoughton, who subsequently published most of his books. One of Watson's elders at St Michael's (introduced in the mid-1970s as a tier of leadership below the clergy but above the Parochial Church Council (PCC) went further than Watson in the late 1970s, urging the congregation in a service at which I was present, to clap in subtle rhythms rather than with enthusiastic abandon – 'not like Pentecostals!' It was, therefore, the more Pentecostal among the fellow travellers at St Michael's who were most likely to depart in later years. Although Watson subsequently became close to John Wimber, the distinctive Wimberist ecstatic thaumaturgy that continues to resonate at the Alpha 'Holy Spirit weekend' was not a characteristic emphasis during Watson's time in York (Percy 1996).

Graham Cray, David Watson's successor (1982–92), subsequently Principal of Ridley Hall Cambridge and then Bishop of Maidstone, chaired the Anglican working group set up in 2002 that produced *Mission Shaped Church* (Cray 2004), a highly influential report promoting the re-imagining of Anglican and Methodist churches. Fresh Expressions was established as an Archbishops' initiative in 2004, and their website cites Cray's reflection on this process.

> The fresh expressions of church which Mission Shaped Church describes are evidence of considerable creative missionary energy within the Church of England. We did not so much write a report telling the Church of England what it needed to do as tell it what it was already doing and point out the potential.[2]

Towards the end of his incumbency, Cray had announced a vision to grow St Michael's to 2,000 regular attenders. After his departure the church experienced slow decline rather than advancing beyond the peak numbers under Watson. Priory Street Baptist, calvinistic and non-charismatic, reported a surprising influx of St Michael's migrants at this time, presumably those indifferent to denominational and pneumatological distinctives who favoured participation in a larger church, or perhaps those disillusioned with second-generation charismatic renewal (Finney 2000; Warner 2003).

Roger Simpson became vicar of St Michael's in 1999, and found the church somewhat disillusioned. He sought to restore the morale and missional focus, but also invested time in the deanery and One Voice York, preferring partnership to St Michael's 'going it alone'. In interview, Simpson stated that he is fully persuaded of the importance of cell church (Neighbour 1990; Beckham 1995) as the means by which to motivate and sustain congregations in mission, claiming that 'Over the next ten years cells will totally transform British church life.' The aim is for Christians to be committed to weekly small groups that intend to multiply as a result of numerical growth. According to Simpson, these cells are 'not very good evangelistically, but they help us keep mission at the heart of the church and have made possible a higher level of lay ministry than ever before'. Nonetheless, and perhaps surprisingly for the leader of the largest Anglican church in the city, Simpson stated 'People are basically happier in small churches.' He would prefer to see ten churches with congregations of 175 than one church of 1,000. He believes that in a larger church more people are lost in the crowd while diminishing numbers are mobilized because public ministry becomes increasingly professionalized. He is also concerned that larger churches can have a 'revolving door', that is a high turnover of short-term attenders. He is therefore pleased that St Michael's has in recent years given away non-stipendiary ministers (NSMs) to two other parishes in York. Over the next two to three years he aspired to establish a church resuscitation, working jointly with an existing parish church; an experimental congregation in a contemporary arts venue; an additional 'high octane' youth and student service at St Michael's; and what he termed a 'cutting edge church for the unchurched', particularly single adults.[3]

Fin de siècle Church Planting

Any account of turn-of-the-century church planting in York would be deficient without recognizing the substantive reconfiguration of the two main Pentecostal churches, both of which had taken over defunct Methodist buildings. The Methodist Chapel in Priory Street (a *locus classicus* of nineteenth-century ecclesiastical competition through church buildings, with Wesleyan, Baptist and Presbyterian buildings cheek by jowl between two Anglican churches, and with Primitive Methodist and Catholic churches built nearby) was sold to the Assemblies of God in the mid-1980s. This church subsequently reconfigured themselves as 'The Rock Church' in the early 1990s, still in membership with the Assemblies of God (AoG), but as a contemporary expression of Pentecostalism, combining rock music with a dance academy that provides street jazz, Latin, ballroom and ballet classes.

> Tastes in music are as diverse as the colours of the rainbow. Most of us gravitate to a style of music that has a specific sound and lyrics that relate to how we feel at any given point in our lives. That's why our music preferences can change dramatically as we tackle the various issues we go through. Here at the Rock we try to cater for all tastes using the various styles and sounds to convey what our relationship with God means to us. Sometimes we want quiet, sometimes we want loud. But to be honest, most of the time, WE WANT IT LOUD![4]

> At 11.15am, in the main auditorium you will continue to experience this life through exciting, contemporary music and spectacular dancing. You won't be able to sit still![5]

The idiom is familiarly Pentecostal, although their moralistic forebears were hardly likely to have welcomed stage make-up and secular dance moves! This emphatic, up-tempo contemporaneity is combined with the conventional Pentecostal-revivalist model of the highly entrepreneurial 'mighty man of God'.

> Anth Chapman is a reformer who will challenge your perspective on life and the Kingdom of God. He passionately believes that we have succeeded in making the most relevant message of the ages irrelevant to the people it was sent to reach. Without reformation the church moves into stagnation followed by fossilisation! He is committed to growing churches with the unchurched. If something is not illegal or immoral, he will probably use it (if he hasn't already!).[6]

The contrast is particularly striking with York Community Church, a recent church plant of similar size, whose Brethren origins are reflected in their deliberate avoidance of any hint of cult of personality. Their minister advised me that he was perfectly happy that neither his photo, nor his name, let alone any profile of his leadership style, was found on the church website.

The Methodist Chapel in Swinegate (built 1910) was subsequently bought by Elim Pentecostal. In 1989 Elim reported an attendance of 170 adults (Gill 2003: 169). However, by 1999 the congregation had declined to 25–30. Their new minister, Graham Hutchinson, subsequently closed the evening service, reinvented Sunday morning as a café-style church, combining coffee and discussion time with 30–40 minutes' preaching, and moved to a school near the university. By 2006 they had grown to 135 adults each week, estimating their total number of regular attenders to be around 200. This church has benefited significantly from the growth of international students and staff at the University of York. In June 2006 they baptized six Chinese and one Briton. Their pastor claims that because Elim is a brand with international recognition, this draws overseas Christians to them, with the consequent international ethos attractive to non-Christians also. They have now negotiated shared use of St Lawrence, an Anglican building, once renovations are completed in 2007–8. By this time Hutchinson hopes to have a weekly congregation of 300.

Not only have these two Pentecostal churches taken entirely different approaches to their cultural reconfiguration, they have adopted opposite approaches to working with other churches. While the Rock Church has a policy of putting all its energy into its own and focused mission, the pastor of Elim has played a key role in One Voice York, of which more below.

The recent Anglican church plant, G2, is an experiment in transition. Conceived as a 'mission station', in practice it has gathered three distinct groups of people: the core team who saw themselves as a continuing part of St Michael's, seeking to reach the unchurched through an experiment in café church; disaffected families at St Michael's, keen to join a congregation that provided Sunday School rather than weekly family services and pleased also to be released from the stresses of Sunday parking in central York; and newcomers to the church and/or the city, for whom G2 is their only current experience of church. Thus far G2 has provided non-liturgical and non-Eucharistic meetings, referring people back to St Michael's for pastoral support. The congregation sit around tables, coffee is on tap, the worship is brief and low-key, and the preaching is broken up by discussion points known as 'table talk'. This extremely informal, effectively post-charismatic approach is designed to be highly seeker friendly. In practice, although G2 has enjoyed steady growth, its actual market seems to be among marginal or even disaffected church attenders. After its summer break for the duration of August 2006, a luxury afforded a mission station but not a church, G2 was yet to determine whether it is still a narrow-band mission station, in which case some of its congregation ought logically be referred to St Michael's or other churches, or alternatively, it will need to reconceive itself as a church plant, entailing the introduction of the Eucharist, preaching designed to build up Christians, and a wider system of pastoral support.

G2 represents a highly significant experiment in contemporary church. It has grown much larger and faster than most Anglican 'Fresh Expressions'. It has avoided replicating the conventional neo-Pentecostal idiom of recent church planting in York. And it has been led by that distinctively Anglican style of leadership – the non-stipendiary priest. On the one hand, unlike most church plants, this means the leader is free to experiment without his salary being dependent on pleasing his congregation in the short term. On the other hand, there may be less available energy to turn a mission station into a self-sustaining church, with all the extra work that inevitably entails. In short, NSMs may enjoy more freedom to experiment but may be less incentivized to establish a fully fledged church.

Future Anglican church planting in York is likely to be shaped significantly by three factors: first, the new Bishop's Mission Order, that came before the

York Synod in 2006, which intends to loosen parish boundary restrictions and give further impetus to experimental church planting; second, Bishop Martin Wallis is considered by his clergy to be aware of the need for new missional initiatives and has approved the sharing of St Lawrence Church with Elim, described by one Anglican vicar as 'Unthinkable even ten years ago!'; and third, the express policy of Roger Simpson at St Michael le Belfrey, with the support of his Bishop, to pursue church planting both in non-ecclesiastical buildings and in redundant churches.

One Anglican clergyman observed in a discussion group, 'There is hardly a school left in York without a church plant.' Another added, 'The more, the merrier.' Nonetheless, the fact that they referred to these new free churches as *house churches* indicates a deliberate and sustained distancing from them. 'House church' was the preferred designation of new churches in the 1970s that originally met in homes. The emergent networks of churches have preferred to be called 'new churches' for around twenty years. Since most of the church plants in York have never met in homes, nor been part of the 'house church networks' of a previous generation, to designate them in such terms is anachronistic. Moreover, one Anglican clergyman described his own church planting aspirations thus: 'We certainly don't want to create another Pentecostal house church!'

Other church plants are listed chronologically in Table 1.

Much of this church planting reflects the fissile tendencies of the free churches in general and Pentecostalism in particular. York therefore exhibits a characteristic of global Pentecostalism identified by Cox – 'the more they fought, the more they multiplied' (Cox 1996; Synan 1997; Anderson 2004). Gateway was originally Acomb Christian Fellowship and broke from St Michael le Belfrey. The Vine Apostolic Church (previously called Living Waters) broke from Christians in York (subsequently called Kings Church). Crossroads Church was formed by most of the previous leadership team of Gateway, which had been disbanded when they joined New Frontiers International (NFI). Hope Church broke from Gateway Church after they left NFI. York Community Church broke from St Andrews Brethren Assembly. York City Church was established with people from Living Waters. Inevitably, in addition to these documented divisions, individuals have continued to migrate between churches in a less overt manner. Even so, many from rural churches are said to supplement the regular evening congregation at St Michael le Belfrey, and, presumably, some turn a regular visit into a change of church. Fluidity has been added to fissiparousness in the character of contemporary church participation (Warner 2006b).

Most of these new and reconfigured churches can be designated Pentecostal or neo-Pentecostal. Indeed, the new church streams of the late twentieth century appear to have been supplanted in York by a new wave of neo-Pentecostalism. Despite the substantive theological diversity among Pentecostals (Anderson 2004) that has been acknowledged as a range of Pentecostalisms (Dayton 1987), this commonality extends much wider than a specific emphasis upon renewing experiences of the Holy Spirit and continuing use of spiritual gifts. Denominationally aligned and independent Pentecostals exhibit similar commitment to a

Name	*Year started*	*Affiliation*	*Average adult attendance 2006*
Gateway Church	1979	Independent Pentecostal – previously New Frontiers International (NFI) 1999–2004	150
York Community Church	1993	Independent	220
The Rock Church	1993	– rebranded existing Assemblies of God	250
The Vine Apostolic Church	1996	Apostolic Church (Wales)	Not given
Kings Church	mid-90s	Ministry without Borders	40
Calvary Chapel	1997	Calvary Chapel	120
York City Church	1999	NFI	200
Crossroads Church	2000	Independent	Not given
Grove Pentecostal	2003?	Independent Pentecostal	Not given
The Ark Church	2003	Independent Pentecostal	50
Hope Church	2004	Abundant Life, Bradford	150
G2	2004	Anglican – fresh expression	50
Manchester Vineyard	2006	Manchester Vineyard	Putative
Leeds Vineyard	2006	Vineyard international	Putative

(Attendance data received from church offices, ministers and websites, and accessed through multiple sources where possible to minimize exaggeration.)

***Table 1:* Recent church plants in York**

measure of experimental contemporaneity, typically combined with enthusiastic music in worship, urgency in mission and aspirations to become a mega-church that impacts the entire city. This last characteristic is expressed on websites, in preaching and in interviews.[7] Despite the fact that the evidence indicates a proliferation of small to medium-sized churches, to become a mega-church remains the dominant dream.

Pentecostals have therefore not only taken over two redundant Methodist buildings in York, but Pentecostalism can be understood as the natural successor to Methodism. Methodist growth until the mid-nineteenth century had supplanted old dissent in York, as it had nationally and internationally (Finke and Stark 1992; Warner 2006b). In the late twentieth century, however, while Methodism in York continued to decline apace, the Baptists have remained essentially static, with two churches in 2006 just as they had in St

Michael's heyday. Baptists are neither suffering the severe continuing decline of other historic denominations, nor have they taken part in the turn of the century surge of experimental church planting. Although the growth of York's free churches around the turn of the century is almost all baptistic, it would be misleading to suggest that Baptists represent the natural focal point. Pentecostalism is more plausibly conceived as the *fons et origo* (source and origin).

The evidence of fragmentation in church planting in York is partly counterbalanced by two factors. First, almost all the neo-Pentecostal churches use Alpha (Calvary Chapel and Hope Church use their own resources). This reflects the paradox of Alpha (Percy 1998; Ward 1998; Hunt 2001; Booker and Ireland 2003; Hunt 2004; MacLaren 2004; Warner 2007). Although the content of the programme is deeply indebted to the conservative apologetic of mid-twentieth-century public-school Anglican evangelicalism, the publicity has been concerned to reach beyond the evangelical sector, securing adoption among mainstream Anglican and Roman Catholic churches. No statistical breakdown has been provided in the public domain concerning the relative success when using Alpha in different kinds of church, by denomination, size or theological tradition. It seems likely that neo-Pentecostal church plants may bring a highly motivated missional urgency, and indeed an ebullient confidence in conservative formulations of the Christian Gospel, to their enthusiastic adoption of this kind of evangelistic programme.

The second factor countering fragmentation is York's distinctive expression of ecumenical co-operation – One Voice York. As with church planting, this reflects an Anglican-Pentecostal axis. Graham Hutchinson, pastor at Elim, arrived in York in 1999, one month before Roger Simpson at St Michael le Belfrey. Hutchinson recalled from that time a lack of cooperation and attitudes of competitiveness between the churches. Less than half a dozen church leaders began to pray together monthly but during the first year their number grew to around twenty and they decided to begin weekly meetings. In due course they adopted the banner of One Voice York, which was already in existence as the mission wing of Churches Together in York. Several mission events were organized, including *Just Ten* with the Anglican evangelist J. John; a barbecue in the grounds of Bishopthorpe Palace to which 500 came; a joint Alpha meal in the Minster attended by 700, for which Roger Simpson secured Nicky Gumbel as the speaker and after which, he recalled, Alpha courses 'really multiplied'. At Pentecost 2005 over 500 attended a prayer event at the Minster, and this grew to over 1,100 in 2006. Also in 2006 Churches Together invited One Voice to organize the Good Friday joint service in the Minster, although this received a mixed response. As Hutchinson observed, 'We represent the majority. However, we need to be inclusive.' A further new initiative launched in 2006 is York School of Theology, in which local leaders will provide lectures for distance-learning students from their churches. The initial courses are from the moderate evangelical Anglican college, St John's Nottingham, but Hutchinson emphasized that this was a united and independent project, free to take the courses considered most suitable from any provider. Given the success of York St John's foundation degree among the traditional churches that have been in the most severe decline (Brierley 2000), it seems likely that the York School of

Theology may secure a strong market, especially if the fissiparous tendencies of neo-Pentecostalism have finally been transcended in York, at least to some degree. Furthermore, the range of co-operative initiatives indicates a willingness to draw upon all resources perceived as appropriate, notably many Anglican resources, whereas traditional British Pentecostalism might be expected to be more overtly dependent upon North American Pentecostal resources (Anderson 2004). Indeed, one neo-Pentecostal church leader identified a key difference between themselves and the Rock Church by suggesting this particular Assemblies of God church was at least to some degree a North American import. When One Voice did recommend a North American author for study across the churches in 2006, it was Rick Warren, the Baptist (and moderately neo-Pentecostal) founder of Saddleback Church, California, who has authored a series of 'purpose-driven' books (Warren 1996, 2003a, 2003b). Neither classical Pentecostal resources from the States nor the distinctive emphases of the 'health and wealth' movement (Anderson 2004) appear consonant with the emphases of One Voice, which is more inclined to assimilate resources with a track record of relative success, irrespective of denominational origin, although perhaps with charismatic Anglican leanings.

One Voice is mostly evangelical and charismatic, but includes some non-charismatics and some non-evangelicals. When Hutchinson was asked to lead One Voice he insisted upon an Anglican co-leader, and David Casswell, vicar of Clifton Parish Church, was appointed. Casswell adopts a Hookerian inclusivity[8] to his conception of One Voice York – 'You are included unless you actively exclude yourself.' Hutchinson and Casswell both believe that the weekly prayer breakfast for clergy and others is essential for constructive ecumenical partnership in mission (although Hutchinson argues for the term 'interdenominational' suggesting that some free-church people suspect 'ecumenical' has come to signify 'interfaith'). Youth leaders have now begun a parallel prayer meeting, which has resulted in regular events for Christian youth groups and a bi-monthly Christian nightclub. Hutchinson recognized that this new attitude of cooperation was not simply down to individuals willing to pray together on a weekly basis: '25 years ago people saw the church doing fine and thought things would continue like that for ever. We're more desperate now.'

Pluralism, Competition and Secularization

Classical secularization theory saw a direct, causal connection between the rise of denominations and the decline of churchgoing. This unconsciously Constantinian (indeed Augustinian) perspective on church life argued that for as long as one Church could claim international, or at least national, supremacy, it could still articulate absolutist claims concerning doctrine and the means of salvation. Once rival forms of church began to mutually acknowledge one another's legitimacy, their various truth claims began to be relativized and the plausibility of their demands of allegiance were irretrievably diminished (Wilson 1966; Bruce 2002). When Berger was still an advocate of classical secularization, he argued that the sacred canopy was fractured by religious pluralism (Berger 1967, 1999). Gill argued that nineteenth-century over-competition was counter-productive in the context of a regulated market with an established church, resulting in over-expansion of seating capacity by unrealistic Free Churches who doomed their successors to a legacy of pews that had never been filled (Gill 1993, 2001, 2003).

Conversely, rational choice theory argued that, in a free religious market, pluralism increased choice and maximized the opportunities for religious consumers to find a provider whose product was consonant with their preferences (Stark and Bainbridge 1985, 1987; Stark and Finke 2000). This American approach has had great difficulty faced with Western Europe, where the decline of existing religious providers ought logically to have produced fertile ground for new religious experimentation (Bruce 1999). This could be explained by David Martin's account of the unintended consequence, to use a Weberian concept,[9] of the Constantinian settlement, in which the greater the proximity between religion and power, the greater the subsequent degree of secularization (Martin 1978, 2005).

Classical secularization theory ought theoretically to have resulted long since in the disappearance of organized Christianity from Western Europe, or at least the demise of the Free Churches – 'even more to the disadvantage of Nonconformist denominations than to the Established church' (Wilson 1966: 14). In fact York confirms the national trend in England, where baptistic and in particular neo-Pentecostal churches have enjoyed numerical advance in the past quarter century, even as Anglicans, Roman Catholics and Methodists have all declined at similarly severe rates (Warner 2006b). As with the national figures, the Baptist Union churches have experienced relative stability compared with other historic denominations, but have a diminishing market share among believer baptizing churches. It is neo-Pentecostal advance that rebuts the prescriptive projections of classical secularization theory. Nonetheless, there is no evidence that this burgeoning church planting has made any substantive impact upon secularized York. There has been a shift of market share towards the neo-Pentecostals, but mostly within the internal market of churchgoers, whether regular or fringe. The de-churched majority seem as little touched by the neo-Pentecostal revolution as by the often-overstated 'spiritual revolution' of the new age (Bruce 2002; Heelas *et al.* 2005). Churchgoing in York has become a marginal leisure activity, even if, as the clergy confidently asserted in interviews, the neo-Pentecostal church planting has achieved a limited measure of conversion growth rather than simply 'recycling the saints' (Bibby and Brinkerhoff 1973, 1974, 1983).

Kelley's account of why conservative churches enjoy relative success has remained influential (Kelley 1972). For Kelly, 'traits of strictness' (*passim*) determine the resilience of such churches, retaining affiliates and motivating them to recruit others. Building on Kelley, Hunter identified significant transitions in the theology and ethics of moderate American evangelicals and concluded that diluted strictness would lead to diminishing numerical success (Hunter 1983, 1987). However, as Smith has demonstrated, late twentieth-century church growth among moderate American evangelicals outstripped that among unreconstructed fundamentalists (Smith 1998). Warner has demonstrated the same pattern among late-twentieth-century English evangelicals (Warner 2007). Even so, in York the strictly conservative churches within calvinistic exclusivism have neither grown nor church planted with the success of Anglican charismatics and neo-Pentecostals.

Although Kay has demonstrated the highly conservative theology prevalent among Elim pastors in the UK (Kay 2000), self-designated fundamentalists have always been suspicious of Pentecostals. This is partly because Pentecostals have roots in pietism, Methodism and Romanticism, affirming the subjective turn in evangelicalism over against the rationalism consequent upon fundamentalism's unconscious derivation from the enlightenment (Bebbington 1989, Murphy 1996, Knight 1997, Dorrien 1998). Moreover, while fundamentalism is instinctively opposed to cultural and liturgical innovation (Marsden 1980, 1987, 1991; Marty, Appleby 1991, 1993a, 1993b, 1994, 1995; Partridge 2001; Percy and Jones 2002), Pentecostals have often been in the vanguard of pragmatic experimentation and cultural engagement (Cox 1996; Synan 1997; Martin 1998, 2002; Scotland 2000; Anderson 2004).

While Barr's polemic treated evangelicals and fundamentalists as more or less synonymous (Barr 1977, 1984), Harris's more subtle and precise account demonstrated that many evangelicals have fundamentalizing tendencies without embracing the cognitive framework or oppositional agenda of fundamentalism (Harris 1998). Even so, while many Pentecostals exhibit fundamentalising tendencies in their theological and ethical conservatism, fundamentalists (and indeed the broader category of calvinistic exclusivists) are surely right to consider their experientialism, missional pragmatism and early-adopter acculturation as indicative of a distinct theological orientation. In contrast with oppositional and pre-critical rationalism they represent a form of late modern modified conservatism. Cox went so far as to argue that the centrality of experiential immanentism in Pentecostalism 'shatters the cognitive packaging' (Cox 1996: 71). This emphasis inevitably subverts the dogmatic certainties of conventional conservative theology, even where these remain central to the formal statements of Pentecostalism. Even so, notwithstanding Guest's account of the ethical conservatism of the congregation at St Michael le Belfrey (Guest *et al.* 2004), charismatic Anglicans exhibit a similar modified conservatism. Contrary to Kelley, if 'traits of strictness' (1972: *passim*) were alone determinative of church growth, more conservative churches in York would have been doing much better than those within the Anglican-charismatic and neo-Pentecostal nexus.

An alternative account is required to explain why moderately conservative, culturally engaged Christianity has been the form least susceptible to decline in the recent Western cultural context. It remains possible that this relative success is in fact a temporary phenomenon, indicative of late-onset decline within an enclave of cultural and religious conservatism, whose late modern appetite for proliferating certainties faces the prospect of postmodern obsolescence. There is certainly national data for England that indicates this possibility (Warner 2007): declining sales of evangelical magazines and Bible reading notes; the decline of evangelical church attendance in the 1990s, albeit not at the rate of non-evangelical decline; and the fact that 74 per cent of churches using Alpha for three or more years are not growing (79 per cent of non-Alpha churches are static or in decline, which is also the performance of churches that have used Alpha for one or two years). In the microcosm of York, more research is required to compile longitudinal data to test the possibility and significance of late-onset decline. In their interviews, Casswell recognized a shift of era – 'Poor Vineyard are struggling now, just like the rest of us' – and Hutchinson observed, 'We are reaching more internationals, but what about the Brits?' A cultural chasm remains unbridged – possibly unbridgeable – between the churches of York and the unchurched majority, secular, pluralistic and post-modern.

Bebbington's quadrilateral of evangelical distinctives has become a normative classification

> *conversionism*, the belief that lives need to be changed; *activism*, the expression of the gospel in effort; *Biblicism*, a particular regard for the Bible; and what may be called *crucicentrism*, a stress on the sacrifice of Christ on the cross. (Bebbington 1989: 3)

Building on the criticism that this categorization is too static and fails to account for evangelical diversity and internecine rivalry, I have argued for a refined model in which, while all evangelicals adhere to these four emphases, different sub-sectors group around two conflictual axes – biblicist-crucicentric and activist-conversionist (Warner 2007). The activists – pragmatic acculturators, experiential and entrepreneurial – are often viewed by their conservative co-religionists as light on the Bible and the cross. In particular, charismatics and Pentecostals exhibit an unremitting optimism allied to convertive piety. This can result in a tendency to juvenile enthusiasm (Hastings 2001), a naïve late-modern mechanical conception of church growth, craving for the latest blueprint that guarantees success. At times they have even shown delusional tendencies, with a triumphalist rhetoric in some songs and mission initiatives that appears to have lost touch with secularized reality (Festinger 1957; Festinger *et al.* 1964; Warner 2007). Notwithstanding these excesses, and irrespective of whether late-onset decline can be demonstrated or falsified, this urgent, insistent, enthusiastic pursuit of experiments in the re-imagining of church, allied to a dogged refusal to embrace defeatism, gives a clue to the resilience and relative success of this kind of church. It is not merely that charismatics and neo-Pentecostals exhibit Tamney's 'modernized traditionalism' (Tamney 2002) and operate in the religious category Heelas and Woodhead have identified as the most viable form of Christianity in post-modern culture, namely 'experiential religions of difference' (Heelas *et al.* 1998: passim). These Christians are convinced they have the potential to succeed in contemporary mission, and the sense of urgent dedication to continue with pragmatic experimentation, however often their initiatives – café church, cell church, rock church, purpose-driven church, male-headship church and Alpha, to name but a few found in York – produce more limited results than had been anticipated. For the neo-Pentecostals, *spes vincit omnia* (hope conquers all).

Since the activist-conversionist axis of evangelicalism has evolved its orthopraxy as a result of pragmatic, cultural bargaining, this has inevitable, even if unintended, cognitive consequences. Just as academic theology has critiqued traditional conservatism, not merely as pre-critical but as culture-bound with enlightenment presuppositions (Barr 1977; Murphy 1996), the more the activists immerse themselves in post-modern mission the more likely their pragmatic indifference to the detail of traditional evangelical theology will increasingly fuse with a new cultural alienation from the conceptual frameworks of their forebears. In short, the unintended consequence of ecclesial experimentation will be the legitimation of doctrinal reformulation. An alliance can therefore be predicted between post-conservative theologians, critiquing and reconstructing the evangelical tradition and post-conservative activists engaged in the re-imagining of church. Although at present most of the charismatic-pentecostal church planting in York is experimental in practice but highly traditional in theology, the pragmatic commitment to cultural engagement ineluctably leads towards doctrinal reflexivity. What remains unclear is whether the gradual dissolution of the residual scaffolding of late-modern certainties will result in the demise of such churches, which may have only subsisted as ghettoes of modernity, or will result in their further invigoration as experiments in progressive orthodoxy. This post-conservative re-combining of the biblicist-crucicentric and activist-conversionist axes seems more likely to occur among some of the Anglican charismatics than among the neo-Pentecostals, among whom many are assertively traditionalist in their theological formulations (Elim Pentecostal churches affirm biblical inerrancy and New Frontiers core leaders have an emphatic, male-only concept of church leadership) and some are, to say the least, remote from academic theological discourse.

The Implications of Proliferating Churches

Troeltsch's model of churches and sects (Troeltsch 1992 [1911]) has sometimes been used polemically to draw a sharp distinction between the respectable form of established religion and its protestant alternatives. The term 'sect' has always been problematic, having a technical meaning in sociological discourse that can be difficult to immunize from its pejorative resonance in ordinary and ecclesiastical usage. While classical secularization theory saw rival sects transmute into mutually accepted denominations as a significant stage in the linear process of secularization (Bruce 1996), Johnson proposed a church-sect continuum, depending upon the degree of cultural assimilation (Johnson 1963). Stark built upon this model to conceive secularization not at the transition from church and sects to denominations but rather as the transition from sects to churches (Stark and Bainbridge 1985, 1987). In this analysis, churches in low tension with their cultural context constitute the mainstream which is always migrating to the sidelines (Finke and Stark 1992) whereas the most viable forms of a religion are always found in relatively high-tension sects. Of course, transferring this theoretical framework to the context of Western Europe, with state-sponsored religious monopolies rather than a free market, is problematic. Nonetheless, by recovering Troeltsch's own alternative terminology we can develop this analysis further. For Troeltsch, church and sect can also be understood as institutional and voluntarist types of church. If this is conceived as an institutional–voluntarist continuum, the types of church we have identified as most likely to grow are voluntarist in ethos, irrespective of denomination. Moreover, whatever the irreducible differences between such churches, those that are not rigorously sectarian have come to recognize one another as partner-voluntarists. As one leader in York observed, 'We wouldn't necessarily enjoy one another's churches, but we pray together. And we almost all do Alpha.'

This voluntarist coalition works very differently to classical secularization theory's conception of denominational pluralism leading to doctrinal relativism. Escott and Gelder's studies of Protestant denominations found the Baptists to be significantly different from Anglicans, Methodists, the URC and the Salvation Army (Escott and Gelder 2002). Baptist attenders were discovered to be younger and more contemporary in their music and worship, more committed to evangelistic outreach, financial support of their church and personal prayer, and placed particular emphasis upon the role played by God and their local church in their lives. However, the denomination was considerably less important to them than to attenders at more institutional churches. If this is the case with Baptist Union churches, which represent a declining and relatively institutional share of the baptistic market, we can assume a still greater degree of post-denominational voluntarism among many of York's neo-Pentecostals (not all, for NFI is emphatically denominational, despite its own rhetoric) and among at least some of the Anglican voluntarists as well. While denominational allegiance may have become increasingly relativized in the voluntarist coalition, their partnership and mutual trust enhance their activist-conversionist commitment and expectancy. The multiplication of voluntarist churches working in partnership appears likely to have reinforced post-denominationalism while strengthening confidence in the non-negotiable essence of the evangelical Gospel.

Roof's identification of a 'spiritual quest culture' (Roof 1999) and Hammond's analysis of the reconstruction of religion around personal autonomy (Hammond 1992) identify a *zeitgeist* that has been conducive to the commodification of evangelical religion. Almost without exception the church plants in York are targeting people groups rather than a geographical parish. The style of worship and preaching is designed to be appropriate to the kind of people the church aspires to attract. This targeted approach has an unintended consequence of course, since the primary consumers of churches in York are committed Christians, who may be inclined, particularly in a post-denominational climate and with a culturally imbued instinct for personal autonomy, to shop around for a church, with their allegiance becoming provisional, contingent upon their needs being suitably met. In the case of G2, a member of St Michael's PCC told me that she thought people should be compelled to return to the mother church if they were not committed to the specific mission of the church plant. However, in practice people have voted with their feet, and families who found a weekly family service unpalatable but wanted to remain within the broad network of St

Michael's chose to gravitate to a congregation that provided separate children's groups. This trend may produce increasing tensions within voluntarist churches, where the preferences of Christian consumers may not necessarily be compatible with the missional vision of the church. Brand loyalty appears to be in decline not only in supermarkets, but also in voluntarist churches. In the brave new world of autonomous religion, the individual religious consumer is king.

Casanova has demonstrated the return of religion to the sphere of public life, negotiating post-Constantinian approaches in pluralistic cultures (Casanova 1994). In the microcosm of York the multiplication of fairly small churches will have rendered voluntarist church life relatively invisible. One Voice York has not yet addressed this issue effectively, although Casswell (co-leader of the organization) expressed the church leaders' hope to develop an interface with the city council. There were protests by some evangelicals in the city against a 'Satan's Grotto' at one tourist venue, and others had campaigned against performances of *Jerry Springer, The Opera*. In both cases One Voice York had declined to be involved collectively, concerned to avoid being pigeon-holed by the media as negative campaigners.

Just as the proliferation of church plants may render voluntarist religion more invisible, the implicit affirmation of personal autonomy is likely to undermine some pan-evangelical leaders' aspirations to homogeneous mobilization with a socio-political agenda. As Smith has demonstrated in the United States, evangelical laity place a higher value on individual liberty of conscience than many self-appointed evangelical public campaigners (Smith 2000). Autonomous religious consumers select among the socio-political concerns voiced within the tradition rather than unquestioningly accepting an ethical package deal. Nonetheless, when voluntarists are invisible in their proliferated churches, and difficult to mobilize, unrepresentative and reactionary campaigners may tar the broad tradition in the media and the public eye with their own highly vocal extremism.

Further research is required concerning the possibility of late-onset decline, fundamentalising tendencies among pragmatic activists, the extent of conversion growth in comparison with 'recycling the saints', and the degree of denominational and local church loyalty among autonomous religious consumers. Such analysis would clarify the extent to which current church planting may operate within late modern categories of pervasive and conservative certainties, resulting in built-in cultural obsolescence with the rise of post-modernity. Research is also needed to test the thesis that functional acculturation in the practice of church is liable to produce an amenable climate for theological reflexivity and the emergence of progressive trajectories among activist-conversionists in theology and ethics.

In 1966 there was a severe division in the UK between Anglican and free-church evangelicals, provoked by the 'pure church' neo-fundamentalist agenda of D.M. Lloyd-Jones (Brencher 2002; Warner 2007). At that time the Anglican–Pentecostal divide was acute. It therefore represents an extraordinary sea-change that the voluntarist evangelical coalition in York is now centred upon Anglican charismatics and neo-Pentecostals. The emerging free market in voluntarist churches, if it is sustained while institutional church life continues to decline apace, will come to denote a major reconfiguration of Christian identity in the city, with post-denominational religious consumers increasingly free to migrate from church to church, according to the missional vision or their own felt needs. Graham Cray's vision for 2,000 Christians at St Michael's has proved untenable: thirty-five years' prominence for that church appears to indicate a maximum capacity of around 800. However, through the proliferating church plants, both Anglican and neo-Pentecostal, Cray's vision may already have been fulfilled. If late-onset decline fails to overturn the voluntarist trajectory, if autonomous religious consumers choose not to undermine missional experimentation, if pragmatic urgency continues to explore fresh expressions of church and if the consequent reconfigurations of post-conservative theology construct a progressive orthodoxy rather than a collapse into institutional anaemia, even in a secularized culture this coalition of voluntarists will continue to experiment with the re-imagining of church as they determinedly innovate, aspiring to missional advance.

Notes

1 The 'Bash' camps were run by Eric Nash as mid-twentieth-century recruitment holidays among public schoolboys for conservative evangelicalism. Prominent participants included John Stott, Michael Green and David Watson.
2 http://www.freshexpressions.org.uk/section.asp?id=46 (accessed 21 June 2006).
3 http://www.rockchurch.org.uk/sunday/ (accessed 21 June 2006).
4 http://www.freshexpressions.org.uk/section.asp?id=46.
5 http://www.rockchurch.org.uk/sunday/.
6 http://www.rockchurch.org.uk/sunday/.
7 York City Church, for example, want to build, in typical NFI style, 'a large New Testament Church in York', http://yorkcitychurch.org.uk/church/vision.php (accessed 21 June 2006).
8 Richard Hooker (1554–1600) developed an inclusive understanding of the Anglican Church, such that all English people were a part of the church unless they actively removed themselves.
9 Max Weber (1864–1920), one of the founding fathers of sociology, developed the concept of an unintended consequence when he traced the advancement of capitalism in the context of ascetic Protestantism (Weber 1958).

References

Anderson, A. (2004). *An Introduction to Pentecostalism: Global Charismatic Christianity* (Cambridge: Cambridge University Press).
Barr, J. (1977). *Fundamentalism* (London: SCM).
—— (1984), *Escaping from Fundamentalism* (London: SCM).
Bebbington, D.W. (1989), *Evangelicalism in Modern Britain: A History from the 1730s to the 1980s* (London: Unwin Hyman).
Beckham, W. (1995), *The Second Reformation* (Houston: Touch Publications).
Berger, P.L. (1967), *The Sacred Canopy: Elements of a Sociological Theory of Religion* (Garden City, NY: Doubleday).
Berger, P.L. (ed.) (1999), *The Desecularization of the World: Resurgent Religion and World Politics* (Washington, DC and Grand Rapids: Ethics and Public Policy Center).

Bibby, R. and M. Brinkerhoff (1973), 'The Circulation of the Saints: A Study of People who Join Conservative Churches', *Journal for the Scientific Study of Religion* 112: 273–85.
—— (1974), 'When Proselytizing Fails: An Organizational Analysis', *Sociological Analysis* 35: 189–200.
—— (1983), 'Circulation of the Saints Revisited: A Longitudinal Look at Conservative Church Growth', *Journal for the Scientific Study of Religion* 22: 253–62.
Booker, M., and M. Ireland (2003), *Evangelism – Which Way Now?* (London: Church House Publishing).
Brencher, J. (2002), *Martyn Lloyd-Jones (1899–1981) and Twentieth-Century Evangelicalism* (Carlisle: Paternoster).
Brierley, P.W. (2000), *The Tide Is Running Out: What the English Church Attendance Survey reveals* (London: Christian Research).
Bruce, S. (1996), *Religion in the Modern World: From Cathedrals to Cults* (Oxford: Oxford University Press).
—— (1999), *Choice and Religion* (Oxford: Oxford University Press).
—— (2002), *God is Dead: Secularization in the West* (Oxford: Blackwell).
Casanova, J. (1994), *Public Religions in the Modern World* (Chicago and London: University of Chicago Press).
Cox, H. (1996), *Fire From Heaven* (London: Cassell).
Cray, G. (ed.) (2004), *Mission Shaped Church* (London: Church House Publishing).
Davie, G. (1994), *Religion in Britain since 1945: Believing without Belonging* (Oxford: Blackwell).
—— (2002), *Europe: The Exceptional Case* (London: Darton, Longman & Todd).
Dayton, D.W. (1987), *Theological Roots of Pentecostalism* (Metuchen: Scarecrow Press).
Dorrien, G.J. (1998), *The Remaking of Evangelical Theology* (Louisville, KY: Westminster John Knox Press).
Escott, P., and A. Gelder (2002), *Church Life Profile 2001:- Denominational Results for the Baptist Union* (New Malden and London: Churches Information for Mission).
Festinger, L. (1957), *A Theory of Cognitive Dissonance* (Stanford, CA: Stanford University Press).
Festinger, L., H.W. Riecken and S. Schachter (1964), *When Prophecy Fails: A Social and Psychological Study of a Modern Group that Predicted the Destruction of the World* (New York and London: Harper & Row).
Finke, R., and R. Stark (1992), *The Churching of America, 1776–1990: Winners and Losers in our Religious Economy* (New Brunswick, NJ: Rutgers University Press).
Finney, J. (2000), *Fading Splendour? A New Model of Renewal* (London: Darton, Longman & Todd).
Gill, R. (1993), *The Myth of the Empty Church* (London: SPCK).
—— (2001), 'The Future of Religious Participation and Belief in Britain and Beyond', in *The Blackwell Companion to Sociology of Religion* (ed. R. Fenn; Oxford: Blackwell), pp. 279–91.
—— (2003), *The 'Empty Church' Revisited* (Aldershot: Ashgate).
Guest, M., K. Tusting and L. Woodhead (eds) (2004), *Congregational Studies in the UK* (Aldershot: Ashgate).
Hammond, P.E. (1992), *Religion and Personal Autonomy: The Third Disestablishment in America* (Columbia: University of South Carolina).
Harris, H.A. (1998), *Fundamentalism and Evangelicals* (Oxford: Clarendon).
Hastings, A. (2001), *A History of English Christianity 1920–2000* (London: SCM).
Heelas, P., D. Martin and P. Morris (eds) (1998), *Religion, Modernity, and Postmodernity* (Oxford: Blackwell).
Heelas, P., L. Woodhead, B. Seel and K. Tusting (eds) (2005), *The Spiritual Revolution: Why Religion is Giving Way to Spirituality* (Oxford: Blackwell).

Hunt, S. (2001), *Anyone for Alpha? Evangelism in a Post-Christian Society* (London: Darton, Longman & Todd).
—— (2004), *The Alpha Enterprise* (Aldershot: Ashgate).
Hunter, J.D. (1983), *American Evangelicalism: Conservative Religion and the Quandary of Modernity* (New Brunswick: Rutgers University Press).
—— (1987), *Evangelicalism: The Coming Generation* (Chicago and London: University of Chicago Press).
Johnson, B. (1963), 'On Church and Sect', *American Sociological Review* 28: 539–49.
Kay, W.K. (2000), *Pentecostals in Britain* (Carlisle: Paternoster).
Kelley, D.M. (1972), *Why Conservative Churches are Growing: A Study in Sociology of Religion* (New York: Harper & Row).
Knight, H.H. (1997), *A Future for Truth* (Nashville: Abindgon Press).
MacLaren, D. (2004), *Mission Implausible: Restoring Credibility to the Church* (Carlisle: Paternoster).
Marsden, G.M. (1980), *Fundamentalism and American Culture: The Shaping of Twentieth Century Evangelicalism, 1870–1925* (New York: Oxford University Press).
—— (1987), *Reforming Fundamentalism: Fuller Seminary and the New Evangelicalism* (Grand Rapids: Eerdmans).
—— (1991), *Understanding Fundamentalism and Evangelicalism* (Grand Rapids: Eerdmans).
Martin, B. (1998), 'From Pre- to Post-modernity in Latin America: The Case of Pentecostalism', in P. Heelas, D. Martin and P. Morris (eds), *Religion, Modernity and Postmodernity* (Oxford: Blackwell), pp. 102–46.
Martin, D. (1978), *A General Theory of Secularization* (Oxford: Blackwell).
—— (2002), *Pentecostalism: The World their Parish* (Oxford: Blackwell).
—— (2005), *On Secularization: Towards a Revised General Theory* (Aldershot: Ashgate).
Marty, M. and R.S. Appleby (eds) (1991), *Fundamentalisms Observed* (Chicago and London: University of Chicago Press).
—— (1993a), *Fundamentalisms and Society: Reclaiming the Sciences, the Family and Education* (Chicago and London: University of Chicago Press).
—— (1993b), *Fundamentalisms and the State: Remaking Polities, Economies and Militance* (Chicago and London: University of Chicago Press).
—— (1994), *Accounting for Fundamentalisms: The Dynamic Character of Movements* (Chicago and London: University of Chicago Press).
—— (1995), *Fundamentalisms Comprehended* (Chicago and London: University of Chicago Press).
Murphy, N. (1996), *Beyond Liberalism and Fundamentalism: How Modern and Postmodern Philosophy Set the Theological Agenda* (Valley Forge, PA: Trinity Press International).
Neighbour, R.W. (1990), *Where Do We Go From Here?* (Houston: Touch Publications).
Partridge, C.H. (ed.) (2001), *Fundamentalisms* (Carlisle: Paternoster).
Percy, M. (1996), *Words, Wonders and Power: Understanding Contemporary Christian Fundamentalism and Revivalism* (London: SPCK).
—— (1998), 'Join the Dots Christianity: Assessing Alpha', *Reviews in Religion and Theology* (May 1998).
Percy, M. and I. Jones (eds) (2002), *Fundamentalism, Church and Society* (London: SPCK).
Roof, W.C. (1999), *Spiritual Marketplace* (Princeton: Princeton University Press).
Scotland, N. (2000), *Charismatics and the New Millennium* (Guildford: Eagle).
Smith, C. (1998), *American Evangelicals: Embattled and Thriving* (Chicago: University of Chicago Press).
—— (2000), *Christian America? What Evangelicals Really Want* (Berkeley and London: University of California Press).

Stark, R. and W.S. Bainbridge (1985), *The Future of Religion: Secularization, Revival, and Cult Formation* (Berkeley: University of California Press).
—— (1987), *A Theory of Religion* (New York: Peter Lang).
Stark, R. and R. Finke (2000), *Acts of Faith: Explaining the Human Side of Religion* (Berkeley and London: University of California Press).
Synan, V. (1997) [1971], *The Holiness-Pentecostal Tradition* (Grand Rapids: Eerdmans).
Tamney, J.B. (2002), *The Resilience of Conservative Religion: The Case of Popular, Conservative Protestant Congregations* (Cambridge: Cambridge University Press).
Troeltsch, E. (1992) [1911], *The Social Teaching of the Christian Churches* (Louisville, KY: Westminster/John Knox Press).
Ward, P. (1998), 'Alpha: The McDonaldization of Religion', *Anvil* 15.4: 279–86.
Warner, R. (2003), 'Ecstatic Spirituality and Entrepreneurial Revivalism', in A. Walker and K. Aune (eds), *On Revival: A Critical Examination* (Carlisle: Paternoster), pp. 221–38.
—— (2006a), 'Fissured Resurgence: Developments in English Pan-Evangelicalism 1966–2001' (unpublished PhD dissertation, King's College, London).
—— (2006b), 'Pluralism and Voluntarism in the English Religious Economy', *Journal of Contemporary Religion* 21.3: 389–404.
—— (2007) *Reinventing English Evangelicalism, 1966–2001: A Theological and Sociological Study* (Carlisle: Paternoster).
Warren, R. (1996), *The Purpose Driven Church* (Grand Rapids: Zondervan).
—— (2003a), *Daily Inspiration for the Purpose Driven Life: Scriptural Reflections from the 40 Days of Purpose* (Grand Rapids: Zondervan).
—— (2003b), *The Purpose Driven Life* (Grand Rapids: Zondervan).
Watson, D.C.K. (1973), *One in the Spirit* (London: Hodder & Stoughton).
—— (1978), *I Believe in the Church* (London: Hodder & Stoughton).
—— (1983), *You are My God* (London: Hodder & Stoughton).
Weber, M. (1958), *The Protestant Ethic and the Spirit of Capitalism* (New York: Scribner's).
Wilson, B.R. (1966), *Religion in Secular Society: A Sociological Comment* (London: C.A Watts).

11

Identity and Religion in Yorkshire Fishing Communities

Stephen Friend

Introduction

This study explores the relationship between identity and religion in Yorkshire fishing communities. Much of the work draws upon nineteenth- and early-twentieth-century material, although a more contemporary perspective is provided by examples drawn from the Women's Voices Project,[1] which is currently engaged in interviewing women in Yorkshire fishing communities. While identity is a much discussed issue today there is relatively little published material that explores the relationship between identity and religion. The present study is a contribution to the debate here.

We begin by exploring the nature of identity, making use of Durkheim's model of social solidarities as a means to understanding the nature of the communities and their development. This is followed by an examination of ritual in fishing communities, before going on to explore the relationship between identity and religious beliefs and practices, especially 'lived religion' (Orsi 2002: xiii) – a term used here in preference to folk religion (Clark 1982) or popular religion (Williams 1999), not least because it avoids the issue of dualism and suggests a more pervasive integration with institutionalized religion.

The Construction and Maintenance of Identity in Yorkshire Fishing Communities

The concept of identity has given rise to innumerable studies. Among these, George Herbert Mead (1934) has argued that we *imagine* ourselves with a particular image; Erving Goffman (1959) proposed that we *act* out our roles; and Anthony P. Cohen (1987) has made us aware of the importance of *symbolism* in the life of a community. The term is also often qualified by an adjective (*personal* identity, *social* identity and *cultural* identity), although Jenkins has argued that it is less confusing to talk simply of 'identity' and to not make distinctions between these various terms (2004: 4). Nevertheless, identity is 'by its nature elusive and ambivalent' (Vecchi, cited in Bauman 2004: 2). At the same time identity is a *process* (Wenger 1998: 215; Jenkins 2004: 4); and the sense of belonging and identity are only really meaningful within a social and cultural context. Hence, avoiding a convoluted definition, we may for simplicity say that *identity is essentially a socially and culturally constructed process, negotiated by the individual and underpinned by contingency.*

Reflecting on his fieldwork in the fishing community on the Shetland island of Whalsey, Cohen argued that communities become very aware of their culture and identity at the boundaries where they engage with others, and especially when they are under threat. A similar point has been made by Delanty who pointed out that

> some of the most powerful expressions of community are often experienced precisely where there has been a major injustice inflicted on a group of people, who consequently develop a sense of their common fate. (Delanty 2003: 48)

At such points behaviour, previously implicit, becomes explicit and is consciously perceived, and people become aware of their culture and distinctiveness. But this is often evident 'not through the performance of elaborate and specialised ceremonial but through the evaluation of everyday practices' (Cohen 1982: 3, 6). Turner, upon whose work Cohen drew, identified liminality ('moments out of time') as an important aspect of symbolic events in which the community reasserts its collective identity (Turner 1969). Such events include, as Delanty (2003: 44) has noted, rites of passage, pilgrimages, rituals, ceremonies and carnivals. When applying Turner's ideas to the study of Whalsay, Cohen went on to argue that 'people can participate in the "same" ritual yet find quite different meanings for it' (Cohen 1987: 55; see also Orsi 2002: xx). The sense of identity, for individuals and the community, is also often reinforced by traumatic events and tragedies, which are recollected in stories, monuments, paintings, tapestries, sculptures and publications, as will be seen in the following discussion.

An excellent example is the tapestry on display in Eyemouth museum, constructed by local women with the help of a professional artist, in which rich symbolism is used to commemorate the effect of the disastrous storm of 14 October 1881 when 129 local fishermen lost their lives. Such an activity does not just record a tragic event but brings the local community together in a commemoration and celebration of its past. Hearing of this use of tapestries in other ports, a group of women in the Yorkshire fishing community of Filey recently got together to develop their own tapestry. In the process of working on this the women have involved many community members such as the local schoolchildren who are invited to add a few stitches under the supervision of the working group. Another Filey group has recently written and produced a play that draws upon the local religious revival of 1823 following which the Primitive Methodists became firmly established in the town. Groups in Hull and Grimsby have also produced plays that draw upon local events; and most fishing communities now hold annual festivals that include music, food, poetry, exhibitions and religious services. All this, however, is not just an exercise in nostalgia, but is important in the process of communities reasserting their identity in the face of significant change.

The sense of nostalgia associated with the modern demise of perceived 'traditional' communities often metamorphoses into a new form of identity while retaining an important link with the past. Hence, as Bauman has argued, identity is often a surrogate reinvention of community (Bauman 2004: 15; see also Delanty 2003: 118–19). It is no accident, therefore, that many fishing communities began developing heritage sites once the fishing industry (in Britain and elsewhere) began to experience decline during the 1970s. Staithes, Whitby, Robin Hood's Bay, Filey and Bridlington have their own museums; Grimsby developed the National Fishing Heritage Centre; Hull's Town Museum has an important section on fishing; and two Scarborough women, from fishing families, are currently developing a local Fishing Heritage Centre. At the same time, while a few festivals are of long standing, such as the 'Penny Hedge' at Whitby, others are more recent developments such as the Nightgown Parade at Staithes, and some are reinventions of lost practices such as the 'Blessing of the Boats' at Whitby and the 'Blessing of the Waters' at Hull. Yet other developments include the Seafest; the Fireman's and Fisherman's Charity Football Match, which takes place on Ladies Day (Boxing Day) in Scarborough; and The 'Lost Trawlermen's Day' annual service at Hull. While the Boxing Day events at Scarborough may be seen as essentially a secular festival there are aspects of it that bear a resemblance to Saints Day festivals such as Orsi has discussed in his book *The Madonna of 115th Street* (2002). This reconstruction and celebration of community identity is a complex process that includes the telling of stories about ourselves and others, and a concern with personal roots, relationships, work, leisure, religion and how people cope with change. But we mislead ourselves if we imagine that such reconstructions and celebrations are merely attempts to resurrect the past.

How, then, do societies 'reconstruct' their past in the light of present circumstances? In the first instance it has to be recognized that the past is perceived as a 'cultural resource', not as a chronological series of events. Cohen has argued that identity on Whalsay is formed and maintained in reference to cultural stability, in a section he entitles 'The "aald days" and the past that never was' (Cohen 1987: 20), and goes on to make the important observation that the past is often perceived symbolically. We also need to be aware that while identity is essentially an *individual* experience that is socially and culturally mediated through the person, it is also a *collective* experience. Jane Nadel-Klein, drawing upon her fieldwork in the Scottish fishing village of Ferryden, has emphasized this point by arguing that 'we continually construct our lives in terms of origin and destination, home and away, places where we belong and places where we are not welcome, zones of comfort and zones of danger' (Nadel-Klein 2003: 216–17). The telling of stories reinforces the construction and reconstruction of our lives – a point made by Doherty who says 'We seem to need stories to position ourselves in the world – to develop a sense of identity' (cited in Nadel-Klein 2003: 216–17). Cohen's argument that identity is formed and maintained in reference to cultural stability is no doubt also true in the wider sense that when people move from one locality to another they tend to seek out people from a similar background. This is a natural biological and psychological trait. The sense of cultural stability is also reinforced via language, dress, customs and stories especially of major events such as great storms and tragedies.

In exploring how identity is maintained it is helpful here to make use of Durkheim's (1894) model of *mechanical* and *organic solidarities* – roughly similar to Ferdinand Tönnies' (1957 [1887]) concepts of *gemeinschaft* (community) and *gesellschaft* (society). These are, of course, ideal types and will not match perfectly any given fishing (or other) community. At the same time the model is not being used here in an evolutionary sense but is being applied to different kinds of communities and societies existing side-by-side. Nor is there any implication of 'primitive' and 'sophisticated' – attention is merely drawn to similarity and difference.

Filey, Staithes and Robin Hood's Bay, during the nineteenth and early twentieth centuries, were among those Yorkshire fishing communities that approximated closely to Durkheim's concept of a mechanical solidarity. Each individual in these communities contributed to the survival of all, and had a *strong* sense of personal identity, with their personal and social identities matching to a high degree. Family, friends, neighbours, teachers and work colleagues were all familiar with the life, experiences and family history of individuals. On the other hand Hull and Grimsby,[2] during the same period, bore a good relation to Durkheim's concept of an organic solidarity where individuals traded their skills within the wider community. Here there was a *weak* sense of personal identity, along with a poor correlation between the individual's personal and social identities.

Scarborough, Whitby and Bridlington perhaps fit mid-way between these two extremes, and contained elements of each. With their long-established fishing communities, like Filey, they had a strong sense of identity. But these fishing communities, although clearly identifiable in terms of space and place, were part of larger social structures. Scarborough, Whitby and Bridlington, unlike Filey, also have harbours that offered good facilities for visiting fishing vessels. When visiting fishermen brought with them new technologies, such as trawling, the indigenous communities (predominantly engaged in line-fishing) responded by rejecting the innovation, sometimes violently. The overall result was that many of the visiting fishermen eventually moved to Hull and Grimsby where they found the facilities more appropriate to their needs, including railway connections west and south that provided a more efficient means of marketing the catches. But some visiting fishermen did stay on, especially at Scarborough, and by the 1891 census the growth in the numbers of fishermen included many whose parents had been born elsewhere (see Appendix 1).

In the large fishing towns of Hull and Grimsby such opposition to new methods of fishing was not initially evident – mainly because there were no long-established and coherent indigenous fishing communities to protest. But as the fishing communities became more established within the towns clashes began to occur that involved the vested interests of various groups. This was especially evident in 1880 when the local owners of fishing firms attempted to enforce all-year-round fleeting (a system of fishing that involved fleets of fishing vessels working for extended periods on the fishing grounds). Edward Gillett has observed:

> The strike began with 90 skippers and mates, but within a week 250 had joined in, as smacks came in, and there were parades through the streets with a band. On the first Sunday 200 fishermen dressed in blue guernseys and smart trousers paraded twice from the club-room in Kent Street to services in St Andrew's church. Soon over 700 men were out and over 400 smacks were tied up in dock. (1970: 266)

St Andrew's church was known locally as the 'Fishermen's Church', and provided a range of support services for the local fishing community. Clearly during this period we can see a stronger sense of local identity emerging, which also embraced the rapidly increasing numbers of religious institutions.

Both the strong and weak senses of identity in Yorkshire fishing communities presented individuals with constraints. The strong sense of personal identity in the smaller communities meant that the constraints on individuals were significant, with innovation being frowned upon. Employment, however, was not normally an issue unless there was a wider economic problem. In Hull and Grimsby, where personal identities were often weak (and multiple), we would expect change to occur more naturally as there was (initially at least) no large coherent culture to resist it (although when there was a major threat that brought together the disparate community, such as involved the major change in fishing methods cited above, there was a united response). However, in these larger communities the generally weak sense of personal identity meant that while the possibility of change was greater, individuals were forced to compete with each other in selling their skills. In this situation we might expect to find remnants of strong personal identities that were hangovers from earlier community experience. Given the larger size of the towns, therefore, innovation could be embraced alongside more traditional activities, although the former was eventually going to influence the latter. In such a situation we would expect change to be more evident in the second and third generations as offspring gradually developed a wider local identity. In Grimsby, the sudden flowering of religious denominations, c. 1870 (the second generation) and the involvement of immigrant residents in local politics (especially in the third generation) bears witness to this change. The religious institutions alongside the temperance societies and various other groups helped to provide a sense of security in a rapidly changing environment, thereby allowing time for the various groups to develop a wider and stronger sense of personal and social identity.

As a general principle it may be said that while change comes about because individuals are psychologically adaptable and are able to embrace change when this is necessary for survival, the nature of the change, whether dramatic or gradual, depends on the nature of the community, and Durkheim's model (although somewhat dated) helps us to understand why and how change takes place in the face of sometimes fierce opposition. In a community with a strong sense of identity change is resisted energetically, but when it does happen it is likely to be dramatic (such as occurred in the 1823 Revival at Filey). In a community with a weak sense of identity, change is likely to be more gradual, but more pronounced, with room for more diversity and innovation (as in Hull and Grimsby) – although there were, as we might expect, occasional outbusts of indignation at proposed changes that would affect the whole community. Change, therefore, is not merely facilitated by the move from a mechanistic to an organic solidarity; rather it is the tension created when the innate need for psychological and social security comes into direct conflict with threats to such security – and while such threats can appear more evident in the smaller communities they also tend to be (initially at least) more strongly resisted there. Clearly, then, Cohen is right when he says that identity becomes most evident when it is under threat (Cohen 1982: 3).

While the model here offers an explanation for the different kinds of change experienced in Yorkshire fishing communities, it only hints at the role of religion. Indeed, it is usually religion in one form or another that offers an explanation for the need of change and thereby legitimates subsequent developments. At the same time, when the religious institutions fail to provide the security they once did, people tend to seek security, a sense of belonging and a feeling of self-worth in other ways. This includes the search for roots via family history, a sense of belonging and attachment in fan clubs and other significant peer groups, and a sense of purpose and hope in fashion, sport, shopping, music, and so on. But such allegiance may not be ultimately as satisfying as the security provided by religious or philosophical frameworks. At the same time we need to acknowledge that the religious institutions do not have a spiritual monopoly. The following section, therefore, explores the range of religious experience and expression that can be found in fishing communities, and in particular illustrates the complex nature of the relationship between identity and religion.

Religion in Yorkshire Fishing Communities

In the close-knit, nineteenth-century community of Filey a significant number of the local population appeared to convert to Primitive Methodism within a few months during the religious revival of 1823. The Primitive Methodist preacher, John Oxtoby, found success only after much preparatory work by others, including the Wesleyan Methodist preachers who, despite local opposition and years of struggle following their arrival in 1806, eventually formed a society in 1810 (Fearon 1990: 75). Even so, progress was slow and numbers did not rise above twenty until 1819, and not above twenty-eight until after 1823 when numbers quickly doubled (Beverley Archives, MRQ 1/36; see Appendix 2). At the same time the Anglican Church does not appear to have lost any members, which suggests that the revival did not simply attract members from one religious institution to another. However, missions to the town were not the only factor that led to the revival. Disillusionment in the wake of the Napoleonic wars, poor harvests and wider social and economic changes also made a significant impact at local level. The combination of earlier missions, social and economic difficulties, and disillusionment with the religious status quo, prepared the community to accept further change. Although there was strong resistance to change, when it did occur in 1823 it included the conversion of approximately forty people (Petty 1880: 188; see

Appendix 2). Such dramatic conversions are generally short-lived, but in some situations with the right local support such change can be more permanent, and this appears to have been the case with Filey, despite fluctuating periods of membership. This account suggests that when change does occur in a *mechanical solidarity* it is more likely to be dramatic – although following on from a period of strong resistance.

Nevertheless, even in the organic solidarities of Hull and Grimsby, members of groups such as Jewish immigrants, and fishermen with strong links to Primitive Methodism in their home towns, found it relatively easy to achieve positions of authority in their adopted towns. At the same time, in some mechanistic solidarities, even relatively innocuous innovations like Primitive Methodism had difficulty in becoming established – Robin Hood's Bay, for example, never had a Primitive Methodist chapel although Wesleyan Methodism remained strong. In general, however, the Methodists, both Wesleyan and Primitive, had a significant impact on the life of Yorkshire fishing communities, although the influence of the Primitives would appear not to have been as great as earlier writers have claimed. In Hull, for example, the Primitive Methodists had more influence among the railway workers than within the fishing community.

Nineteenth- and early twentieth-century fishing, like farming, was determined by the seasons, which were closely linked to religious holy days and festivals. In Filey the year began with the Spring Fishery (January to Easter), during which period the fishermen relocated with their families to the East Anglian ports where they worked in yawls (larger fishing vessels) with a crew of between five and seven, supported on shore by their women. Returning to Yorkshire after Good Friday the fishermen worked in their cobles (small, open fishing vessels), and the women collected limpets (known locally as flithers) along the seashore for baiting the fishing lines. This was followed by the herring season between June and November, conducted in their yawls. When the herring season came to an end the yawls were tied up for repairs and refitting, leaving the fishermen to work in their cobles over the Christmas period. Scarborough followed a similar pattern, although with the growth of the North Sea fishing industry during the 1850s there was a good deal of movement and relocation between the ports, especially to Hull and Grimsby where the trawling industry grew rapidly during the mid-nineteenth century and involved lengthy trips away for the deep-sea fishermen. The much smaller fishing communities, such as Robin Hood's Bay, had just three seasons: line fishing in winter, lobsters and crabs in early spring, and salmon in the summer. And perhaps not surprisingly there was also a stronger link here between fishing and farming. In the larger fishing communities of Hull and Grimsby, fishing during any one season was diverse with yawls, smacks and steam vessels engaging in line fishing, trawling, seine netting and so on – although trawling gradually became the dominant activity. By the end of the nineteenth century steam-powered fishing vessels became the dominant mode of transport in the larger towns, with hardly any sailing smacks left, with the result that very few fishermen could look forward to one day owning their own vessels.

Given the complex and rapidly changing nature of life, especially in the larger fishing communities, it was important that clergy and ministers understood the fishing seasons, and were able to respond as change occurred. It was also important for them to have some knowledge of local customs, especially when it came to the spheres of labour divided between the men and women. Valenze, for example, has pointed out that the local customs in Filey were longstanding and complex, and that 'wives, widows, sisters, and daughters managed every aspect of work outside the boat' (Valenze 1985: 251–52). In Staithes the women were responsible for both landing and launching the vessels, a point reinforced by the Rev. Arthur Pettitt in his *Guide to Filey* (1868), where he says 'The men have only to catch the fish, their labour as a rule being over as soon as the boat touches sand' (cited in Valenze 1985: 252). And this division of labour had an important effect on the lives of women. Thompson, for example, has pointed out that by removing the fishermen to sea for increasing periods of time, this situation made them not only 'peculiarly dependent on the work of women ashore', but also gave the women more responsibility and 'the possibility of more power, both in the home and in the community' (Thompson 1985: 3).

As the main carriers of tradition it is the women who knit ganseys, make dresses, tell stories, pass on traditions to their children and support the religious institutions. But there has been relatively little academic study here other than for a few notable exceptions, especially those studies carried out during the 1970s such as Frank's study of women in Yorkshire inshore fishing communities (in *Oral History* 1976, updated and published as a chapter in *Yorkshire Fisherfolk*, 2002); Clark's work in Staithes (1982); and the work of Thompson, Wailey and Lummis (1983), based on their research in Scotland, Lancashire and East Anglia; and Lummis's (1985) work in East Anglia. Thompson also made some important observations in his article 'The Roots of Power between the Sexes' (1985). Religion, too, generally receives only a passing mention – usually with reference to the institutional aspects of religious life, although Clark's work is again a significant exception.

Clark's study remains definitive. His *Between Pulpit and Pew: Folk Religion in a North Yorkshire Fishing Village* was the end result of extended fieldwork in Staithes during the period April 1975 to July 1976, where he became 'deeply immersed in the minutiae of village life' (Clark 1982: viii) and, like Lummis in East Anglia, was able to draw upon local memories extending back into the late nineteenth century. On the nature of religion in the village he observed:

> Without its particular form of religion, Staithes would be a very different place. Indeed I hope to show that religion not only provides a means whereby Staithes people make sense of their individual lives but also contributes to the way in which they create a sense of communal identity in relation to the rest of society. (Clark 1982: vii)

He went on to note that a considerable amount of religious activity here occurred outside the religious institutions, and he therefore used the term 'religion' in an inclusive sense, drawing extensively upon what he termed 'folk religion'. This approach is important when we consider that from the perspective of the churches and chapels generally, irregular attendance at services meant a lack of commitment and questionable religiosity, whereas from the perspective of working-class people, attendance at church services and functions was part of a broader cultural religiosity where morality and religious duty embraced the church but was not restricted to it. Indeed, regular attendance at religious services was often seen by working-class people as unhealthy and indicative of hypocrisy – there was a sense in which the participants were seen to be trying too hard to prove their piety.

Among Nonconformists, Primitive Methodism was more sympathetic than many religious denominations to the matrix of popular religious beliefs and practices, including magic, folklore, superstitions and a generally held diffusive Christianity. To the more 'educated' people (including many clergy) such beliefs and practices were often incoherent and abhorrent, although, as Rodney Ambler has said, their lack of coherence 'paralleled the wider experiences of the people among whom they had greatest credence' and should not be allowed to obscure their importance as a series of observations that helped individuals over difficult periods in their lives (Ambler 1984: 242). Yet, at the same time, there was also often a loosely held allegiance to the established church. The situation in Filey was summed up well by a writer in the *Yorkshire Post*, of 29 October 1961 (cited in Valenze 1985: 247), who pointed out that the local fishermen had religion in 'three layers' – they were Primitive Methodists, they gave the local church its due, and they were steadfastly superstitious. A major underlying factor here is a concern with ritual, the performance of which plays a significant role in the daily lives of working people.

Rites and Rituals

Van Gennep's analysis of the three core stages of separation, transition and reincorporation has been important in helping scholars to understand the nature and significance of rites of passage (Gennep 1960). Building on Gennep's work, Turner (1969) explored the nature of liminality (referring to the stage of transition as 'betwixt and between'), and was especially interested in the symbolism present within the rituals. His results provided scholars with a framework to help further analyse ritual and threshold rites in a wide range of social activities. But, as Clark (1982: 112) observed, sociologists have not made as much use of these concepts as anthropologists, although, as he pointed out, there were two notable exceptions in the work of Bocock (1974) and Leonard (1980). While Leonard concentrated on courtship and weddings, Bocock applied the concept of ritual to a wide range of practices in contemporary society, and thereby conducted one of the first such analyses of ritual from a sociological perspective. For the purpose of the present study, therefore, I adopt Bocock's definition of ritual as '*the symbolic use of bodily movement and gesture in a social situation to express and articulate meaning*' (Bocock 1974: 37). Nevertheless, the main rites of passage, of birth, marriage and death, provide a good starting point for the examination of ritual, as it is here that the interplay between spirituality and our material, everyday lives is made most explicit. Even so, we should bear in mind that the stylization of these rites of passage can have the negative effect of emphasizing and celebrating the supernatural and downplaying the natural.

Despite their reticence regarding weekly attendance, most working-class people did attend church and chapel services in the past for at least the three major rites of passage of birth, marriage and death. It was, however, common for fisherfolk in Filey to hold such rites of passage in the parish church, while continuing to attend services at the Methodist churches, even after it became possible for such rites to take place in Nonconformist buildings (marriages, for example, could take place in licensed Nonconformist buildings following the passing of the Dissenting Marriages Act of 1836). At the same time, the burial ground in Filey was attached to the Anglican Church (whose clergy held the monopoly on the conduct of services in churchyards up until 1880 when the Burials Law Amendment Act was passed). Interestingly, despite occasional revivals such as that at Filey in 1823, there was no general swing from Anglican to Nonconformist allegiance in the fishing ports. In Robin Hood's Bay, Filey and Staithes there was indeed a strong attachment to the Methodists; but in Scarborough the fisherfolk initially attended St Mary's Church, and later, St Thomas' Church (opened 1840), which had been especially built for the fishing community. In Hull there was a strong attachment to the local Fishermen's Bethel (Port of Hull Society), while families attended St Barnabas Church for the rites of passage. Grimsby fisherfolk held their family celebrations at St Andrew's or St John's Church, both of which had been built in the 1870s specifically for the fishing community and were known as 'fishermen's churches'. The nature of the support here appears to have been for the ministers and clergy rather than for the institution, and attendance was in any case irregular. This practice of attending services infrequently is still evident in that a recent Scarborough interviewee stated 'I'm just a births, deaths and christenings and things' (sic). The 'and things' apparently refers to other special occasions (Women's Voices Project 22MP05, 5 October 2005).

While the major rites of passage were important social occasions, they were also associated with a wide range of popular beliefs and practices, many of which were incorporated into the official practices of the religious institutions, as Clark (1982), Williams (1999), Sykes (1999) and others have observed. Until the 1960s the mother, following the birth of her child, especially in working-class communities, expected to be 'churched'. This liminal process, while often considered a folk practice, has been a Christian purification rite and an act of thanksgiving after childbirth from Christianity's early days. But at the same time a variety of superstitions and popular practices have also been associated with the ceremony, such as the belief that social contact with an unchurched mother, or for her to be allowed back into her house prior to the ritual, would result in bad luck for the family (Obelkevich 1976: 273; Clark 1982: 115; Williams 1999: 89). Although the service was usually performed quietly during the week, a witness was often required, especially if the child was baptized at the same time. Similar services were performed in Nonconformist chapels, as Clark has noted, and in this particular case the woman was 'churched on the first occasion that she attended chapel after the birth of a child' (Clark 1982: 119). Other accounts have been provided in recent interviews (Women's Voices Project 02RJ04, 25 November 2005 and 11DN05, 23 June 2006 in Scarborough; 09MH05, 08 June 2005 in Hull). Clark also pointed out that while for the clergy the service was seen as an opportunity for thanksgiving, the women were more concerned with the issue of purification, a point that is backed up in the Women's Voices Project interviews.

The service of baptism for children came to be known in the popular mind as a 'Christening' (the giving of a Christian name), and was thought to be of physical and spiritual benefit to a sick child (Smith 1969: 183). But in the smaller fishing ports such as Filey, Staithes and Robin Hood's Bay, the giving of nicknames (known in Filey as Bye-names) was also essential as a means of distinguishing people in a community where many were related. There are overtones here of the ancient superstition that letting an evil spirit know your real name was tantamount to letting it have some control over your life. Even so, there was until recently some reticence in letting outsiders know an individual's nickname, although today there is less reticence and nicknames even appear on gravestones. (Perhaps we should not forget that both Christian names and surnames in the past have served similar functions with regard to identity and character as nicknames. It should also be noted that some religious groups, such as the Mormons, place an important emphasis on secret names.) Nicknames usually also describe some characteristic of the individual or family, such as the name 'Tint', which recalled the individual saying 'ti'n't' as a further abbreviated form of 'It isn't' or 'It aint' (Women's Voices Project 03AW05, 9 May 2005). That nicknames are now appearing on fishermen's gravestones all around the British coast indicates their importance, as individuals can be clearly identified in death as well as in life. It should also be mentioned here that the naming of vessels was also an important rite, with many of their names having biblical and other religious links.

The rites of marriage and death were also subject to numerous traditions and customs in which the liminal aspect was reinforced. These were occasions for a readjustment in family relationships as well as being important symbolic occasions for the community. Michael Fearon (1990) provides an example from an account of a funeral procession in Filey in 1908:

> I saw a solid mass of people coming at a foot pace down the slope towards the other end of the bridge from where I stood. In front was a group of thirty or forty fishermen, four abreast, all in their spotless dark blue knitted jerseys, all slowly stepping on, and all joining in Dr Watt's well-known hymn 'There's a land of pure delight' . . . Behind them the coffin, with one or two wreaths of flowers upon it, was carried by six stalwart brother toilers of the deep, and it was followed by the widow and the more distant relatives of the deceased, while closing the procession came the wives and sisters of the fishermen, and other sympathising friends. (Fearon 1990: 125–26)

Filey ravine separates Yorkshire's North and East Riding, with St Oswald's Church (Anglican) on the north side and the fishing communities on the east. The church may be reached by the bridge mentioned in the above account. As with other rites of passage, funerals were often held at St Oswald's church, even though many of the fishermen were Methodists. One recent interviewee provided an insight into the symbolism of the ravine:

> [T]he fishermen, if there were any funerals or anything, they used to carry the coffin across the bridge, . . . they wouldn't have a hearse ... and they all had their own saying, . . . If you said 'how's Mr so-and-so today?', or called them by their name, they would say 'oh, he's about ready fo't' North Riding'. (Women's Voices Project 03AW05, 9 May 2005)

Loss of life was (and remains) very high among fishermen, and it was (is) believed that the lost souls would seek to return home. This belief is evident in the various tales told by women who have lost relatives. One interviewee recalled her encounter as a child with a woman whose husband had recently been lost at sea:

> [I]t was the [woman] next door but one to granny who lost her husband and two sons, and it was often talked about. We used to go to the house . . . and this lady used to burn a candle in her upstairs window . . . the theory was that when they [the souls] turned up they'd know where the house was. As children we used to ask what the candle was for . . . But that's what they used to do, you see . . . believed that . . . when you haven't got a body, I suppose, you never completely lose hope. (Women's Voices Project 16MT05, 22 July 2005)

With no body to bury, and the possibility of the missing relative still being alive, there could be no formal service, a situation that naturally increased the sense of loss for the relatives. The exception here was when several lives were lost, for example in a storm, when a formal service was held to commemorate those lost and missing.

Numerous practices and beliefs were associated with such loss. In Grimsby, for example, up until the 1960s, curtains were closed and the door of the house was left open for the soul's return. For those whose loved-ones had been lost at sea and when all optimism for their return had gone, there was the hope that the body would eventually be washed up or caught in a trawl net. Were this the case the decomposed body could be identified by the pattern, and sometimes the initials, on the fisherman's gansey, and the remains returned to the relatives so that the various rites could be performed.

While the study of ritual tends to focus on rites of passage, life cycles, festivals and the sacraments, of which there are many in fishing communities, as can be seen from the few examples cited above, ritual can also be found in what would at first sight appear to be more mundane activities. These include setting off for sea, visiting the pub following a trip to sea, the wives of fishermen gathering at the company's office on Fridays to collect payment (deducted from their husbands' settlings), washdays, the telling of stories by the men (yarning) during the quiet periods on board ship and in the pubs (it was normal in the trawler towns for many fishermen to visit their local pub before returning home), and of course there were the innumerable superstitions. Alec Gill provides an example of a 'leaving ritual' performed by a Hull fisherman's daughter, who, as a child, would throw her father's slippers at the front door after he had left – to '*ensure that he'd come back safely to wear them again*' (Gill 2003: 151). Newly married women in Hull and Grimsby were encouraged to join other women outside their terraced homes in the street during the evenings where they 'gossiped' (Women's Voices Project 02RJ05[2], 9 December 2005, Scarborough). This initiation into the world of the local women symbolized acceptance by the local community and provided ongoing support for the fisherman's wife.

Such rituals in popular culture have a similar function to those performed in church services. For example, in the Eucharist and in 'yarning' an important focus is found in the symbolic act of communicating and the presence of interest from others, and a sense of empathy resulting from the unburdening experienced by the story-teller. Orsi (2002: 161) makes this same point when he refers to the many stories of 'favours bestowed by the Virgin' told by correspondents from great distances, and reproduced in the parish bulletins of the church at Mount Carmel in Harlem. In other words, the events are important primarily for the communicators where 'hope' also plays an important role. This is not to demean the nature of the Eucharist; indeed, it should be remembered that the churches' symbolic and stylized rite has its foundation in a meal shared by Jesus and his friends where conversation, no doubt, centred on the group's experience.

All this, while merely scratching the surface, indicates a wide range of beliefs and practices, many of which are not normally considered to be aspects of formal religious activities. Indeed, when we explore these along with other rites and rituals within the spheres of magic, folklore and superstition, we find there are closer links with religion than might at first be thought.

Religion, Magic, Folklore and Superstition

The established churches have embraced a range of customs and practices that were previously disapproved of, yet the churches struggled, and continue to struggle, with the pervasiveness of what they see as other, less acceptable, popular beliefs and practices. Wesleyan Methodism, too, by the beginning of the nineteenth century had become more respectable and rejected 'superstitious practices' (Davis 1997). But Wesley himself had been accused of dabbling in magic when he approved the visions and trances of members. The Primitive Methodists, and other offshoots from the Wesleyans, especially the 'Magic Methodists' led by James Crawfoot, were initially supportive of the range of popular beliefs and practices, including 'some elements of folk culture, such as visions, dreams, omens, magic, witchcraft and exorcism' (Johnson 1993: 73) Even the joint founders of Primitive Methodism, Hugh Bourne and William Clowes, embraced popular beliefs and practices, and Bourne travelled to London to visit Joanna Southcott where he was impressed with her medicines and cures. Clowes, too, performed an exorcism in Harrishead (Johnson 1993: 74, 75).

Not only the practice but also the terminology of magic and religion was and remains very fluid, and scholars have argued over the relationship. James Frazier (1890) proposed that religion involves action via an intermediate figure and is therefore to be distinguished from magic as this involves direct action; Durkheim (1976: 44) proposed that religion and magic have different social functions: religion serves the group, while magic serves the individual; and Malinowski (1948) argued that the psychological function of religion is paramount in that religion is concerned with the present, while magic concerns itself with the future. But such attempts to distinguish magic from religion have not been very successful, and a number of anthropologists have argued that religion and magic are both aspects of the same belief system (see, for example, Jarvis 1980: 292).

Folklore, like magic, has also been interpreted in a variety of ways. During the nineteenth century (and not unusually in the twentieth) the term 'folk' has been understood to refer to peasant society and has often been used in a derogative sense. Nineteenth-century folklorists also tended to dismiss the beliefs of 'folk cultures' as magic and superstition rather than religion. But folk-beliefs, as Patrick Mullen has pointed out, 'often functioned in ways similar to organised religion' (Mullen 2005: 314; see also Nadel-Klein 2003: 216). For Alan Dundes (1989), too, 'folk religion' and 'popular religion' can be seen as synonymous, while 'folklore' and 'popular religion' have a significant overlap.

The commonly perceived idea that folklore, superstition and magic are, like religion, part of the life of pre-scientific and primitive societies, in which there was no sharp distinction between the sacred and the secular, gradually gave way to a more rationalist perception in which the 'primitive' was contrasted sharply with the 'modern'. In contrast to this view, folklore in fishing communities remains very much a part of the local picture, although few take the stories and legends literally. The tales, however, should not be written off as meaningless as they play an important role in reinforcing the local sense of identity. Some traditions, for example, serve to account for the *origins* of activities, geographical features and major natural disasters. Hence, it is said that the ammonites (sometimes called 'St Hilda's stones'), found at Whitby and Robin Hood's Bay, are fossils of snakes that St Hilda banished from the surrounding land (Gutch 1901: 13–14). In Filey, in order to cause the destruction of ships and the death of sailors, it is said that the devil set about building the promontory known as Filey Brigg (Cole 1828). In the process he dropped his hammer and when retrieving it caught a haddock, making what looks like a thumbprint, which is still evident today. When his work was completed he flew over the parish church and dropped the haddock over the tower where it still survives as a weather vane. The tale draws upon a number of traditions, not least the concept of the fish as an early Christian symbol. Hence, the story links the local trade, and by implication the community, with Christian symbolism. Other tales serve the function of *defining ourselves by defining others*. We are told, for example, that should a Filey resident lead a dissolute life, the devil would arrive in his carriage to collect the soul of the deceased person – and deliver it to Scarborough. This example (there are many others) of symbolic boundaries helps to reinforce personal and social identities by emphasizing differences.

Superstition, too, has closer links with orthodox religious belief and practice than many have been prepared to admit, although some scholars have tended to refer to non-orthodox religion as 'mere superstition' (Abercrombie *et al.* 1973: 93). Hence, superstition is generally defined with reference to irrational belief (Jarvis 1980: 296). The problem of definition has been noted by scholars such as Jahoda who offered a somewhat tautological definition from the perspective of psychology: 'the kind of belief and action a reasonable man in present day Western society would regard as being "superstitious"' (Jahoda 1969: 10). On the other hand, Jarvis (1980) places his definition within the sphere of 'folk religion' and then goes on to distinguish folk religion from institutionalized belief systems. It is this distinction that is being called into question here.

The failure of modern scholarship to take superstition seriously has tended to reinforce the isolation and separateness of orthodoxy, thereby perpetuating the dualistic perception of the sacred and the secular. Many superstitions have nevertheless been incorporated into Christian practices and then reinterpreted within a Christian framework (Hutton (1996) provides innumerable examples). At the same time superstitions usually have a functional basis, and in fishing communities these often relate to the male and female spheres and help to reinforce distinctions, with the women often acting as protectors of the fishermen – this is an interesting reversal of the Enlightenment perception of men as the protectors of women (see Abrams 2002: 22ff. for a discussion on this point). It should also be remembered that boats are referred to as 'she', to which the fisherman trusts his life. On leaving home (the domestic sphere of his wife or mother) the fisherman enters the boat (the sphere of his 'mistress'), and he is hardly likely to upset the latter if she is going to take care of him at sea. It is important, therefore, that the domestic and work spheres are kept separate (although the wives of the fishermen took on many the responsibilities normally associated with the sphere of 'work', in that they were responsible for the family finances, networking in the community, baiting the lines, purchasing household items, doing household repairs, even negotiating all aspects of the move from one house to another). The women were not encouraged to wave the men off to sea nor were they normally allowed onto the fishing vessels, and at Staithes, throughout the nineteenth century, it was traditional for the women to turn their backs on the fishermen when they saw them going down to the harbour where their cobles were berthed (Anson 1965: 104). While such practices have overtones of magic and superstition, there are also psychological implications for the well-being of the fisherfolk in that should the ritual be ignored the resulting tension and stress emanating from feelings of guilt could have dire effects upon the family.

The clothes worn by the fisherfolk also have superstitious links, as Anson has recorded: 'There was a feeling, not always clearly defined, that they lost their efficacy to withstand the forces of evil if they did not conform to traditional patterns, handed down for generations' (Anson 1965: 26). While most women in fishing communities simply used clothes handed on from one generation to the next until they fell to bits, the women in the older fishing communities had their own styles of dress, such as the 'Staithes bonnet' (still worn by some women in Staithes, and for festival occasions in other Yorkshire fishing ports). Arthur J. Munby has provided one of the few accounts of the dress and daily lives of fisherwomen along the Yorkshire coast during the 1860s – in particular in Flamborough, Yorkshire, he referred to 'Molly's lilac hood-bonnet' – and gave details of fisherwomen's clothes in other parts of the country (Hudson 1974: 256, 292).

Although it was not unusual for some men to knit – for some fishermen this was an extension of net-making – the responsibility for producing clothes normally rested with the women, who, through this and other tasks, tried to ensure a sense of continuity, security and protection for the men. The ganseys worn by the men (pink ones were sometimes worn by the women) were ubiquitous throughout the nineteenth century and up until the 1950s. Both men and women kept one gansey for Sunday best, and in Scarborough it was common for the men to wear a white neck warmer on Sundays, rather than the coloured one worn during the week. While clothes were therefore integrated with the religious life of the community, they were important, too, as significant elements in rites of passage, not just in death but also for children as they received their first gansey (and in some cases a smock), with their own unique identifier, at just a few years old; and the girls were introduced by their mothers to the skills of knitting ganseys as soon as they could hold a needle. The patterns were not written down but passed on from mother to daughter by example, thereby preserving a sense of mystery in the garment's production. The single length of wool (ganseys were made as a complete item, not sections sewn together) also suggests a symbolic link between the women on shore and the men at sea. The gansey thus became an important symbol of individual and communal identity.

Other material arts also contain important symbolic elements. In the fishing port of King's Lynn, in Norfolk, residents (men and women) made rag-rugs with a red diamond in the centre – to deter the devil from entering their houses. No similar record has been found for rag-rugs along the Yorkshire coast, although one elderly lady, who grew up in Robin Hood's Bay during the 1920s, stated that when making rag-rugs for the home the fisher-folk always began with a blue diamond in the centre. Unfortunately, the origin and purpose of the practice appears to have been lost (Women's Voices Project 23NW06, 8 April 2006). Nevertheless, the colour red did have an important local spiritual significance as fishwives wore red petticoats to ward off evil. There was also a practical purpose in that the hem of the dress was hooked up into the waist so that it did not get dirty, leaving just the petticoat to be washed – and to be more obvious to passing evil spirits. Such activity may be written off as 'mere superstition' but to do so disregards the fundamental spiritual importance of material culture to the community, and fails to acknowledge the integration of the spiritual and the material, and the importance of such traditions for the formation and maintenance of identity in fishing communities..

The ritual aspects of these various practices clearly have an important function, too – a view supported by Colin Campbell, who has argued that the essence of these ritual acts lies in their symbolism, and as such they have intimate links with religious beliefs and practices (Campbell 1996: 151–66). In support of this argument he has pointed to the sense of unease a person feels when the ritual has not been properly conducted.

Alongside the ritual, superstitious beliefs and practices in fishing communities involve the widespread use of charms and tokens, such as the caul (sometimes known as a 'kell' or 'smear') – the gossamer-like covering sometimes covering a baby at birth (Gutch 1901: 51). Many fishermen also wore a gold ring in the left ear – to pay for a 'proper funeral' should the need arise. It was also common, well into the twentieth century, for fishermen to empty their pockets of coins before setting off to sea, although some coins were kept and placed in the cork floats attached to the nets to 'pay for the fish' (Gutch 1901: 47). Should there be a series of poor voyages the skipper may walk around the boat with a lighted torch – to 'burn out the witches'. Other skippers were more conventionally religious and would exclaim 'Praise the Lord!' when casting the net – in the hope of a good catch.

Despite these and innumerable other links between religion and superstition, the latter was, and is, often seen negatively as pre-scientific and irrational, something that stretches credulity. But, as a coping mechanism, superstitions may be seen as having a positive and constructive function, a point made by Malinowski when he observed that superstition reduces anxiety (Malinowski 1948: 31). The essence of superstition, then, would appear to be in its psychological function of helping to reduce anxiety in the face of uncertainty. In this sense the ritual aspect of superstitious belief and practice is the most potent, although, unlike the standard forms of ritual within orthodox religion, the ritual of superstitious belief and practice does not require standardization. Nevertheless, Malinowski's views have come in for some criticism.

In his research among the Trobriand Island fishermen during the period 1915–20, Malinowski observed that superstition was more prevalent where the risk was greater, and he argued that risk here was directly correlated to magic ritual:

> It is significant that in the lagoon fishing, where man can rely completely upon his knowledge and skill, magic does not exist, while in the open-sea fishing, full of danger and uncertainly, there is extensive magical ritual to secure safety and good results. (Malinowski 1948: 31)

Later researchers questioned whether the function of taboos in reducing anxiety is essentially correlated with a *lack of economic security or with a fear of personal danger*, but found it difficult to reach a consensus. Mullen's 1969 study of Texas coastal fishermen, for example, concluded that the correlation is basically with the need for *economic security*; while Poggie *et al.* (1976: 258 note) argued for *personal danger* being the predominant factor.

The various theories were subsequently applied to a study of British East Anglian fishermen conducted via oral interviews by Lummis (1985). Of the three main types of fishing engaged there (trawling, drifting and inshore fishing) it was the driftermen who proved to be the most superstitious, followed by the trawlermen and then the inshore fishermen. This observation raised the question that, as the trawlermen were more likely to face personal danger than driftermen, one would expect (on the basis of Poggie, Pollnac and Gersuny's research) to find that trawlermen were the more superstitious. On the other hand, if superstition is directly correlated to both personal risk (Poggie *et al.* 1976) *and* economic insecurity (Mullen 1969), one would expect superstitious practice to be equally prevalent in both situations – but this was not the case.

According to Lummis, the situation is far better explained with reference to *economic uncertainty* than to *personal risk*. The driftermen were the most economically precarious group in the past, largely because they did not understand the movements or breeding habits of the herring, upon which they mainly depended for a livelihood. This explanation could also be usefully applied to the women and children who shared the economic risk of the men at sea. But where economic security is the norm it seems likely that anxiety-reducing superstitious practices will be directly correlated with *personal risk*. It would seem reasonable, therefore, to suggest that inshore fishermen are less superstitious than trawlermen and driftermen (i.e. the degree of personal risk is smaller, and there is less economic uncertainty).

Lummis (1985) also pointed out that most interviewees said they were not as superstitious as the older generation. Two points are important here. First, given that modern fishing techniques and safety methods, including life-saving equipment, ship-to-shore radio and radar, are vastly improved over that of the previous generation, we should perhaps expect to find a less superstitious younger generation. Lummis confirms this point when he says that the most superstitious fishers are those who work alone, far out at sea. Second, fishermen and fishing communities, in post-World War II Britain, were also less isolated and a less self-perpetuating group than formerly. Nevertheless, there may also be a certain degree of embarrassment in admitting to an active belief in superstition in the face of a sceptical world. This point also seems to be borne out in Lummis's research when a fisherman of the older generation would not admit to being personally superstitious (Lummis 1985: 156).

Conclusion

There are, of course, methodological problems in trying to measure superstition (similar to the problems evident in measuring religious belief), which cannot be adequately explored by the observation of practices alone. Lummis's approach using qualitative analysis clearly helps as a means of testing various theories, as also does the approach used in the Women's Voices Project (2005–), which makes use of a personal narrative methodology such as that used in 'grounded theory' (Strauss and Corbin 1998). Both approaches help to provide us with an opportunity to balance personal memories with a variety of records. And in the case of the records it is possible to balance the qualitative data with the records of personal accounts – as in the case of the Filey revival of 1823. But no methodological procedure is foolproof, although there does appear to be a good deal of consistency between the recorded accounts from the early nineteenth century and the present-day accounts provided by women in Yorkshire fishing communities.

While focusing on the Yorkshire fishing communities we have briefly explored a range of beliefs and practices relating to 'lived religion'. And from the foregoing we can see that superstition, like other aspects of lived religion, especially evident in folklore, magic, festivals, customs, dress and language, performs a number of important social, psychological and economic functions that provide a sense of security and help people make sense and meaning of their lives. But more importantly we need to recognize that the dualistic perspective often advocated by orthodox Christianity serves to prevent the acknowledgement of the variety and vitality of the wide range of religious experience and expression, and such expressions of belief do not disappear simply because orthodoxy chooses to write them off as 'mere superstitions'. The concept of 'lived religion' provides us with a useful counterbalance to the dualistic perspective often common in formal religion, especially Christianity.

While fisherfolk may appear to have had only a perfunctory relationship with the religious institutions we should be wary of making such a judgement on the basis of irregular attendance at services. The situation is far more complex than that. Some Christian institutions, for example, especially the 'fishermen's churches', 'fishermen's chapels' and Bethels, attracted a more sustained commitment. At the same time, regardless of attendance, fisherfolk generally held the religious institutions and clergy in high regard. Indeed, it is not unusual to hear those (perhaps the majority) who attend only for special events refer to the local church or building as 'our church' – indicating an important family and community link. Clearly such links were and remain important as part of the matrix of beliefs and practices that are significant in the construction and maintenance of personal and social identities. Such links were evident in the local 'fishermen's churches/chapels and Bethels' in terms of active and ongoing pastoral engagement with the local community, a willingness to take the diversity of lived religion seriously, a willingness to adapt to the local situation and an avoidance of criticism. Such overt empathy with the local community can be extreme in some cases – such as when the vicar of St Andrew's Church, Grimsby, regularly visited the North Sea fishing fleet in the 1870s (well before the advent of more formalized organizations such as the Mission to Deep Sea Fisherman).

On a day-to-day basis, however, many clergy and church members often failed to meet the ongoing needs of local people, and were critical of what were considered to be unacceptable beliefs and practices. Nevertheless, it is the ubiquity of lived religion that played (and perhaps continues to play) the greater role in the formation and maintenance of identity, where a wide range of beliefs and practices were associated with the performance of ritual and the need for security in an insecure world.

Appendix 1: Birthplaces of fishermen

Grimsby (Gby), Scarborough (Scar) and Filey (Fy) fishermen – birthplaces (by county)

	Gby *1851*	*Scar*	*Fy*	*Gby* *1871*	*Scar*	*Fy*	*Gby* *1891*	*Scar*	*Fy*
Not Known				8	2		151	1	
London	1			101	1	1	324	3	
Berkshire				1					
Bedfordshire							5		
Buckinghamshire							3		
Cambridgeshire	1			4			26		
Cheshire				1			4		
Cleveland		1							
Cornwall							1		
Cumberland							3		
Derbyshire				1			4		
Devon		6		26	5	1	37	1	
Dorset				1					
Durham		1		1	1		7		
Essex				104	1		157	3	
Gloucestershire							10		
Hampshire		1		3			24	1	
Hertfordshire				1			3		
Kent		6		74	8		83	8	1
Lancashire				8	3		69	2	
Leicestershire				1			10	1	
Lincolnshire	14	2		116	7	2	570	8	
Norfolk		9	3	50	70	17	170	48	4
Northamptonshire							3		
Northumberland							4		
Nottinghamshire				4			33		
Oxfordshire				1			4		
Rutland				1					
Staffordshire					1		10	1	
Somerset				4			2	4	
Suffolk		4		15	8		56	8	
Sunderland								1	
Surrey				4		1			
Sussex		1	1	3	2		10	1	
Tyne & Wear					1			2	
Warwickshire				3			17		
Wiltshire							1	1	
Worcestershire	1						1		
Yorkshire		128	142	51	247	177	216	356	180
Ireland			3	3	1	2	7	1	3
Scotland				2		1	13	2	
Shetland				2					
Wales				2			4		

	Gby 1851	*Scar*	*Fy*	*Gby 1871*	*Scar*	*Fy*	*Gby 1891*	*Scar*	*Fy*
Isle of Man							2		
Isle of Wight				1			1		
Guernsey							1		
Australia							1		
Belgium							1		
Denmark				1			8		
East Indies							2		
Finland				1					
France				1			2		
Germany				1			13		
Holland									
Iceland				1					
India							2		
Malta							1		
Newfoundland				3			1		
Norway							13		
Sweden							1		
USA							6		
Zetland									
Town Date	**Gby 1851**	**Scar**	**Fy**	**Gby 1871**	**Scar**	**Fy**	**Gby 1891**	**Scar**	**Fy**
Total Fishermen	**17**	**158**	**149**	**646**	**358**	**202**	**2,216**	**453**	**188**
Fishermen born in the town	7	96	131	26	196	160	239	315	171
Population of towns	**9,055**	**12,158**	**1,511**	**22,302**	**22,391**	**2,267**	**52,058**	**33,376**	**2,481**

Notes:

1) The figures here are based on the census data and generally include only those fishermen at home on census day.
2) The population figures for Grimsby do not include Cleethorpes, Scartho and Humberston.
3) Determining the numbers of fishermen registered at each fishing port for the nineteenth century is fraught with difficulties. Even interpreting the census data presents us with problems. For example, a 'Smack Owner' may or may not go to sea. I have, however, included these among the fishermen.

Appendix 2: Attendance figures for Filey Primitive Methodist Church

Filey was part of the Bridlington Circuit during the period 1835–1863, and thereafter an independent circuit.

The membership figures here are based on March quarterly figures (except for 1862 and 1889, which were June and December respectively).

1823	40	1844	79	1865	256	1886	306	1907	341
1824		1845	72	1866	255	1887	287	1908	340
1825	50	1846	84	1867	248	1888	275	1909	303
1826		1847	83	1868	301	1889	258	1910	283
1827		1848	111	1869	274	1890	235	1911	290
1828		1849	95	1870	262	1891	242	1912	256
1829		1850	104	1871	242	1892	237	1913	263
1830		1851		1872	262	1893	220	1914	237
1831		1852		1873	244	1894	218		
1832		1853		1874	295	1895			
1833		1854		1875	319	1896	233		
1834		1855		1876	316	1897	205		
1835	50	1856		1877	326	1898	226		
1836	36	1857		1878	337	1899	240		
1837	35	1858		1879	333	1900	241		
1838	34	1859		1880	350	1901	229		
1839	31	1860		1881	353	1902	208		
1840	32	1861		1882	323	1903	311		
1841	33	1862	208	1883	339	1904	297		
1842	71	1863	248	1884	347	1905	325		
1843	74	1864	254	1885	299	1906	340		

Sources: Beverley Archives: MRQ 1/36
Northallerton Archives: Quarterly Schedules, MIC 3893 1/1/6-8
Figures for 1823 from Petty 1880: 189
Figures for 1825 from Woodcock 1889: 9

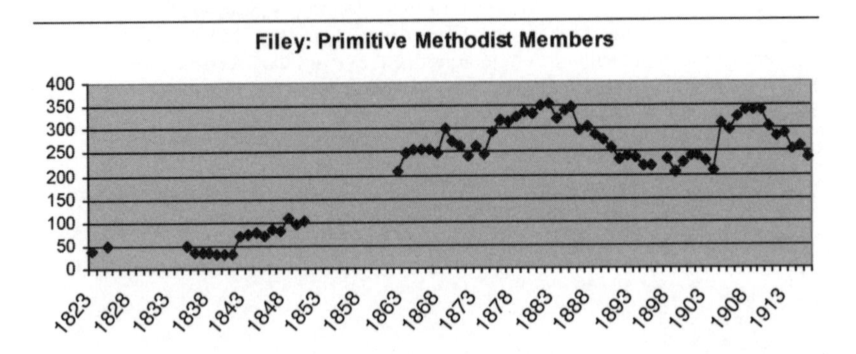

Notes

1 S. Friend and S. Parkes, 'Women's Voices Project', was established at York St John University in April 2005, and makes use of a personal narrative approach in that the women are encouraged to to tell their own stories about life in Yorkshire fishing communities. The recorded material is thus an important resource for community members, scholars and academics. The project is currently investigating how the women make sense and meaning of their lives within the communities, and this lends itself naturally to an exploration of 'lived religion'. The interviews referred to in this chapter represent the first published use of the material.

2 Grimsby is, of course, in Lincolnshire, not Yorkshire. Nevertheless, its history is so closely tied to the Yorkshire fishing industry that its exclusion here would result in a distorted picture.

References

Abercrombie, N., J. Baker, S. Brett and J. Foster (1973), 'Superstition and Religion: The God of the Gaps', in D. Martin and M. Hill (eds), *Sociological Yearbook of Religion in Britain*, III (London: SCM Press), pp. 93–129.

Abrams, L. (2002), *The Making of Modern Woman* (London: Longman).

Ambler, R. 'Social Change and Religious Experience: Aspects of Rural Society in South Lincolnshire with Specific Reference to Primitive Methodism, 1815–1875' (unpublished PhD thesis, University of Hull, 1984).

Anson, P.F. (1965), *Fisher Folk-Lore* (London: The Faith Press).

Bauman, Z. (2004), *Identity* (Cambridge: Polity, 2004).

Bocock, R. (1974), *Ritual in Industrial Society: A Sociological Analysis of Ritualism in Modern England* (London: George, Allen & Unwin).

Campbell, C. (1996), 'Half-belief and the Paradox of Ritual Instrumental Activism: A Theory of Modern Superstition', *British Journal of Sociology* 47.1 (March): 151–66

Clark, D. (1982), *Between Pulpit and Pew: Folk Religion in a North Yorkshire Fishing Village* (Cambridge: Cambridge University Press).

Cohen, A.P. (1987), *Whalsey: Symbol, Segment and Boundary in a Shetland Island Community* (Manchester: Manchester University Press).

Cohen, A.P. (ed.) (1982), *Belonging: Identity and Social Organisation in British Rural Cultures* (Manchester: Manchester University Press).

Cole, J. (1828), *History and Antiquities of Filey in the County of Yorkshire* (Scarborough: J. Cole).

Davis, O. (1997), 'Methodism, the Clergy, and Popular Belief in Witchcraft and Magic', *History* 82.226 (April).

Delanty, G. (2003), *Community* (London: Routledge).

Dundes, A. (1989), *Folklore Matters* (Knoxville: University of Tennessee Press).

Durkheim, E. (1976), *The Elementary Forms of the Religious Life* (London: George Allen and Unwin).

—— (1984), *The Division of Labour* (trans. 1894 by W.D. Halls; New York: The Free Press).

Fearon, M. (1990), *Filey, From Fishing Village to Edwardian Resort* (Beverley: Hutton Press).

Frank, P. (1976), 'Women's Work in the Yorkshire Inshore Fishing Industry', *Oral History* 4.1: 57–72.

—— (2002), *Yorkshire Fisherfolk* (Chichester: Phillimore).

Frazier, J. (1993) [1890], *The Golden Bough* (London: Wordsworth).

Gennep, A. Van. (1960), *The Rites of Passage* (London: Routledge & Kegan Paul).

Gill, A. (2003), *Hull's Fishing Heritage: Aspects of Life in the Hessle Road Fishing Community* (Barnsley: Wharncliffe Books).
Gillett, E. (1970), *A History of Grimsby* (Hull: University of Hull Press).
Goffman, E. (1959), *The Presentation of Self in Everyday Life* (London: Doubleday Anchor).
Gutch, Mrs (1901), *Country Folk-Lore*, Vol. 11. The Folklore Society: David Nutt, London: 13–14.
Hudson, D. (1974), *Munby, Man of Two Worlds* (London: Abacus).
Hutton, R. (1996), *The Stations of the Sun: A History of the Ritual Year in Britain* Oxford: Oxford University Press).
Jahoda, G. (1969), *The Psychology of Superstition* (London: Allen Lane, The Penguin Press).
Jarvis, P. (1980), 'Towards a Sociological Understanding of Superstition', *Social Compass* 27: 285–95.
Jenkins, R. (2004), *Social Identity* (London: Routledge).
Johnson, W. (1993), 'Between Nature and Grace: The Folk Religion of Dissident Methodism in the North Midlands, 1780–1820', *Staffordshire Studies* 5: 73–76.
Leonard, D. (1980), *Sex and Generation* (London: Tavistock).
Lummis, T. (1985), *Occupation and Society: The East Anglian Fishermen 1880–1914* (Cambridge: Cambridge University Press).
Malinowski, B. (1948), *Magic, Science and Religion* (Illinois: Glencoe).
Mead, G.H. (1934), *Mind, Self and Society* (Chicago: Chicago University Press).
Mullen, P.B. (1969), 'The Function of Magic Folk Belief among the Texas Coastal Fishermen', *Journal of American Folklore* 82: 214–25.
Mullen, P.B. (2005), 'Folklore', in *Encyclopedia of Religion*, V (ed. J. Lindsey; Thompson Gale, Farmington, USA, 2nd edn).
Nadel-Klein, J. (2003), *Fishing for Heritage: Modernity and Loss Along the Scottish Coast* (Oxford and New York: Berg).
Obelkevich, J. (1976), *Religion and Rural Society, South Lindsey 1825–1875* (Oxford: Clarendon Press).
Orsi, R. (2002), *The Madonna of 115th Street: Faith and Community in Italian Harlem, 1880–1950* (New Haven: Yale University Press).
Pettitt, Rev. A. (1868), *Guide to Filey* (Sheffield).
Petty, J, (1880), *The History of the Primitive Methodist Connexion from its Origin to the Conference of 1880* (rev. edn by James MacPherson; London: John Dickenson).
Poggie, Jr, J.J., R.B. Pollnac and C. Gersuny (1976), 'Risk as a Basis for Taboos among Fishermen in Southern New England', *Journal for the Scientific Study of Religion* 15: 257–62.
Smith, A.W. (1969), 'Popular Religion', *Past and Present* 40 (July): 181–86.
Strauss, A., and J. Corbin (1998), *Basics of Qualitative Research: Techniques and Procedures for Developing Grounded Theory* (London and New Delhi: SAGE).
Sykes, R.P.M. (1999), 'Popular Religion in Dudley and the Gornals c. 1914–1965' (unpublished PhD thesis, University of Wolverhampton).
Thompson, P. (1985), 'The Roots of Power between the Sexes', *Comparative Studies in Society and History* 1: 3–32.
Thompson, P., with T. Wailey and T. Lummis (1983), *Living the Fishing* (London: Routledge & Kegan Paul).
Tönnies, F. (1957) [1887], *Community and Society* (New York: Harper).
Turner, V. (1969), *The Ritual Process: Structure and Anti-structure* (New York: Aldine de Gruyter).
Valenze, D. (1985), *Prophetic Sons and Daughters: Female Preaching and Popular Religion in Industrial England* (Princeton: Princeton University Press).
Wenger, E. (1998), *Communities of Practice: Learning, Meaning and Identity* (Cambridge: Cambridge University Press).

Williams, S. (1999), *Religious Belief and Popular Culture in Southwark c. 1880–1939* (Oxford: Oxford University Press).
Woodcock, H. (1889), *Primitive Methodism on the Yorkshire Wolds* (London, n.p.).

Interviews

Scarborough
22MP05, 5 October 2005
02RJ04, 25 November 2005
02RJ05(2), 9 December 2005
11DN05, 23 June 2006

Hull
09MH05, 8 June 2005

Filey
03AW05, 9 May 2005
16MT05, 22 July 2005

Whitby
23NW06, 8 April 2006

Archives

Beverley archives, MRQ 1/36
Northallerton Archives, Quarterly Schedules, MIC 3893 1/1/6-8

12

An Examination of the Sikh Community in York

Richard Noake

Introduction

York is said to be the second most visited city in England next to London. It has a rich history, particularly boasting Roman, Viking, mediaeval and Georgian periods. The religious tradition of York is long and well documented, dominated by the large Cathedral, York Minster. To the casual observer York's population is mono-cultural and it is presumed mono-faith. It comes as something of a surprise to many to discover that York has a diverse ethnic and religious population. In addition to the many Christian groups and denominations in York, we can discover from the 2001 census statistics that York is home to Buddhists, Hindus, Jews, Muslims and Sikhs. It also has a Ba'hai community and a large Chinese community. In number terms, of the minority religious groups only the Muslims total more than one thousand and have more than one place of worship – two in fact. However, the other communities are becoming more visible and beginning to impact on the life of the City.

This chapter considers the experiences of those living in York who identify themselves as Sikh. This experience, for most, is a diasporic experience, of moving, of relocating. For some it has involved a move from a different continent. For others, a move from a larger, more culturally diverse context in the United Kingdom. For all it has been a move from a more established Sikh community. This chapter examines issues relating to the maintenance of a Sikh identity in a predominantly mono-cultural, mono-faith context.

On Using the Term Diaspora to Describe the Sikh Condition

Throughout this chapter I will refer to the Sikh experience as one that is explained best as a diaspora experience. Various scholars (Tololyan 1996; Clifford 1994; Kokot, Tololyan and Alfonso 2004) have debated the concept of diaspora, and 'Diaspora Studies' has become a growth area in academia. Amongst scholars of diaspora studies some might argue against using the term in relation to Sikhs. Certainly, in using the term diaspora it is recognized that in its original context – pertaining to the experience of the Jews – the term conveyed a negative, forced experience of removal from one geographical context (often referred to as 'homeland') to another, or even from a settled context to a nomadic life experience of constant removal and relocation. It might be argued that the Sikh experience does not contain these extremes therefore the term diaspora should not pertain to Sikhs.

Perhaps a more accurate term for the experiences of York-based Sikhs would be 'migration' (and indeed Migration Studies has also been an area of research in the academy); however, following debates proffered by Harvey and Thompson and taking account of the possible life experience of some Sikhs (which have been punctuated with traumatic episodes of forced relocation), 'diaspora' offers a more holistic description. As they argue:

> There is no linguistic law that says 'diaspora' must now and always refer to unwanted or forced movement whilst other words, such as 'migration', must be used for the welcome or intentional kind. 'Diaspora' can also refer to a deliberate scattering of seed, a distribution, diffusion or dissemination; it is possible to use it to refer to something that produces abundant and fecund growth. (Harvey and Thompson 2005: 1)

Therefore, we might argue that 'diaspora' is a term that can be used to describe both the positive and less positive experiences of Sikhs, containing as they do stories of both 'unwanted or forced movement' and 'abundant and fecund growth'.

Certainly, this is true for Sikhs in York. For amongst those who reside in the City are some who can tell stories of the events of the 1947 partition of India, of living in refugee camps and, for some, of leaving Africa during the time of the large-scale evacuations due to the totalitarian, Africanization regimes of the 1970s. These stories, in part, echo the traditional understanding of diaspora as 'forced relocation', although, as already stated, some have argued that the Sikh diaspora experience is not as strongly predicated on stories of forced relocation, for either economic or political reasons (R. Singh 2000: 19). Nevertheless, there are many who can vividly recall the events of partition, which did bring about forced relocations from what is now Pakistan to India, and that these relocations were fundamentally as a result of politics and economics. The Sikh context does not rely solely on these stories of trauma; there are also more positive stories of relocation: to pursue education, to take up new employment opportunities and to increase economic stability.

Safran, who in seeking a more specific use of the term diaspora, not linked to 'any group of expatriates', makes the case that 'diasporas comprise special kinds of immigrants because they have a retained a memory of, a cultural connection with, and a general orientation toward their homelands' (2004: 10). This categorization strengthens the case for a Sikh diaspora as it could be argued that for many Sikhs a preoccupation with the land of origin, the Punjab, has, certainly since the events at Amritsar in 1984, been a given, and hence the notion of diaspora in this context is made even stronger.

In presenting these various debates, it could be argued that the case is made to label the Sikh experience a diasporic one. In general terms and in relation to the Sikhs of York, the range of the experiences, including forced relocations for political and economic reasons, suggests there is a Sikh diaspora.

A Short History of the Sikh Diaspora

Sikhism originated in the Punjab, northern India, and from its earliest times (from Nanak, born 1469 CE) to the start of British rule (1858 CE) that is the place where most Sikhs lived. Brian Axel informs us that when the Sikh movement began, it '*did not*, for the most part, follow the dictates of the system of indentured servitude that, between 1833 and 1920, was responsible for the migration of people from all over the subcontinent to other colonies' (2001: 2, original emphasis). He argues that most Sikhs, and almost all were men, travelled as members of the services, either the army or police, or a few as 'students, scholars, adventurers, and "free" laborers' (ibid.). This is supported by Brown who adds that the relatively positive experiences of Sikhs in the British Army (many of these being from the *Jat* caste, or *zat*), who would have engaged in extensive overseas travel, inspired other family members to take up the opportunities made available by the Empire, with Sikhs, for example, being prominent in the Hong Kong police from the 1860s into the twentieth century (2006: 20). Kalsi supports this and, in commenting on the movement of Sikhs, identifies that many Sikh soldiers relocated to various parts of the Empire including Singapore, Hong Kong and Malaya, whilst others migrated to Australia, Fiji and Canada (2005: 116ff.). He notes that upwards of 5,000 Sikhs moved to Canada and the United States respectively in the early 1900s, but that immigration policies curtailed the development of these communities until the 1960s.

One exception to the indentured labour experience was in relation to the Sikhs who travelled to East Africa between 1897 and 1920 to work, effectively as a forced workforce, on the East African railways. Initially, most of these were craftspeople, being from the *Ramgarhia* caste. As the Empire developed in East Africa, more Sikhs relocated to countries like Kenya, Uganda and Tanzania, not just to work on the railways but to provide essential clerical support, effectively in the form of a civil service.

A watershed for many Sikhs was the 1947 partition of India to form Pakistan. Despite Sikh representatives at the time putting forward a 'resolution demanding "a Sikh independent sovereign state"' (K. Singh 1999b: 253) their demands were rejected. Partition brought about the forced relocation of Sikhs, and for many, they had to leave their homes in West Punjab, the new Pakistan, either to live in East Punjab or to move away from the north of India altogether. Many found themselves with nothing, having lost all their possessions, and they were placed for some time in refugee camps. Despite such devastation, through hard work, many of the Sikhs that relocated to East Punjab prospered.

One Sikh interviewed in York had personal experience of the partition. He spent his formative years living with his parents and siblings in Tanzania, where his father prospered and amassed something of a fortune. In the 1940s they relocated to West Punjab and lived in a large house. At partition they had to leave and found themselves in a refugee camp. Rather than move to East Punjab the family returned to Africa and managed to re-establish themselves socially and financially.

Migration to Africa continued until the early 1950s, by which point there were thriving Sikh communities in these countries. Kalsi comments that the majority of the Sikhs in East Africa were of low caste, being craftsmen. In the Punjab they would have worked for the *Jat* (land-owning caste) Sikhs (2005: 119). But in East Africa they became established and developed a new identity, one not restricted by caste boundaries and expectations. This allowed them to build *Gurdwaras* and led to them asserting 'their Ramgarhia Sikh identity' (ibid.). By the 1960s many had 'secured key and highly visible roles for themselves in the economies of these areas, as traders, managers, technicians and artisans' (Brown 2006: 46). With the arrival of independence from British rule these African countries developed policies which would see the mass relocation of South Asians, including Sikhs, primarily to Britain. Cole explains that the African Sikhs were sometimes 'third-generation settlers who had never visited India and even now had no intention of going there' (1989: 263). He makes the point that having worked with the British in East Africa there was more of a social relationship with Britain than the Punjab or Punjabi Sikhs. When these Sikhs arrived in Britain they sometimes 'joined existing Sikh communities but they were not afraid to distance themselves geographically, setting up businesses and their homes in white areas which had no previous experience of Asians' (ibid.).

Sikhs in Britain

The history of a Sikh presence in Britain can be traced back to 1854 and the arrival of Duleep Singh, the exiled son of the Maharaja Ranjit Singh. It is Ranjit Singh who brought some sense of stability to the Punjab in the early part of the nineteenth century when he ruled over the region as Maharaja from 1799 to 1839. However, British occupation of the Punjab from 1849, and the subsequent Anglo-Sikh wars, brought an end to this period of stability. His son, who was declared Maharaja, was eventually ordered out of the Punjab and he relocated to England, having renounced Sikhism prior to arrival (Cole 1989: 261). He bought an English estate in Elveden in Suffolk and, having converted to Christianity, lived the majority of his remaining life in Britain (K. Singh 1999b: 101) although it is argued he did re-convert to Sikhism (Cole 1989: 261).[1] More notable signs of a Sikh presence in Britain can be traced to the development of the first *Gurdwara* in 1911 in Putney (Cole 1994: 155), although Peach and Gale (2003: 477) suggest 1908 in Shepherd's Bush. Sikh involvement in World War I brought some Sikhs to Britain and Ballard states that 'by the late 1920s small groups of Bhatra pioneers could be found in Britain's seaports' – *Bhatra* Sikhs belonging to the traditional occupational caste of the hawkers and peddlers (2000: 127). There was also some influx in between the world wars, with *Jat* Sikhs, traditional land-owning Sikhs (and the highest caste), but blessed with entrepreneurial skills, joining their *Bhatra* brothers. Ballard suggests by 1939 there were probably several hundred male Sikhs in Britain, divided roughly equally between *Bhatra* and *Jat* caste. Ballard also mentions that one consequence of World War II on these Sikh entrepreneurs was that conscription brought an opportunity for them to enter employed status in the place of those having gone off to war (2000: 128).

However, the majority of Sikh movement to Britain happened after World War II, with increased numbers beginning to arrive in the late 1950s and onwards. Brown mentions that immediately following World War II Britain was the only country to have an open-access policy to those from South Asia, due to the Commonwealth ties (2006: 24). However, the politics and policies in the 1960s 'of immigration, race relations and the need for skilled labour swung the pendulum the other way' (2006: 25). This had the potential to severely curtail the migration of South Asians to Britain. Nevertheless, during the 1950s and 1960s Sikhs continued to arrive in Britain, especially dependants, who came to join husbands and fathers.

Cole suggests that the normal pattern of migration to Britain was for males to arrive having chosen a destination where employment was available (2004: 156ff.). They would help other men to relocate having found them employment through persuading employers to take them on and later their families would join them. Rait comments that initially Sikhs settled in cities which were primarily industrial, like London, Birmingham, Leeds, Bradford and Coventry (2005: 4). With a concentration of Sikhs came the development of *Gurdwaras*, places of worship, sometimes houses being purchased for this specific purpose. Cole notes that such practices were developing as early as the late 1950s (1989: 262).

Cole mentions the 'myth of return' – the notion migrants had that they would eventually relocate back to their 'home' – being a factor in the Sikh context as in other South Asian contexts (2004: 159). So, if they intended at some point to return why did they arrive? We have mentioned some of the political crises which might have forced them to come to Britain, but there were other factors at play. Rait (2005: 6) argues that it was not necessarily because of poverty, as is often presumed, but rather 'it was the Sikh tradition of migration that led many Sikhs to migrate. Their history shows them to be adventurous, hard-working and risk takers by nature' (ibid.). Cole states 'Migration among Sikhs is not a new or even recent phenomenon' and links this 'migrant' tendency back to Guru Nanak, the first Sikh Guru, who in the late 1400s and early 1500s took journeys inside and outside of India to promote his vision (2004: 156).

One York Sikh, who had relocated from the Punjab, expressed his notion of a migrant community; that Sikhs were outward looking and that they did not shy away from the opportunities to travel and live in other countries. He comments:

> One characteristic of the [Sikh] community is [it is] very outgoing, outward looking, [a] progressive community . . . even if people have not moved out [of the Punjab] their outlook by nature is very progressive . . . some links you can draw back to the teachings of the Sikh Gurus, very revolutionary, challenging the status quo, moving forward, believing in hard work, believing in sort of, in making your own destiny, those are things that you find in our teachings. Now that has really cast a shadow on the way people think and the way people lead their lives and that comes back and gets ingrained in and reflects in your character and reflects in your attitude. For

> example, I didn't think twice when it came to me . . . that I'd be moving . . . from home. It was an opportunity and I said yes, alright. (Ramindar, 17 October 2006)

An important factor in relation to those original migrant workers, in addition to their perception that they would return to their home, was that they also sent money back home to dependents to ensure a rise in lifestyle when they did return. Ballard mentions this trait and comments that

> Sikh emigration . . . was an entrepreneurial activity, and its participants were overwhelmingly drawn from moderately well off families of peasant stock. As such their central objective was usually to catch up with, and better still to overtake, those of their kin who were better off than they themselves. (2000: 130)

A perception that many have, and it seems to be borne out, is that Sikhs in Britain are generally aspirant and high achievers. Rait comments that a trend amongst established Sikhs in Britain has been for them to move 'into more affluent and suburban areas' and to buy 'better and expensive properties' (2005: 4).

In reality, most Sikh migrants to Britain did not move back to the Punjab. Clearly, those coming from East Africa were unlikely to move back to the Punjab, but even the Punjabi Sikhs failed to return in any sizeable numbers. A contributing factor to the non-return was the increasingly strict British immigration laws which forced most South Asians to make a decision: to either stay and to bring the family to Britain or to return to the Punjab and possibly lose the opportunity to return to Britain. Ballard suggests that a further persuasive factor in encouraging Sikhs to stay was literally strength of numbers, due to increased immigration, despite tightening British controls, which brought about the possibility that they could build 'a Punjabi moral order in the midst of what had hitherto been regarded as a wholly alien environment' (2000: 132). This saw the development of *Gurdwaras* and the establishment of a strong Sikh community in cities such as Leeds, Bradford, Coventry, Southall, Birmingham and London.

An important fact in this story of the Sikh diaspora to Britain is that the Sikh communities, developing in the 1960s and established today, are not a homogenized community. Whilst they are all Sikh, the boundaries and distinctions based on caste and the impact of the place of origin prior to migration to Britain is significant. The majority of *Bhatra* and *Jat* caste arrived from the Punjab. They were undereducated and lacked a strong command of English. The majority of *Ramgarhia* (craftsmen) Sikhs came to Britain from East Africa. They and their families were respectively highly educated and having worked with the British in East Africa had a good command of English, and as Ballard states, they were used to living as a migrant community (2000: 134ff.). This has led to East African Sikhs becoming by far the most affluent group in Britain, although they represent the minority within the Sikh community. This is not to suggest that Sikhs from other backgrounds have not achieved.

Through hard work and a frugal attitude 'the lifestyles now enjoyed by the vast majority of British Sikhs can only be described as comfortable and broadly middle class' (Ballard 2000: 135). So, what has been the increase in Sikhs in Britain over the last forty to fifty years? Peach and Gale, working with previously published data generated from the General Register Office of Places of Worship, have determined, by working back from the 2001 census details, that it is possible to estimate the number of Sikhs, based on ethnic categorizations, living in the UK in 1961, as being in the region of 16,000 (2003: 479).

The United Kingdom 2001 census, having included for the first time a question on religion, can provide us with more than an estimate. It showed that of a total population of 58.7 million people, just over 42 million, 71.6 per cent, professed to be Christian. Of the remaining categories of religion, Sikhism was listed, with 336,000 identifying themselves with this label, some 0.6 per cent of the total population.

On Determining a Possible Baseline for Sikh Identity

In attempting to explore the extent to which Sikhs in York maintain their identity, it would be useful to try and determine what common factors, if any, contribute to the development of a Sikh identity. The renowned scholar of Sikhism, Hew McLeod, whose own substantial exploration of Sikhism began in the 1960s, was asking the question 'Who is a Sikh?' in his seminal and, for some, controversial work[2] of 1989 of the same title. In his book, of which the subtitle 'The Problem of Sikh Identity' signals the challenge facing the scholar setting out to make any sense of this youngest of world religions, McLeod offers a useful guide to the tradition that is Sikhism. McLeod's work, and indeed most guides to the Sikh religion, identifies some central features that might aid the development of a baseline of orthodoxy and orthopraxy in relation to Sikhism.

McLeod identifies the genesis of the tradition, through the personhood of Nanak, born in 1469, and later identified by Sikhs as the first in a line of ten earthly Gurus. In the Sikh context the Guru is identified as more than a holy man, and is believed to embody both a religious and political leadership dynamic (1989: 7ff.). In stark contrast to the notion of guru as removed from society, as a wandering ascetic, the Guru of Sikhism is a universal exemplar of living *in* the world, an imperative that Sikhism still embodies today. Nanak's campaign, to refocus attention on the divine and to move away from certain rituals and practices prevalent in Hinduism, began after a brief period of 'revelation', where Nanak was supposedly transported to the place of the divine (Kalsi 2005: 17). Nanak's life mission after this event was given over to preaching his message, a message which sought to re-capture the notion of the divine for humanity and to emphasize the possibility of a relationship with Akal Parukh (essentially God) that could bring about the ultimate aim of release from the constant cycle of transmigration through birth, death and rebirth.

Oberoi argues that Nanak and his followers did not establish a separate religious identity and suggests that 'For much of its early history the Sikh movement . . . had shown little enthusiasm for distinguishing its constituents from members of other religious traditions' (1994: 47). In line with other scholars, Takhar takes issue with Oberoi and suggests his 'views should not be pressed as far as to accept too blurred an identity for early Sikhs' (2005: 5). What most Sikhs will agree on is that Nanak developed a tradition, which others took up, where, meditating on the name of God, *nam simran*, was central, where 'The emphasis . . . must be laid firmly and exclusively upon inner devotion as opposed to external observance' (McLeod 2000: 29). The first words of the Sikh scriptures are ascribed to Nanak and form the beginning of the most important saying of Nanak, known as the *Mul Mantar*; here Nanak declares that there is one God, *Ik Oankar*, and that God is truth. For religious Sikhs, this is at the heart of the Nanak legacy and in discussions of identity forms the basis of a faith adherent's understanding of their God and consequently affects their devotion to God.

In addition to this devotional focus, Sikhs also point to Nanak as instigating a position of equality for women, a radical view to the prevalent one of his day, and of being against divisions in society based on caste, again this being contrary to the Hindu view at that time; although McLeod argues that caste distinctions were tolerated even by the Gurus in the area of marriage (1989: 21).

McLeod (1989: 23ff.) and many other scholars (Mansukhani 1989; Narang 1989; Grewal 1994; K. Singh 1999a; Kalsi 2005; Nesbitt 2005) provide a detailed exploration of the historical development of the tradition from Nanak through the other nine Gurus. In attempting to identify central features for an understanding of Sikh identity, the period of the Gurus provides the majority of the key elements. Sikhs argue that all Gurus contributed in a fundamental way to the development of the Sikh tradition, with a core belief being that the same *jot*, or 'indwelling divine light' (Cole 2004: 177), illuminated all ten Gurus; however, in relation to distinctive contributions that exemplify Sikh identity, some Gurus' actions stand out. The third Guru, Amar Das (Guruship 1152–1574), established the practice of *langar*, of communally prepared food to be shared with all, following devotional activity. In the act of preparation, what Sikhs view as an act of *sewa* or voluntary communal service and a key Sikh ethic, men and women work together and all people, regardless of gender or caste, sit together, traditionally on the floor, to share the meal. This practice, in the Guru period and today, is meant to emphasize the ethic of service and the notion of there being no distinction between male and female, high caste and low caste. The fifth Guru, Arjan (Guruship 1581–1606), compiled the Sikh scripture, the *Adi Granth*, and also built the Harimandir Sahib, the Golden Temple, completing both in 1604. Both are key to an understanding of Sikh identity, the former providing as it does many of the prayers and hymns of the Sikh tradition and also the primary focus at the conclusion of the human Guru tradition and the later being a focus for spiritual authority. The final human Guru, Gobind Rai (Guruship 1675–1708), at the 1699 Vaisakhi ceremony, initiated the development of the *Khalsa Panth*, with the central elements including: the initiation rite of *amrit*; the wearing of the symbols of faith; the keeping of the *panj kakkar* – the five Ks; and the taking of the name *Singh* (lion) for a man and *Kaur* (princess) for a woman. Cole highlights the significance of the new names and argues 'that by adopting the names Singh and Kaur, members were effectively declaring that the names by which their social group could be recognised were irrelevant and unacceptable among Sikhs' (2004: 42). This development then is seen as a move against maintaining caste distinctions. Gobind Rai is also, some argue, responsible for the establishing of the turban, or in Punjabi, *pag*, as an outward feature of a Sikh (Cole 1973: 51).

This *Khalsa* ('brotherhood', although 'sisters' were also included) *Panth* (path) becomes a major organization within Sikhism and many, although not the majority, join the *Panth* in a show of allegiance to the Guru, who becomes known, from this point on, as Gobind Singh, taking on his Sikh male identifier. Takhar argues that the development of the *Panth* 'was critically important for Sikhism since the formation of the *Khalsa* endeavoured to provide Sikhs with a final distinct identity from both Hindus and Muslims, as much by outward appearance as inward philosophy' (2005: 11). It has been argued that in the development of the *Khalsa*, Guru Gobind Singh instigates the now familiar figure of the Sikh as the 'saint-solider', combining the spiritual and corporeal.

To join the *Khalsa*, Sikhs undertook, as they still do today, an initiation ceremony, known as *amrit sanskar*, which included the drinking of *amrit*, sugared water, which had been blessed with the *Khanda*, a double-edged sword and a central symbol of the Sikh emblem. All *Khalsa* Sikhs, known as *amritdhari* Sikhs, in engaging in this initiation ceremony, agree to keep the symbols of the tradition as well as to live a certain lifestyle, epitomized by a high degree of moral and spiritual rectitude. These symbols, the *kakkar* or five Ks, are, for many, the visible symbols of the religion: the *kara* or iron bangle; the *kesh*, the uncut hair; the *kangha*, the comb; the *kirpan*, the sword; and the *kachha*, cotton breeches. The turban is not one of the *kakkar*; 'however, it is integral to male Khalsa Sikhs' expression of their commitment' (Nesbitt 2005: 51) and it is not just the preserve of men, as some Sikh women also wear the turban. These post-*amrit* expectations for Sikhs form the major part of the *Rahit* or code of discipline for all *Khalsa* Sikhs.

Guru Gobind Singh also breaks with the tradition of appointing a human successor and establishes the Sikh scriptures, the *Adi Granth*, as the final and everlasting Guru, known from that time as the Guru Granth Sahib. From the end of the reign of the human Gurus the sacred scripture, the Guru Granth Sahib, becomes the focus for the community and plays a central part in Sikh worship.

In relation to the *Khalsa*, as has been mentioned, not all Sikhs in 1699 joined and not all Sikhs today are *Khalsa* Sikhs. In making this statement we are challenged, alongside writers like McLeod, to ask the question about Sikh identity and what makes a Sikh a Sikh. If an initiation has not been undertaken then can you be called a Sikh? Kalsi agrees it is difficult: 'Defining Sikh identity is complex and problematic. Originally, people chose to enter the Sikh *Panth*, but nowadays children born into Sikh families are regarded as Sikhs and usually have "Singh" or "Kaur" as surnames; and this includes clean-shaven Sikhs' (2005: 6). Within the Sikh community there are known phrases that relate to certain typologies: *amritdhari* Sikhs, those having gone through initiation into the Khalsa; non*amritdhari* being any Sikh that has not engaged in initiation and these can be subdivided into *keshdhari*, keepers of the uncut hair; and non*keshdhari* or *mona* Sikhs, clean shaven. A further term which might be used is *sahajdhari* which indicates a Sikh who is on the road to initiation, the term literally meaning a 'slow adopter' (Kalsi 2005: 6). At the time of Guru Nanak the term Sikh was used to imply a 'searcher after truth', one who is 'having instruction, guided by teaching' (Oberoi 1994: 56). This was a label ascribed to an individual. It was only later, through the work of the other Gurus, that the term came to be used as an identifier for the community.

Therefore, from a purely religious perspective we have the possibility that Sikh identity is somehow bound up in: believing in one God; in the inspiration and leadership of the ten human Gurus; in the scriptures as the final and forever Guru; in the notion of initiation into the *Khalsa* and afterward the keeping of the five Ks and other disciplines associated with the *Rahit* or code of conduct which include not smoking and not eating Halal meat. McLeod provides a detailed account of the *Rahit* as practised after 1699, outlining subtleties in interpretation and questioning the various versions that existed and some of the sources (1989: 23ff.; 2000: 103–35). It is not the purpose of this chapter to delve into these details. From the late 1800s onwards various Sikhs tried to produce a definitive version of the code of discipline for initiated Sikhs. The fact that a version was on the table by 1931, produced by the Shiromani Gurdwara Parbhandhak Committee (an elected body charged with managing Sikh Gurdwaras and a group with significant power in the Sikh world today) and took until 1950 to be published, as the Sikh Rahit Maryada, highlights the difficulty and complexity of the task and consequently the challenge in attempting to provide a definition of a Sikh, albeit a *Khalsa* Sikh. McLeod does suggest that all orthodox Sikhs will accept these markers of identity and 'although they may not actually undergo initiation, they will at least observe the basic requirements of the Rahit'. He adds that 'Those who decline to accept the basic requirements of the Rahit can still be accepted as Sikhs, but only on the understanding that they are failing to discharge customary duties' (McLeod 1989: 121).

We have determined a set of religious values that Sikhs may subscribe to and consequently might act as markers of identity. We must turn, briefly, to the discussion of caste within Sikhism, for this provides another dimension in the discussion of Sikh identity. As Kalsi states 'it is generally believed that the Sikhs are a casteless brotherhood . . . On closer investigation one finds, however, that instead of a single Sikh community, there is a situation of complex plurality' (1992: 25). Commentaries on the Sikh tradition do contend that the Sikh Gurus made pronouncements about there being no hierarchy and hence no caste. However, it is also generally accepted that the eradication of caste distinctions did not happen in the Guru period and has not been achieved since. So, we have a tradition that makes some claims about a casteless society but in truth practises caste distinctions, particularly in relation to the acquiring of marriage partners; there are also a significant number of *Gurdwaras* in Britain that are established by particular caste groups and include the caste name in the name of the *Gurdwara*. It is unnecessary and impossible to list the many different caste names that exist within the Sikh tradition. Some significant caste markers are *Jat*, *Ramgarhia*, *Bhatra*, *Chamars* and *Khatri*.

A further area that impacts on Sikh identity is the relationship between Sikhism and the Punjab and the Punjabi language. As has already been stated, the tradition began in the Punjab and its formative history is bound with that region. The common tongue of the Sikhs is Punjabi, with the scripture being written in this language (whilst acknowledging that the vocabulary is very varied), its form known as *Gurmukhi*. Devotion in the Gurdwara is still delivered in Punjabi. However, in Britain it is the case that a majority of the younger generation certainly cannot read Punjabi and many also struggle to speak it.

In mentioning the Punjab it is necessary to also comment on the extent to which ongoing concerns about Sikh nationhood, the development of a Sikh homeland in the Punjab and the struggle for the creation of Khalistan impacts upon notions of Sikh identity. It is pertinent here to mention the watershed experiences of June 1984 in the tragic happenings at the Golden Temple in Amritsar, where the Indian Army, ordered by the then Prime Minister, Indira Gandhi, attacked what they considered to be Sikh militants and terrorists who had taken refuge in the Temple. These events, called 'Operation Bluestar', led to the death of hundreds of Sikh men and sparked violent action amongst Sikh communities around the globe. Gandhi's action was undoubtedly the reason for her assassination by her two Sikh bodyguards. This in turn led to severe action by officials against Sikhs in the Punjab, including torture and death. A number of writers (Wolffe 1993: 108; Axel 2001; Barrier 2006: 33–56; Tatla 2006: 57–58) cite this event as a catalyst for a reappraisal of Sikh religious, cultural and political identity. At the time it led to many becoming involved in Sikh militancy, in the wearing of saffron-coloured turbans (Tatla 2006: 67) and reprisal activities. It still is the subject of heated debate, for scholars and Sikhs alike, and it seems to be at the centre of ongoing militancy in the Punjab region itself. Axel provides details of this aspect of Sikh experience. He mentions that 'Since 1984 . . . although certainly not supported by all Sikhs, the idea of Khalistan has nevertheless become intimately linked to the transformation of British Sikh life' (2001: 178). This provides a focus for young British Sikhs and encourages their growing interest and concerns about the land of their origins and the formation of a separate homeland. One can add to these stories of trauma the related but distinct experiences of Sikhs post-9/11, commented on by writers such as Verma (2006: 89–101), where Sikhs, males in particular, have experienced discrimination as a result of false identity because they are turbaned and wear beards (and therefore supposedly resemble Bin Laden).

In attempting to determine a baseline for Sikh identity we have introduced a number of key themes. There are markers relating to religious adherence, to orthodoxy and orthopraxy. These raise questions about *Khalsa* Sikhs and non-*Khalsa* Sikhs. The *Rahit Maryada* would link both orthodoxy and orthopraxy to being a *Khalsa* Sikh; however, the weight of written opinion suggests that those who practise a religious adherence and yet are not *amritdhari* are nevertheless accepted as Sikhs, albeit seen as moving towards the 'standard'. There is also the theme of caste and whether this is a dimension of Sikh identity and how it is discussed and explained when there would appear to have been a directive to abandon caste distinctions. There is the theme of the Punjab and the hoped-for dream of some that there will be the establishment of a separate homeland for the Sikhs. There are areas that have not been discussed, not least the existence of various groups amongst the Sikh tradition. Takhar explores the major ones, providing a useful guide to this subject and states that 'the very existence of different groups who have varying beliefs and practices within the Sikh Community . . . illustrate aptly that the *Panth* is not homogenous' (2005: 1).

These debates relate to the process of identity formation in relation to religious adherence. The inclusion of discussions about caste and statehood broaden out the base for identity and introduce cultural and political dynamics. There are also factors in relation to ethnicity, which to date have not been discussed. The dialogue here includes the ways in which Sikhs label themselves – are they Punjabi, Indian, Asian, British or an amalgam of these, for example British Asian or British Sikh? We have also suggested that Sikh women are afforded equal rights and responsibilities within the tradition and this marker will be an interesting one to explore.

In the opening paragraphs of this chapter it was suggested that York is predominantly mono-cultural and mono-faith. The story of the Sikhs in York, in the same way as the story of any minority group, is both an interesting and important one to tell. If the City considers that its minority religious and cultural groups are an integral part of the life of the City then the ways in which these groups understand themselves and their potential role in the City is fundamental. In today's current climate the opportunity and ability to dialogue with others is seen by politicians, educators and, increasingly, religious leaders too, as fundamental to the future harmony and cohesion of our communities. In examining the Sikhs in York this chapter will now ask a number of questions: Who are they? Where are they from? What brought them to York? How do they view themselves as individuals and as a community? In exploring these questions, notions of identity, in relation to the identified markers, will be considered: religion – in asking in what ways are you Sikh in terms of religious adherence; culture – in so far as caste and gender impacts on self identity and experience; politics – the significance or not of the establishment of a Sikh state; ethnicity – the ways in which this marker impacts on life experience in York.

The Sikhs in York

The United Kingdom 2001 census provides details of religious affiliation for many of the towns and cities of Yorkshire. It serves, in a way, as a wake-up call to those who believe that the adherents of the Indian religions – Hindu and Sikh (and indeed other religions other than Christianity) are only located in the urban centres of South and West Yorkshire, with the largest communities being in Leeds and Bradford (see Kalsi 1992; Knott and Kalsi 1994: 161ff.). It takes very little effort to discover that the case is somewhat different. Whilst in percentage terms the more rural Yorkshire locations have very small numbers of Hindus and Sikhs, it is nevertheless interesting to note that some kind of migration has been taking place, whether from contexts outside of the UK directly to these places or, more likely, from the urban areas to the rural idylls of North Yorkshire which, it could be argued, includes the City of York, sitting as it does in the essentially rural Vale of York.

Table 1 demonstrates two present-day realities, the first being the one most known, that places like Leeds and Bradford have large Hindu and Sikh communities, with the Sikhs of Leeds being the largest single community at over 1 per cent of the total population of the city. The second reality comes as a surprise to some – it certainly did to the Sikhs in York – that Sikhs and Hindus now reside in areas that have not been the usual localities for them to inhabit. In my interviews, all Sikhs found it hard to believe there were ninety-five Sikhs in the City. On hearing this news the common response was to start counting whom they knew and no one was able to account for all of them. My research into the Sikhs of York began through the good grace and support of the two Sikh advisers to York St John University College (as it was then), Dr Darminder Singh Chadha and Mrs Gurdeep Kaur Chadha. They were the first Sikh inhabitants of York, arriving in 1976. They have lived and worked in the City from their arrival, raising a family in the same house they occupy today. Whilst the Chadhas might be seen as the premier family of the Sikhs in York, they do not claim to know all Sikhs who live in the City and as my initial research relied heavily on their contacts, it proved somewhat difficult to locate the remaining Sikhs – for their contacts had scant details of other Sikhs.

In conducting my research I carried out semi-structured interviews. The majority of these were face-to-face interviews in the interviewees' homes, although any and all follow-up discussions were carried out on the telephone. In total I conducted interviews with an approximately 15 per cent sample of those Sikhs living in York.[3]

All direct quotes are dated as to the interview date; however, names are pseudonyms. From interviews and discussions with interviewees about other Sikhs

Table 1: **Population totals for locations in Yorkshire**

Location	*Total*	*Hindu*	*Sikh*
Leeds	715,402	4,183	7,586
Sheffield	513,234	1,675	773
Bradford	467,665	4,451	4,748
Wakefield	315,172	617	266
Doncaster	286,866	448	798
Rotherham	248,175	260	192
Hull	243,589	257	227
Barnsley	218,063	177	180
York	181,094	347	95
Harrogate	151,336	101	49
Scarborough	106,243	75	9

Source: ONS 2001

whom they knew but who did not want to contribute to the research, the Sikhs in York comprise a number of families. Most of these families have an 'acquaintance' relationship to each other, with a small number comprising an extended family network, although there has not, until recent times, been any homogeneity about the Sikhs in York, therefore it would be difficult to call them a community in the traditional understanding of the term. These families range in age from couples in their thirties with no children to those with young and growing families, to some couples whose children have left home and left York.

There are some older Sikhs in York who actually have a forced relocation story, although these experiences were not the reasons such Sikhs arrived in York. There are also a number of younger Sikhs, in their thirties and forties, who can tell stories of forced relocation of parents or grandparents and for whom, therefore, the diaspora experience is part of their ancestral memory. However, the majority of Sikhs in York have relocated for economic reasons, as their employment is based in the City. A small number have come directly from the Punjab to work for one of York's largest employers, Nestlé Rowntree. Others have experienced living in other cities in the United Kingdom before coming to York. In all these cases the other cities, such as Leicester, Leeds and Nottingham, have provided an established UK-based Sikh community.

In her chapter in this edited collection, Esther McIntosh provides a critique of John Macmurray's work on community in relation to New Labour's policies. In her work she offers a useful distinction, drawn from Macmurray, between community and society and states that 'both societies and communities are characterized by the intentional relations of human beings, but it is the type of union informing the relationality of people, in addition to the intentionality, that marks the difference between a community and a society'. She quotes Macmurray and his distinctions between peoples that co-operate for specific purposes and peoples who share and are bound by 'something deeper than any purpose'. On the spectrum of relationality upon which society and community sits, it might be argued a true community is therefore one where there is a bond deeper than practical reasons to relate to each other.

In this sense it is important to ask what kinds of relationships appear to be experienced by Sikhs in York and to what extent is there evidence for a Sikh community in York? In relation to communities other than Sikh, all those interviewed spoke about being members of different communities in York, both work and social. They all expressed that they liked York; one woman interviewed said it was 'friendly, peaceful and clean' (Manjit, 17 October 2006) – although the same woman then said that being in York was isolating; when challenged to say how it can be isolating and yet friendly, the 'friendliness' was explained as 'politeness', that all the neighbours were polite and said hello, but there was not an open-door policy, like there would be in a predominantly Sikh community.

This sense of isolation was a common theme for some women, particularly those who had raised families in York. One woman explained that on moving to York,

> we were on a constant of getting out of York for 10 years. I was very unsettled, very isolated, especially when the children came along. There was a lack of a Sikh community and hard work of travelling to Leeds for our temple and trying to make friends in the Sikh community . . . we found it was very difficult as the Sikh community didn't exist in York and we also found it very difficult making social interactions in Leeds as we found the community in Leeds to be inward looking . . . they had their own family and they had an extended family and they didn't really befriend outsiders. In the end that's why we have stayed in York to make the best of what we have. (Guninder, 12 September 2006)

This interviewee also spoke about feeling a sense of cultural and religious isolation: 'I missed the interactions with the Sikh community and the discussions at the Gurdwara'. This contrasts with others who in discussing their reasons for coming to York explained that they 'needed' to relocate, for emotional, psychological and spiritual reasons, to escape what they described as the rather claustrophobic and suffocating experience of living in close-knit and intensely introspective and intrusive communities elsewhere. These Sikhs admitted to not being particularly religious and yet, in choosing a label for themselves, they felt happiest with British Sikh. It might be deduced from this that their understanding of being Sikh extends beyond purely religious markers.

In discussing with one recent migrant from the Punjab the extent to which he and his family had been accepted by his work and local community, he was positive about the levels of acceptance, although he noticed there was a very different mentality amongst the indigenous population of York (which in many senses sums up white Britain):

> We find quite a different social environment and society, people are within themselves, everybody lives their own life. People at work are very friendly, no issues; you go to market, interaction; when we go to school no issues at all, people say hello, you don't feel you have been discriminated . . . not one percent do I feel because you are Asian you have been discriminated . . . but I don't live the same lifestyle, come Friday people go to the pub, but I say no, come Friday I spend time with my family. (Ramindar, 17 October 2006)

In relation to these responses it might appear that Sikhs in York experience membership of groups – work and social, but do not talk, in the McIntosh sense, of belonging to communities that are bound by something deeper. However, it would be improper to make this assumption fully as not all interviews pinpointed the nature or extent of community adherence other than in relation to Sikhism. Certainly, until recent times, any construction of Sikh community identity seems to have happened at a distance from York, with the majority travelling to Leeds for family and/or religious reasons and some even travelling to London to visit relatives. This would happen, in the case of Leeds, on a weekly basis. Those who travelled for religious reasons commented that once children had arrived the intensity was greater as they did all they could to provide a regular Sikh encounter, immersing them in the language, culture and religious tradition.

In ascribing an identity to oneself through the use of labels, the majority of those interviewed preferred British Sikh, rather than Asian or Indian. Recent migrants from the Punjab felt Sikh best described them, even when offered the possibility of Punjabi – this label being too generic as it included members of other faith communities. The majority of those interviewed had links with East Africa. Some were born in East Africa and migrated to Britain in early adulthood or childhood and for others their parents were born or based in East Africa and migrated to the UK prior to their birth. Despite this, none felt any affinity for Africa and would not have described themselves as African. One woman who had lived in Africa explained that even though she had lived there she had existed in an Indian environment so she did not relate to an African way of thinking or living.

All expressed a desire to see the Sikhs in York become more visible and more supportive as a community. Some expressed how important it was for a strong Sikh community to exist in York if they were to ensure that their children received a positive experience of living as a Sikh that did not rely on constant travel to more established centres like Leeds. However, most thought the number of Sikhs in York, particularly those who were interested in the cultural and religious, would necessitate working with the Hindus to create a culturally supportive network, although some hoped that the development of a *Gurdwara* might be possible which would significantly enhance the profile of the Sikh community.

In respect of religious observation and the maintenance of a Sikh tradition, none of those interviewed were *amritdhari* or fully baptized Sikhs. Some saw it as a possible future state but none perceived it as essential to being Sikh. All were very modest about their religious observance, some because they were not observant, others because they did not perceive themselves to be particularly observant, when in reality their daily acts of devotion suggested otherwise. One household has a Guru Granth Sahib: This requires that a room in the house is given to the book and that the book is kept in the same way as if it was at the *Gurdwara*. The level of observance needed to house a Guru Granth Sahib cannot be underestimated.

In relation to the outward signs of the tradition not all males in York are *keshdhari* (keep the long hair) but it appeared that all females were. Not all males wear the turban. Those who are *mona* Sikh were keen to state that it makes no difference in their religious observance. Of those who do wear the turban, at least one male saw it as an important symbol of his heritage, that he was proud to be a Sikh and to be seen wearing the turban. He claimed it meant he was easily recognized in York and that was important to him. Interestingly this male admitted he did not keep the code of discipline besides wearing the turban and maintaining the long hair and that he was not a particularly religious observant Sikh.

Despite the positive tone of at least one male Sikh to wearing the turban, it is often the case that the outward vestiges of a religious tradition can be a potential barrier to community cohesion, incorporation and integration. It might be perceived that being a Sikh in York would be challenging, particularly being an Asian/Indian/Punjabi Sikh. Not only are you visibly different by virtue of ethnicity but you are also, potentially, and particularly if you wear the turban, different in dress. As a Sikh in York, or for that matter away from the Punjab, is your difference, your distinctiveness, a determining psychological factor in what makes you Sikh? It would seem that for this one interviewee this was the case.

The positive experiences expressed by one adherent have been hard won over the years. Many Sikhs in the past have experienced discrimination as a result of their turban. Today there are still media reports about Sikhs suffering discriminatory action. Such discrimination is despite the 'liberal politics of recognition' (Hall 2004: 116) seen throughout the 1980s in attempts to generate a truly multi-cultural and tolerant society. These policies have been in stark contrast to the earlier experiences for Sikhs, in the 1960s and 1970s, where they had to do battle in court because of 'Britain's increasingly restrictive nationality and immigration acts' (Hall 2004: 115). The turban in particular has been the subject of court action, with the Sikhs initially winning the argument and being allowed to wear the turban in all contexts (what could have also been seen as a victory too for the Race Relations Acts). Although, Singh makes the point that 'Sikhs were able only to secure *indirect* protection for their religious practices' and cites legal cases against British Steel (1993), British Rail (1985) and Nestle where Sikhs, demanding the right to wear turban and beard, lost their cases (G. Singh 2005: 166–67, original emphasis). The parallels at the time of writing, late 2006, with the debates about the wearing of the veil by Muslim women, is both interesting and apposite.

Despite the battles won by the Sikhs over the wearing of the turban, discrimination is still perceived to be a problem in relation to community cohesion. Weller suggests:

> if it is not tackled in a vigorous and coherent way, then religious discrimination will continue to constrain the full participation of Hindus and Sikhs . . . in the social, political, economic and cultural life of the country and deprive the wider society of the full potential of the contribution that religious communities, organisations and individuals can make to its stability and well-being. (2004: 493)

What is pleasing to note is that none of the Sikhs interviewed had experienced what they would have classed as being religious or racial discrimination, in either work or social contexts. However, some of those with younger children or contemplating family life were concerned that children might be discriminated against at school and this made some of them question whether they would make sons wear a turban.

There are studies available on the discourses of gender and in particular the issues inherent in being a woman from an Asian culture and more particularly from a Sikh background (Paur 1994; Rait 2003). Arguments about the position of women in western society are well rehearsed, with some commenting that there is a lack of equality in relation to men. Debates about the position of women in Asian cultures are also well documented; in Sikhism we have a rhetoric which puts women on an equal basis to men: 'Sikhism advocates sex equality and accords women an equal place in society' (Rait 2003: 35). Nevertheless, Rait in her own work and the research of others (Paur 1994) found that many Sikh women did not feel there was absolute equality. Despite such concerns none of the women interviewed considered that they experienced anything but equality in relation to life in York, although it is difficult to know how open they were, given my own male, white identity.

The subject of caste was mentioned on two occasions without a prompt. In one interview the issue emerged in relation to parental identity where all parents of a couple had been *Ramgarhia*. I asked whether this had been a factor in them marrying and they admitted it was 'in those days' but the comment was forcefully made that 'we don't believe in that anyway . . . if you're a Sikh it doesn't matter what caste you're in' (Narinder, 16 October 2006). The other context was again in relation to marriage where a young married couple volunteered that they were both *Ramgarhia* and that this had been a factor in their marriage. This bears out the literature which clearly shows that caste, if anywhere, is prevalent in the area of marriage. Those who responded to a question about caste felt it was an outmoded cultural phenomenon but admitted that despite it being outmoded it seemed to be, some identified with regret, an increasing factor in relation to marriage. Of those interviewed the majority were *Ramgarhia* caste, which is perhaps to be expected given the strong links of many to East Africa.

In relation to political interests in the homeland none of those interviewed admitted to being involved in campaigning for a separatist state, for a Khalistan. Some acknowledged that it was an issue which could polarize Sikhs, and others were reluctant to discuss it as it was political and I suspect they did not want to mix what they perceived to be discussion about identity in relation to religion with a discussion of political identity. One Sikh male suspected that his young adult son was intensely interested in the issue and that this interest was encouraged by his contemporaries. He explained that although his son wore none of the outward symbols of Sikhism he was becoming increasingly interested in being a Sikh and spent much of his spare time with Sikhs in Leeds, where the discussions involved the cultural and political. For many though the subject of a Sikh homeland was a subject that they were aware of and followed at a distance but they were neither involved in or committed to this aspect of Sikh dialogue.

It can be seen from these few extracts of interviews conducted with Sikhs in York that there is clearly some level of diversity in their individual experiences. From an outward perspective some looked more Sikh than others, in the keeping of *kesh* and wearing of the turban, although some of the *keshdhari* Sikhs did not profess to be strongly religious in practice and, in contrast, those who were non*keshdhari* spoke about carrying out daily prayers and regular attendance at a *Gurdwara*. The majority of those interviewed expressed the fact that they would like the Sikhs of York to be more visible and to act more as a community. Some were already involved in the realization of this goal and others committed themselves to it in the future. Most of those interviewed mentioned, without prompting, the work of York St John University as being significant in the recent upsurge of interest by the Sikh and more generally South Asian community in things cultural and religious. Therefore it is to this development that the chapter finally turns.

More Recent Developments: The York St John Factor

In number terms the South Asian communities of York have not seen any significant change since the 2001 census. However, since 2004, the profile of minority religions has begun to increase and the involvement of one of the City's Higher Education institutions, York St John University,[4] has been significant to this development.

In 2003 York St John College, as it was then called, a Higher Education Institution with an Anglican Foundation, based in the heart of the city, began to explore the possibility of engaging members of regional faith communities in the work of its Chaplaincy. This was motivated by a desire to make real the rhetoric of community dialogue and working together that the institution had expressed for some time but not fully implemented. With the encouragement and support of the College Principal, Professor Dianne Willcocks, the College Chaplain, Rev. Jeremy Clines, wrote to various faith centres, places of worship and, where the information was available, named individuals, asking for names of respected adherents who lived in York who might be interested in working, in a voluntary capacity, with the College. The objective at the time was to create a team of faith advisers from the different faith communities represented in and around York. These advisers would work with the Chaplaincy team, and others in the institution, to provide advice and support to students and staff who might be adherents of these specific faiths. Their role would also include awareness building of the multi-faith context of York through the possible staging of cultural and religious events using the facilities of the College.

In 2004, Dr Darminder Singh Chadha and Mrs Gurdeep Kaur Chadha, and Mr Mahendra Verma and Mrs Usha Verma, respectively agreed to represent the Sikh and Hindu faith communities, as part of a fourteen-strong team of new faith advisers appointed by York St John. From the time of their appointment these two couples have worked with Chaplaincy and other members of York St John to raise awareness amongst University staff and the City at large of the minority South Asian communities based in the City. In April 2004, the first 'Faith Event' was a Gurdwara Day, where a Guru Granth Sahib was brought to the College by Harbans Singh Sagoo[5] and members of the Guru Nanak Nishkam Sewak Jatha[6] Gurdwara in Leeds. It was installed in a room adjacent to the College Chapel, and various members of the Asian community of York, together with members of the College community, attended readings from the Guru Granth Sahib as well as a music recital and langar, the sharing of food.

York St John then provided a multi-faith prayer room in the College for those of faiths other than Christian. This was opened in May 2004, thus providing for some minority religions, including Sikh and Hindu, the first formal worship space in the City. In October 2004, the second 'Faith Event' attracted substantially more people, where in excess of 150 people, consisting of British Asians, white British and other nationalities, attended the first ever public Divali celebration to be staged in York, held at York St John. Divali has been celebrated each year since 2004, with increasing numbers of attendees from both British Asian and white British communities.

As a result of the positive outcomes engendered by the work of the faith advisers and members of the University College, the institution looked to the City to embrace these developments and make more concrete its own involvement. An initiative was mooted: York: City of Faiths, and in March 2006, it was launched at York St John. Addresses were given by the University College Principal, the Archbishop of York, Dr John Sentamu, the Lord Mayor of York, Councillor Janet Greenwood and the nationally renowned Sikh, Dr Indajit Singh OBE, Director of the Network of Sikh Organisations UK. The initiative hoped to encourage positive change to York's ethos and values through promoting ongoing inter-religious cooperation. In this it stated four key purposes: 'to make the people of York aware of the ongoing inter-religious collaboration and cooperation in the City; to encourage York citizens to take part in these initiatives; to support the joint statement of commitment to this ongoing work; and to help people of all faiths to feel a common pride in the City of York'.[7] At the launch of the initiative these purposes were endorsed by all faith advisers and the panel representatives through the signing of a Statement of Intent.

One positive way of maintaining and developing the identity of the Sikh community was to continue with the staging of Faith Events. In May 2006, the Sikh Advisers and other members of the Sikh community, together with staff and students of the institution, hosted a Baisakhi celebration which attracted over 250 Sikhs, Hindus, other Asians, and people from the City. As with the Divali celebration in 2004 this was the first public celebration of Baisakhi in York. Also in May 2006 the Sikh Advisers began monthly meetings based in the prayer room, which included some devotional activity. These were offered throughout 2006 and attended by some members of the York Sikh community.

The role of the faith advisers and the University in the advancement of community cohesion and profile raising for those from a Sikh and Hindu context cannot be underestimated. A majority of those Sikhs interviewed for this study were keen to see the Sikhs in York become more supportive of each other and to create a more cohesive community. All mentioned the recent developments facilitated by York St John as a sign of a willingness to create a more vibrant, inclusive and visible community.

For one couple who only recently relocated to York from a larger city where there had been a strong and visible community, York St John had been pivotal in them creating links with the Asian community in York: 'we went to the Baisakhi festival at St John's and that's where we began to meet people' (Satwant, 18 October 2006). The Hindu and Sikh faith advisers have also cited the activities located at the University as being a catalyst to the development of a non-faith-based organization located in York which celebrates the culture of

India: The Indian Cultural Association. As a direct result of the Divali and Baisakhi celebrations the South Asians in York asked for more regular community meetings to share all aspects of Indian culture leading to the creation of this Association. This is not the first attempt by South Asians to meet, there being an Asian Association in the early 1970s and an Indian Society in the late 1980s; however, these organizations had ceased all activity.

The Faith Adviser actions proved to be the catalyst to a re-energizing of the community. In the development of the Indian Cultural Association in York we see Sikhs and Hindus working together, in a sense, to provide strength in numbers. We have the joining of the two communities to share the common elements of their cultures: they swap memories of India, even if for second-generation Asians they are more ancestral memories; they take opportunities to speak native languages; they share food; they celebrate Indian art, music and culture through poetry recitals, Indian dancing and lectures. This is not an uncommon practice where Indian communities have been in evidence. Burghart (1987) comments on this not being a new phenomenon, stating that in minority communities, Hindus and Sikhs have been found to work together in the furtherance and celebration of Indian culture. He mentions the Hindu and Sikh communities in Bradford who in the early 1980s joined together to re-establish some sense of community homogeneity.

Conclusion

What are we to say about the Sikh 'community' in York and how they as individuals and as a group maintain their sense of Sikh identity? It has been suggested that the Sikh experience in Britain is a diasporic one. The Sikhs in York do contribute to that wider story, in that they are able to tell of their own or generational experiences of Indian partition, conflicts in East Africa, and migrations to and within Britain.

The 2001 census identifies that there are Sikhs in York and that these form part of a wider South Asian group which includes a minority Hindu community. As a percentage of the total population of York the Sikhs might be considered to be insignificant; however, the recent involvement by Sikhs in the cultural and religious expression of the city might signal that they are significantly engaged and are contributing in positive ways to the diversity of the city.

Drawing on the work of scholars, I have suggested that there are a set of markers that might help in constructing a baseline for Sikh identity. A number of these markers relate to religious orthopraxy and orthodoxy and initiate a debate about the status of Sikhs compared to a construction of Sikh orthodoxy found in the *Rahit Maryada*. It is here that a Sikh is identified as a *Khalsa* Sikh incorporating as it does the maintenance of the five symbols of initiation and a lifestyle that contains various injunctions and expectations. In relation to these markers none of the Sikhs interviewed turned out to be *amritdhari*; however, none of them saw that construction as necessary to being identified as a Sikh, and the weight of scholarship would appear to support them in this fact, and all those interviewed, irrespective of their religious commitment, saw themselves as being Sikh. Whilst the Sikhs in York demonstrate a diversity of religious adherence and commitment it is significant in our discussion about maintenance of a Sikh identity that the majority engage in some form of religious expression.

In relation to other markers of identity that involve a more cultural and political dimension, most notably caste and nationhood, the Sikhs in York were all aware of these markers but did not particularly want to engage with them. This might indicate a reluctance to discuss with an outsider issues that are clearly complex; however, the impression gained is that these markers, whilst an undoubted factor in Sikh identity, were not markers that they considered fundamentally important to their own individual or community identity.

In relation to any sense of there being a community it would not be unfair to say that until recent times there has been no sense of there being a community; either a community of like-minded people who meet together for cultural stimulation, exchange and support or a community of believers practising their faith. Any sense of Sikh community has been maintained through regular travels to places like Leeds and Bradford to the *Gurdwaras* and the Sikhs who live there in large, self-supporting communities. What has occurred until recently has been individuals within the Sikh and more generally South Asian communities meeting with each other for social support.

In her chapter in this collection McIntosh poses the notion that 'a necessary condition of a community [is] that the people within it are involved in face-to-face or direct relations with one another; community cannot exist at a distance or among people who never meet'. The recent story of the Sikhs in York is of a majority of those present engaging in face-to-face relations. McIntosh also argues that 'Communities come into existence in order to satisfy a fundamental human need for familiarity and intimacy; hence, communities cannot be artificially created'. Of those Sikhs interviewed, most seem to have expressed a need for more 'familiarity and intimacy' and some have commended the recent work of the faith advisers and York St John University in providing contexts for a community to be genuinely encouraged to develop.

The challenge is set, if they are interested in being a community, for those from the South Asian communities to find ways to meet face to face, both as separate faith traditions and as peoples who share a cultural heritage. It will be interesting to see how far the City, which committed itself in principle to the notion of a City of Faiths, can find the resources to support its rhetoric.

Notes

1 Duleep Singh, as the last sovereign leader of the Sikhs, has been the subject of scholarly interest for some years, with biographies being written (Alexander and Anand 2001) and the erection of a statue in 1999 on Butten Island in Thetford in his memory. Ballantyne (2004) argues that the Dalip Singh story is an important one in the understanding of the Sikh/British relationship

2 For some Sikhs, and some of them scholars within the tradition of Sikh Studies, McLeod's objective, analytical approach went too far and he managed, through his writing and lecturing, to offend a considerable number. His own response to this can be found in his work *Exploring Sikhism* published by Oxford (2000).

3 Based on the census data statistics.

4 In 2006 York St John gained full university status and became York's second Uni-

versity changing its title in October 2006 from York St John University College to York St John University. This was its second title change in a year having already changed title from 'College' to 'University College' upon achieving taught degree awarding powers.

5 Mr Sagoo is in charge of the Leeds *Gurdwara*.

6 Detailed exploration of this group is found in Takhar 2005: 38–58.

7 The signed statement and full text of the speeches can be found at http://www2.yorksj.ac.uk/default.asp?Page_ID=3407.

References

Axel, B.K. (2001), *The Nation's Tortured Body: Violence, Representation, and the Formation of a Sikh Diaspora* (Durham and London: Duke University Press).

Alexander, M. and S. Anand (2001), *Queen Victoria's Maharajah: Duleep Singh 1838–93* (London: Phoenix Press).

Ballantyne, T. (2004), 'Maharaja Dalip Singh, History and the Negotiation of Sikh Identity', in P. Singh and N.G. Barrier (eds), *Sikhism and History* (New Dehli: Oxford University Press), pp. 151–75.

Ballard, R (2000), 'The Growth and Changing Character of the Sikh Presence in Britain', in H. Coward, J.R. Hinnells and R.B. Williams (eds), *The South Asian Religious Diaspora in Britain, Canada, and the United States* (Albany, NY: State University of New York Press), pp. 127–44.

Barrier, N.G. (2006), 'Trauma and Memory within Sikh Diaspora: Internet Dialogue', *Sikh Formations: Religion, Culture, Theory* 2.1: 33–56.

Brown, J.M. (2006), *Global South Asians: Introducing the Modern Diaspora* (Cambridge: Cambridge University Press).

Burghart, R. (ed.) (1987), *Hinduism in Great Britain: The Perpetuation of Religion in an Alien Cultural Milieu* (Cambridge: Tavistock).

Clifford, J. (1994), 'Diasporas', *Cultural Anthropology* 9.3: 302–38.

Cole, W.O. (1973), *A Sikh Family in Britain* (Oxford: Pergamon).

—— (1989), 'Sikhs in Britain', in P. Badham (ed.), *Religion, State, and Society in Modern Britain* (New York: Edwin Mellen Press), pp. 259–76.

—— (1994), *Sikhism: Teach Yourself Series* (London: Hodder and Stoughton).

—— (2004), *Understanding Sikhism* (Edinburgh: Dunedin Academic Press).

Grewal, J.S. (1994), *The New Cambridge History of India: The Sikhs of the Punjab* (New Dehli: Cambridge University Press).

Hall, K.D. (2004), 'The Ethnography of Imagined Communities: The Cultural Production of Sikh Ethnicity in Britain', *The Annals of American Academy of Political and Social Science: Being Here and Being There* 595: 108–21.

Harvey, G. and C.D. Thompson (eds) (2005), *Indigenous Diasporas and Dislocations* (Aldershot: Ashgate).

Kalsi, S.S. (1992), *The Evolution of a Sikh Community in Britain: Religious and Social Change among the Sikhs of Leeds and Bradford* (Leeds: University of Leeds).

—— (2005), *Religions of the World: Sikhism* (Philadelphia: Chelsea House).

Knott, K., and S.S. Kalsi (1994), 'The Advent of Asian Religions', in A. Mason (ed.), *Religion in Leeds* (Stroud: Alan Sutton Publishing), pp. 161–79.

Kokot, W., K. Tololyan and C. Alfonso (eds) (2004), *Diaspora, Identity and Religion: New Directions in Theory and Research* (London: Routledge).

Mansukhani, G.S. (1989), *A Book of Sikh Studies* (New Delhi: National Book Shop).

McLeod, W.H. (1989), *Who is a Sikh? The Problem of Sikh Identity* (New Delhi: Oxford University Press).

—— (2000), *Exploring Sikhism: Aspects of Sikh Identity, Culture and Thought* (New Delhi: Oxford University Press).

Narang, G.C. (1989), *Transformation of Sikhism* (New Dehli: Kalyani Publishers, 5th edn).
Nesbitt, E. (2005), *Sikhism: A Very Short Introduction* (New York: Oxford University Press).
Oberoi, H. (1994), *The Construction of Religious Boundaries: Culture, Identity and Diversity in the Sikh Tradition* (Chicago: University of Chicago Press).
ONS (Office for National Statistics) (2001), http://neighbourhood. statistics.gov. uk/dissemination/.
Paur, J.K. (1994), 'Resituating Discourses of "Whiteness" and "Asianness" in Northern England: Second-generation Sikh Women and Constructions of Identity', *Socialist Review* 24.1/2: 21–53.
Peach, C. and R. Gale (2003), 'Muslims, Hindus, and Sikhs in the New Religious Landscape of England', *The Geographical Review* 93.4: 469–90.
Rait, S.K. (2003), *Sikh Women in Leeds: Religious, Social and Cultural Beliefs and Traditions* (Leeds: Wisdom House Publications).
—— (2005), *Sikh Women in England: Their Religious and Cultural Beliefs and Social Practices* (Stoke-on-Trent: Trentham Books).
Safran, W. (2004), 'Deconstructing and Comparing Diaspora', in W. Kokot, K. Tololyan and C. Alfonso (eds), *Diaspora, Identity and Religion: New Directions in Theory and Research* (London: Routledge), pp. 9–29.
Singh, G. (2005), 'British Multiculturalism and Sikhs', *Sikh Formations: Religion, Culture, Theory* 1.2: 157–73.
Singh, K. (1999a), *A History of the Sikhs Volume 1: 1469–1839* (New Dehli: Oxford University Press).
—— (1999b), *A History of the Sikhs Volume 2: 1839–1988* (New Dehli: Oxford University Press).
Singh, R. (2000), *Sikhs and Sikhism in Britain: Fifty Years On, the Bradford Experience* (Bradford: Bradford Libraries).
Takhar, O.K. (2005), *Sikh Identity: An Exploration of Groups among Sikhs* (Bodmin: Ashgate).
Tatla, D.S. (2006), 'The Morning After: Trauma and Memory and the Sikh Predicament since 1984', *Sikh Formations: Religion, Culture, Theory* 2.1: 57–88.
Tololyan, K. (1996), 'Rethinking Diaspora(s): Stateless Power in the Transnational Moment', *Diaspora* 5.1: 3–36.
Verma, R. (2006), 'Trauma, Cultural Survival and Identity Politics in a Post 9/11 Era: Reflections by Sikh Youth', *Sikh Formations: Religion, Culture, Theory* 2.1: 89–101.
Weller, P. (2004), 'Hindus and Sikhs: Community Development and Religious Discrimination in England and Wales', *Studies in the History of Religions: South Asians in the Diaspora: Histories and Religious Traditions* 101: 454–97.
Wolffe, R. (1993), *The Growth of Religious Diversity: Britain from 1945: A Reader* (London: Hodder and Stoughton).

13

Adolescent Attitudes in York towards Muslims and Islam

A.A. Brockett, N. Noret, S. Harenwall, P.D. Baird and I. Rivers[1]

Introduction

This chapter is an empirical study of York adolescents' attitudes towards Muslims and Islam from the perspectives of age, gender and type of educational institution. It presents and discusses the adolescents' responses to six questions from a questionnaire, thereby seeking to illustrate some of the causes of tension in the interactions between religious communities and wider society, and so contribute to a deeper understanding of communal conflicts.

The chapter begins by introducing the broad issue of anti-Muslim attitudes and 'Islamophobia'. This is followed by sections on the aims and the methods of this research project. The next section presents a context for the adolescents' responses by considering the level of their knowledge about Muslims and Islam, and the sources of their information. The results of their responses to the six questions are then presented in subsequent sections, followed by some discussion and a summary conclusion.

It is commonplace to hear that Islamophobia is increasing in the UK. But what is it? The -phobia suffix primarily signifies fear, as in agoraphobia, fear of the marketplace, or arachnophobia, fear of the spider species, but one response to fear is hatred, thus some -phobia suffixed words signify hatred rather than just fear, e.g. xenophobia, hatred of foreigners; homophobia, hatred of homosexuals.

So, according to the Runnymede Trust Report the term depicts 'an intense and unwarranted dread or hatred of Islam resulting in Anti-Muslim prejudice'. This Report, along with its updates in 2001 and 2004, then developed an analysis based on closed or open views. The -phobia suffix in the then-little-used neologism signified an intensity of feeling, but since then the word has become much more common – 20% of the York year 10 and 12 schoolchildren in the survey under discussion knew of it in 2003, for instance – and it can now also refer to less intense feelings.

If one aspect of prejudice is stereotyping, then the term Islamophobia itself could be said to be self-fulfilling, in that Islam is multi-faceted and takes many forms, rather than being monolithic. Arachnids can be precisely defined so 'Arachnophobia' can also be reliably defined and perhaps treated, but 'Islam' is so vast a concept, spanning huge swathes of the world's population, territory and history, to be almost meaningless on its own. Some say that Islamophobia doesn't exist as such, but that it is a myth that is taking on a life of its own, or if not a myth, then – quoting Alibhai Brown – 'an excuse . . . to . . . blackmail society' (Malik 2006). Pipes, who considered himself an 'Islamism-ophobe', argued that, 'while prejudice against Muslims certainly exists, "Islamophobia" deceptively conflates two distinct phenomena: fear of Islam the religion, and fear of radical Islam, the ideology'.[2]

Since the McPherson Inquiry into the murder of Stephen Lawrence (presented to Parliament, February 1999), if a victim believes they have been attacked for racist reasons, the police have to treat it as such. Now that offences can be classed as religiously aggravated as well as racially aggravated, whether or not to onlookers Islamophobia exists in given situations or places, and to what level of intensity, is to an extent irrelevant if it is perceived to exist by Muslims. A substantial number of Muslim students in Higher Education in Britain, for example, are in no doubt that Islamophobia exists, both in Higher Education and British society at large (FOSIS 2003: 2). Other research claims to show that British Muslims in general are experiencing an increase in religious prejudice since 9/11 (e.g. Sheridan and Gillett 2005).

The second element in the Runnymede Trust Report's definition quoted above – 'dread or hatred of Islam resulting in anti-Muslim prejudice' – points to another major way of viewing Islamophobia – as a form of cultural or religious *racism*. This view has recently been argued strongly by Modood (2005). An earlier proponent of this view was Fred Halliday (1996), who preferred to use the terms Muslimophobia or anti-Muslimism. In his opinion few people are hostile towards the ideology or belief system itself, i.e. Islamophobia, but rather towards the people who adhere to it, i.e. Muslimophobia, anti-Muslimism. 'Once again it would appear to be secular, contemporary, political concerns such as strategic influence and immigration that provide the real occasion for anti-Muslimist ideology, rather than an animosity that is timeless and religiously based' (Halliday 1996: 170). By means of an extensive demonstration that both Islam and the Muslim world are extremely varied, Halliday argued forcefully against the theory of the clash of civilizations simplistically propounded by many right-wing and evangelical authors and speakers.

Nonetheless, they and others continue to promote the theory, and indeed the British National Party (BNP) in recent years has focused much of its rhetoric on Islam, and at times debates Qur'anic doctrine in relatively fine detail. Considering its former race-based discourse, it is possible to infer a latent anti-Muslimism or Muslimophobia behind this 'pure' Islamophobia, thus this chapter includes some discussion on adolescent attitudes towards the BNP. Many Muslims appear to perceive this rhetoric as an attack against them both on account of their beliefs and their ethnicity, so it may not be possible to disentangle the two.

Muslims also now perceive politics to be part and parcel of Islamophobia. Non-recognition of Muslims in certain areas of the law was the last in the list of examples of Islamophobia given by the Runnymede Trust Report (CBMI 1997), although legislation enacted soon after 11 September can be seen as tacit recognition of Muslims by the law, albeit in a negative sense. The Anti-Terrorism, Crime and Security Act 2001 has been seen as political Islamophobia. Statistics from a survey of Muslims carried out by the Forum Against Islamophobia and Racism[3] show that between 11 September 2001 and 30 June 2004, 609 people were arrested under the Act; 99 were charged; 15 convicted; about 95% of all those arrested have been Muslim; yet most of those convicted have been non-Muslim. 25% of the survey's participants said that these statistics proved Muslims were being criminalized under the legislation. 20% of the participants noted that the continuous arrests across the country have exaggerated the threat of terrorism and led to the Muslim community being perceived as the 'enemy within'.

One categorization could therefore divide Islamophobia into actual/ perceived anti-Muslim/Islam:

1 prejudice – opinions, attitudes
2 behaviour – harassment, violence
3 politics – public discourse, political ideology, 'war on terror'.

These correspond to classic definitions of the dimensions of racism, such as that of Wieviorka (1995):

1 prejudice
2 behaviour
3 politics.

This study concerns the first of these categories.

These results are part of a larger study, the principal aims of which were to investigate the nature of adolescents' attitudes towards Muslims, Islam, Arabs and the Middle East, and, where necessary as a result, contribute to the improvement of intervention schemes supporting Muslim and Arab inclusion in UK society.

Research Method

Participants

1,515 pupils (55.4% female, 44.6% male) from years 10 and 12 participated in the survey, comprising approximately 30% of the total of these two cohorts in the city. Disregarding dropouts this total was 5,010, according to the September 2003 school census and individual private school data. 11 out of the 17 mainstream schools, and Sixth Form and FE colleges in York accepted the invitation to take part in the survey, providing an even geographical and socio-economic distribution across the city. Participants' ages ranged between 13 and 24 years (mean = 16.14, sd = 1.38). The 13–15 year-old group comprised 32.15% numbering 487 participants, the 16–18 group 65.74% numbering 996 and the 19+ group 1.79% numbering 27 (five did not specify their age).

Table 1 shows how closely the sample represented the overall religious affiliation of the population of the city, as recorded in the 2001 census when the population comprised 181,094 people. The only apparent divergence is in the first three categories ('Christian', 'No religion' and 'Religion not stated') which when added together total York City 98.6%, Sample 96.21%. The assumption

Religion	*York City*	*Sample*
Christian	74.4	52.4
No religion	16.6	43.81
Religion not stated	7.6	0
Muslim	0.6	0.4
Buddhist	0.2	0.4
Hindu	0.2	0.07
Jewish	0.1	0.07
Sikh	0.05	0.13
Pagan	0	0.4
Other	0.3	2.33

Table 1: **Percentage religious affiliation**

therefore is that the sample's 43.81% 'no religion' would largely have come from Christian heritage. The number of Muslim participants in the sample was only six or seven, the seventh not acknowledging their affiliation explicitly.

The Instrument

The survey employed an instrument consisting of a questionnaire of 68 questions, approximately half quantitative and half qualitative. It was split into three sections. All participants completed section 1, questions 1–52; non-Muslim participants completed section 2, questions 53–59; and Muslim participants completed section 3, questions 60–68.

The questionnaire went through a rigorous development over a period of nine months from July 2003 to March 2004. Following a method of arriving at quantitative measures from qualitative sources (Lankshear 1993; Hoppe *et al.* 1995; Gibbs 1997), focus groups were employed to develop questions and concepts for the questionnaire. Thus the start point of the design was a series of focus groups of 1–2 hours with the relevant age group in four separate schools. The first was with a class of twenty 15–16 year olds in London in July 2003, who were asked to discuss in groups of three the questions they would ask to find out their peers' attitudes towards Muslims, Islam, Arabs and the Middle East and write them down. Any imposition of the researchers' own questions and/or biases were studiously avoided. Following the Delphi Method/Technique developed in the 1950s the questions they wrote down were collected and with minor editing drawn up into a list. This list, amended each time, was then distributed for discussion with target-age focus groups in three further schools in Bradford and York in October–November 2003, along with one of a slightly older age group of Muslim students at York University. Comparison was also made with two other similar surveys, those of the IQRA MORI poll conducted in 1990 (IQRA Trust) and of Modood, Berthoud, *et al.* (1997). At this stage the list of questions was converted into a questionnaire with Likert scale tick-boxes and/or spaces for other answers. Following word-by-word scrutiny by an expert on questionnaire design – a Principal Lecturer in Psychology at York St John – it was sent out to seven external academic referees, and the Chief Executive of the Kirklees Racial Equality Council. The instrument was then formally piloted with whole 10 and 12 year classes in three schools in Dewsbury and Bradford with an approximate 50/50 mix of 'White' and 'Black and Minority Ethnic' participants in January 2004 to test for comprehension and timing. The results of this pilot survey were entered into SPSS (Statistical Package for the Social Sciences) and analysed and reports sent to the three schools, but fall outside the dataset for York – the subject of this chapter. In all, the questionnaire went through 14 major iterations in the 9 months preceding distribution.

Survey Procedure

Questionnaires were distributed to the 11 schools/colleges in York by the research team in March–April 2004 and were completed during class time. In some cases administration of the questionnaire was carried out by the research team, but where not, supervising staff in all cases had been carefully instructed orally and in writing on the precise procedure to follow. Strict participant confidentiality was maintained throughout and peer discussion was prevented. In some schools/colleges the filling-in of the questionnaire was immediately followed by a session led by the teacher on the issues raised in the questionnaire, but this was always after the sealing of the questionnaires in the envelopes. The questionnaires were then collected by the research team for data input and analysis and each school was provided with a report highlighting the main findings from the survey, comparing their school's data with that of the city as a whole.

The Level of Respondents' Knowledge and their Sources of Information

Elsewhere in the questionnaire respondents were asked several factual questions, suffice one as an example: Which of the following are forbidden and not allowed in Islam: eating meat; eating beef (cow); eating pork (pig); drinking alcohol; shaving the beard (men); having the face uncovered (women)?

The category which the largest percentage of adolescents believed was forbidden by Islam was that women must not have their face uncovered (69.35%). This was followed by drinking alcohol (53.87%). Eating pork (45.66%) and males shaving the beard (43.91%) were also considered to be forbidden by a large number of respondents. Smaller percentages thought that beef (31.85%) and meat (22.85%) were forbidden in Islam.

Respondents were asked where they get their information about the religion of Islam from, whether Parents, Friends, At school (from teachers and/or class), The Mosque, TV, Radio, Newspapers, Internet, Books, or Other. 77.67% of respondents said their knowledge of Islam came from school. A further 47.5% said that they got their information from TV and 30.25% from newspapers. Parents counted for 17.95%, and 15.85% said their information came from books. 12.45% cited their friends as sources of information and only 9.52% cited the Internet. Less than 2% of respondents said their knowledge of Islam came from the Mosque (1.22%) which equates to the small proportion of Muslim participants.

Respondents were asked which newspaper they get most of their information about the religion of Islam from. Of those who reported that they got their information about Islam from newspapers, their most-read type was the national broadsheets (n = 308). Almost four times less cited were the national tabloids (n = 80) which, in turn, were almost two and a half times more than the local and evening papers (n = 33). Sunday broadsheets were cited 19 times and the Sunday tabloids had nine readers. Other named newspapers were cited seven times and included such titles as *The Arab News* and *The Big Issue*, while 18 citations of other non-specific papers were included.

Respondents were asked which TV channel they watch the news on most often (see Table 2). A large percentage of respondents said that the channel they mostly watched the news on was BBC1 (44.64%) and more than a quarter of respondents said that they watched the news on ITV (27.68%). Of the remaining terrestrial channels, 6.82% watched Channel 4 and 1.92% and 1.59% watched Channel 5 and BBC2 respectively. Sky News was watched by 5.23%, whilst 2.12% watched other satellite channels. The least-watched news channel was CNN, with only 0.33% of respondents. A noticeable percentage of respondents (9.67%) said that they did not watch the news at all.

Channel								
BBC 1	*BBC 2*	*ITV*	*Ch. 4*	*Ch. 5*	*Sky News*	*CNN*	*Other satellite channels*	*I don't watch the news*
%								
44.64	1.59	27.68	6.82	1.92	5.23	0.33	2.12	9.67

Table 2: **Which TV channel do you watch the news on most often?**

Conclusion about the Level of Respondents' Knowledge and their Sources of Information

A high level of ignorance about basic Muslim practices was displayed. The only two practices forbidden by Islam in the list are drinking alcohol and eating pork; however, these aspects were thought to be forbidden by only around half of the respondents. Conversely, large percentages of respondents erroneously believed that Islam prohibits women from having their face uncovered and men from shaving their beards.

The vast majority of respondents (77.67%) said that their knowledge of Islam came from school, which was 30.17% more than those in the next most often cited source: the television. Less than 20% of respondents said that their information about Islam came from their parents (17.95%) which was less than half the number that cited the television (47.5%) and 12% less than those who cited newspapers (30.25%) as their source. When all the media types – television, radio and newspapers – are added together, they constitute a source of information to a much larger percentage of adolescents (90.49%) than any other source. Of those who answered the question with a qualitative statement, a number of respondents expressed a blatant lack of interest (n = 8), which equates to around 10% of this group. One which stood out was 'Why would I want to know about Islam?! I'm Christian'. However, many more individuals indicated that they did not receive information about Islam (n = 45), possibly highlighting a shortfall in the availability of information for these individuals. The vast majority of newspapers read by the respondents were the national broadsheets (n = 308), four times more than the national tabloids. However, memoranda from FAIR (e.g. 2004) document problems in the media's portrayal of Muslims whether in broadsheet or tabloid.

Of all the television channels, BBC1 was cited as the channel on which most respondents watched the news (44.64%), followed by ITV (27.68%). A noticeable percentage of respondents said that they did not watch the news at all (9.67%).

These results highlight considerable ignorance about Islam amongst York adolescents. The media and school/college were the main sources of information cited by respondents, which underlines the need for better sources of information for journalists and for curriculum development in respect of religious and cultural differences.

Question 1: Respondents were asked on a six-point Likert scale whether their attitudes towards Muslims after 9/11 had got: much worse; worse; stayed the same; improved; or improved a lot

Adolescents' Attitudes According to Age

Figure 1: **Adolescent attitudes towards Muslims following 9/11, according to age[4]**

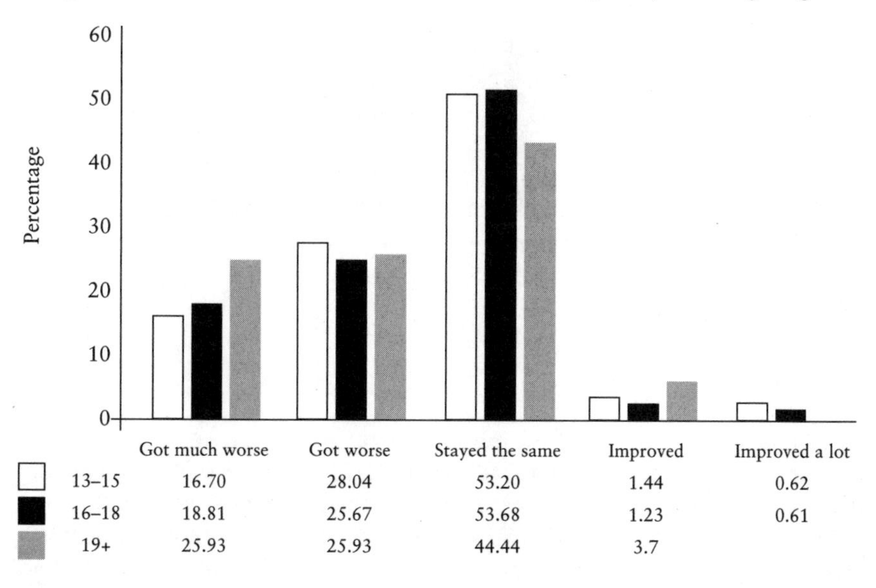

	Got much worse	Got worse	Stayed the same	Improved	Improved a lot
13–15	16.70	28.04	53.20	1.44	0.62
16–18	18.81	25.67	53.68	1.23	0.61
19+	25.93	25.93	44.44	3.7	

The majority of respondents in each age group stated that their attitudes towards Muslims remained the same following 9/11: more than half of 13–15 year olds (53.2%) and 16–18 year olds (53.68%) and almost half of those aged 19+ (44.44%). In all cases, there was a much higher percentage who reported that their attitudes had worsened than those who said their attitudes had improved. Of those who said their attitude had 'got worse', the 13–15 age group was the largest (28.04%), which was more than 11% higher than those in the same age group who said their attitude had 'got much worse'. Conversely, in the age group 19+, equal numbers (25.93%) had answered 'got worse' and 'got much worse'; however, seven times fewer people in this age group had said their attitude had improved (3.7%; one being Muslim) which is nonetheless higher than the other age groups. Thus the 19+ age group indicated the most improvement in attitude as well as the overall worsened attitudes (51.86%).

Adolescents' Attitudes According to Gender

Figure 2: **Adolescent attitudes towards Muslims following 9/11, according to gender**

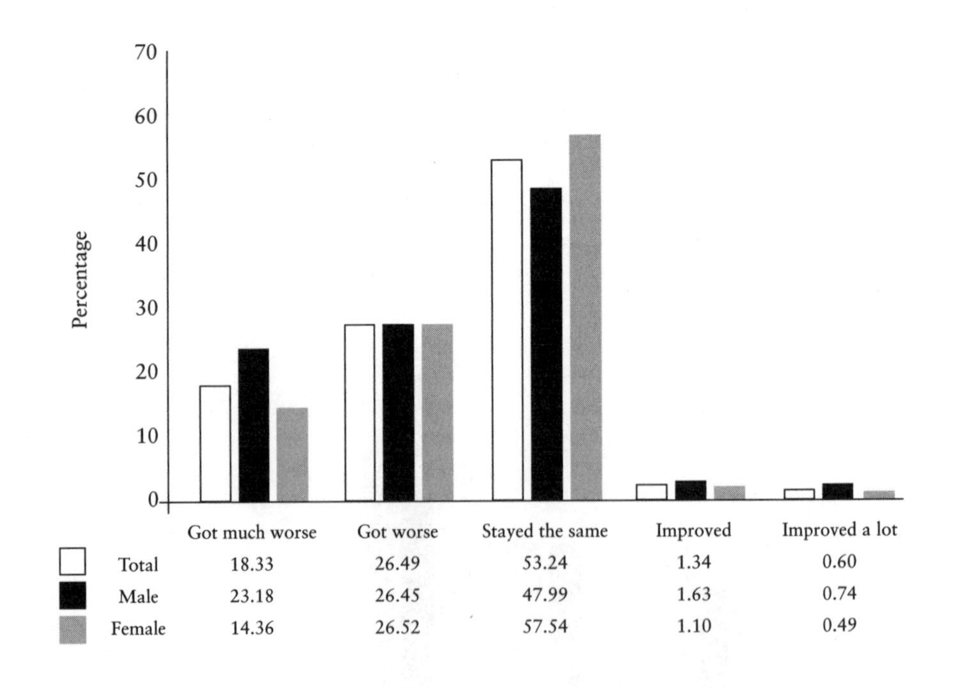

	Got much worse	Got worse	Stayed the same	Improved	Improved a lot
Total	18.33	26.49	53.24	1.34	0.60
Male	23.18	26.45	47.99	1.63	0.74
Female	14.36	26.52	57.54	1.10	0.49

Although more than half the sample (53.24%) reported that their attitudes towards Muslims had not altered following 9/11, the majority of the remainder of the respondents (44.82%) reported worsening attitudes with more males (23.18%) than females (14.36%) stating that their attitudes had 'got much worse'.

Adolescents' Attitudes According to Type of Educational Institution

Figure 3: **Adolescent attitudes towards Muslims following 9/11, according to educational institution**

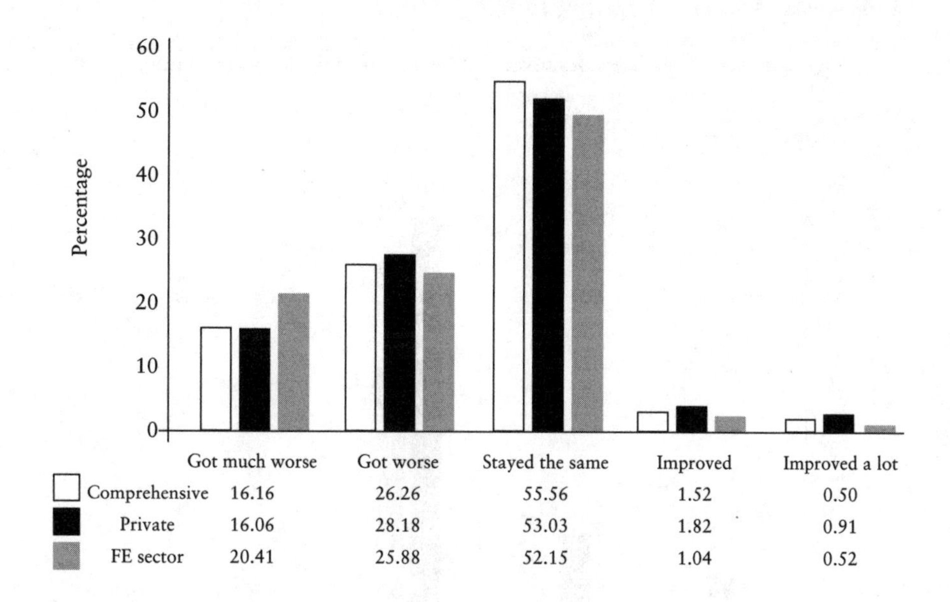

Over half of all respondents in each type of educational institution said that their attitudes towards Muslims had not changed following 9/11 (comprehensive 55.56%; private 53.03%; FE sector 52.15%). Of the remainder, more than a quarter of respondents in each group said that their attitudes had 'got worse' (comprehensive 26.26%; private 28.18%; FE sector 25.88%) and a further 16.16%, 16.06% and 20.41% respectively said that their attitudes had 'got much worse'. In all, less than 2% of respondents in each school type said that their attitude had 'improved' and less than 1% said that their attitude had 'improved a lot'.

Question 2: Respondents were asked on a six-point Likert scale whether their attitudes towards Muslims after the invasion of Iraq had got: much worse; worse; stayed the same; improved; or improved a lot

Adolescents' Attitudes According to Age

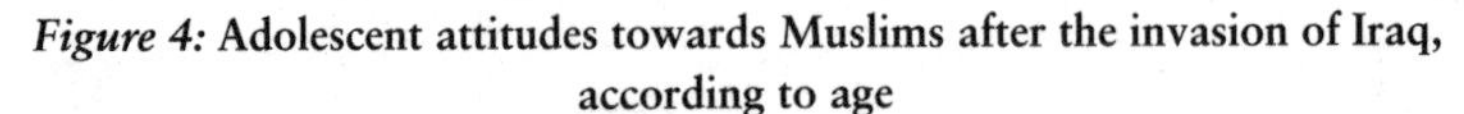
Figure 4: Adolescent attitudes towards Muslims after the invasion of Iraq, according to age

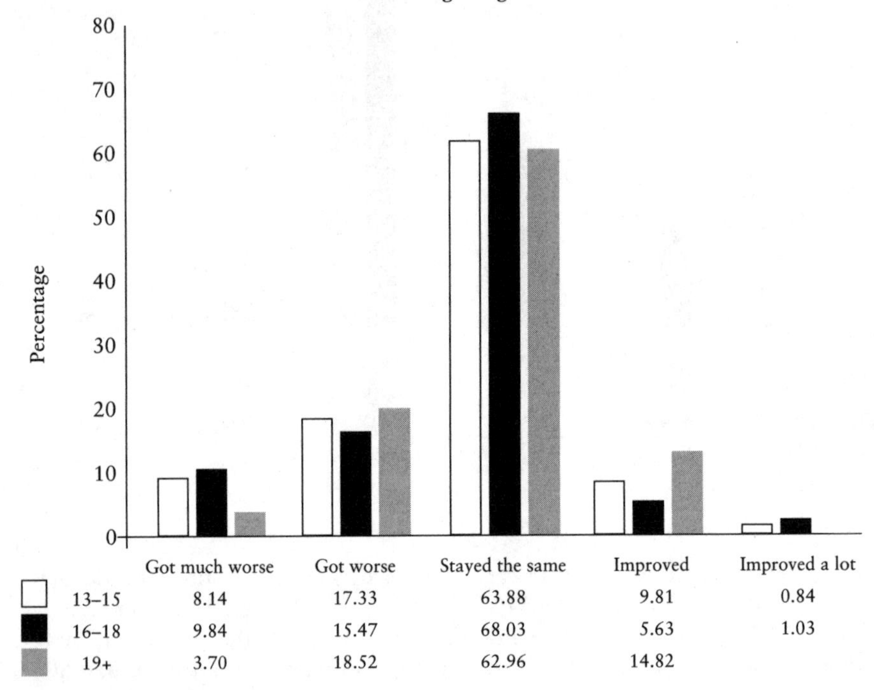

In a similar pattern to the reports of changes in attitude towards Muslims following 9/11, more than half the respondents in each age group stated that their attitudes had stayed the same. Furthermore, although the majority of the remainder of the respondents indicated that their attitudes towards Muslims had worsened, fewer said this than had said so following 9/11. Of those respondents who said their attitude had improved, the largest group was the 19+ age group which, at 14.82%, was a four-fold increase on those of that age group who said their attitude had improved after 9/11.

Adolescents' Attitudes According to Gender

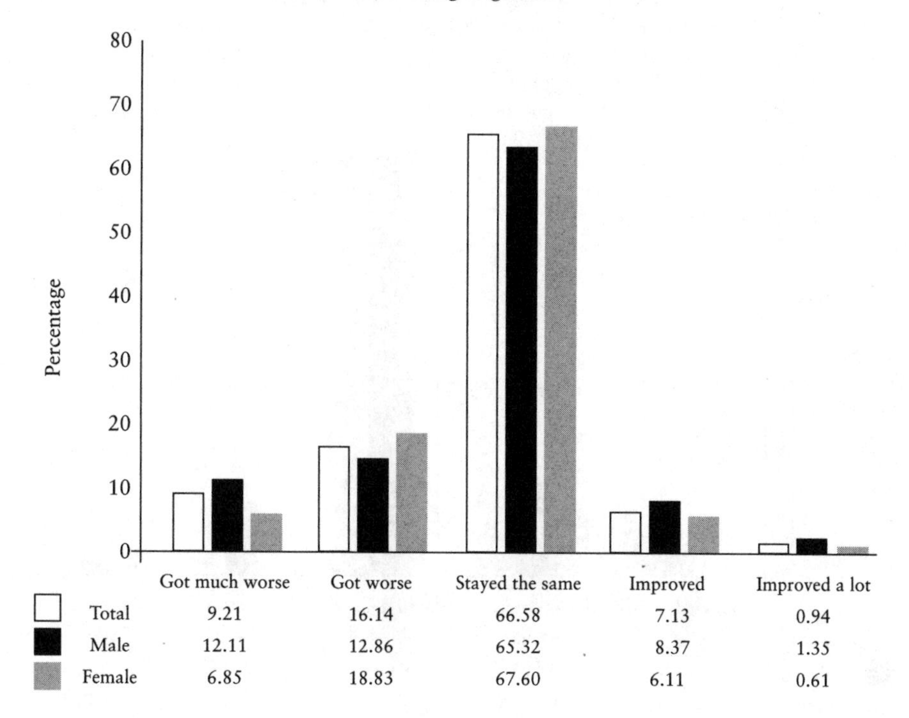

	Got much worse	Got worse	Stayed the same	Improved	Improved a lot
Total	9.21	16.14	66.58	7.13	0.94
Male	12.11	12.86	65.32	8.37	1.35
Female	6.85	18.83	67.60	6.11	0.61

Figure 5: **Adolescent attitudes towards Muslims after the invasion of Iraq, according to gender**

The majority of both sexes said their attitude had not altered after the invasion of Iraq, with more than half overall (66.58%) saying so. However, although the larger proportion of the remainder of the sample (25.35%) said their attitudes had worsened (16.14% 'got worse'; 9.21% 'got much worse'), a small percentage (8.07%) reported improved attitudes towards Muslims, the majority of whom were male.

Adolescents' Attitudes According to Type of Educational Institution

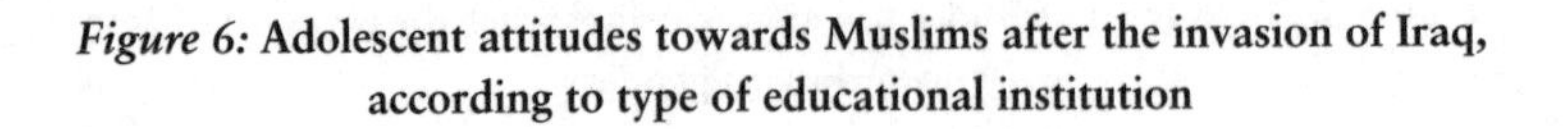

Figure 6: **Adolescent attitudes towards Muslims after the invasion of Iraq, according to type of educational institution**

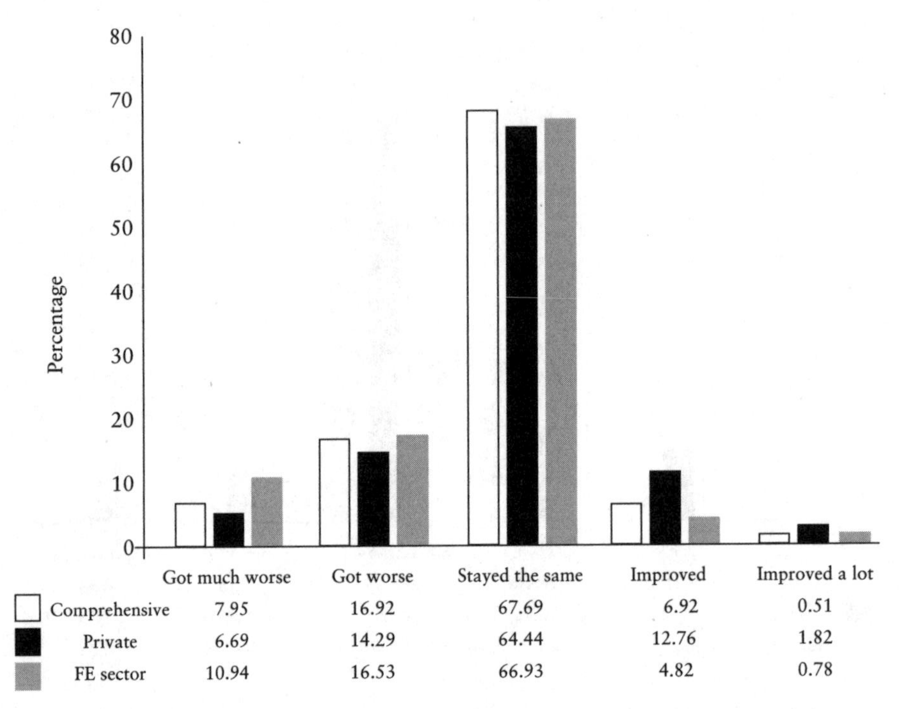

	Got much worse	Got worse	Stayed the same	Improved	Improved a lot
Comprehensive	7.95	16.92	67.69	6.92	0.51
Private	6.69	14.29	64.44	12.76	1.82
FE sector	10.94	16.53	66.93	4.82	0.78

Over two thirds of respondents in comprehensive schools (67.96%) and the FE sector (66.93%) and almost the same amount in private schools (64.44%) reported that their attitudes had remained the same following the invasion of Iraq. The majority of the remainder said that their attitudes had 'got worse' (comprehensive 16.92%; private 14.29%; FE sector 16.53%) and whilst the 'got much worse' and 'improved' categories comprised similar percentages of respondents, almost twice as many private school respondents (12.76%) than comprehensive (6.92%) and almost three times more than the FE sector (4.82%) said that their attitudes had improved since the invasion of Iraq.

Question 3: Respondents were asked on a six-point scale whether they: strongly disagreed; disagreed; were neutral; agreed; or strongly agreed with the views of the British National Party (BNP), or didn't know enough to comment

Due to the BNP's known attitudes towards Islam it was predicted that there would be a relationship between adolescents' positive attitudes towards the BNP and deteriorating attitudes towards Muslims and Islam following 9/11 and the invasion of Iraq.[5]

To test the prediction a Spearman[6] correlation was performed between attitudes towards the BNP and towards Muslims after 9/11 ($r_S = -.374$, $p < 0.01$). The result indicates that participants whose attitudes deteriorated after 9/11 are also more likely to agree with the views of the BNP. The correlation was also performed between attitudes towards the BNP and attitudes following the invasion of Iraq. This revealed a similar result ($r_S = -.307$, $p < 0.01$) with adolescents who agree with the views of the BNP being more likely to display a deterioration in attitudes towards Muslims following the invasion. These figures exclude those who didn't know enough to comment.

Adolescents' Attitudes According to Age

***Figure** 7:* **Adolescent attitudes on the views of the BNP, according to age**

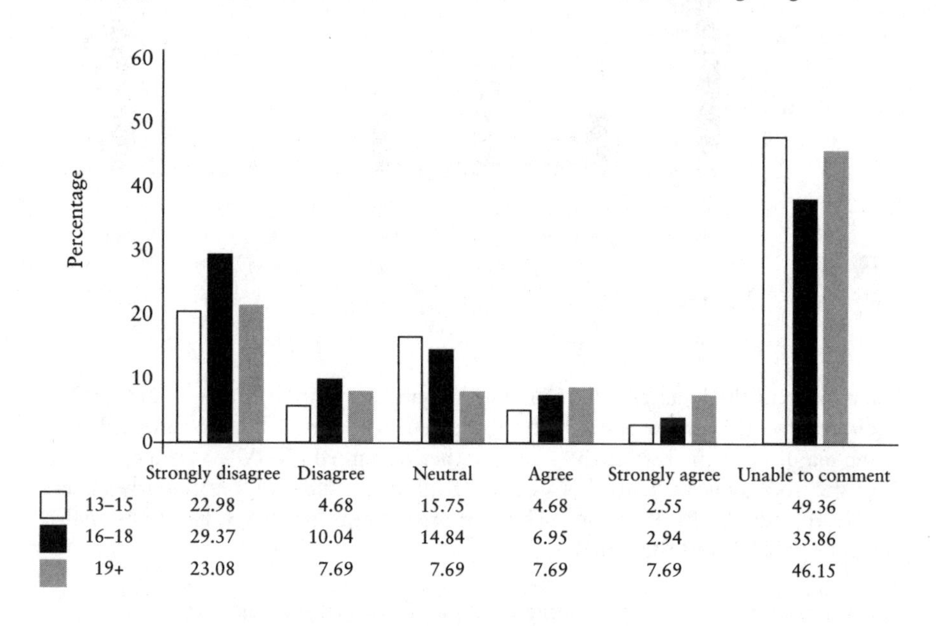

	Strongly disagree	Disagree	Neutral	Agree	Strongly agree	Unable to comment
13–15	22.98	4.68	15.75	4.68	2.55	49.36
16–18	29.37	10.04	14.84	6.95	2.94	35.86
19+	23.08	7.69	7.69	7.69	7.69	46.15

Almost half the 13–15 age group (49.36%) and 19+ age group (46.15%) and over a third of the 16–18 year olds (35.86%) felt unable to comment on the views of the BNP. Of the remainder, the largest percentages indicated that they 'strongly disagree', the largest group being the 16–18 year olds (29.37%). With the exception of the 'strongly disagree' category, the percentage of 19+ responses (7.69%) were identical in each of the remaining categories, giving a combined total of 15.38% sympathizing with BNP views. The same proportion of 13–15 year olds (4.68%) answered both 'disagree' and 'agree'; however, fewer said that they 'strongly agree' (2.55%) whilst a much larger percentage remained neutral (15.75%). Of all those able to comment, the 16–18 age group showed the largest variation in their responses (29.37% strongly disagree; 10.04% disagree; 14.84% neutral; 6.95% agree; 2.94% strongly agree).

Adolescents' Attitudes According to Gender

Figure 8: **Adolescent attitudes on the views of the BNP, according to gender**

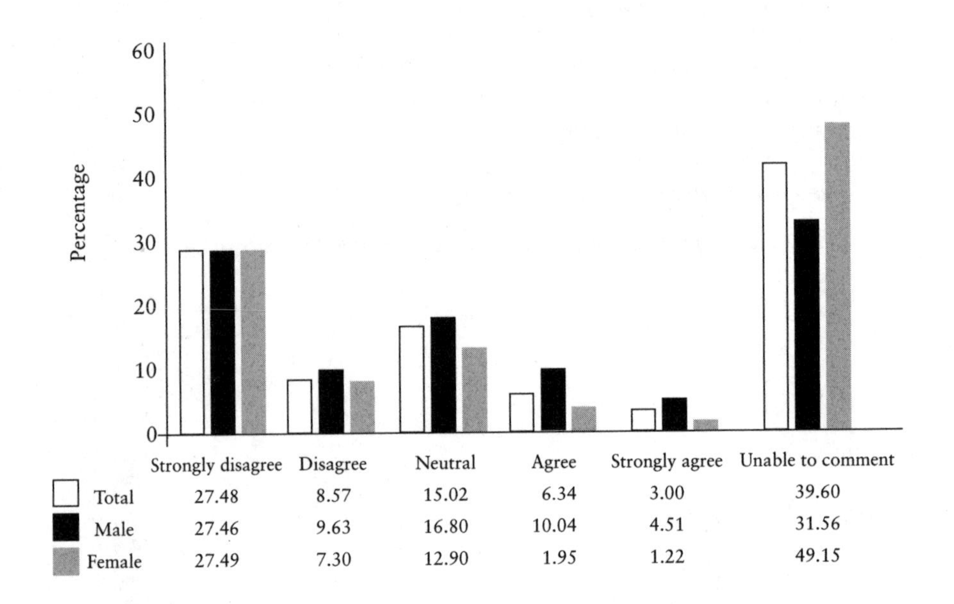

	Strongly disagree	Disagree	Neutral	Agree	Strongly agree	Unable to comment
Total	27.48	8.57	15.02	6.34	3.00	39.60
Male	27.46	9.63	16.80	10.04	4.51	31.56
Female	27.49	7.30	12.90	1.95	1.22	49.15

Almost half the females (49.15%) and just under a third of the males (31.56%) did not feel they knew enough about the beliefs of the BNP to comment. While the majority of the rest of the sample either disagreed (36.05%) with the views of the BNP or were neutral (15.02%), a minority (9.34%), particularly males, agreed with the BNP's views. This minority comprised 14.55% of the males but only 3.17% of the females.

Adolescents' Attitudes According to Type of Educational Institution

The majority of respondents (comprehensive 44.12%; private 36.2%; FE sector 39.24%) said that they did not know enough about the BNP to comment about its views. The majority of the rest of the respondents (comprehensive 24.02%; private 33.03%; FE sector 26.37%) reported that they 'strongly disagree', with a small percentage saying that they 'strongly agree' (comprehensive 2.94%; private 3.17%; FE sector 2.95%). In the 'disagree' category, there was a larger percentage of private school respondents (12.67%) than comprehensive (7.35%) or FE sector (7.17%). Of those respondents who remained neutral about the beliefs of the BNP, the private schools yielded the smallest percentage (8.14%) compared to the comprehensive schools (17.65%) and FE sector (17.09%).

***Figure 9:* Adolescent attitudes on the views of the BNP, according to type of educational institution**

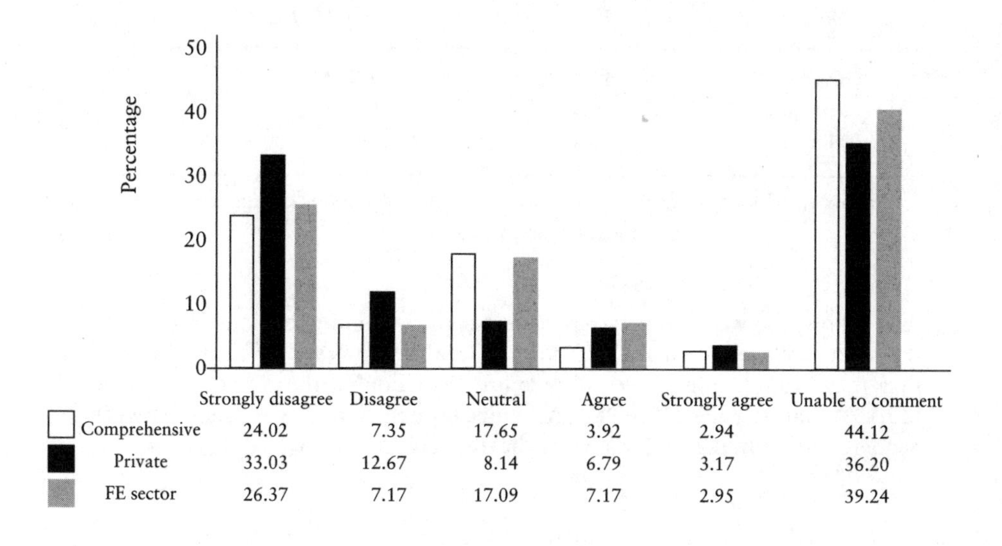

Question 4: Respondents were asked whether or not they would mind if girls in their school/college wore a headscarf

Adolescents' Attitudes According to Age

Age	*Would mind*	*Wouldn't mind*
13–15	16.30%	83.70%
16–18	16.02	83.98
19+	16.67	83.33

***Table 3:* Adolescent attitudes towards girls in their school or college wearing a headscarf, according to age**

The great majority of adolescents said that they would not mind if girls in their school or college wore headscarves. Furthermore, there was very little difference in the percentages of each age group and there was no significant association between age and minding if girls in their school or college wore headscarves x^2 (2) = 0.023, p = ns.

Adolescents' Attitudes According to Gender

Gender	*Would mind*	*Wouldn't mind*
Total	16.06%	83.94%
Female	10.55	89.45
Male	23.10	76.90

Table 4: **Adolescent attitudes towards girls in their school or college wearing a headscarf, according to gender**

As a whole, the vast majority reported that they would not mind girls in their school or college wearing a headscarf (83.94%); however, of those that said that they would mind, there were more than double the number of males (23.1%) than females (10.55%). A significant association was found between gender and minding if girls wore headscarves in school x^2 (1) = 41.41, $p < 0.001$.

Adolescents' Attitudes According to Type of Educational Institution

School type	*Would mind*	*Wouldn't mind*
Comprehensive	14.25%	85.75%
Private	21.34	78.66
FE sector	14.76	85.24

Table 5: **Adolescent attitudes towards girls in their school or college wearing a headscarf, according to type of educational establishment**

More than three quarters from each school type said they would not mind girls wearing headscarves in school or college (comprehensive 85.75%; private 78.66%; FE sector 85.24%). Nevertheless, a significant association was found between school type and minding if girls wore headscarves in school or college x^2 (2) = 8.334, $p < 0.05$.

Question 5: Respondents were asked on a six-point scale whether they: strongly disagreed; disagreed; were neutral; agreed; or strongly agreed with the statement that Muslims should adopt Western culture when living in the UK

Figure 10: **Adolescent views on whether Muslims should adopt Western culture when living in the UK according to age**

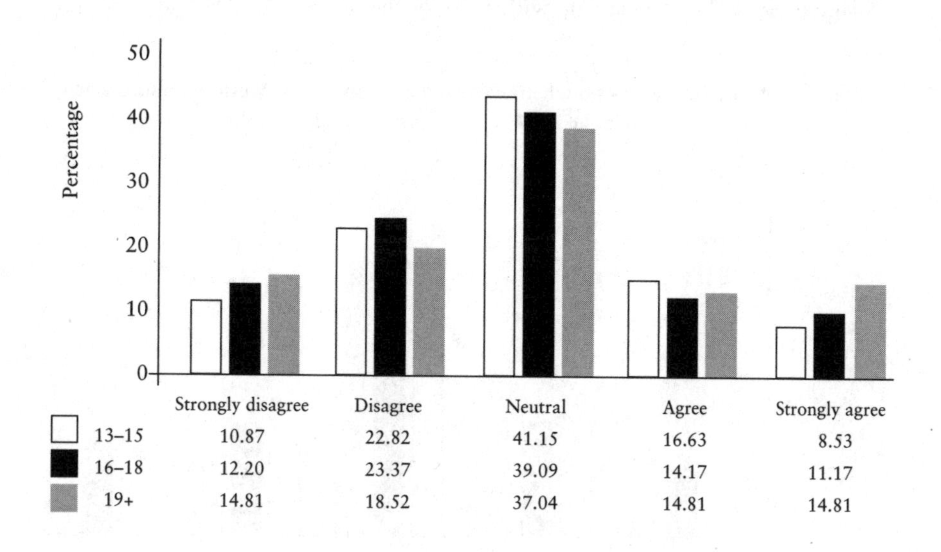

	Strongly disagree	Disagree	Neutral	Agree	Strongly agree
13–15	10.87	22.82	41.15	16.63	8.53
16–18	12.20	23.37	39.09	14.17	11.17
19+	14.81	18.52	37.04	14.81	14.81

Adolescents' Attitudes According to Age

Adolescents' views on whether Muslims should adopt Western culture when living in the UK were predominantly neutral, with all age groups showing a majority of more than one third in this category (13–15 years – 41.15%; 16–18 years – 39.09%; 19+ – 37.04%). Of the remaining categories, the largest percentage of respondents said that they disagree, the majority of these being the 13–15 (22.82%) and 16–18 (23.37%) age groups. The remainder of these two groups reduces in each subsequent category from 'agree' (13–15 years – 16.63%; 16–18 years – 14.17%) to 'strongly disagree' (13–15 years – 10.87%; 16–18 years – 12.2%) to 'strongly agree' (13–15 years – 8.53%; 16–18 years – 11.17%) respectively. This pattern is not matched by the respondents in the 19+ age group who, apart from the 'disagree' (18.52%) and neutral (37.04%) categories, were all equal (14.81%).

Adolescents' Attitudes According to Gender

For the most part, adolescents' views as to whether Muslims should adopt Western culture when living in the UK were neutral (males = 35.11%; females = 43.33%). Nevertheless, gender differences were apparent with fewer females (6.3%) than males (15.65%) agreeing strongly that Muslims should adopt Western culture. These differences are also noticeable when comparing the combined percentages of females in the agree categories (18.4%) and the disagree (38.27%) respectively with those of the males: 34.19% and 30.7%.

Figure 11: **Adolescent views on whether Muslims should adopt Western culture when living in the UK according to gender**

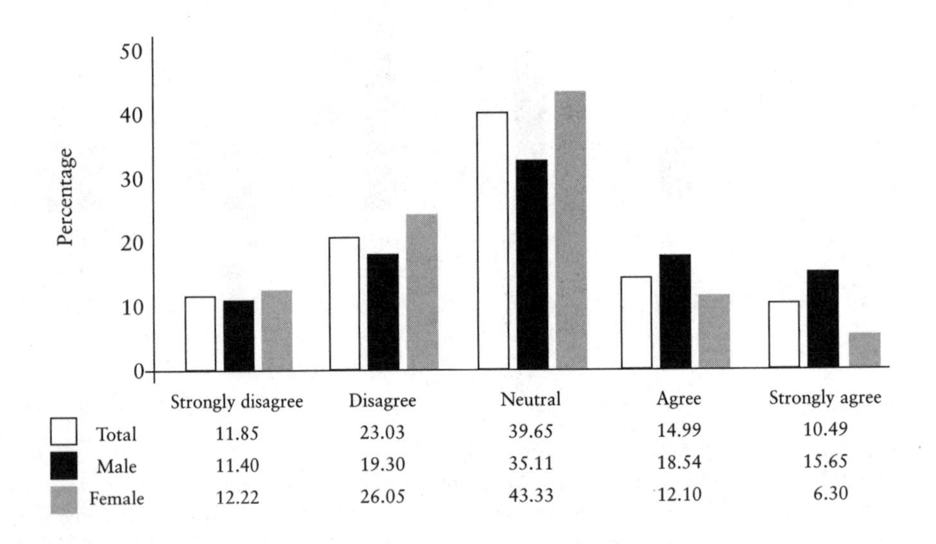

Adolescents' Attitudes According to Type of Educational Institution
The majority opinion on whether Muslims should adopt Western culture when living in the UK remained neutral (comprehensive 46.19%; private 30.28%; FE sector 40.4%). The category with the highest percentage of the remainder of the respondents was 'disagree' (comprehensive 21.79%; private 26.91%; FE sector 21.97%), followed by 'agree' (comprehensive 13.91%; private 18.65%; FE sector 13.95%). Combining the 'strongly disagree' with the 'disagree' and the 'agree' with the 'strongly agree' gives the percentages shown in Table 6.

Figure 12: **Adolescent views on whether Muslims should adopt Western culture when living in the UK according to type of educational institution**

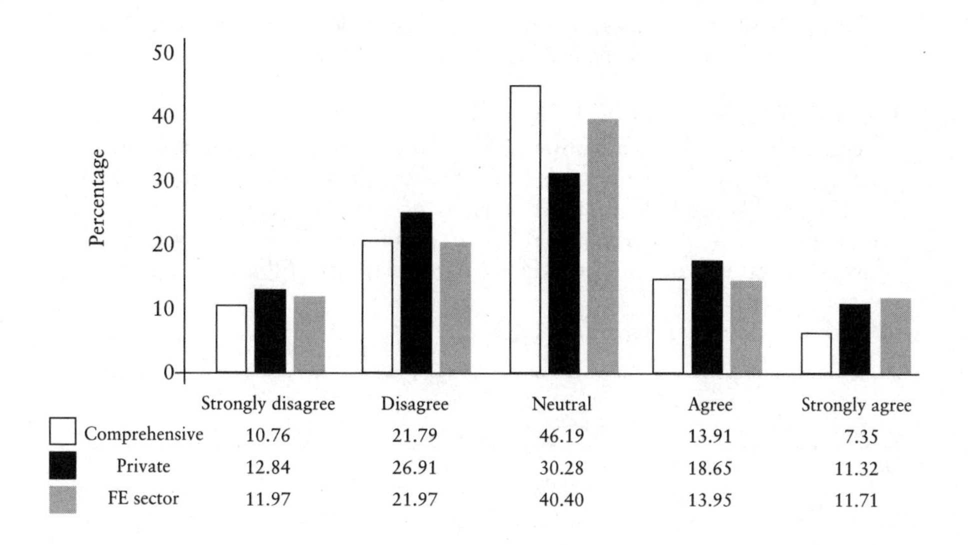

	Strongly disagree + disagree	*Strongly agree + agree*
Comprehensive	32.55%	21.26
Private	39.75	29.97
FE sector	33.94	25.66

Table 6: **Adolescent views on whether Muslims should adopt Western culture when living in the UK, according to type of educational institution**

Question 6: Respondents were asked whether they thought it was right or wrong to show a video on TV of Saddam Hussein, the former president of Iraq, having a medical examination

Adolescents' Attitudes According to Age

Age	*Right*	*Wrong*
13–15	66.96%	33.04%
16–18	58.00	42.00
19+	64.00	36.00

Table 7: **Adolescent views on the broadcasting of Saddam Hussein's medical examination on national television, according to age**

The predominant view of the broadcasting of the footage of Saddam Hussein undergoing a medical examination was that the media were right in doing so. In all age groups, the majority fell into this category with two-thirds of the 13–15 year olds (66.96%), almost as many of the 19+ age group (64%) and over half the 16–18 year olds (58%). A significant association was found between age groups and thinking the media were right x^2 (2) = 10.36, $p < 0.01$.

Adolescents' Attitudes According to Gender

Gender	*Right*	*Wrong*
Total	61.09%	38.91%
Female	53.33	46.68
Male	70.52	29.48

Table 8: **Adolescent views on the broadcasting of Saddam Hussein's medical examination on national television, according to gender**

The general perception was that the media were right to broadcast. However, substantially more males (70.52%) held this view than females (53.33%). A significant association was found between gender and thinking the media were right to show the footage x^2 (1) = 43.08, $p < 0.001$.

Adolescents' Attitudes According to Type of Educational Institution

School type	*Right*	*Wrong*
Comprehensive	67.84%	32.16%
Private	56.51	43.49
FE sector	59.61	40.39

Table 9: **Adolescent views on the broadcasting of Saddam Hussein's medical examination on national television, according to type of educational institition**

The majority of adolescents thought that the media were right to show the video of Saddam Hussein undergoing a medical examination (comprehensive 67.84%; private 56.51%; FE sector 59.61%). Furthermore, a significant association was found between type of educational institution and thinking the media were right to show it x^2 (2) = 10.529, $p < 0.01$.

Discussion

Age

As expected, the majority of participants' responses in all age groups fell into neutral categories: attitudes remaining the same, not knowing enough to comment on the BNP, neutral on adopting Western culture and not minding if girls wore headscarves in school. The exception was the ethical issue whether or not the media should have broadcast the video of Saddam Hussein which the majority of adolescents regarded appropriate.

Most adolescents whose attitudes did not stay the same after 9/11 reported that they 'got worse' or 'got much worse'. The 19+ age group seem to have been more affected by the 9/11 event than the other age groups both negatively (51.86%) and positively (3.7%), deviating further from the norm with 7.12% more negative attitudes than the 16–18 year olds and 7.38% more than the 13–15 year olds. Noticeably few respondents said that their attitudes had 'improved' or 'improved a lot' after 9/11 which supports Sheridan and Gillett's (2005) findings of an increase in ànti-Muslim feeling following 9/11.

Over 60% of the participants said that their attitudes toward Muslims did not change after the invasion of Iraq. In contrast to 9/11, the 19+ age group displayed the least negative attitudes (22.22%) compared to the other age groups (13–15: 25.47% and 16–18: 25.31%); however, consistent with attitudes after 9/11, they also had the greatest improvement in attitudes here (14.82%) compared to the other age groups (13–15: 10.65 and 16–18: 6.66%). Participants seem to be less affected by the invasion of Iraq than the 9/11 attacks.

Due to the significant negative correlation between attitudes towards the BNP and towards Muslims following 9/11 and the invasion of Iraq it can be presumed that those sympathizing with the BNP are more likely to hold negative attitudes toward Muslims and Islam than those who do not. A large proportion of the sample did not know enough about the BNP to comment on their policies (mean = 43.79%). Of the remaining participants, however, 7.69% of those aged 19+ agreed with the views of the BNP, which was higher than younger participants (4.68% of the 13–15 year olds and 6.95% of the 16–18 year olds). Nevertheless, the 19+ age group was more than twice as likely to strongly agree than those aged 16–18 and more than three times as likely to strongly agree than those aged 13–15. The 16–18 year olds were more likely to disagree with the views of the BNP (39.41%) than those from other age groups (30.77% of those aged 19+ and 27.66% of the 13–15 year olds) as well as being more able to comment on the BNP (64.14%) than the other age groups (53.85% of those aged 19+ and 50.64% of the 13–15 year olds).

The vast majority of adolescents of all three age groups said that they would not mind if girls in their school wore headscarves (each in the 83% range, differing at the most by 0.65%); the similarity between groups is supported by statistical analysis revealing that there was no significant association between age and minding if girls wore headscarves.

Although the majority of the sample was either neutral or disagreed with the statement that 'Muslims should adopt Western culture', over 25% thought that they should. Overall, the 19+ group had the least tolerant view with 29.62% agreeing with the statement compared to 25.16% of the 13–15 group and 25.34% of the 16–18 one.

On the ethical issue of the broadcast of Saddam Hussein's medical examination, the majority view of all age groups was that the media were right in showing the footage with the strongest opposition among the 16–18 year olds (42%) followed by those aged 19+ (36%) and the 13–15 year-olds (33.04%). A statistically significant association was found between age groups and thinking the media was right/wrong in showing the footage of Saddam Hussein undergoing a medical examination ($p < 0.01$) with 16–18 year olds being more likely to disagree with the media.

Apart from the question about Saddam Hussein there seem to be no significant differences between the younger groups (13–15 and 16–18); however, the older group (19+) seems to deviate more from the norm on most questions. It should be noted when interpreting the results, however, that the older group (19+) contains six-year spans (19–25), whereas the younger groups contain only three each.

Gender

While the majority of both sexes' responses fell into neutral categories – excepting the question about Saddam Hussein which most considered to be right – there were some differences between the sexes' positive and negative attitudes towards Muslims and Islam.

Almost half the males (49.63%) said that their attitudes towards Muslims had got worse or much worse after 9/11 compared with 40.88% of the females. Only 2.37% of the males and 1.5% of the females said that their attitudes had improved since 9/11. The above worsening of adolescents' attitudes towards Muslims after 9/11, especially males', lends further support to Sheridan and Gillett's (2005) findings of increased racial prejudice against groups perceived to share the values of perpetrators of major world events. The data show that 19.47% more adolescents displayed either neutral or favourable attitudes towards Muslims after the invasion of Iraq than did so following 9/11. A higher number of the females' attitudes (67.6%) stayed the same after the invasion compared to the males' (65.32%); however, more females than males said that their attitudes had got worse since the invasion (25.68% and 24.97% respectively). Also fewer females expressed improved attitudes than males (6.72% and 9.72% respectively). A larger proportion of females than males felt that they did not know enough about the views of the BNP to comment (49.15% and 31.56% respectively). Of the rest, males were more than five times as likely to agree (10.04%) and nearly four times as likely to strongly agree (4.51%) with the views of the BNP than their female counterparts (1.95% and 1.22%).

Reasons why this percentage of the males appeared to favour radical opinion are unknown, particularly when a large proportion of their peers did not: 27.46% of males and 27.49% of females strongly disagreed with the views of the BNP.

Although the majority did not mind girls wearing headscarves in their school or college, more than twice as many males (23.1%) as females (10.55%) said that they would mind if girls in their school or college wore a headscarf. This association was statistically significant at the level of $p < 0.001$ indicating that male adolescents in York are more likely to mind girls wearing headscarves than females. Male and female adolescents' views on the statement 'Muslims should adopt Western culture when living in the UK', although in the main neutral, diverged when it came to agreeing or disagreeing. Over one third of the males agreed with the statement (34.19%) whereas less than a fifth of the females did so (18.4%) indicating almost 50% less tolerance from males than females. Gender differences are again apparent in the adolescents' views on the broadcasting on national television of Saddam Hussein undergoing a medical examination. Less than one third of the males thought that the media was wrong in broadcasting Saddam Hussein's medical examination (29.48%) compared to 46.68% of the females. This association between gender and thinking the media were right in showing the footage was significant at the level of $p < 0.01$ and adds further support to the trend which denotes a more tolerant attitude towards Muslims and Islam in females than in males.

Apart from change in attitudes following the invasion of Iraq (where females' attitudes had deteriorated more than males, but by only less than 1%) gender differences suggest that tolerant attitudes are more prevalent in females than in males. Sotelo (1999) discovered similar gender differences in relation to political tolerance.

School Type

Despite the majority of adolescents' answers falling into the neutral categories – attitudes staying the same, not knowing enough about the BNP to comment, remaining neutral on whether Muslims should adopt Western culture – some differences between the school types are discernible from answers which were favourable towards Islam and Muslims – improved attitudes after 9/11, disagreeing with the BNP, etc. – and those which were unfavourable. Overall, a larger proportion of participants from the FE sector said that their attitudes had worsened (46.29%) after 9/11 than those from private schools (44.24%) and from comprehensive schools (42.42%). The attitudes from the FE sector had also improved the least (1.56%), whereas attitudes in private schools had improved the most (2.73%).

Adolescents' attitudes were much less negative after the invasion of Iraq than they were following 9/11. Nevertheless, the FE sector reported least improvement (5.6%) and most deterioration (27.47%) in attitudes towards Muslims following the invasion, followed by comprehensive schools (7.43% and 24.87% respectively) with private schools displaying the most overall improvement in attitudes (14.48%) as well as the least deterioration (20.98%).

Adolescents' views on the BNP produced the widest diversity of answers. A large proportion of the sample felt unable to comment, with those from private schools being most informed (63.8%) followed by those in the FE sector (60.76%). The least informed were from comprehensive schools (55.88%).The FE sector was somewhat more likely to sympathize with the BNP (10.12%) than private (9.96%) and comprehensive schools (6.86%).

The vast majority of adolescents in each of the three types of educational institution were tolerant towards girls in their school or college wearing headscarves. However, a considerably higher number of those attending private schools said that they would mind (21.34%) than in comprehensive schools (14.25%) or the FE sector (14.76%). The association between type of educational institution and minding girls wearing headscarves was statistically significant on the level of $p < 0.05$, with those attending private schools minding more than their counterparts.

Although a large proportion of the participants were neutral regarding the statement 'Muslims should adopt Western culture when living in the UK', there were some differences in attitudes between the types of educational institutions. Those attending private schools deviated further from the norm than the others with 39.75% disagreeing and 29.97% agreeing with the statement, and the comprehensive schools appearing to be less demanding with only 21.26% agreeing that Muslims should adopt Western culture when living in the UK.

A substantial majority of respondents believed that the media were right to show the footage of Saddam Hussein's medical examination on national television, with nearly two thirds of those in comprehensive schools agreeing so (67.84%) followed by the FE sector (59.61%) and private schools (56.51%). A significant association between type of educational institution and thinking the media was right in showing the footage of Saddam Hussein was found indicating that those attending comprehensive schools are more likely to agree with the media on this issue. Although there were some striking similarities between the school types, there were also some differences. Overall, comprehensive schools displayed the most tolerant attitude towards Muslims and Islam and the FE sector the least.

Conclusion

Although the majority of the sample favoured neutral views, some less tolerant views were found in some of the questions and the groups. The two most prominent questions in this regard concerned, first, attitudes after 9/11, where over 50% of those aged 19+ and nearly 50% of all males said that their attitudes towards Muslims had deteriorated, and second, if it was right to show the video footage of Saddam Hussein undergoing a medical examination, where over 60% of the whole sample said it was. In general, the 19+ age group demonstrated a less tolerant attitude towards Muslims and Islam than the younger groups; males were less tolerant than females, and those attending the FE sector were less tolerant than those in private and comprehensive schools, the latter appearing to be the most tolerant.

In order to further understand the causes of tension in the interactions between religious communities and wider society, and so contribute to ways of resolving communal conflict in this area, future research should focus on establishing a more robust, reliable and valid measure of Islamophobia in the UK. Two specific elements of this would be further investigation into the more tolerant overall views towards Muslims and Islam found in comprehensive schools – as opposed to the more expected differences in attitudes between gender and/or age – and, more importantly, further investigation into the correlation between attitudes towards the BNP and towards Muslims.

Notes

1 The authors gratefully acknowledge the work of Bahar Ala-eddini, who helped carry out the survey as a Research Assistant.

2 http://www.danielpipes.org/article/3075.

3 FAIR: http://www.fairuk.org/policy12.htm.

4 In some figures, percentages may add up to more than 100% as respondents were asked to indicate multiple responses to some questions.

5 Participants who did not know enough to comment on the BNP were excluded from the Spearman correlation (see note 6 for definition).

6 Spearman's rank correlation coefficient, named after Charles Spearman (1863–1945) (http://en.wikipedia.org/wiki/Charles_Spearman), is a non-parametric measure (http://en.wikipedia.org/wiki/Non-parametric_statistics) of correlation (http://en.wikipedia.org/wiki/Correlation) indicating the strength and direction of a linear relationship between two random variables. The further away the correlation deviates from zero (higher or lower) the more significant the correlation. The correlation can only vary between –1.0 and +1.0; the closer the number is to 1, the greater the relationship. Anything below .29 is seen as low (Cohen 1988).

References

CBMI (Commission on British Muslims and Islamophobia) (1997), *Islamophobia, A Challenge for Us All* (London: Runneymede Trust).

—— (2001), *Addressing the Challenge of Islamophobia: Progress Report, 1999–2001* (London).

—— (2004), *Islamophobia: Issues, Challenges and Action* (Stoke-on-Trent: Trentham Books).

Cohen, J. (1988), *Statistical Power Analysis for the Behavioral Sciences* (Hillsdale, NJ: Lawrence Erlbaum Associates, 2nd edn).

FAIR (Forum Against Islamophobia and Racism) (2004), *Memorandum Submitted by FAIR to the House of Commons Home Affairs Committee*, http://www.fairuk.org/useful.htm (accessed 10 November 2005).

FOSIS (The Federation of Student Islamic Societies in the UK and Ireland) (2003), *Islamophobia on Campuses and the Lack of Provision for Muslim Students* (UK: The Federation of Students' Islamic Societies).

Gibbs, A. (1997), 'Focus Groups', *Social Research Update* 19 (Winter): 1–7.

Halliday, F. (1996), *Islam and the Myth of Confrontation* (London: I.B. Taurus).

Hoppe, M.J., E.A. Wells, D.M. Morrison, M.R. Gilmore and A. Wilsdon (1995), 'Using Focus Groups to Discuss Sensitive Topics with Children', *Evaluation Review* 19.1: 102–14.

IQRA Trust (n.d.), *Research Report 1: Research on Public Attitudes to Islam* (MORI; London: IQRA Trust) [interviews conducted December 1990].

Lankshear, A.J. (1993), 'The Use of Focus Groups in a Study of Attitudes to Student-Nurse Assessment', *Journal of Advanced Nursing* 18: 1986–89.

Malik, K. 'The Islamophobia Myth', HYPERLINK "http://www.kenanmalik.com/essays/islamophobia_prospect.html accessed 7 Apr 06" http://www.kenanmalik.com/essays/islamophobia_prospect.html (accessed 7 April 2006).

Modood, T. (2005), *Multicultural Politics: Racism, Ethnicity and Muslims in Britain* (Edinburgh: Edinburgh University Press).

Modood, T. *et al.* (1997), *Ethnic Minorities in Britain: Diversity and Disadvantage* (London: Policy Studies Institute).

Sheridan, L.P. and R. Gillett (2005), 'Major World Events and Discrimination', *Asian Journal of Social Psychology* 8.2: 191–97.

Sotelo, M.J. (1999), 'Gender Differences in Political Tolerance among Adolescents', *Journal of Gender Studies* 8.2: 211–17.

Wieviorka, M. (1995), *The Arena of Racism* (London: Sage Publications).

Index

Diagrams are given in italics.